The Bulfinch
Illustrated Encyclopedia of

The Bulfinch
Illustrated Encyclopedia of
ANTIQUES

CONSULTING EDITORS
PAUL ATTERBURY   LARS THARP

A BULFINCH PRESS BOOK
LITTLE, BROWN AND COMPANY
BOSTON • NEW YORK • TORONTO • LONDON

First North American Paperback Edition, 1998

ISBN 0–8212–2506–5
Library of Congress Catalog Card Number 94–75734

CONTRIBUTORS

Pottery and Porcelain	Deborah Scott, Gordon Lang, Lars Tharp
Glass	Deborah Scott
Silver	Tim Forrest
Furniture	Tim Forrest
Clocks and Watches	Richard Garnier
Oriental Wares	Jonathan Bennett
Project editor	Gwen Rigby
Assistant editor	Heather Magrill
Designer	Frances de Rees
Researcher	Alastair Owens
DTP assistant	Pennie Jelliff
Picture editor	Elizabeth Loving

Marshall Editions would like to thank Edward Schneider, Tessa Trethowan
and Margarita Crutchley of Christie's Images for their help in the creation
of this encyclopedia.

Conceived, edited, and designed by
MARSHALL EDITIONS
170 Piccadilly, London W1V 9DD

Bulfinch Press is an imprint and trademark of Little, Brown and Company (Inc.)
Published simultaneously in Canada by Little, Brown & Company (Canada) Limited

Printed in Italy

PAGE 1 *Three 19th-century mantel clocks,* left to right: *German Biedermeier
ormolu clock; French Second Empire porcelain and brass clock; Austrian silver-
gilt clock set with gems.*

PAGE 2 *This magnificent morning room at Saltram House in Devon, England
was designed by Robert Adam. It was furnished in 18th-century taste and features
a fine mahogany dining table, gothic-style chairs, an English lacquer cabinet and
a gilded side table with an inlaid top. In the center of the dining table is a Chinese
punch bowl of the same period.*

CONTENTS

FOREWORD

From the time I was a boy, I have been mad about English furniture and, indeed, about furniture made anywhere else in the world. I have spent all my career as an auctioneer and, since I joined Christie's, furniture has formed a major part of my life – I derive great pleasure from examining, cataloguing and writing about fine furniture and, probably above all, from living with it. I also greatly enjoy discussing it with those who share my passion, for one never ceases to learn more about one's favorite subject, whether it be furniture, silver, ceramics, glass, clocks or Oriental works of art.

All of these are discussed in depth in this magnificently illustrated encyclopedia. The aim of covering most aspects of the decorative arts in a single volume is ambitious, and to have encapsulated so much in one book is a rare feat. This is an excellent introduction to a variety of diverse subjects. The text is both authoritative and easy to understand, the captions are concise but informative, and the illustrations have been selected with great skill. It is not only a splendid book but also a rewarding one – I wish that it had been available when I first became interested in the subject of antiques.

The decorative arts are, happily, no longer just the preserve of collectors, auctioneers and the fine-art trade, art historians and museum curators. There is vast interest in the works of art and objects created by our forebears, and a plethora of books and articles has been published on every art-historical subject. These have engendered wide general interest, which has been augmented by popular television and radio programs. Inevitably, however, such publications are becoming more and more specialized, so a wide-ranging and informative book such as this will fill a growing public demand.

Most of the photographs here have been selected from Christie's Images, the company's photographic library, and from departmental records at Sotheby's. Christie's have been delighted to collaborate with the compilers of the book, since we feel strongly that the visual records we are fortunate enough to have amassed should be more widely appreciated. The consistently fine quality of the photography and the erudition displayed in our catalogs reflect the high standards we endeavor to set ourselves, for the catalogs form our primary link with our clients and, indeed, with a much wider public.

Apart from their main aim of promoting worldwide the works of art that the company has been instructed to sell, the catalogs are a reservoir of expertise, whether the research and scholarship be established or current. In fact, the auction houses have unwittingly assumed a curatorial function, which in itself leads to the accumulation of accessible knowledge; time always hones and refines this, but it is exciting to be, day in day out, at the cutting edge.

I hope that this encyclopedia may nurture the instinct to collect in some of its readers. If it does, I beg you to do your homework and take advice before you plunge into the market-place. The decorative arts market is not for those who want to get in and out quickly, showing a profit, but in time your purchases can prove an excellent investment. Read up your subject, take the best advice you can, enjoy what you have bought and, one day, you or your heirs may reap a rich harvest.

Anthony Coleridge

ANTHONY COLERIDGE
CHAIRMAN, CHRISTIE'S
SOUTH KENSINGTON, LONDON

LEFT *Auctions, or the public sales where items are sold to the buyer offering the highest bid, occur at all auction houses. The cartoon by Thomas Rowlandson, the English painter and caricaturist, is of a sale at Sotheby's in London in the late eighteenth century. It shows all the important features of an auction: the display of the item up for sale, in this instance a book; the prospective buyers looking on and bidding; and the auctioneer, gavel in hand, conducting the proceedings.*

ABOVE *Although a little more formal, the photograph taken almost 200 years later of an auction at Christie's, London, is of exactly the same procedure; here the painting* Le jeune garçon au chat *by Renoir is coming under the hammer. The only major difference is that, to the left of the auctioneer, bids are being taken over the telephone from people who are absent or wish to remain anonymous.*

INTRODUCTION

William Morris, the great nineteenth-century designer and thinker, once wrote: "Have nothing in your house except what you know to be useful or believe to be beautiful." Most antiques, at least at the time they were made, fulfilled one, and sometimes both, of these demanding criteria; but with time they have shifted inexorably toward different standards of value and judgment.

The passion for antiques is universal, part of a reverence for the past that has traditionally been used as a yardstick for the present, and those who share this passion may well be convinced about the beauty of the objects they love, even if usefulness is rarely of any importance. An appreciation of antiques is a particular, personal way to preserve the past, both in the form of the objects themselves and in the information such objects convey. All antiques, of whatever period, are in effect time capsules, and their survival carries with it a vision of other worlds, other times. The pleasures generated by the search for antiques are, therefore, infinitely varied and valuable as a basis for an understanding of the past.

An encyclopedia of antiques cannot hope to show everything, but it should, in its selection of illustrations and its text, present a detailed appreciation of its chosen area. It is only by seeing together so many objects, of such diversity, that the changing patterns of style, taste and social habits can be broadly understood. And no antique, however splendid or valuable, can stand on its own, for everything has to be seen as part of the society that formed it.

The categories of antiques are today so broad, stretching as they do from the artefacts of ancient Egypt and other pre-Christian cultures to the products of the modern industrial age, that they are beyond the scope of any one book. This book concentrates on the primary area of interest, namely those centuries from the Renaissance to the early twentieth century that witnessed the development of culture and civilization in Western Europe and North America. The antiques represented are in the more traditional fields of furniture and woodwork, ceramics and glass, silver, clocks and watches, for it is the appreciation of these fields above all else that creates an awareness of the past, and a knowledge of the social context that brought these objects into existence. At the same time, the book contains a detailed study of the antiques of the East, the cultures whose products have been most influential in the development of style and taste in the West.

Concepts of beauty are, like style and fashion, constantly changing, and many of the antiques shown here have survived a number of radical changes in the reactions they provoke. The canons of taste that prevailed in the eighteenth century seem safe and reliable today, but those of the nineteenth century still arouse uncertainty and even hostility. Yet beauty was there at the time each object was created, both in the mind of its creator and in the market for which it was made, and one of the pleasures to be drawn from an appreciation of antiques is exactly that need to question established and predictable judgments. Most of the antiques included in this book were also designed to be useful in the broadest sense, and this has to be understood, even if reverence and the needs of conservation have made many of them useless today.

The history of antiques is all about form and function, and the changes imposed on these essentials by style and taste. William Morris may have been a high-minded idealist, but the essential simplicity of his views about usefulness and beauty can still be applied to many of the antiques in this book, and these views should be used as the basis upon which each piece can be judged, both in the context of its own time and in the way it is perceived today.

Knowledge is both valuable and pleasurable. It is also the vital foundation upon which any appreciation of antiques is based, and the need for access to knowledge is shared by the scholar, the historian and the amateur enthusiast. The greater the depth of knowledge, the greater the pleasure to be derived from it; that is the primary justification for producing any encyclopedia of antiques.

◀ **INTERIOR WITH EMPIRE FURNITURE**
Vilhelm Hammerschøi, a Danish painter who lived from 1864 to 1916, specialized in painting quiet interiors in muted colors, principally gray with stronger accents. He always featured furniture from the French First Empire period (1799–1815), and his paintings epitomized a reverence for the refined and timeless styles of the past, a reverence felt as strongly today as it was in Hammerschøi's time.

	1550	1600	1650	1700	1750

STYLE

GOTHIC (TO 1620)	BAROQUE (1620–1700)	ROCOCO (1700–60)

GREAT BRITAIN AND IRELAND

TUDOR	JACOBEAN	CAROLEAN	COMMONWEALTH	RESTORATION	WILLIAM & MARY	QUEEN ANNE	EARLY GEORGIAN	MID-GEORGIAN

ELIZABETH I (1558–1603) JAMES I (1603–25) CHARLES I (1625–49) CHARLES II (1660–85) JAMES II (1685–88) WM & MARY (1688–94) WM III (1694–1702) ANNE (1702–14) GEORGE I (1714–27) GEORGE II (1727–60)

UNITED STATES

EARLY COLONIAL (TO 1700)	WILLIAM & MARY STYLE (1700–25)	QUEEN ANNE STYLE (1725–55)

FRANCE

HENRI IV (1589–1610)	LOUIS XIII (1610–43)	LOUIS XIV (1643–1715)	REGENCE (1715–23)	LOUIS XV (1723–74)

NORTHERN EUROPE

RENAISSANCE (TO 1650)	BAROQUE (1650–1730)

ROCOCO (1700–60)

MEDITERRANEAN EUROPE

RENAISSANCE (TO 1650)	BAROQUE (1650–1730)

MANNERISM (ITALY)

MOORISH INFLUENCE (SPAIN)

CHURRIQUERESQUE (SPAIN)

ROCOCO (1700–60)

CHINA

MING DYNASTY (1368–1644)	QING DYNASTY (1644–1912)

JIAJING (1521–66) LONGQING (1566–72) WANLI (1572–1620) TIANQI (1620–27) CHONGZHEN (1627–44) SHUNZHI (1644–61) KANGXI (1661–1722) YONGZHENG (1722–35) QIANLONG (1735–96)

JAPAN

MOMOYAMA (1573–1615)	EDO (TOKUGAWA) (1615–1867)

1550	1600	1650	1700	1750

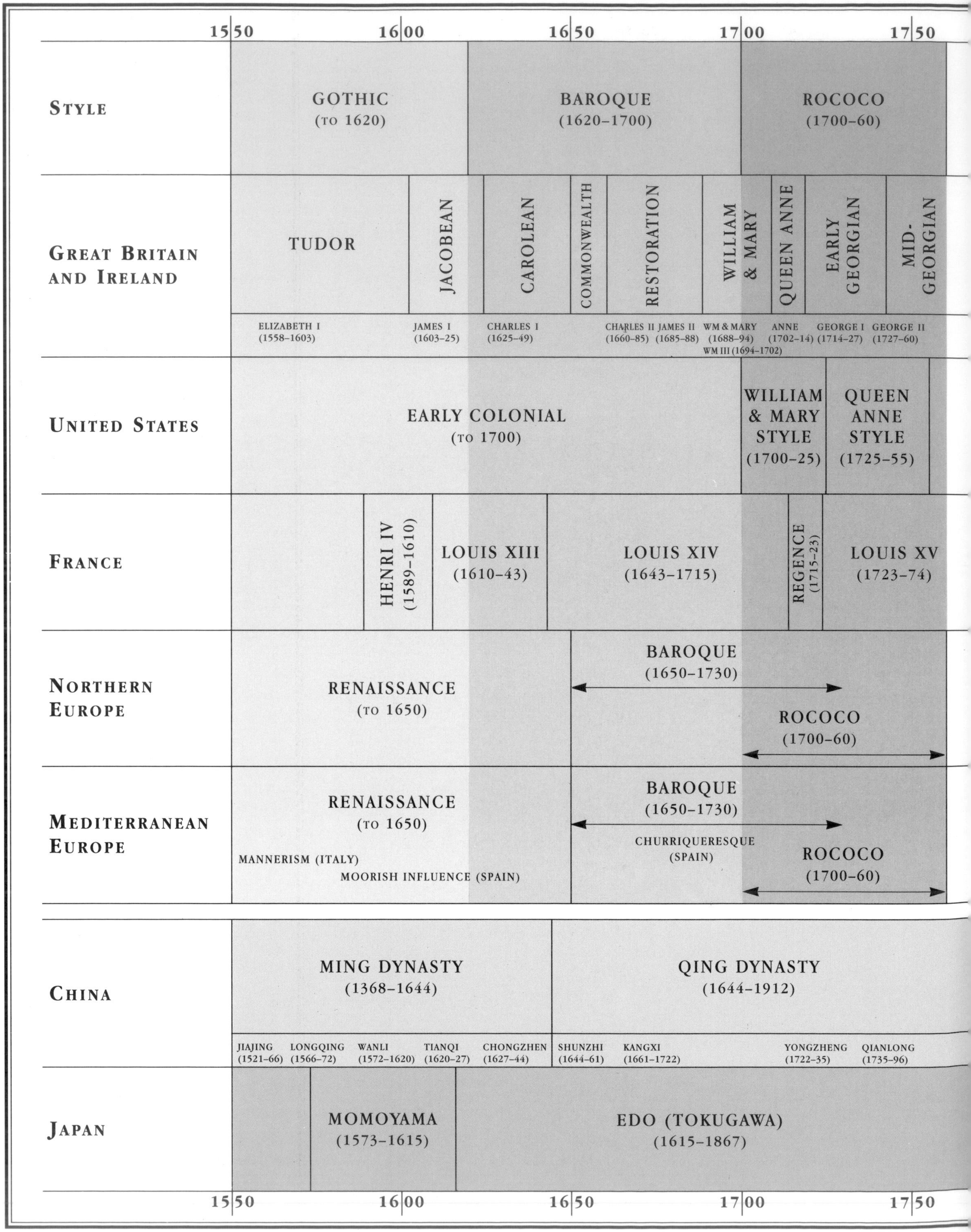

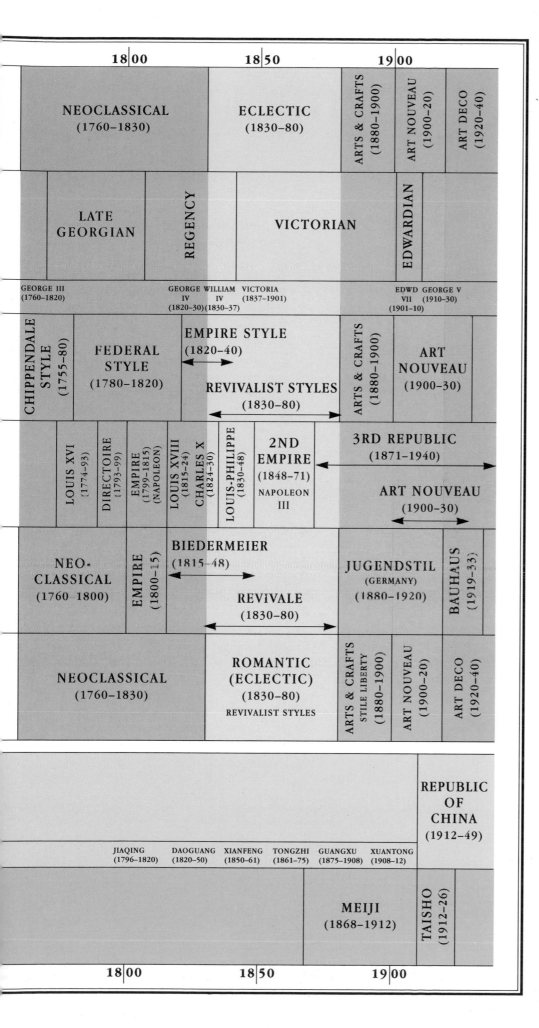

This chart shows the major styles that were prevalent in a particular period. Each general style is given a particular color which follows through Europe and the United States; China and Japan are completely separate.

The chart allows broad comparisons to be made between countries and allows movements, such as the Jugendstil in Germany, to be placed in a stylistic context and linked with similar movements across Europe. It also illustrates the fact that styles in the United States were, until Independence (1776), dominated by those in Britain, although they tended to lag about 20 years behind.

Both the individual British monarchs and the general style names are shown since they are used interchangeably. A piece may, for instance, be described either as James I or Jacobean.

The chart also includes the Chinese dynasties, together with the reigns of individual emperors, and the Japanese periods.

CHAPTER ONE

POTTERY AND PORCELAIN

Ceramics is the umbrella word covering all pottery and porcelain – objects made of clay and usually hardened by drying or "firing." The story of ceramics is as complicated and interwoven as the societies and people who discovered and evolved the different ceramic materials and techniques.

Early humans were hunters and followers of herds, a lifestyle that permitted few artefacts except for the most basic and portable tools needed for making clothing and shelter, and for hunting. Such implements were of stone, bone and wood. Water might be carried in skins or gourds. Occasionally, when invoking the spirits for a forthcoming hunt in a sacred place, such as the painted Stone Age caves of Europe, effigies of the intended quarry, often bison, were modeled from locally available clay for the purposes of magical propitiation. Such magical totems were, no doubt, forerunners of the small portable figurines of female fertility gods made of clay and bone and hardened in the fire, which appear on Stone Age sites dating to between 10,000 and 20,000 years ago.

Only when societies became more settled did clay emerge as a material useful for making vessels in which to store essential food produce from one harvest to the next. The presence of pottery vessels at such neolithic sites usually points to established farming communities, which formed the basis of cultures based on cities: "civilizations." The early development of ceramic technology was, therefore, an important part of the subsequent material human culture.

In Sumeria, baked clay tablets provided the medium for written records and accounting. In most societies, a further stage of technology developed when, on firing, certain clays accidentally surrendered their metal ores. Pottery thus gave birth to the technologies of working copper, tin, bronze, iron, silver and gold. In producing metal objects, the ceramic technology was itself often enhanced, since clay was essential in modeling and casting. As can be seen in China from the Shang Dynasty right up to the Qing, the forms of vessels created in bronze and in pottery are often interchangeable throughout successive centuries.

The discovery of glaze, too, was accidental: certain ashes, when sufficiently heated, imparted a glassy texture to anything they touched. Not only could a porous vessel be rendered watertight by such contact, but its unglazed clay surface took on a different color and texture. In this way, societies discovered a new and hygienic method of storing liquids, either *in situ* or for transportation. At the same time, the colors and designs that could be achieved with different glazes and pigments raised ceramics from mere utility objects into an art form.

Ceramics thus became trade commodities, with certain types avidly pursued by societies not yet able to produce their own. Among the most notable of these industries was that of the Chinese who, having evolved porcelain over 1,000 years ago, found ready markets in Persia and eventually Europe. Only in the early eighteenth century did Europeans succeed in producing a similar material, at the famous Meissen factory in Germany. Although used initially for tableware, its figures of idealized virtues and allegory were soon commissioned for weddings, important banquets and state feasts celebrating political alliances.

Since their first recorded forms as ritual sculpture, ceramics have evolved into an infinite variety of forms central to human functions, from magic to storage wares, to tablewares, to objects of beauty, to electrical transmission insulators and even protection for spacecraft. As ceramics are utilized in ever more complex technologies, cultures and trades, it is not surprising that they are as varied as the times, places and peoples who created them. Learning to identify ceramics, and their time and place in the history of design and function, gives an insight into the cultures of the world and also an enjoyment of one of its most versatile creations.

▶ **16TH-CENTURY MAIOLICA DISH**
The istoriato, *or "history painting," on this maiolica dish (c.1535) from Urbino depicts the death of Achilles. While the hero kneels in the temple of Apollo, Paris shoots an arrow into his heel. The ruined city of Troy is visible through the arch. Diam. 10½in/26cm*

All pottery and porcelain is made of clay hardened by fire, but few clays are used by potters in a raw state, straight from the ground. Most require refinement, by weathering and straining, and need mixing with other clays and minerals to achieve a "body," or "paste," with a particular plasticity, color and firing qualities. Impurities and air bubbles must be driven out to prevent malformation or explosions in the kiln.

Ceramic bodies fall into two basic types: porous earthenwares and nonporous stonewares and porcelains. The first of these are fired to temperatures of, typically, 900–1,500°F/500–800°C; the individual grains of the clay body adhere to each other but remain intact. Stoneware and porcelain clays are fired to c.2,400°F/1,300°C, whereupon the grains of the body melt and fuse, causing the ware to become impervious.

Porcelain, also called china, is distinguished from stonewares by its whiteness and translucency. It can be divided into hard-paste, or true porcelains (the first of which emerged in China) and soft-paste, or artificial porcelains. The latter are European imitations of Chinese porcelains, made from a variety of materials, resulting in a much softer paste. The term "bone china" was applied to a particular type of soft-paste porcelain whose major ingredient is bone ash, developed in Staffordshire in the late 1700s and adopted by most English factories by the early 1800s.

Learning to distinguish and recognize the physical nature of the material is the most fundamental stage in learning to identify, and date, ceramics; hence the importance of examining the bottom or "foot" of an object, where the unglazed clay may be visible.

Color and glaze

The next most important constituent of a piece is the glaze. By applying a glaze, a thin glassy layer, the potter modifies or covers the body. A clear lead glaze will enhance the buff color of a Staffordshire slipware dish to a mellow honey tone, while an opaque tin glaze will cover a red earthenware clay in a white "skin," on which enamel color may be painted. Glazes form another basis for the categorization of ceramics.

▶ **RUSKIN POTTERY**
A vase made in England in the early 1900s. The russet color of the Chinese-inspired flambé glaze was derived from oxides of copper.

▼ **POTTER AT WORK**
The technique of throwing pots on a revolving wheel was for centuries the standard method of manufacture from the raw clay. Today, most pottery and porcelain is cast from molds, so throwing is now a characteristic of studio pottery and sometimes of the making of very basic wares, such as the flower-pots being thrown here.

Decoration follows body and glaze in importance. Lead-glazed earthenwares lend themselves to in-glaze color stains, such as the famous "three-color" wares of the Tang Dynasty in China and the Staffordshire Whieldon-type vegetable molded wares of the 1700s. Chinese potters developed and perfected a range of different monochrome glazes: *temmoku* black; tea-dust brown; *junyao* blues; *geyao* and *guanyao* cracklewares; and, later, *sang-de-boeuf* and *flambé* redwares.

Porcelain glazes are often transparent and colorless, showing off the whiteness of the material as well as giving it sparkle. In the fourteenth century, the Chinese found that cobalt blue, painted on a porcelain surface before the application of the glaze, matured to a strong blue color when fired to c.2,400°F/1,300°C. This was one of the most influential discoveries in all ceramic art, which has been copied everywhere in both porcelains and earthenwares, all of which are known as blue and white wares. Such metallic oxides, applied and fired under the glaze, are known as underglaze pigments. The precise shade of an underglaze blue and its reaction with the glaze above may be a helpful indicator of date and origin.

The next type of decoration was painting or enameling on top of the glaze. Such wares include

▲ GILDING: THE FINAL STAGE IN ORNAMENTATION
The painted and glazed vase is enriched by hand with an applied paste or coating of pure gold, which is then generally fired at low temperature and, finally, burnished.

▲ TRANSFER PRINTING SPODE'S ITALIAN PATTERN
An engraver finishes off the copper plate, from which prints will be taken on the special tissue paper seen hanging over the drier and then transferred by hand to the surface of the unglazed ware.

Italian maiolica (tin-glazed) wares bearing classical narrative, or "*istoriato*," subjects; Royal Worcester porcelains painted in enamels with miniature landscapes; and Berlin porcelain plaques copying well-known paintings. Again, the colors of on-glaze enamel decoration, taken in conjunction with body and glaze, will point to certain factories or kilns and eliminate others.

Ceramics may be painted by hand or decorated by a mass-production technique such as transfer-printing. Dazzling metallic lusters, such as those on the Hispano-Moresque wares of the 1300s, may be deposited on the surface using complex kiln firing sequences or via metallic glazes, and gilding may be applied in several ways.

Construction and molded decoration

The clues to the process by which a piece has been created are also helpful in establishing its origin and age. The first neolithic vessels were made by building up coils of clay, or by pulling up the sides of the vessel, but some pieces were slab constructed. Later came the potter's wheel and throwing and, later still, slip-casting, in which liquid clay is poured into a porous mold so that the water escapes to leave a thick skin of clay.

Some forms may require elements to be made separately and then assembled. The inside of a figure or vase is more likely to divulge the method of construction than the exterior, which would have been finished to disguise the assembly process.

Molded ornament can be cut out, impressed, scored or stuck on while the clay is plastic, prior to firing. Early neolithic pots were often decorated with impressed fabric or cord; the characteristic classical friezes were "sprigged," or applied, to Wedgwood vases, while

imitations may incorporate the reliefs in an all-in-one slip mold. Doulton vases may be impressed and incised with natural leaves; Sèvres vases may be worked in the *pâte-sur-pâte* cameo technique; Devon slipware may be cut out and combed in *sgraffito* technique.

Pots may be fired in a number of ways, from a hole in the ground, to Chinese multichambered "dragon" kilns; from Staffordshire "bottle"-shaped kilns to the modern tunnel kiln. Kiln type and management (knowing when the right temperature has been reached) have a direct bearing upon the sort of ware that can be manufactured on a repeatable basis.

▶ "SPRIGGING" AT THE WEDGWOOD FACTORY
The relief decoration on jasperware, Wedgwood's most famous product, is cast separately in a different coloured clay from the base, to which it is attached, or "sprigged," before firing.

POTTERY AND PORCELAIN WARES AND PERIODS

	0	500	1000	1500	1600

EARTHENWARE

EUROPE, MIDDLE EAST AND UNITED STATES

NEOLITHIC AND PRE-COLUMBIAN CULTURES (c. 10,000 BC–c. AD 1500)

MIDDLE EASTERN SLIPWARES (800–1100)
NISHAPUR (800–1100) MESOPOTAMIA
SAMARQAND (900–1100) MESOPOTAMIA

MIDDLE EASTERN EARTHENWARES
IZNIK (1500–) TURKEY

EUROPEAN LEAD-GLAZED EARTHENWARES (700–)
BEAUVAIS (1500–1600) FRANCE
HAFNER (1500–1600) GERMANY

EUROPEAN TIN-GLAZED EARTHENWARES
HISPANO-MORESQUE (1300–1500) SPAIN
MAIOLICA (1400–) ITALY
FAIENCE (1500–) FRANCE, GERMANY
DELFTWARE (1500–) HOLLAND, ENGLAND

CHINA AND JAPAN

CHINESE LEAD-GLAZED TRADITION (200 BC–)
HAN (200 BC–AD 200)
TANG (600–900)
POST-TANG (900–)

JAPANESE LEAD-
RAKU (1550–)

STONEWARE

EUROPE, MIDDLE EAST AND UNITED STATES

SALT-GLAZED STONEWARES (1200–)
WHITE, GRAY AND BROWN STONEWARE (1200–)
RHINE REGION, GERMANY

CHINA AND JAPAN

CHINESE STONEWARES (200 BC–)
YÜEH WARE (200 BC–AD 900)
HENAN PROVINCE BROWN WARE (700–1200)
JIEN WARE (1000–1300)

JAPANESE
SHINO WARE (1550–)
ORIBE WARE (1550–)

PORCELAIN

EUROPE, MIDDLE EAST AND UNITED STATES

EUROPEAN
FLORENCE

CHINA AND JAPAN

CHINESE WHITE WARES (700–)
YINGQING, DINGYAO (700–1300)   BLANC-DE-CHINE (1300–)

CHINESE SONG DYNASTY MONOCHROMES (900–1200)
GEYAO, GUANYAO, RUYAO, CELADON (900–1200)

CHINESE ENAMELED PORCELAINS
FAMILLE VERTE (1450–1720)
DOUCAI (1450–1900)
WUCAI (1500–1700)

	0	500	1000	1500	1600

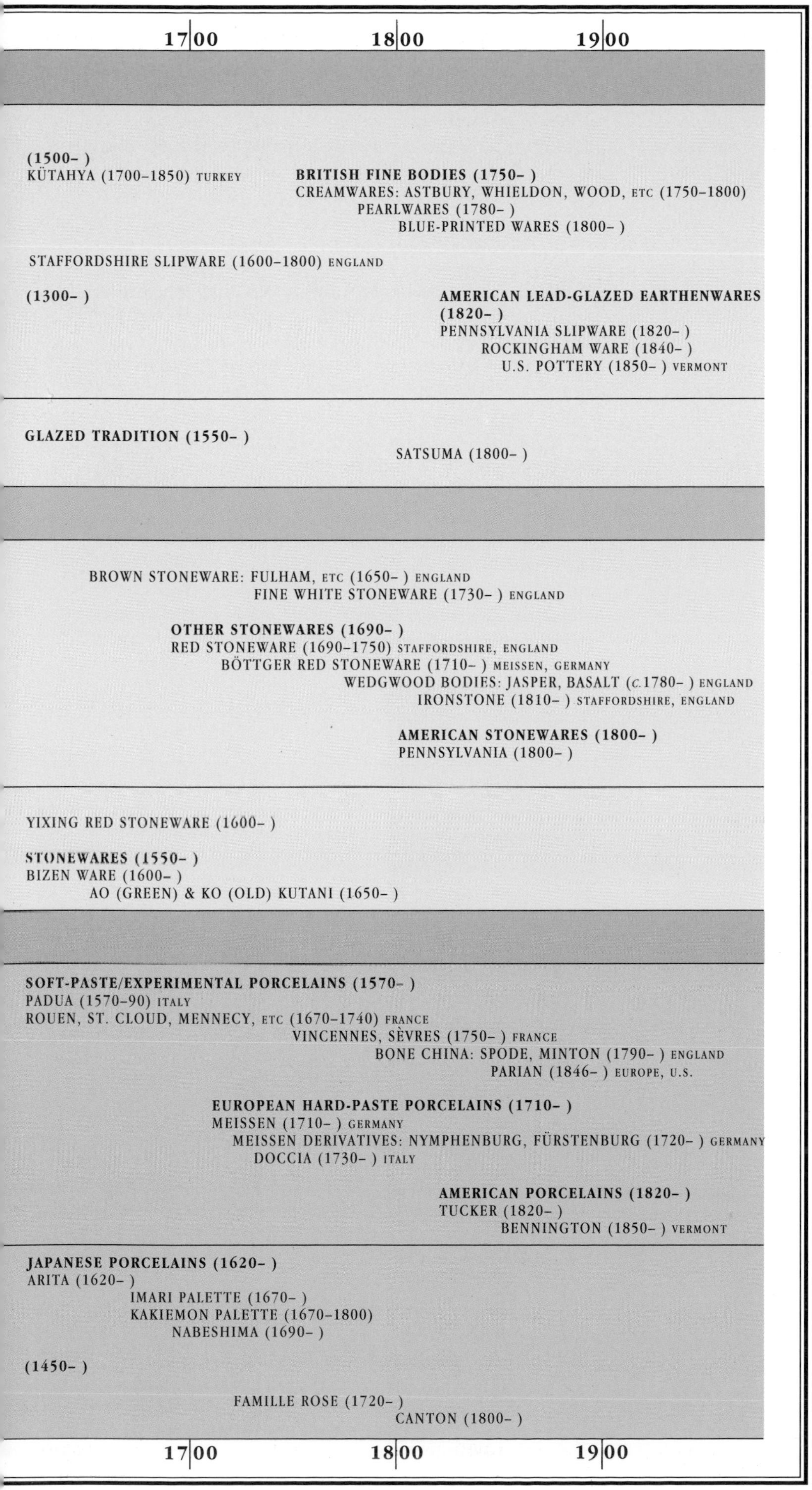

17	00	18	00	19	00

(1500–)
KÜTAHYA (1700–1850) TURKEY BRITISH FINE BODIES (1750–)
CREAMWARES: ASTBURY, WHIELDON, WOOD, ETC (1750–1800)
PEARLWARES (1780–)
BLUE-PRINTED WARES (1800–)

STAFFORDSHIRE SLIPWARE (1600–1800) ENGLAND

(1300–) AMERICAN LEAD-GLAZED EARTHENWARES
(1820–)
PENNSYLVANIA SLIPWARE (1820–)
ROCKINGHAM WARE (1840–)
U.S. POTTERY (1850–) VERMONT

GLAZED TRADITION (1550–)
SATSUMA (1800–)

BROWN STONEWARE: FULHAM, ETC (1650–) ENGLAND
FINE WHITE STONEWARE (1730–) ENGLAND

OTHER STONEWARES (1690–)
RED STONEWARE (1690–1750) STAFFORDSHIRE, ENGLAND
BÖTTGER RED STONEWARE (1710–) MEISSEN, GERMANY
WEDGWOOD BODIES: JASPER, BASALT (c.1780–) ENGLAND
IRONSTONE (1810–) STAFFORDSHIRE, ENGLAND

AMERICAN STONEWARES (1800–)
PENNSYLVANIA (1800–)

YIXING RED STONEWARE (1600–)

STONEWARES (1550–)
BIZEN WARE (1600–)
AO (GREEN) & KO (OLD) KUTANI (1650–)

SOFT-PASTE/EXPERIMENTAL PORCELAINS (1570–)
PADUA (1570–90) ITALY
ROUEN, ST. CLOUD, MENNECY, ETC (1670–1740) FRANCE
VINCENNES, SÈVRES (1750–) FRANCE
BONE CHINA: SPODE, MINTON (1790–) ENGLAND
PARIAN (1846–) EUROPE, U.S.

EUROPEAN HARD-PASTE PORCELAINS (1710–)
MEISSEN (1710–) GERMANY
MEISSEN DERIVATIVES: NYMPHENBURG, FÜRSTENBURG (1720–) GERMANY
DOCCIA (1730–) ITALY

AMERICAN PORCELAINS (1820–)
TUCKER (1820–)
BENNINGTON (1850–) VERMONT

JAPANESE PORCELAINS (1620–)
ARITA (1620–)
IMARI PALETTE (1670–)
KAKIEMON PALETTE (1670–1800)
NABESHIMA (1690–)

(1450–)

FAMILLE ROSE (1720–)
CANTON (1800–)

17	00	18	00	19	00

This chart allows the major types of ceramics, and where and when they were made, to be compared and contrasted. It is divided into the three main groups of ceramic body – earthenware, stoneware and porcelain. China and Japan are separated from the Western world within each of these categories.

This arrangement shows graphically how advanced the Eastern traditions were. It also means that the development of wares can be followed. For example, with stoneware it is possible to see where it was first perfected; when it was introduced in the United States; how Wedgwood fits in; and how long stoneware was in use in Europe before hard-paste porcelain was discovered.

The type of Chinese enameled porcelain known in Europe as Canton is generally called "rose medallion" in the United States.

As ceramics are evolved, rather than invented, dates are often approximate, especially for early wares. In every instance, the start date is given for the production of the different wares. For types of pottery and porcelain that are still being made, no end date is given.

HISTORICAL SURVEY

The history of ceramics is a dazzling and complex weave: a warp of continuous and broken traditions crossed by an ever-changing weft of imported ideas. In this rich brocade, several broad patterns emerge.

For perhaps thousands of years, clay was used only in its plastic state, for modeling animals, figures and totems, often for ritual purposes. At some time within this prehistoric period, it was discovered that the clay could be "fixed" by drying it in the sun and, presumably by accident, that fire could create a more lasting effect. The potter's art was born. Thereafter, different clays were sought, treated and perhaps mixed with fluxes to promote fusion and improve the quality of the material, making it easier to manipulate and fire. Vessels were pinched into shape, coil-wound, battered or assembled from slabs. The type of clay used was a basic earthenware, a porous clay fired to modest temperatures.

By refining new clay bodies and firing techniques, higher firing temperatures were achieved, so creating a harder, more robust material: stoneware. Vessels in this material were also watertight and required no coating of pitch or resin, unlike the earlier retsina-carrying amphorae of the Mediterranean.

The discovery and development of glaze was another major advance. Not only did a clear glaze seal and enhance the color of the underlying body, but it could itself be colored by including a metallic oxide, leading to an almost infinite variety of glaze colors and textures.

These developments occurred in many places, and at different times, by local evolution, conquest or cultural influence. No culture was more prolific in its steady invention and evolution of ceramic traditions than China, where the development of the potter's wheel in the second millennium BC encouraged the improvement in clays needed for "throwing" techniques.

The gradual emergence of the Chinese empire was, by the Han Dynasty (206 BC–AD 220), accompanied by a dramatic rise in the use of pottery for elaborate burial ceremonies. At first, ranks of life-sized sculptural figures, such as the famous "terracotta armies" at Xiang, were made, clay replacing the ancient custom of human and animal sacrifice. Then, in the Tang Dynasty (618–907), figures were scaled down in size, and "three-color" – the so-called egg-and-spinach – lead glazes were introduced, providing a sudden bloom of color after the plain green lead-glazed wares of the Han Dynasty. Added to this came an early production-line technique of press-molding repeated elements, such as limbs, trunks and heads for the camels, horses, courtiers and grooms to accompany the dead into the afterlife.

During the Tang Dynasty, the gradual refinement also occurred of the stoneware tradition into the white

◀ **LADIES TAKING TEA**
Although tea was still a precious commodity, at the time this picture was painted by the Flemish artist Jan Josef Horemans the Elder (1682–1759) the custom of drinking tea had already been adopted by the European bourgeoisie. The small blue and white cups without handles, the large saucers, from which the tea was drunk, and the bowl may have been Chinese, but were more likely Delftware.

▶ THE DINING ROOM AT
SALTRAM HOUSE
*A side table in the dining room at
Saltram, a fine country house near
Plymouth, England, with part of a
green-flowered faience dinner
service set out on it. Reflected in the
mirror, the dining table can be seen
with other items from the dinner
service, which bears the arms of the
Parker family and was specially
made in Marseilles c.1750–70 for
use at Saltram.*

and magically translucent material today known as porcelain, or china. It was to take another 1,000 years and dozens of occasionally successful experiments in "soft paste," or artificial recipes, before a gifted European alchemist succeeded in producing porcelain. This took place at the Meissen factory near Dresden, Saxony, from materials approximating the Chinese "hard-paste" ingredients of china clay and china stone.

It was the growing awareness of Chinese porcelains in the 1300s to 1600s that gave impetus to porcelain-inspired alternative traditions, in both Islamic lands and renaissance Europe. Thus the addition of ashes of tin to a clear lead glaze rendered buff-colored pottery white, allowing it to be painted and giving rise to some of the most sought-after European pottery, maiolica.

This technique was introduced by the Moors into Spain, where it flourished in the 1300s and 1400s as the Hispano-Moresque tradition, based in Valencia and exporting armorial chargers to Italian princes and potentates. When potters in northern Italy started to produce their own maiolica wares, they developed a dazzling palette of additional colors perfectly suited to the print-derived landscapes and *istoriato* scenes epitomized on Urbino wares. These products were later to be made in the Low Countries (Delftware), in France (faience), in Germany and Scandinavia (*fayencen*), and in England (delftware).

Once trade with the Orient was under way, the arrival of Chinese and Japanese blue and white porcelain was the most influential factor to affect the earthenware and stoneware industries of Europe. It

inspired not only technical experiments to produce a porcelain body, but also many artistic imitations of blue and white, of Kakiemon and Imari. From *c.*1700, competition from Chinese potters brought about a refinement of the lead-glazed earthenware clays made in Staffordshire. This was further encouraged by the East India trade, from which stemmed the increase in wealth, as well as household display, of the aristocracy and the rising middle class.

While European princes began to set up Meissen imitators, it was a potter in earthenware, Josiah Wedgwood, who brought the Industrial Revolution to ceramics. He introduced technical improvements in clay bodies and firing techniques; set up production-line manufacture; and used modern marketing techniques to advance his products at home and abroad.

Three other leaps in ceramic technology in the late 1700s gave added advantages to Staffordshire potters: transfer-printing (*c.*1760); the creation of a hybrid "bone china" body; and slip-casting, which allowed figures and flat wares to be mass-produced by pouring liquid clay into molds, so doubling the effectiveness of liquid bone china. These factors, allied to the political decline of China's Qing Dynasty after 1790, gave the European industry, especially in England, trading supremacy.

As for the life of the anonymous potter, another century was to pass before the deadly lead glazes, in use for more than 2,000 years, were – in Staffordshire – replaced by safer alternatives, raising life expectancy well beyond the meager 35 years as happened at the beginning of the nineteenth century.

China has the most celebrated ceramic lineage in the world. In a tradition dating from before the dawn of recorded history, the Chinese potter has been at the birth of every major innovation and development.

From the neolithic cultures came the use of colored pigments and the wheel, which enabled potters to make more sophisticated forms with sharply defined contours. During the Shang Dynasty, the first in Chinese history from which records survive, the potter borrowed technology from the bronze industry to build more advanced kilns and, for the first time, white-bodied wares and glazed pottery were made.

Developments during the Han Dynasty included lead glaze and high-fired stoneware. By the Tang Dynasty, the basic green and ocher lead-glazed wares were enriched by the brilliant *sancai* (three-color) palette found on tomb figures and wares, and the the first porcelain was made, a warm cream-colored ware from northern China.

Song Dynasty wares included refined stonewares and porcelains that often relied simply on perfection of form and glaze to delight the eye; this is epitomized by the classic Jun and Ru wares of northern China. The introspective classicism of these wares continued when the Song Court was forced to flee south to Hangzhou in Zhejiang province. The celadons and Guan wares made there were the last classic stonewares, which carried the Song spirit forward into the more exuberant Yuan Dynasty.

Chinese dynasties

Xia	2205–1766 B.C.
Shang	1766–1122 B.C.
Zhou	1111–255 B.C.
Qin	221–206 B.C.
Han	206 B.C.–A.D. 220
Six Dynasties	220–589
Sui	581–618
Tang	618–907
Five Dynasties	907–960
Northern Song	960–1127
Southern Song	1127–1279
Yuan	1206–1368
Ming	1368–1644
Qing	1644–1912

1 NEOLITHIC MORTUARY JAR
A typical example of the Yangshao culture of Gansu province in western China. This pot, hand built from fine pinkish-buff clay, dates from the third millennium B.C.; it was burnished by rotating it on a cloth on a flat surface. The pot is painted in chocolate-brown and red with a characteristic motif that probably represents the edible water frog. H 17½in/44cm

2 MODEL OF A GRAIN MILL
When this model was made in the Han period (206 B.C.–A.D. 220), the red clay body would have been covered in a thick, brilliant dark green glaze, but the damp conditions of the grave from which it was recovered have broken down the glaze and blanketed it in an iridescent coating. W 10in/25cm

3 JUNYAO NARCISSUS BOWL
This stoneware relies for its effect on a heavy glaze, which can be lavender, sometimes enhanced with purple splashes, blue or soft green. Vessels are usually based on conservative or archaic forms – this 13th-century bulb bowl takes its shape from a bronze original. Diam. 8in/20cm

4 TANG FIGURE OF A HORSE
Made for the tomb of a dignitary or an official, this finely modeled Fereghan horse (A.D. 688–906) is decorated in the sancai palette of chestnut-brown, green and cream glazes on an almost white body. Tang potters achieved great naturalism in their tomb sculptures, and this horse shows spirit, energy and realism. H 29in/74cm

5 CIZHOU STONEWARE VASE
A typical example of a tall, slender narrow-mouthed Cizhou stoneware meiping, or blossom vase, dating from the 12th century. It is decorated with painted flowers and bamboo and, in the central zone, with the characters for flower, wind, snow and moon vigorously incised through the white slip to a brown ground. H 14½in/37cm

6 LONGQUAN CELADON BOTTLE
The elegant pear-shaped body and trumpet neck of this early 14th-century vase are typical of many later Song and Yuan wares. The intentional splashes of iron-brown are uncommon, as is the crackled olive glaze; the usual celadon color is a subtle sea-green without crackle. H 10in/25cm

7 GUANYAO STONEWARE DISH
In some ways, the elegant simplicity of many Guanyao forms, based on bronze shapes or flowers, continued the tradition of the north; it was the body and the glaze that differed. There were two types of Guan ware: a fine dark-bodied clay and a paler clay, both very thickly glazed and with a pronounced intentional crackle. This dish probably dates from the 13th or 14th century. Diam. 5½in/14cm

8 CELADON GROUP
Figures are rare in Longquan ware and usually take the form of a divinity or a sage, here on a water buffalo. For a fairly late 15th-century Ming piece, this soft yellow-green is a good color; the best Song pieces are bluer. Strong red oxidization can be seen on the animal's feet. H 10½in/27cm

◄ **DINGYAO DISH**
One of the classic wares of the Northern Song Dynasty in the 11th–12th centuries, Ding ware was a thinly potted porcelain fired in a coal-fueled kiln, which produced a distinctive ivory glaze. Most extant Ding pieces are bowls or dishes, sometimes decorated by carving or molding. Here, a lotus pattern has been carved in a fluent, calligraphic style, in contrast to the more rigid decoration of molded pieces. Because the dish was fired upside down on its unglazed rim, this has been sheathed in copper. Diam. 8in/20cm

1

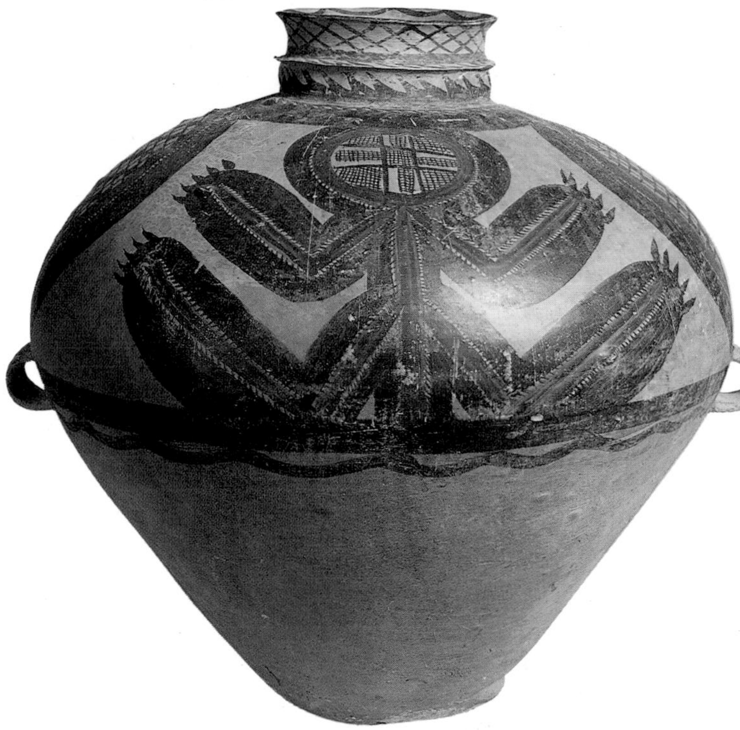

2

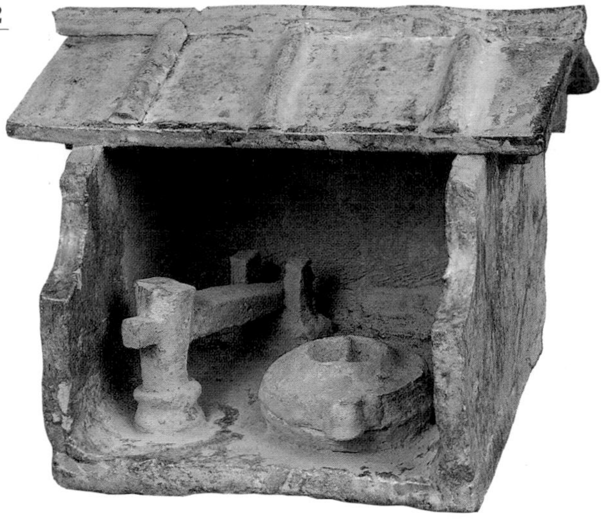

3

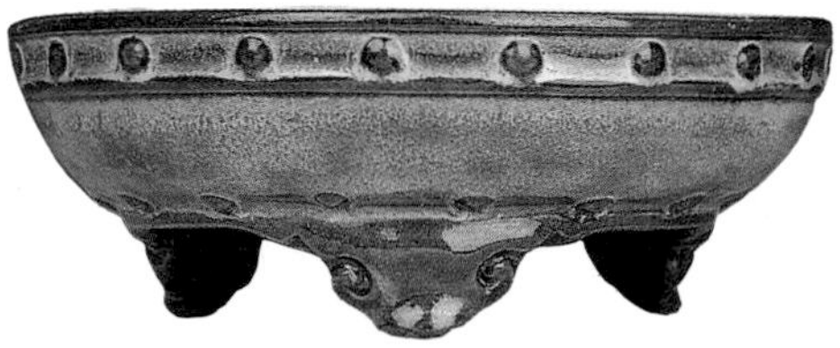

4

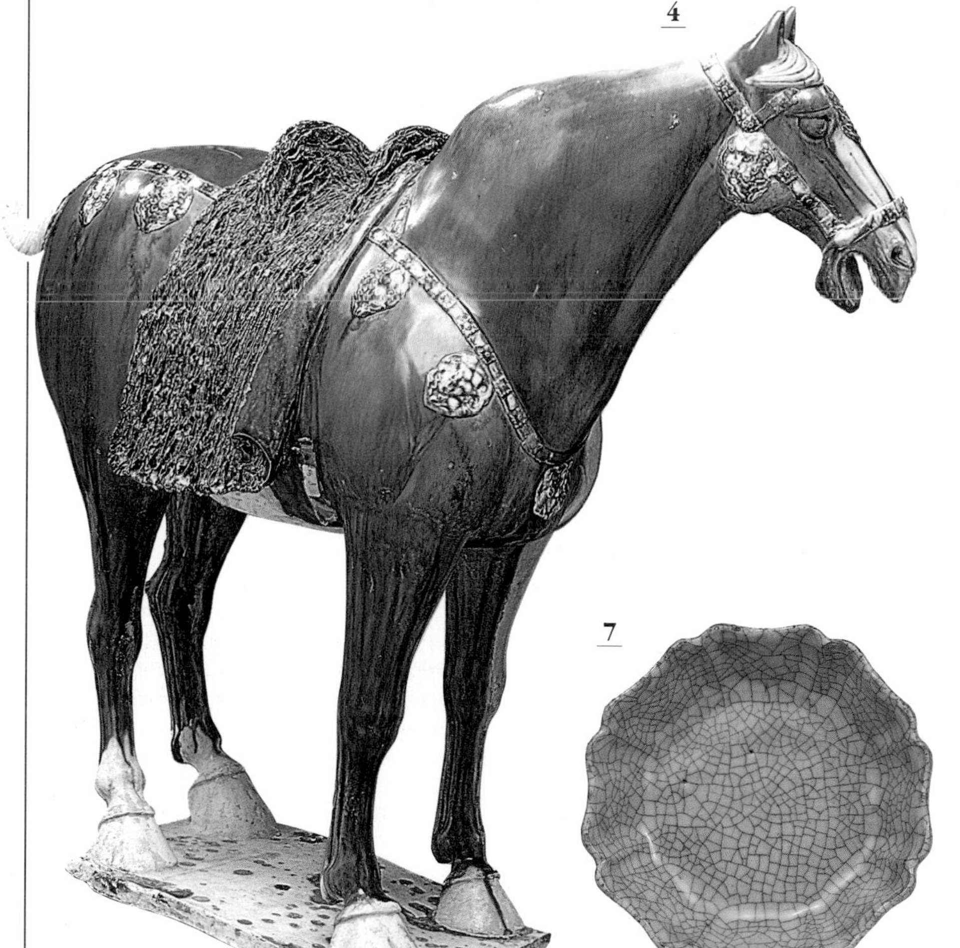

5

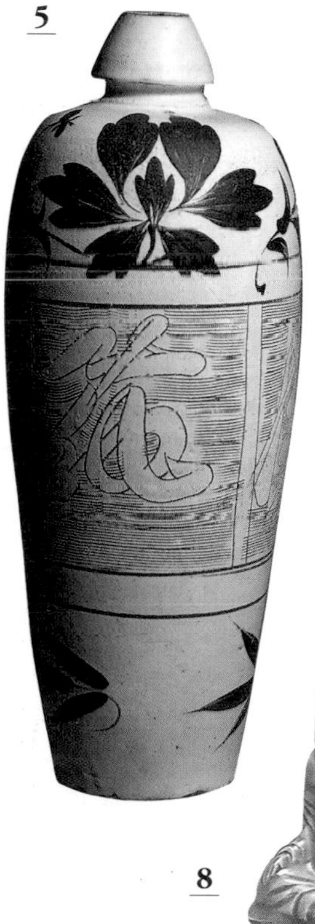

6

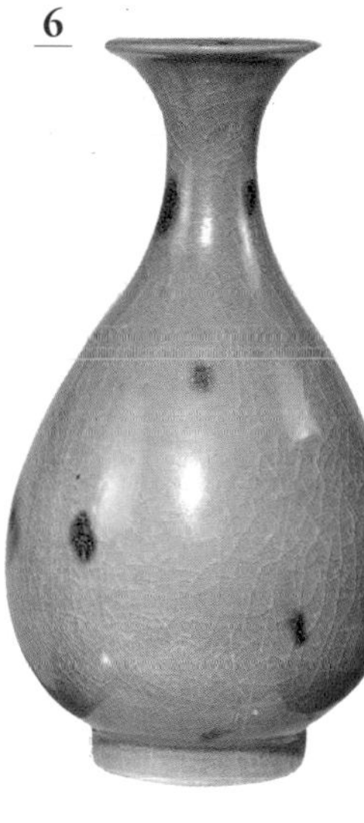

7

8

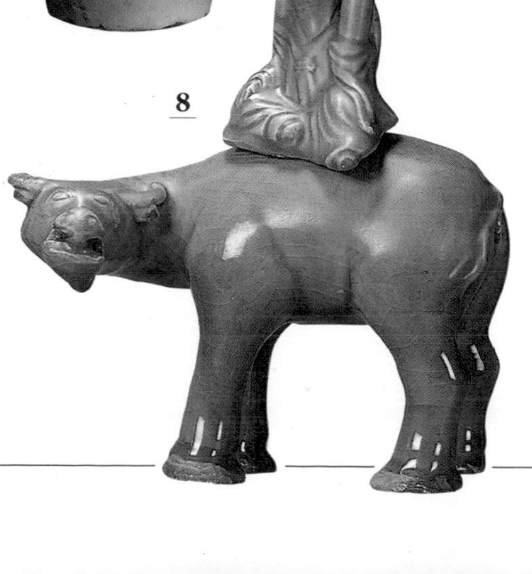

Although many fine monochrome wares, such as celadon and black-glazed stonewares, were made during the Song Dynasty (960–1279), the finest single-color pieces were produced during the Ming and Qing dynasties (1368–1912). Most of these pieces were made with a fine white porcelain body which, although occasionally left plain, was usually glazed.

The earliest glazes included cobalt-blue and a rather unreliable copper-red. During the first half of the Ming Dynasty (before c.1500), yellow, turquoise and celadon, a greenish shade, were added to this range of glazes. Later in the same dynasty, apple-green, eggplant, iron-brown and iron-red also became available. Some pieces were lightly incised with a pattern that sometimes can only be seen by looking closely.

During the Qing Dynasty (1644–1912), considerable advances were made in the manufacture of ceramics. This led to a revival of some wares and glazes which, due to technical problems, had fallen out of favor in the late 1400s. In addition, several new glazes were introduced.

◀ BLANC-DE-CHINE BUDDHA
The large figure of the Buddha in a rather formal position, with his left arm held against his chest and holding a pearl in his hand, stands on a double lotus base. Dating from the 17th or 18th centuries – more accurate dating is difficult – it carries the impressed mark of the maker, He Chaozun. The white of blanc-de-Chine wares has a surprisingly wide tonal range, from a pinkish-ivory color, through the slightly bluish tone of this statue, to dead white. H 33in/84cm

Chinese blanc-de-Chine
This fine white porcelain (*below*) has been made around Dehua in the southern province of Fujian since the Song Dynasty. Dating *blanc-de-Chine* is difficult because little documentation concerning its production remains.

Since this clay is extremely plastic, molds were used extensively in the manufacturing process. Most of the output was of figures, usually with some Buddhist significance. Some of these figures were sculptural masterpieces with crisply modeled flowing robes and fine detailing.

The Qing glazes
As firing technology improved during the Qing Dynasty, several new glazes were introduced. "Peach bloom" (**3**), a subtle varicolored glaze derived from copper, was difficult to fire and so was used only on small vessels for the scholar's table. Other Qing glazes included the pale blue, so-called *clair-de-lune*; "mirror black"; "tea-dust" (**8**), a muddy, deep olive green; and "robin's egg," a purple-speckled turquoise.

1 IMPERIAL YELLOW BOWL
Yellow as an overglaze enamel monochrome was probably first used after c.1450. This type of enameling could be added to an earlier piece without damaging the porcelain, so dating can be difficult although, as a guide, the Imperial yellow of the 15th and first half of the 16th centuries tends to have a warm tan tone. The circled six-character mark is for the Hongzhi period (1488–1505). Diam. 6½in/16cm

2 PAIR OF BLUE-GLAZED VASES
High-relief elephant's-head handles break the hard lines of these square violet-blue vases, which bear the mark of Qianlong (1735–96). H 12in/30cm

3 "PEACH BLOOM" WATER POT
One of the major innovations of Tsang Ying-hsuan, the superintendent of the Imperial kilns in the reign of Emperor Kangxi, "peach bloom" was an extremely temperamental glaze used only for a small number of objects. On good-quality pieces, such as this taibo zun, or water pot, the soft pinkish glaze is suffused with tones of moss-green. The pot is dated by the mark of Kangxi (1661–1722). Diam. 5in/13cm

4 INCISED SHALLOW BOWL
Dating from the 17th century, this eggplant-glazed bowl, with an everted rim, has a molded ring on the outside which divides two bands of incised lotus decoration. Diam. 6in/15cm

5 PEAR-SHAPED VASE
Guan, or "official," ware was a highly refined stoneware covered in a thick, crackled gray glaze. It developed near Hangzhou, the center of the Southern Song Court (1127–1279). This item dates from the 18th century. H 5½in/14cm

6 FLAMBÉ-GLAZED MEIPING
Designed to hold a single stem of cherry blossom, meiping-form vases had narrow necks and bulbous shoulders. Made in the 18th century, this piece has a variegated flambé glaze (a red or purplish color suffused with flashes of gray or blue), which developed during the Qing Dynasty and required great skill in kiln operation. H 7½in/19cm

7 LEMON-YELLOW GLAZED BOWL
A traditionally shaped bowl with the Yongzheng mark (1722–35). It is an early example of this glaze, unknown before c.1725. Diam. 5in/13cm

8 "TEA-DUST" GLAZED JARDINIÈRE
Resembling the dust of green tea, this green glaze, saturated with tiny yellow flecks, was usually reserved for rather large objects. It bears the seal mark of Qianlong (1735–96). Diam. 8in/20cm

9 LARGE LIVER-RED STEM BOWL
Originally developed in the early Ming Dynasty, this glaze fell out of use in the late Ming and was revived in the Qing. This piece was made during Yongzheng's reign (1722–35). Diam. 7in/18cm

10 LARGE BLUE-GLAZED BOTTLE VASE
This shape, popularly used for 18th-century monochromes, was developed by Yongle (1402–24). It bears the mark of Qianlong (1735–96). H 22in/56cm

UNDERGLAZE BLUE AND RED

The technique of painting a color under a glaze developed during the Tang Dynasty (618–907). At first, the clean crisp patterns were considered vulgar, and it was some time before the celadon wares were superseded by underglazed porcelains. The most important center for ceramics in China was the Imperial kiln at Jingdezhen in Jianxi province, and it was here that expertise in this form of decoration matured.

Underglaze painting evolved on the *Qingbai* porcelain body, the ware mentioned in *The Travels of Marco Polo*, in which the word "porcelain" was first used. The earliest Jingdezhen porcelain painted in underglaze almost certainly dates from *c.*1330 and is the ancestor of the Western "willow pattern," still familiar today.

The "green," or unfired, porcelain is left until it is dry enough to be handled and is then painted in underglaze cobalt-blue, copper-red or, in extremely rare cases, iron-brown or black. When the color has dried, the piece is immersed in, or brushed with, glaze before the object is fired in the kiln. This method has been refined over the centuries, gradually eliminating many of the flaws which marred earlier production.

It is, however, the characteristic flaws of each period that help with dating Chinese porcelain. Reign marks are unreliable, but they can be useful in conjunction with an understanding of calligraphy and the stylistic trends and key motifs of the reigns.

CHINESE REIGN MARKS

The six-character mark indicates the period of production by giving the name of the reigning emperor. This mark is for the Ming Emperor Xuande (1425–35) (1).

Emperor's second name — Character for "Great"

Made in the reign of — Dynasty

— Emperor's first name

Reign marks should not be used as the sole method of dating Chinese porcelain, since some potters reused marks from an earlier, more respected, period.

---

1 EARLY MING BLUE AND WHITE BOWL
Within 100 years of the first underglaze wares being made, this heavily potted but beautifully proportioned bowl was produced. The painter has shown skill in balancing the sprays of fruit with the contours and space allowed. The bluish tone of the thick glaze, the blurred or "soft-focus" effect of the design, and the blackened pigment in areas are characteristic of early Ming wares. The mark is of Emperor Xuande (1425–35). Diam. 11in/28cm

---

◀ **FINE UNDERGLAZE COPPER-RED DISH**
After his accession to the throne, the Ming Emperor Hongwu (1368–98) closed the ports and temporarily restricted trade. Imported cobalt, used to produce underglaze blue, became difficult to obtain and so the native copper-red ore was used as a substitute.

Rarely successful as a color, copper-red had a tendency to fire to a dirty mushroom pink or to the grayish color of this dish. In the center of the wide shallow base is a painting of a chrysanthemum spray surrounded by six scrolling peony blooms. The straight everted rim is decorated with a key-pattern band. Diam. 8in/20cm

---

2 MING BLUE AND WHITE PEN TRAY
The Wanli mark (1572–1620) identifies this piece as late Ming, a period when the standard of both decoration and material declined. The dragons are sketchily drawn and casually placed, with the head and a claw of the smaller dragon touching the frame. In addition, the rim is chipped, a common flaw on porcelain of this period. L 7½in/19cm

3 LATE MING "KRAAK" ARMORIAL DISH
The term "kraak," coined by the Dutch who raided Portuguese ships (carracks) for their cargoes of porcelain, is used to describe early Chinese export wares (c.1570–c.1650). In the early 1500s, the Portuguese became the first Europeans to establish maritime trading links with China, and much porcelain was shipped to the West. This dish from the Wanli era (1572–1620) depicts a hydra with seven heads. The compartmentalized rim is typical of kraak wares. Diam. 17in/43cm

4 UNDERGLAZE BLUE AND RED VASE
The pear-shaped body and flared neck of this vase were popular in the 14th and 15th centuries. In the early 1700s when this vase was made, many techniques and styles were revived or reinterpreted, and although rather mechanically painted, this piece has traditional underglaze copper-red and cobalt-blue decoration. H 15in/38cm

5 BLUE AND WHITE EXPORT DISH
The fenced garden and willow tree on this typical 1730s export dish show the inspiration behind the patterns designed by Worcester, Bow, Lowestoft and other English factories in the mid-18th century. Diam. 16in/41cm

6 "TEMPLE-PATTERN" MEAT DISH
The shape of this dish (c.1770) is based on a silver form of the French Régence period, but the decoration is fantasy. In China, such landscapes were painted, whereas Western "willow-pattern" designs were printed. W 16in/41cm

7 BLUE AND WHITE SPILL VASE
The rigid design, of scrolling vegetation with Buddhist emblems, on this piece is typical of mass-produced, late 19th-century wares. H 11in/28cm

8 LATE QING JAR AND COVER
The design of prunus blossom against a cracked-ice background, in vogue in the Kangxi period (1661–1722), was revived in the late 1800s. H 13in/33cm

POTTERY AND PORCELAIN

◄ **RETICULATED BALUSTER VASE**
Complexity was the keynote of porcelain forms and decoration from the middle of the 18th century until well into the 19th century. The outer shell of this double-walled vase is elaborately decorated, in the intricate manner characteristic of the Qianlong period (1735–96), with seven different decorative bands of plantains, scrolling vegetation and eye-catching small formal motifs; the opaque turquoise and yellow are typical of famille-rose *enamels.*

The inner vase, just visible through the pierced panels of fruiting branches, is painted in underglaze blue in early Ming style. There is no evidence of the porcelain at all; indeed, this vase could easily have been made of enameled metal. H 16in/41cm

Fahua
The term means outlined decoration, in which the design is effected in a raised trail of slip, or clay (**1**). These ridges act as boundaries, which separate the colors and prevent them from running together. *Fahua* resembles cloisonné work (*see pp.304–6*) and has the same bold feel. The colors employed are rich dark blue, purple, turquoise, yellow and green.

Resist technique
Semi-wet porcelain clay is incised with the design, which is then carefully covered in a resist medium to prevent the glaze from sticking to it (**2**). After firing, the design is painted in a translucent enamel, sometimes with part of the decoration extending on to the surrounding glaze.

1 16TH-CENTURY FAHUA WINE JAR
Most existing pieces of fahua are large-scale hollow wares, such as this wine jar (guan), *blossom vases* (meiping) *or barrel-shaped garden seats. The decoration in white slip, infilled with turquoise, yellow and blue, shows the Eight Daoist Immortals, a favored theme in the middle and later Ming periods. Diam. 14in/36cm*

2 MING GREEN DRAGON BOWL
A bowl decorated in the resist technique with two brilliant green dragons pursuing each other. Such pieces were made from the Chenghua period (1465–87) until the end of the Zhengde period (1506–21). Diam. 7½in/19cm

3 LATE MING WUCAI DISH
A Wanli period (1572–1620) saucer dish painted in a typically bold, slightly cluttered style. Figure subjects, usually depicting religious subjects of Daoist significance, became more common in the 16th century. The loosely drawn, almost cartoon-like, figures and the enclosing calligraphic clouds were also standard decorative forms. The languid, undulating foliage and highly stylized lotus are strongly outlined.

4 FAMILLE-VERTE SCROLL WEIGHT
The brilliant polychrome painting on this unusual object from the Kangxi period (1661–1722) is a fine example of famille verte. The dense carpet of peony and bamboo on a seeded green ground is employed mostly on large ornamental export wares. L 14in/36cm

5 DOUCAI SAUCER DISH
This style of painting originated in the classic Ming reign of Chenghua (1465–87), but was seldom used until its revival in the latter part of the reign of Kangxi (1661–1722). Both the large leafed plants and the fruiting branches on the underside of this dish from the early 1700s are outlined in underglaze blue and filled in with subtle colors heightened in red. Diam. 6½in/16cm

6 FAMILLE-ROSE YUZHI BOWL
Meticulously potted in highly refined porcelain, this plain rounded bowl is typical of many Imperial pieces from the Kangxi period (1661–1722). The new famille-rose palette was used for the heavy brocade-type decoration, with the somewhat stiff but detailed roses that are typical of this group of overglaze wares. Diam 6in/15cm

7 FAMILLE-ROSE BOTTLE VASE
The decorative theme of bats and ribbons among clouds on this vase parallels contemporary cloisonné. Indeed, many examples of turquoise ground porcelains from the Qianlong period (1735–96) are direct copies of metalwork. H 25½in/68cm

8 FAMILLE-ROSE HU-SHAPED VASE
A heavy, baluster-form vase, dating from the early 1900s, when potters attempted to re-create fine, 18th-century Imperial famille-rose wares. Many such pieces are deceptive, but the soft pastel shades and rather weak painting confirm the late date of this vase (1916). H 6½in/16cm

The technique of painting ceramics in overglaze color was developed *c.* AD 1200 on the Cizhou stonewares of northern China. At first, the palette was limited to three colors, red, green and yellow; black and brown were added later.

Enameling on porcelain appears to have begun in the early fifteenth century; it was soon refined to such a degree that, by the reign of Emperor Chenghua (1464–87), the potters of Jingdezhen were able to produce such delicate pieces as the *doucai* wares. *Doucai* is a method of painting whereby the outline of the design is drawn in underglaze blue and then filled in with washes of overglaze enamels in red, green, yellow and purplish-brown. Black was sometimes used, mainly for detailing.

In the 1500s, *doucai* was abandoned for the *wucai,* or five-colored, palette, which was used until the late 1600s. Despite the name, iron-red, yellow, green, black, cobalt-blue and manganese-brown comprise the full *wucai* color range. *Wucai* wares of the later Ming Dynasty are much cruder than their *doucai* predecessors. Blue was used like any other color, as a wash or for detail, rather than merely for outlining.

1
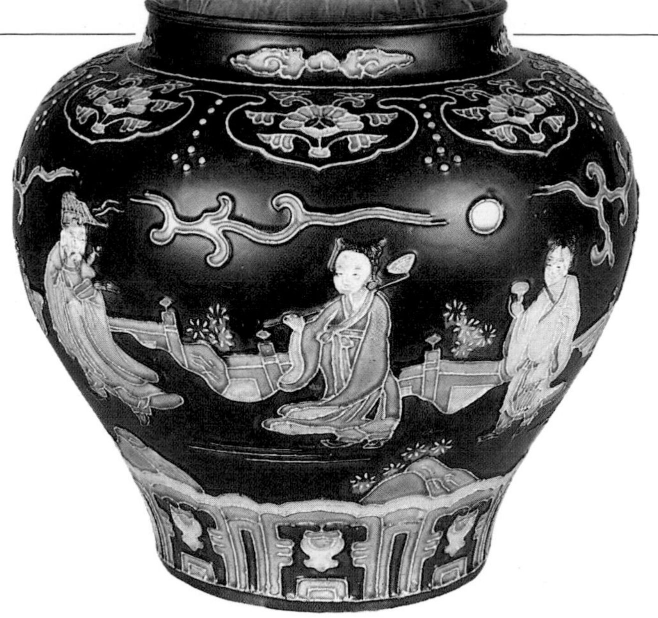

2
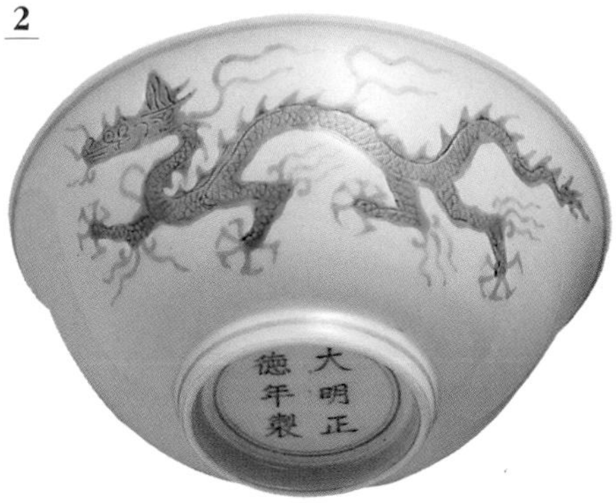

3
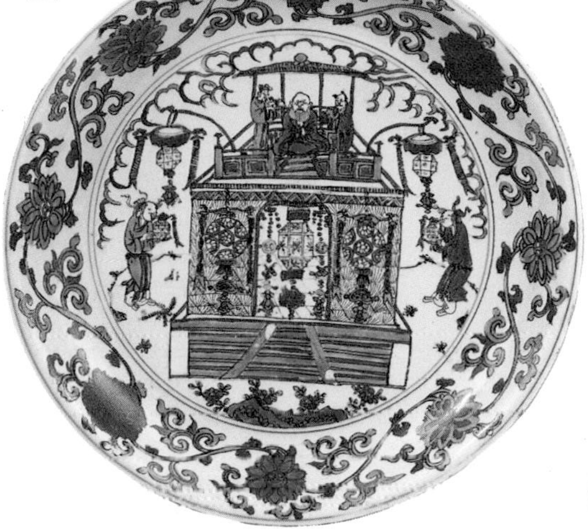

4
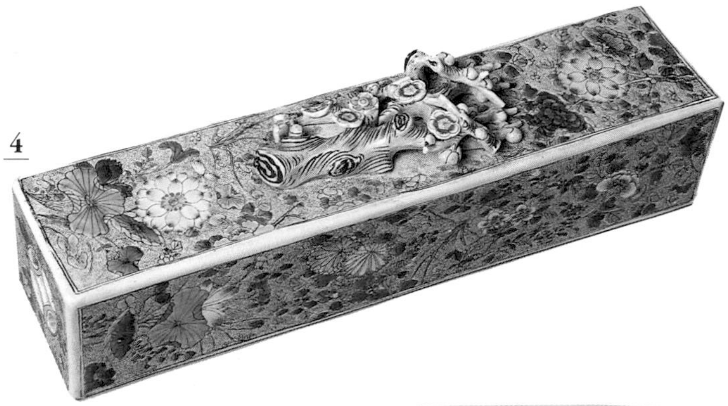

5
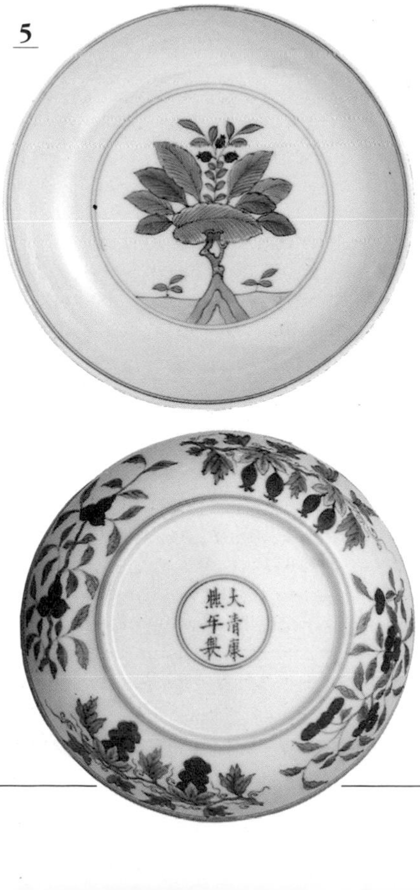

6
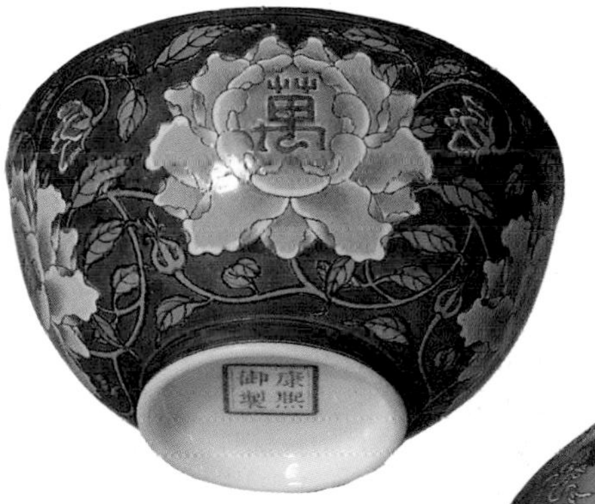

7
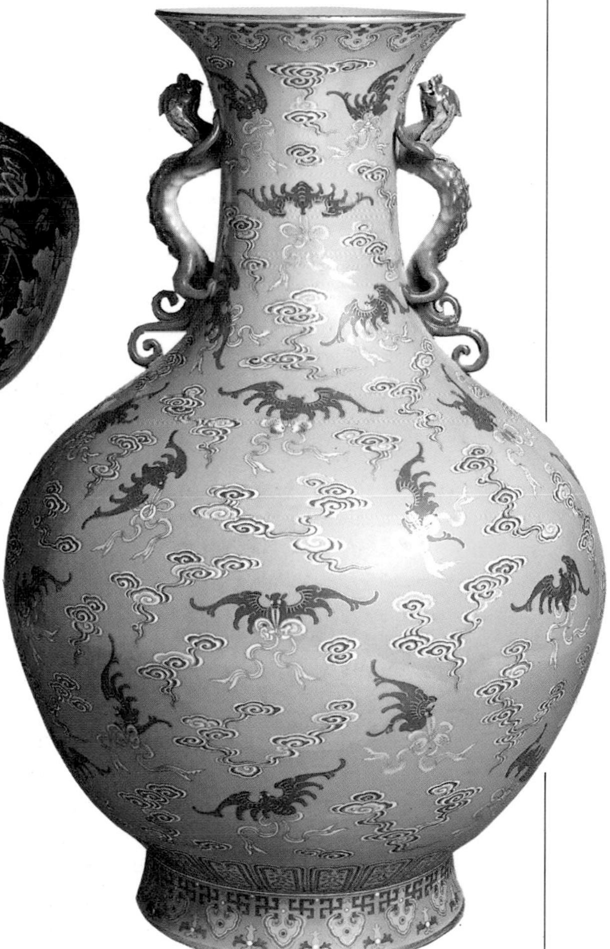

8
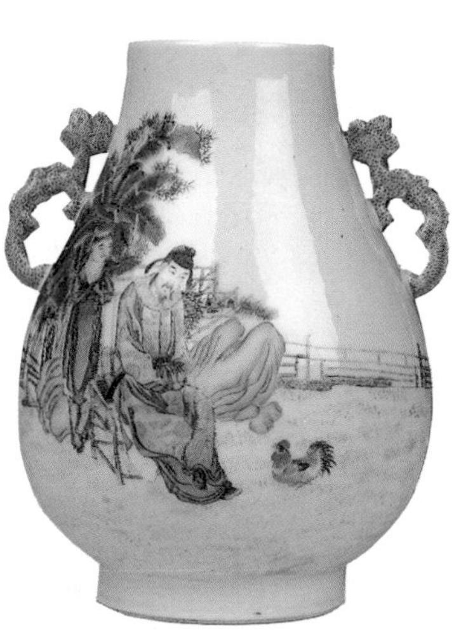

During the reign of Kangxi (1661–1722), *wucai* was replaced with the *famille-verte* palette, a somewhat lighter, more refreshing color scheme, in which green of varying tones generally plays a larger part. In the *famille-verte* palette, underglaze blue was discontinued in favor of a brilliant, almost purple, overglaze blue, which gives great vibrancy to these porcelains.

Finally, *c*.1720, *famille verte* gave way to *famille rose*, which, as the name suggests, used rose-pink – a color introduced from Europe – in its range. These more intimately painted wares were rendered in opaque enamels rather than with the fresh translucency of the *famille-verte* group. *Famille rose* has remained in vogue and is, perhaps, best known from the porcelains decorated in Canton for the export market during the nineteenth and early twentieth centuries. In contrast to the academic and exacting standards required in wares made in the Chinese taste for the home market, porcelain intended for export was more casually decorated in rather gaudy colors.

While Chinese potters quickly adopted European shapes and decorative styles, much export ware was gilded and painted with elegant Mandarin family scenes, landscapes, flowers and birds that conjured up an image of China for an eager occidental market. Although the symbolism of such subjects as the deer, bamboo and *lingzhi* fungus on the dish below, which allude to longevity, would largely have been lost on Westerners, they had great appeal.

Armorial wares

The earliest armorial porcelain – export wares decorated with coats-of-arms – dates from the 1500s, shortly after the Portuguese began trading with China. By the 1700s, many Westerners were commissioning dinner services, and armorial porcelain (3) was found in wealthy households all over Europe.

1 CHINESE IMARI-STYLE EWER
This unusual ewer, part of a set with a shell-shaped basin, is an example of a European silver form in late baroque style translated into porcelain, c.1720–40. The palette was copied from colorful Japanese Imari porcelain, which was enjoying great success. Similar sets were supplied to the Portuguese market.

▼ FAMILLE-ROSE EXPORT GROUP
Export porcelain dating from the Qianlong period (1735–96). Left to right (front): "Rockefeller" pattern plate and saucer, diam. plate 8in/20cm; snuffbox of European form, which suggests that it was specially commissioned, W 3in/7cm; large teapot and cover, with typical enameled decoration, H 10in/25cm.

Left to right (back): Octagonal deep dish painted with deer, bamboo and fungus, diam. 12½in/32cm; meat dish in a form common in French silver of Louis XIV's reign, the central bouquet painted in European style, L 15in/38cm.

2 FAMILLE-ROSE SAUCER DISH
A refined and sophisticated piece in finely potted "eggshell" porcelain from the Yongzheng period (1722–35), when Chinese potters were at their most skillful. It shows an exceptional range of colors and meticulous brushwork.

3 ARMORIAL CHARGER
Made in 1722–35 for Lord Archibald Hamilton, sometime Governor of Jamaica. This dish bears the family coat-of-arms in iron-red, gilding and famille-verte *enamels. The same border design is found on other export porcelain. Diam. 16in/40cm*

4 FAMILLE-VERTE DISH
A fine example of export porcelain (1661–1722). The central medallion within a wide border of rectilinear panels is sumptuously painted in typical early 18th-century style. The theme here is floral, but landscapes, figures or even objects were used in a similar layout. Diam. 15in/38cm

5 A DUTCHMAN AND HIS WIFE
Most porcelain exported from China was functional or decorative. The few figures included birds, animals and Daoist or Buddhist deities. Secular figures of Westerners, such as these from the periods of Yongzheng or Qianlong (1722–96), are extremely rare. H 10in/25cm

6 TOPOGRAPHICAL PUNCHBOWL
Punchbowls were essential to entertainment in Georgian England. This bowl (c.1805) shows an accurate view of the Mansion House, home of London's Lord Mayor. The neoclassical influence is evident in the restrained border and monochrome treatment of the main subject. Diam. 16½in/42cm

7 CANTON FAMILLE-ROSE VASES
A fusion of East and West. Typical Chinese-style Mandarin figures, butterflies and flowers have been added to a neoclassical urn shape in these early 19th-century vases. This style of decoration was used throughout the 1800s. H 18in/46cm

8 CRACKLED PORCELLANEOUS VASE
The poor quality of some late pieces is exemplified by this vase (c.1870). The body has been covered in a crackled glaze to simulate age, the painting is poor, and the figures have been covered in iron-brown wash to suggest bronze, inferring costliness. H 12in/30cm

The formal gathering of a few individuals to drink tea in a calm, secluded location conducive to meditation was introduced into Japan by Ch'an Buddhist priests in the thirteenth century. Its origins lie hundreds of years earlier in the Buddhist monasteries of southern China, where the drinking of tea was seen as a useful stimulant during long periods of contemplation or prayer.

In Japan, the "tea ceremony" quickly attracted a wider, secular following, and by the fifteenth century it had been adopted by the nobility, samurai and government officials alike. Although, over the centuries, the ceremony has become ever more elaborate and exclusive, it remains an integral part of life for many Japanese.

The ceremony takes place in a small outhouse (*chashitsu*), designed to create the correct atmosphere of tranquillity in which to appreciate the subtle elements of the rites. Most of the vessels needed are made of pottery, although other materials were occasionally used. The equipment includes a large storage jar for the tea leaves (*chatsubo*); a small tea caddy (*cha-ire*) to hold powdered tea leaves for immediate use; a fresh-water jar (*mizusashi*) for replenishing the kettle; and a waste-water jar (*kensui* or *mizukoboshi*). Other items are a flower holder; incense burners and holders; dishes for the small meal (*kaiseki*) eaten immediately prior to tea drinking; and above all, the tea bowl (*chawan*), the most-used vessel in the ceremony.

▲ **THREE TEA CEREMONY ITEMS**
In the foreground is a small ovoid cha-ire, *or tea caddy, with a lathe-turned ivory cover. It was made in the 18th century from close-grained Bizen stoneware, which has been informally dressed in a lustrous wood-ash glaze to create a type of rustic simplicity in keeping with the tenets of the ceremony.*

To the left is a chawan, *or tea bowl. It has a traditional low-bellied form, and the low-fired brick-like body is a deep salmon-pink, with splashes of gray. It is signed by Ryonyu from the ninth generation of a family of noted potters.*

The large gourd-shaped Raku vessel on the right is a mizusashi, *or fresh-water jar, dating from the late Edo period in the 19th century. H 2½–6in/6–15cm*

Tea ceremony wares
In the early years, Japanese tea masters would use vessels in Chinese or Korean stoneware as well as native ceramics. By the late 16th century, Japanese potters were being patronized and actively encouraged by the great tea masters to produce appropriate pieces. However, this aim induced a more contrived style to wares that were formerly made by humble, unselfconscious potters. This latter group includes the celebrated wares of Raku (*above*), Shino (**2**), Oribe (**1, 5**), Seto (**6**), Bizen (*above*) and Karatsu. Inherent in all tea ceremony wares should be the two aspects of *sabi* and *wabi*, loneliness and tranquillity.

1 MOMOYAMA-PERIOD ORIBE TEA BOWL
Furuta Oribe (1544–1615), when he was chief tea master, gave his name to these buff- or brown-bodied wares, decorated in copper-green or dark brown with geometric patterns. His anti-organic forms were considered eccentric at the time. W 5½in/14cm

2 SHINO-WARE BOWL
Early Shino wares are distinguished by their generally crude potting, coarse reddish clay, and the frequent use of an irregularly applied feldspathic glaze. This example, a late 16th-century food bowl used for the small meal (kaiseki) taken before drinking tea, is typically painted gray under the crackled clear glaze. Diam. 8in/20cm

3 SHIGARAKI WAISTED JAR
A large waisted storage jar, or tsubo, made at Shigaraki, south of Kyoto, where there were a number of kilns. This hand-coiled jar, dating from the 17th century, is composed of a local red clay saturated with feldspar and quartz, which gives it a curious "snowflake" effect. A grayish-green ash glaze, typical of Shigaraki pottery, partially covers the shoulders and drips down the sides. H 10in/25cm

4 GROUP OF FIVE TEA CADDIES
A tea caddy, or cha-ire, held finely powdered tea leaves. These examples, all of which have ivory covers, range in date from the 1600s to the 1800s. They are decorated in various types of brown and black glaze, which can be traced back to the Chinese temmoku wares of the 10th–13th centuries. H 2–4in/5–10cm

5 ORIBE MUKOZUKE DISH
Of characteristic geometric form, this late 17th- or 18th-century dish is decorated with stylized vegetation and fencing in the usual Oribe color combination of copper-green and iron-brown. Mukozuke dishes were used to hold condiments during the meal that preceded the drinking of tea. W 5½in/14cm

6 SETO-WARE FRESH-WATER JAR
The square form of this mizusashi, *with a dark brown body covered in crackled cream-colored glaze, was derived from an archaic Chinese jade vessel. A late 19th-century piece, it shows the continued interest of the Seto potters in Chinese and Korean work and in the revival of early Seto wares. H 7in/18cm*

JAPANESE PORCELAIN: 1

Porcelain was probably first made in Japan in the second decade of the seventeenth century by the potters of Arita, a small town on the island of Kyushu. Its development was strongly influenced by both the Koreans and the Chinese.

In the 1590s, a contingent of Korean potters was brought back to Japan after Emperor Hideyoshi's abortive campaign in Korea. They practiced and taught their skills in Japan, with the result that the earliest Japanese wares reflect native Korean style. Many years elapsed before Japanese porcelain developed its own original style.

Colorful Imari and Kakiemon porcelain began to appear in the late 1600s, but these wares were costly and in relatively short supply compared to Chinese porcelain. The bold and dynamic Imari style encouraged solid displays, while Kakiemon provided a subtle, more intimate counterpoint. These wares were avidly collected in the West and both, especially Kakiemon, had a major influence on early European porcelain factories: much of the output of the Meissen, Chantilly and Chelsea factories was either copied or adapted from such designs.

Japanese porcelain is known by these polychrome types, although blue and white wares were also produced. These were, however, mainly for export and were rarely of the same standard as Chinese pieces. Japanese porcelain is undated, making it difficult to construct a history of the wares, although some early European inventories exist which help the process.

Early Japanese export ware

The demise of the Ming Dynasty in the mid-17th century and the virtual cessation of production at Jingdezhen, the home of Chinese porcelain, gave the Arita potters an unexpected boost. The Dutch turned to the infant Japanese porcelain industry to fill their export orders (*below, 2, 8*), and since the European market was attuned to Chinese blue and white porcelain, it seemed obvious to copy these wares.

1 KO-KUTANI-STYLE DISH
Although known as Ko-Kutani – literally "old Kutani" – wares such as this late 17th-century dish were made not in Kutani, but in Arita. The palette is entirely Japanese, but the leaf-shaped border was borrowed from the Chinese. The predominant iron-red enameling is common on early Arita porcelain intended for the home market. Diam. 8½in/21cm

2 ARITA BLUE AND WHITE GROUP
As soon as the Dutch had established the trade in porcelain with Japan, they requested European forms such as these. Both the barber's bowl, painted with a man and his attendant standing near a stream, and the pair of ewers date from the Genroku period (1688–1704). All three are in a debased form of the Chinese "transitional" style which had been popular about 40 years earlier. Diam. plate 12in/30cm; H ewers 9in/23cm

◀ **ARITA CHARGER**
Made for the European market, this late 17th-century blue and white charger is based on the Chinese "kraakporselein" style, recognizable by the compartmentalized border. This piece differs from the original in the rather loose, or schematic, rendering of the ho-o bird and foliage. The designs on Arita export porcelain can also seem somewhat blurred due to the thick bubbled glaze. The VOC monogram of the Dutch East India Company (Vereenigde Oostindische Compagnie) is unique to Japanese porcelain. Diam. 14in/36cm

3 SMALL KAKIEMON OCTAGONAL BOWL
Delicately enameled in the restrained manner associated with Kakiemon decoration, this bowl is typical of the late 1600s. A combination of turquoise, sky-blue, iron-red, yellow and a little black was used to enhance the fine porcelain. Faceted forms, such as this octagonal bowl, are fairly common in Japanese porcelain. W 5in/13cm

4 ARITA POLYCHROME WRESTLERS
Japanese porcelain makers in the 17th and 18th centuries specialized in useful and decorative wares. Human figures, such as these wrestlers, were extremely rare. These two groups have been dated to c.1688 because another group, probably from the same mold, was recorded in an inventory at Burghley House in England taken in that year. H 12in/30cm

5 ARITA FIGURE OF A TIGER
Animals modeled by the Japanese seemed always to have a cartoon-like or humorous element: this colorful, stylized tiger has the mien of a pet. The markings and palette are typical of late 17th-century Arita wares. H 7½in/19cm

6 IMARI JAR AND VASE
Although the antithesis of the subtle and spacious Kakiemon style, Imari wares also appealed to Europeans. This bulbous covered jar and tall beaker vase are part of an early 18th-century garniture. They are decorated in underglaze blue, iron-red, enamels and gilding. The panels feature birds, plants, rocks and waterfalls. H jar 33in/84cm

7 NABESHIMA SAUCER DISH
Made for the nobility of the Nabeshima clan, this type of porcelain was of higher quality than export pieces. Meticulously decorated with colored enamels within an underglaze blue outline, this 18th-century piece is a fine example of the timeless and often asymmetrical designs associated with Nabeshima wares. Diam. 4½in/11cm

8 MID-18TH CENTURY IMARI PLATE
From the earliest days of the trade with Japan, the Dutch supplied the Japanese with models and designs they wanted copied. The draftsman Cornelis Pronk was commissioned to design this rather sassy European version of a Japanese girl, known as "La Dame au Parasol." Diam 9in/23cm

POTTERY AND PORCELAIN

The decline of the Dutch East India Company's trade in porcelain from *c.*1750, and its eventual demise, meant that Japanese factories had to turn to the home market. But the absence of records because of a fire that devastated Arita in 1828 makes it very difficult to ascribe much to the 100 years before 1854, when Commodore Perry forced the Japanese to resume trade with the outside world.

By the mid-nineteenth century, a great number of factories had been established, not only on Kyushu, the traditional home of Japanese porcelain, but also on Honshu. Many manufacturers had also started marking their output, which makes it possible to attribute most pieces from this period.

In addition to the continuation of standard styles in Imari and Arita blue and white, there emerged some more innovative types of ware, especially at the end of the nineteenth century. This was probably a response to the demands of the increasingly sophisticated markets in America and Europe, although the exponents of the Aesthetic Movement and Japanese style were also partly responsible. A few discerning collectors led the way in distinguishing the small number of beautiful and refined wares from the poorer quality goods that swamped the market.

Japanese eggshell services
During the 20th century, the Japanese exported many thousands of eggshell services (8). The name is derived from the fact that the pieces were extremely thinly potted which, paradoxically, contributed to their survival, since many people were too nervous to use them. Most, although not all, of these sets were rather crudely decorated, and even those bearing the phrase "hand painted" were painted over printed outlines. Another mark commonly found on these sets is "genuine Samurai china."

1 FUKUGAWA BLUE AND WHITE VASE
Although established in Arita in the late 1680s, the Fukugawa factory only came to prominence during the Meiji period (1868–1912). Fukugawa wares, although noted for refined potting and glazing, rarely broke away from pastiches of earlier Imari types. This large, overcrowded oviform vase and domed cover, made in the late 19th century, was embellished in cold lacquer, a technique that had become something of a fashion at the time. The panels of decoration show a group of red-capped Manchurian cranes standing among bamboo canes and flowering plants. H 3ft 4in/1.02m

2 LARGE FUKUGAWA VASE
Japanese wares often display a sublime indifference to form, line and balance, as the awkward angular shoulders and exaggerated trumpet neck of this late 19th-century vase show. The enamel decoration of carp in turbulent waters was a favorite theme of the Fukugawa factory. H 3ft 6in/1.07m

◄ **FINE MAKUZU KOZAN VASE**
Meticulously potted by Makuzu Kozan of Yokohama, this baluster vase is a fine example of the individual pieces made for a small elite. The brilliant yellow ground was added to the underglaze palette of grayish-red, blue, green and white that developed during the Meiji period (1868–1912). The petals have been enhanced with lightly carved detail. Makuzu Kozan produced blue and white porcelain as well as polychrome wares such as this. H 20in/51cm

3 FUKUGAWA TRUMPET-SHAPED VASE
One of a pair, this fine 19th-century vase was made in a traditional form that dates from the late 17th century. The main decoration is rather unusual, since it imitates the style of Ming landscape paintings. The borders, however, cling to the contemporary urge to over-elaborate and feature panels of flowers and foliage picked out in enamels and gilt. H 24in/61cm

4 IMARI-STYLE BOTTLE VASE
Painted in the traditional Imari-style underglaze blue, iron-red and gilding, which developed in the late 17th century, the design of this Meiji-period vase is not far removed from original Imari themes. The compressed globular bottle form and tall straight neck, however, are taken from Chinese porcelain and never appeared on old Imari wares. H 10in/25cm

5 PAIR OF IMARI VASES
These globular vases are decorated with a pattern of trees in a garden. Upon close inspection, the glaze can be seen to be slightly crazed, which can decrease the value. H 12in/30cm

6 HIRADO SAUCER-SHAPED DISH
During the 1800s, the Hirado factory produced some of the finest Japanese porcelain. These dishes in Kutani style are a dramatic rejection of their heritage: the solid ground and circular panels owe more to the old Ming kinrande style – characterized by iron-red and gold decoration – than to the subtle underglaze-blue wares for which the factory is known. Diam. 24in/61cm

7 NORITAKE CUP AND SAUCER
Made for the European market, these early 20th-century pieces have been decorated with a rather "esthetic" theme of isolated butterflies, an icon for longevity in Japan. This type of decoration was also found on some contemporary Japanese cloisonné.

8 NORITAKE EGGSHELL COFFEE SET
Although most early 20th-century Japanese porcelain was technically advanced, the designs were often weak and insipid. On this eggshell coffee set, made in the European style, the Noritake factory has employed a heavy, brocade-type decoration which makes an interesting change from the "geishas in gardens before Mount Fuji" designs that tend to clutter Western china cabinets.

Satsuma Ware

Composed of a fine, chalk-white body under a clear or straw-colored glaze which is usually densely crackled, Satsuma ware is the Western name for a type of Japanese pottery that was exported throughout the Meiji period (1868–1912). Potters have been active in the district of Satsuma in western Kyushu, the southernmost island of Japan, since the 1500s. The earliest wares were akin to simple rustic types found all over the country, and it was only at the end of the eighteenth century that the finely potted earthenwares, painted in the delicate polychrome enamels typically associated with the name Satsuma ware, were made.

A number of items exist bearing date marks from the early nineteenth century. They are painted in strong, thick enamels, and differ so greatly from both the earlier Satsuma wares and those that are known to date from the second half of the nineteenth century that some authorities consider the authenticity of these marks to be doubtful.

While some Satsuma wares are decorated with a fine judgment of space and form, many pieces, especially those with lavish gilding made in the late 1800s and early 1900s, are overly ornate for modern taste. Favorite subjects for decoration include flowers, with the chrysanthemum being the most common; figures, usually of samurai, geishas and *rakan* (holy men or sages); and seasonal landscapes. Unlike Japanese ceramics dating from before 1800, most Satsuma is marked in blue or red overglaze enamel or gilding.

Sobei Kinkozan

One of the best-known Satsuma potters, Sobei Kinkozan (5), established a factory in Kyoto to produce vast quantities of Satsuma ware for export. Hidden away, but on the same site, was a small studio where he crafted superb individual pieces for discerning collectors. He is now regarded as one of the three best makers of the period, the others being Yabu Meizan (*below*) and Ryozan.

1 EARLY 19TH-CENTURY SATSUMA JAR
This handsome jar, signed Meigado Kizan, is painted in the bold colors typical of wares dating from the early 19th century. Apart from the gilding, the dominant colors are the deep blue and blood-red that characterize this pottery. The range of ceramic, bronze and lacquer vessels scattered decoratively over the surface recalls similar arrangements on Chinese porcelain of the Kangxi period (1661–1722). The diaper motif on the shoulders is derived from the pattern on a turtle's shell. H 10½in/26cm

2 BEAKER VASE
Trumpet-shaped vases were popular from the 17th century in Japanese ceramics, but were probably based on a much older design for Chinese bronze vessels. The enamel decoration on this 19th-century vase depicts a continuous line of cranes standing on the seashore. Cranes, which symbolize longevity, are a favorite theme in the Far East, especially in Japan. H 14½in/37cm

◀ **SATSUMA VASE**
Yabu Meizan (1853–1934) was an important porcelain painter who specialized in the Satsuma brocade style. This vase, decorated by him in the late 19th century, features a continuous landscape with fishing villages on islands in a lake with mountains beyond.

It is rare for the boxes in which these wares were exported from Japan to have survived, but inside the lid of this box is a label bearing the words "Yabu Meizan. Painter of the Finest Satsuma Porcelain. Osaka, Japan." H 5in/13cm

3 MID-19TH CENTURY VASE
A vase of classic ovoid form, richly decorated with enamels and gilding in typical Japanese style. The different-sized mon, or family badges, enclose a variety of subjects, including a ho-o bird, a rain dragon, butterflies on a cobweb, flowers and landscapes on a ground of "calm-water" (seigaha) pattern. This design was used extensively on textiles from the medieval period. H 15in/38cm

4 TRUMPET-NECKED VASE
Enamel and gilt decoration dominate the vase, from the foliate-rimmed lip and dragons on the neck, through the tasseled rope tied around the neck, to an elaborate scene depicting a rakan – a holy man or sage. Rakan were popular subjects on ornate Satsuma wares made for the export market in the late 19th century. The vase is signed by Ryokuzando. H 24in/61cm

5 PAIR OF SATSUMA PLATES
Plates telling a story were relatively uncommon, and the design for these examples, which are part of a series of seven depicting the Tale of the Forty-seven Ronin, was probably borrowed from contemporary Meiji woodblock prints. The meticulous style and yellowish-tone palette are characteristic of the period, c.1900. Each plate is signed by the maker, Kinkozan. Diam. 8½in/21cm

6 KYOTO KORO AND COVER
Although the koro originated as a bronze incense burner, it was a popular form in both pottery and porcelain. On this piece, the artist Nambo has conjured up images of spring and summer with women in flowering gardens. The interior, which can be seen through pierced oval openings, was painted with fruit and flowers, perhaps symbolizing longevity and fruitful marriage. The dense flowerhead and foliage decoration is common on many refined pieces made in the late 19th century. H 7in/18cm

7 PAIR OF SLENDER VASES
Delicately painted in purple and gilding, these vases feature a favorite Japanese theme of birds either flying or perched among drooping wisteria. H 10in/25cm

YABU MEIZAN.
PAINTER OF THE FINEST
SATSUMA PORCELAIN.
No.197, Naka Ni-chome, Dojima,
OSAKA, JAPAN.

ISLAMIC POTTERY

◄ **IZNIK WARES**
These pieces date from c.1530–c.1600, the classic period of Iznik pottery, made in Turkey. Left to right: Rare blue, white and turquoise saucer, c.1530. Diam. 8in/20cm

Lions, deer and a rabbit on a green roundel decorate this dish. Diam. 12in/30cm

A brilliant white, bulbous, narrow-necked water bottle, painted with blue hyacinths and red carnations c.1565. H 18in/46cm

Barbed-rimmed dish, c.1555, with palmettes and flower sprays in the "Damascus" palette. Diam. 14½in/37in

3 SYRIAN RAKKA-WARE BALUSTER JAR
An early 13th-century piece, this heavily potted jar is painted in a bold manner far removed from the intricacies found on many Kashan wares. The pot is made of a granular whitish body and has a typical, broadly crackled translucent glaze which stops well above the foot. H 12½in/32cm

4 KASHAN MOLDED-BORDER TILE
The technique of luster decoration probably developed in Mesopotamia in the 800s and traveled to Islamic Spain and then Italy at the turn of the 16th century. This type of decoration allows no shading, but the painter has enhanced the raised inscription with a dense ground of scrolling foliage. 14 x 13in/36 x 33cm

5 LAJVARDINA POTTERY BOWL
Made in Persia in the 1300s, the time of Mongol rule, lajvardina, or lapis-lazuli, wares are among the most elaborately decorated of Islamic ceramics. The leaf-shaped panels on this bowl, painted in red and white on a lapis-blue ground, are heightened in gold leaf, suggesting inlaid metalwork. Diam. 8in/20cm

6 IZNIK POTTERY DISH
An example (c.1560) of underglaze cobalt blue and turquoise in a design taken from a 15th-century blue and white dish. Clusters of grapes were a common theme, but the border, which earlier would have been of swirling waves, has been reduced to tight scrolls. Diam. 14in/36cm

7 16TH-CENTURY DAMASCUS DISH
This pottery was made by the Turkish potters who had produced the tiles for the Dome of the Rock in Jerusalem, using much the same palette. The blemishes in the center of the dish show where small clay stilts kept the pieces apart in the kiln. Diam. 12½in/32cm

8 LATE 16TH-CENTURY IZNIK PITCHER
Perhaps the most common form of Turkish vessel at this time. The painter has deviated from the usual saw-edged leaves and stylized vegetation to create a bold, vivacious scheme on a rich cobalt ground. H 10in/25cm

9 TURKISH KÜTAHYA POTTERY FLASK
The fine whitish body of this 18th-century flask from Anatolia is painted in a slightly primitive manner with figures in red, cobalt, turquoise and yellow, with black details. H 6in/15cm

The Islamic countries, occupying a region at the crossroads between Europe and Asia, have, as would be expected, one of the world's most diverse cultures. This is reflected in their ceramic wares, but it was not until about the ninth century that ceramics were appreciated in the Middle East as anything more than utilitarian. It was probably the presence of Chinese ceramics, introduced mainly by trade in the eighth and ninth centuries, that encouraged their reappraisal and the development of more sophisticated wares.

Although no porcelain or stoneware was manufactured, in a tradition dating back to the early classic wares of Syria and Persia, the region spawned a particularly rich variety of pottery. These wares achieved considerable status among the applied arts of the Islamic world.

The output includes the early luster wares of Mesopotamia, Egypt and, particularly, Persia – with bold and highly abstract slipware from Nishapur and Aghkand, and the thinly potted wares of Kashan with their unique turquoise glaze. These were followed by the intricate Minai wares of Rayy and Kashan, also in Persia, and the derivative, but nonetheless brilliant, blue and white wares of Iznik and Damascus.

These distinctive and important contributions to international ceramic culture inspired Western potters, from those of Malaga and Valencia in Spain in the 1600s to William de Morgan at his Fulham pottery in London in the late 1800s.

China and Islam
Some 800 years of trade between China and the Islamic world is echoed in Iznik wares, especially in the predominance of cobalt blue. The large dish (*above right*) is of a type based on early 15th-century Chinese blue and white ware. But the loosely scrolling flowers and the addition of turquoise created a refreshing image.

In an interesting reversal, the shape of the tall bottle (*above*) inspired Chinese potters during the mid-17th century "Transitional" period. Painted only in blue and white, such flasks were exported to Europe as "knotted flasks."

1 KASHAN POTTERY
The forms of all these 13th-century pieces are based on metal originals. The turquoise glaze on the two ewers and the lampstand, which has, typically, tumbled irregularly toward the foot, was much favored. The iridescence on some items is probably due to their burial in adverse conditions. H lampstand 12in/30cm

2 AGHKAND DISH
Only three signed dishes of this type of 12th-century ware exist; this one is inscribed "Amal Suleyman" (the work of Suleyman). The outline of the design was incised (sgraffito work) and the details painted in with translucent green and ocher lead glazes. Similar techniques were used in China and in renaissance Italy. Diam. 7in/18cm

EARLY TIN-GLAZED EARTHENWARE

◄ **HISPANO-MORESQUE ARMORIAL DISH**
The vine-leaf pattern, with alternating leaves of blue and gold, which decorates this large dish was the most popular background for this type of armorial pottery. The rampant lion in the center probably represents the arms of the city of León in northern Spain. The dish dates from c.1450–75. Diam. 18in/46cm

1 ORVIETO EWER
The green and brown (manganese) decoration on this ewer (c.1470) is typical of wares made in a number of centers in Tuscany and Umbria from the 13th century. It is known as Orvieto ware, although this was just one of the towns producing it. H 11in/28cm

2 FLORENTINE ALBARELLO
Highly abstract designs were favored on early maiolica, as this late 15th-century albarello shows. The ocher and blue zigzag lines, known as San Bernadino rays, are taken from the badge of San Bernadino, patron saint of Siena. The inscriptions on this jar, "Casandra" on one side and "Sperointe" on the other, set it apart from similar examples and add to its value. H 10½in/26cm

3 DELLA ROBBIA PLAQUE
This relief-molded plaque is of the type made famous by Luca Della Robbia and his family at the end of the 15th century. Typically, the relief was white on a blue background, although this early 16th-century example also uses yellow and green. The architectural gilt-wood frame, with Greek pediment and paterae, is contemporary with the plaque. H 19in x W 13in; H 48cm x W 33cm

4 FAENZA WET-DRUG JARS
Known as Famiglia Gotica, or Gothic floral, the style of decoration on such wet-drug jars (c.1500) flourished in Florence and Faenza in the late 15th and early 16th centuries. It is characterized by emblems, scrolls and flowers executed in bright colors. The name of the drug is inscribed beneath the spout. H 7½in/19cm

5 DERUTA DISH
Portrait dishes such as this, showing beautiful women set within vigorous background designs, were particular to Deruta, Italy. Made c.1500, this dish shows the vivid oranges, yellows and blues typical of Deruta ware. Diam. 13in/33cm

6 HISPANO-MORESQUE BOWL
Painted in pink copper luster with a design of stylized birds against a background of leaves, this early 16th-century dish from Moorish southern Spain shows the vitality and feeling of movement that is exhibited by all Hispano-Moresque decoration. Diam. 15in/38cm

Coating earthenware with a white tin glaze produced the ideal background for highly colored decoration, hence its popularity and widespread use. Tin-glazed wares have different names in different countries, but the technique is fundamentally the same though decoration varies dramatically. It is probable that it developed in the Middle East, spread to Moorish Spain, and then to Italy and the rest of Europe.

Spanish tin-glazed earthenware, known as Hispano-Moresque, was made from about the twelfth century; however, surviving examples, usually dishes, vases and drug jars, date from the fifteenth to the eighteenth centuries. They are generally decorated with a pinkish or golden luster, sometimes with the addition of blue.

Maiolica, as tin-glazed earthenware is called in Italy, enjoyed its most creative period during the Renaissance. Using a palette characterized by cobalt blue, manganese purple-brown, green and (from the fifteenth century onward) yellow, styles of decoration developed that were radically different from the freely painted Hispano-Moresque work.

Major centers of maiolica production included Florence, Faenza and Orvieto, and, in the sixteenth century, Urbino, Deruta and Siena. Maiolica was made predominantly for the luxury market and was notable both for its superb design and meticulous execution, rather than for any remarkable developments in form.

Della Robbia

A pioneer of the Renaissance style, Luca Della Robbia (1399–1482) was born, and lived, in Florence. Originally a sculptor of marble, he began to work in earthenware c.1440. Della Robbia successfully transferred the art of sculpture to earthenware, developing its potential as an artistic medium.

In addition to large relief plaques (**3**), Della Robbia made some figures, and glazed all his pieces with a mixture of tin, antimony and other minerals. He established a family studio and, upon his death, was succeeded by his nephew Andrea (1435–1525) and later by his grand-nephew Giovanni (1469–1529).

In 1894, a "Della Robbia Company" was set up in England at Birkenhead, near Liverpool. It made tiles, plaques and vases in the Arts and Crafts style, using lead, rather than tin, maiolica-type glazes.

Drug jars

Among the most common items made of tin-glazed earthenware were drug jars, used for the pharmaceutical products of the time. A waisted, wide-necked pot, or albarello (**2**), was for dry drugs, such as herbs and powders, while syrups and potions were kept in jugs with narrow necks, shoulder spouts and loop handles (**4**). A well-equipped pharmacy required hundreds of jars, which accounts for their relative profusion today.

As migrant workmen took their skills to other parts of Europe during the sixteenth century, maiolica techniques spread from Italy. In France, faience (the French term) began to be made in various towns; the most successful of these in the first half of the seventeenth century was Nevers. Here, grand show pieces were made, painted with themes taken from engravings of fine paintings; another development was *Bleu de Nevers*, or *Bleu Persan* (2).

By the late 1600s, faience tablewares were becoming fashionable as an alternative to silver or pewter, and factories sprang up all over France to respond to this demand. Large dinner services were commissioned, and new designs were developed suitable for decorating the many different pieces in a service. Decorative style and palette changed in response to the growing taste for delicate, floral decoration in softer colors than those of traditional maiolica. Among the most successful French factories in the 1700s were Rouen, Moustiers and Strasbourg.

The production of tin-glazed earthenware suffered as a result of the success of porcelain in the late 1700s, and many factories in northern Europe closed. A hundred years later, the technique enjoyed a revival, however, as art potters sought both to re-create archaic forms and to use tin glaze in a modern idiom. At Moustiers for instance, factories which had been closed for many years have reopened, and the industry is again flourishing.

Istoriato painting

The term "*istoriato*" meaning, literally, "history painting," is used to describe a characteristic style of decoration for maiolica (1). Either the well or the whole surface of the plate or dish is used as the painter's canvas, and a classical or mythological scene is depicted in the typical polychrome palette.

The Italian city of Urbino was particularly renowned for *istoriato* painting, but the fashion soon spread to France where, in the late 1500s and early 1600s, Italian migrant workers at Lyons, for instance, were producing *istoriato* wares. Later, a distinctive north-European style of *istoriato* developed.

Majolica

This is the name given to a type of ware developed at the Minton factory in England in the mid-1800s. It owed something to the palette of true maiolica, but was decorated with lead-glaze, not tin-glaze, colors. Large sculptural shapes were favored, such as plant stands and *jardinières* (see p.258). Similar ware was made at other places in Britain, America and France.

▼ **STRASBOURG DUCK TUREENS**
Tureens in the shape of animals, birds or vegetables in baroque style were fashionable in the mid-18th century as decoration on sideboards and dining tables. These duck tureens were made c.1755 at Strasbourg, where the factory was notable for the realism such pieces display. W 15½in/39cm

1 URBINO DISH
This spectacular dish was made in Urbino in the late 16th century. It combines a central roundel bearing istoriato *decoration of a classical scene with the delicately painted grotesques, hunters, animals, trees and birds for which Urbino was famed. Diam. 18½in/47cm*

2 BLEU PERSAN GARNITURE OF VASES
The name Bleu Persan *refers to this type of earthenware, in which the tin glaze is stained blue and overpainted in white tin pigment, typically with chinoiseries. Most was made at Nevers in France between 1630 and 1700. H 14½in–23½in/37cm–59cm*

3 CASTELLI PLAQUE
In the 18th century, the factory at Castelli, in the Abruzzo region of Italy, developed a reputation for fine figure and landscape decoration. This was the specialty of the Grue family, in whose workshop this delicately painted plaque depicting the Flight into Egypt was painted c.1730. H 8in x W 10½in; H 20cm x W 27cm

4 APRICOT DISH
Faience lends itself to trompe-l'oeil, such as this pretty plate filled with naturalistically modeled and painted apricots. This piece probably comes from Montpellier in France (c.1780–1800), but there are similar examples from several other European countries. Diam. 10in/25cm

5 IZNIK-TYPE CHARGER
The great French potter Theodore Deck (1823–91) was inspired by 16th- and 17th-century Iznik ware from Persia and devised his own brilliant colors to imitate it. He made and signed this dish c.1870. Diam. 16in/41cm

6 ITALIAN MAIOLICA INKWELL
This late 19th-century reproduction of 16th-century Italian maiolica, made by Carlo Ginori, is typical of such reproductions. It employs maiolica colors and uses powerfully molded grotesque forms. H 7in/18cm

7 DE MORGAN VASE
William De Morgan, who was part of William Morris's circle in the late 1800s, made some use of tin glazes and luster in his pottery. This is an example of his "Persian faience" (c.1885), which copies the rich blue palette of the original. H 15in/38cm

POTTERY AND PORCELAIN

The production of tin-glazed earthenware spread to the Netherlands at the beginning of the sixteenth century. Initially, it was made in Antwerp and imitated Italian maiolica; it was not until the seventeenth century that a distinctive Dutch style emerged as more factories started up, including many at Delft.

The blue and white Chinese porcelain imported by the Dutch East India Company was extensively copied. Oriental designs became gradually absorbed into a Dutch-Oriental style that flourished between c.1650 and 1750, especially in Delft. European designs were also used and became extremely popular in the early eighteenth century. The factories at Delft were highly productive, and eventually the town's name was given to all such ware, whether Dutch or English.

Under the influence of the polychrome *famille-verte* and *famille-rose* enameled porcelain being imported from China, the potters also developed a technique for enameling in color on tin glaze, which they employed in the early 1700s.

A small quantity of tin-glazed earthenware was made in Germany from c.1520 onward, but the finer German pieces date from the late seventeenth century and take their style mainly from Dutch-Oriental wares, not Italian maiolica. Many faience factories, notably those in Nuremberg, Frankfurt, Ansbach and Hanau, were set up in the early eighteenth century. By the middle of the century, in an attempt to counter the growing demand for porcelain, they developed the use of enamel colors as the Dutch had done.

Earthenware tiles

One of the best-known types of tin-glazed earthenware from northern Europe is the tile. They were a specialty of the Dutch, but were also made in French and German faience and in maiolica in Italy and Spain.

At Delft, pictures were created by painting a design on a panel made of many tiles; tiles were also individually decorated with landscapes, ships and so on, but with corner ornaments that made a pattern when the tiles were butted up. In Germany in particular, tiles were extensively made for stoves and were produced by the Hafner potters (4).

▼ **GERMAN FAIENCE**
Although Frankfurt dominated the production of tin-glazed earthenware in Germany from the mid-17th century, fine wares were also made at many smaller factories, as this group shows.

Left: a caster imitating a silver shape, from Hannoversch-Münden c.1760.

Center: three pieces from Frankfurt: a large, Dutch-type nine-lobed dish decorated in Oriental style c.1700; a würzbierschüssel, or covered dish, with Chinese-inspired decoration in a palette of manganese purple, green and blue-green c.1740; and a tiny taperstick, an earlier rarity dating from c.1690.

Far right: a pair of candlesticks, dated 1818, from Kellinghusen, where small factories continued to produce wares in peasant style well into the 19th century. Diam. large dish 13½in/35cm; H caster, candlesticks 6½in/17cm; taperstick 6in/15cm

1 DELFT TULIP VASES
The town of Delft was well known for vases with a number of holes in them to take the individual stems of tulips. These vases commonly took the form of a brick, but exotic shapes were also made, including tall towers, pagodas and bizarre Turk's heads such as these, made c.1680. H 10in/25cm

2 DUTCH DELFT PLATES
Both Chinese and European decoration in blue and white were still in use at the Delft factories in the 1700s. This pair of plates (c.1720) is painted in a rather inky blue, and the border design is more successful than the densely painted center. Diam. 5½in/14cm

3 DELFT DORÉ PLATE
This beautifully painted plate is an example of Delft polychrome enamel painting with gilding, a technique known as Delft doré. The decoration on this plate (c.1750), with the arms of one G.V. Leeuwen, is copied from Chinese famille-verte. Diam. 13in/33cm

4 HAFNER-WARE JUG
A baluster jug made in Nuremberg c.1580. The relief decoration and the glaze colors, which were influenced by Italian maiolica, are typical of a group of early pottery wares known as Hafner ware. H 13in/33cm

5 HANAU FAIENCE JUG
A Birnkrug (pear-shaped jug) with a pewter cover, dating from 1708. It is an example of "Hausmalerei": the Hausmaler were independent artists who decorated the wares of various factories (see p.62). Their work is seen largely on faience made in Frankfurt and Hanau. H 9in/23cm

6 SET OF GERMAN VASES
Garnitures, usually of five vases, were fashionable in the late 1600s and early 1700s. Inspired by Chinese porcelain, versions in blue and white earthenware were made at Delft and in Germany; this set is from Brunswick c.1720. H 16½in, 17in; H 42cm, 43cm

7 ERFURT TANKARD
This is an example of one of the most typical shapes in German faience, the tankard, or Walzenkrug, with a pewter cover. It dates from c.1765 and is painted with Harlequin holding his hat and slapstick. H 10½in/26cm

ENGLISH DELFTWARE

Tin-glazed earthenware was made in England from the mid-sixteenth century. During the 1700s, it became known as delftware after the famous Dutch Delft.

Although early examples, made in London, owe more to Italian maiolica and French faience in design, the major inspiration in English delftware decoration was the then fashionable Chinese and Japanese porcelain. Later in the seventeenth century, England's increasingly close bond with Holland gave Dutch Delft a strong influence on English versions, which continued until about 1740. Ship's bowls and commemorative ware appeared in the 1700s along with other pieces decorated with European landscapes and floral designs.

There were several centers for English delftware, and correct attribution is often difficult. In London it was made at Southwark and later, in the eighteenth century, mostly at Lambeth. Apothecaries' drug jars, pill slabs, and wine bottles were staple products of the London potteries.

Bristol and Liverpool were the other major centers. Wares from the former were characterized by a pinkish body and a bright palette, including purplish manganese. In Liverpool, the body was beige, and plates occasionally have a red edge; transfer-printed decoration was also used in the late 1700s.

The production of porcelain and increasingly sophisticated pottery, such as creamware and salt-glazed stoneware, put an end to the manufacture of English delftware by about 1800.

"Blue-dash" chargers

An edging of blue dashes (*below, 3*) is characteristic of many large dishes, or chargers, designed for decorative purposes in the 17th century. Typically, these "blue-dash" chargers have polychrome decoration featuring either Adam and Eve, naive portraits of ruling monarchs, or boldly stylized tulips. Most examples date from 1650–80; they are keenly collected.

Posset pots and caudle cups

In the 1600s, these vessels (*below, 4*) were made to hold the warm drinks favored at the time. Posset was warm milk with ale or wine and spices, while caudle was a more substantial gruel, perhaps intended for invalids, which included eggs, sugar, spices and oatmeal, as well as wine or ale. Caudle cups had either one or two handles, and some also had lids and saucers.

▼ **LONDON-MADE DELFTWARE**
Two posset pots with spouts are shown here. The left-hand one (c.1690) is highly elaborate, with serpents on the handles and a complex knob; the simpler one on the right (c.1674) has a false bottom, which allows a different liquor to be sipped from each spout. The Adam and Eve "blue-dash" charger dates from c.1660; the flower vase modeled as the somewhat grotesque head of a child from c.1685. The caudle cup with a portrait of Charles II was made at Southwark in 1661. H posset pot 13in/ 33cm; Diam. charger 17in/43cm

1 MALLING JUG
One of the earliest examples of English tin-glazed earthenware, this silver-mounted jug dates from 1570–90. The glaze is speckled with blue and manganese in imitation of fine German stoneware. The first was found at West Malling, in Kent, England, but they are thought to have been made in London. H 10½in/26cm

2 WINE BOTTLE
A staple product of the London potteries, wine bottles were often decorated with the name of the contents, the date, and sometimes initials. This fine example shows Charles II in armor, complete with a "golden" crown floating above his head. H 6in/16cm

3 PLATES AND CHARGER
"Merryman" plates were made in 1648–1742 in sets of six, each bearing a line from an old rhyme; these two are dated 1721. In the center is a London "blue-dash" charger, adorned with tulips, which were fashionable in the 18th century. Diam. plates 9in/23cm; charger 10½in/26cm

4 CAUDLE CUP
Chinese porcelain was the foremost inspiration for delftware, and the decoration on this caudle cup clearly copies a Chinese underglaze blue design, although crudely. The cup bears a coat of arms and is dated 1674.

5 LIVERPOOL TILES
Transfer printing was a popular form of decoration from the 1750s, and John Sadler in Liverpool used this technique on pottery. These tin-glazed tiles (c.1775) showing The Sailor's Farewell and The Sailor's Return are typical examples of his style.

6 SHIP'S PUNCH BOWL
The good fortune of ships was toasted in punch mixed in bowls such as this, commissioned by ship's captains. Many were made in Liverpool and Bristol in 1750–75. This one, with the ship's flags picked out in red, was made in Liverpool c.1760. Diam. 10½in/26cm

7 BALLOONING PLATE
Great events, from coronations to weddings, were often commemorated on delftware. One of the most exciting was England's first balloon ascent by Vincent Lunardi in 1784, shown on this plate. Diam. 9in/23cm

EUROPEAN LEAD-GLAZED POTTERY

The technique of using a lead oxide (or sulfide of lead) to glaze pottery was first practiced in Roman times and was widely applied in Europe during succeeding centuries. Lead glaze is bright and transparent and can be stained with metal oxides, usually copper for green and iron for yellow and brown. It was often combined with decoration in liquid clay, or slip, which was sometimes tinted, again using metallic oxides. The slip was trailed or painted over the pottery surface and could be worked in various ways to create particular effects – solid blocks of color, marbling and feathering, as well as figurative and repetitive patterned decoration.

Lead-glazed pottery was made all over Italy, especially from the fourteenth century onward. Incised decoration (*sgraffito*) was common and was often combined with colored glazes, especially orange or yellow and green. Much of Germany's early lead-glazed earthenware comprised tiles made for domestic stoves. The best of these, made in the sixteenth and early seventeenth centuries, were molded in relief and green-glazed, or, later, decorated in polychrome. In France, lead-glazed pottery found skilled and specialized expression, particularly in the work of Bernard Palissy and in the pieces from Saint-Porchaire.

The discovery of the method of making fine porcelain in the 1700s and its rise to popularity with more affluent members of society meant that lead-glazed pottery was relegated to a peasant art form in most of Europe. In England, however, in the guise of creamware, it emerged as a valid competitor to porcelain.

▲ **PEASANT WARES**
These dishes date from the 18th century. They are decorated with slip in the typical palette and coated with a lead glaze, which imparts a pale honey color. Elements of the design are outlined using the sgraffito technique. The two smaller dishes were probably made in Upper Austria c.1790. The large dishes, with inscriptions and the date 1733, are German-made. Slipware often bears commemorative inscriptions and initials. Diam. 12½in, 20in, 19in, 11½in; Diam. 31cm, 51cm, 48cm, 29cm

Saint-Porchaire wares

French lead-glazed earthenware made in Poitou is known either by the later name of the region, Saint-Porchaire (**5**), or as Henri II ware. Shapes were sophisticated and included those of Renaissance inspiration as well as architectural forms. It is usually claimed that the decoration (often yellow or brown) is inlaid, but this has been disputed. Relief ornament, such as masks, was often added.

Bernard Palissy

The innovative work of this artist (**2**) was sufficiently admired in his own time for it to be imitated, a process that continued into the 1800s (**3**). Working in the late 16th century in France, he developed a mastery of colored glazes. He was also a naturalist with a particular enthusiasm for reptiles and insects. These he managed to portray in pottery in a most life-like manner, creating dishes like pools, full of pond-life of every sort covered with green, blue, gray and brown glazes.

1 SOUTH GERMAN STOVE TILE
The popularity of relief decoration is evident in this 15th-century green-glazed tile. Other examples, also in Gothic arch form, have a figure depicted in relief within the niche. H 11½in/29cm

2 PALISSY DISH
A dish typical of Palissy's wares, made in the late 1500s. It is molded in relief, with fish swimming inside a rich blue border of leaves and animals, all depicted in vivid glaze colors. W 19½in/50cm

3 PALISSY-STYLE DISH
The Palissy style of decoration was extensively revived during the 19th century, especially in Mediterranean regions. In this example, probably made in Portugal, the effect is more fussy and overworked than Palissy's.

4 BOLOGNA PITCHER
Incised decoration, or sgraffito, was used widely in Europe from the 1400s. This late 15th-century pitcher shows how the technique could be combined with green and ocher glazes. Although the drawing here is crude, much finer figurative depictions appear on other examples. H 8in/20cm

5 SAINT-PORCHAIRE SALT CELLAR
Salt cellars had hierarchical significance in the Middle Ages, which explains the architectural grandeur of this sophisticated piece, made by the potters of Poitou (now known as Saint-Porchaire) in the early 1500s. The fine white clay is decorated with brown scrolls in the typical manner and lead glazed, with a touch of color around the masks. H 4½in/11cm

6 HUNGARIAN MARBLED BOWL
The technique of marbling with colored slip has been widely used by country potteries throughout Europe since the 17th century. This late 19th-century bowl in the traditional style is enlivened by multicolored slips. Diam. 8in/20cm

7 FRENCH PROVINCIAL JUG
Traditional decorative styles on French provincial lead-glazed pottery have remained unchanged since the late 17th century. This slip-decorated jug, made in northern France in the late 1800s, is of characteristic form and color, and is typical of a wide range of domestic wares. H 7in/18cm

Lead, or galena, glaze was widely used in England from the Middle Ages onward. Though cooking pots were left unglazed, many other simple household bowls and pitchers had a green lead glaze applied. More decorative vessels were made during the thirteenth and fourteenth centuries, with applied and incised decoration.

In the seventeenth and early eighteenth centuries, slipware flourished in England. The reddish clay vessels were decorated with liquid clay, or slip, of various colors. The piece was then finished with a lead glaze. Designs were formed by trailing or brushing the slip, using applied molded patterns or incising.

In the eighteenth century, the Staffordshire potter Thomas Whieldon developed the technique of using glazes colored with oxides to decorate services and ornamental wares; this was imitated by many other potters. On early pieces from the 1750s, the palette is limited to brown, gray, gray-blue and green; later on, yellow appears. Whieldon's early partner was Josiah Wedgwood, who went on to develop creamware, the most successful pottery of the late 1700s.

Toward the end of the century, pottery figures from Staffordshire were decorated with underglaze colors, and later with bright overglaze colors. At Minton, in the mid-nineteenth century, majolica was developed. Using a cane-colored body to set off thick, brightly colored glazes, it echoed the strong palette and relief work of early Italian maiolica.

Toby jugs

The familiar Toby jug is one of a long line of novelty jugs and drinking vessels, including Staffordshire owl jugs (2) and German jugs in the form of bears. The name probably derives from the nickname – "Toby Philpot" (or "Fillpot") – of Harry Elwes, a well-known ale-drinker.

The first jugs in the shape of a rotund figure in a three-cornered hat (which formed the lid) were made by the famous Staffordshire potter Ralph Wood in the mid-1700s. Later, these jugs were produced by most English pottery factories, and many different forms are known. Early examples are decorated with translucent colored glazes of muted colors: green, brown, gray and ocher. Pieces made after c.1790 (3) were modeled less carefully, and much brighter overglaze enamel colors were used.

▼ MEDIEVAL POTTERY

There were wide local variations in the body, or "fabric," used during the medieval period, as the different colors here show. The two pitchers on the left, dating from the 15th or 16th century, are ovoid, while the earlier one on the right, from the 14th or 15th century, is of typical baluster shape. They have loop handles and pinched spouts. In front is a small 15th-century ointment jar. All the pieces have a transparent, green lead glaze applied to some or all of the piece. H 6in, 5½in, 7½in, 3in; H 15cm, 14cm, 19cm, 8cm

1 WROTHAM TYG

Slipware such as this tyg, or many-handled cup, is typical of pieces made in Wrotham, Kent, in the 1600s. The dark body is decorated with white slip and pads of white clay, impressed with the date 1643 and the initials TI, for its maker, Thomas Ifield. H 5½in/14cm

2 OWL JUG

The plumage of this handsome owl was made by combing two colors of slip together to create a feathered effect. Trails and beads of slip depict the wings, eyes and feet. Owl jugs (the head acts both as a cover and a cup) were also made in Germany, but this rare example (c.1700) comes from Staffordshire. H 8½in/22cm

3 STAFFORDSHIRE TOBY JUG

Later Toby jugs, such as this one of a sailor made in the mid-1800s, were more crudely modeled and painted than earlier examples. A standard blue and white transfer print has been used for the hat and coat. H 7½in/19cm

4 WHIELDON-TYPE EWE AND LAMB

This beautifully modeled group, with brown, gray and green glazes, dates from c.1765. Whieldon was best known for his use of colored transparent glazes, applied over relief-molded vessels as well as figures. W 6in/15cm

5 STAFFORDSHIRE SPANIELS

Early Staffordshire dogs, such as these spaniels (1850–75), were modeled in the round; later versions intended to sit on a mantelpiece were made with a flat, undecorated back. Early dogs were colored rusty-red, followed by brown and, in the 1880s, black. H 9½in/24cm

6 FIGURE OF GARIBALDI

The Italian revolutionary leader is renowned for his contribution to the unification of his country. This well-modeled piece dating from 1860, when he conquered the kingdoms of Sicily and Naples, is one of the best Staffordshire figures of the period. H 15in/38cm

7 MINTON MAJOLICA TEAPOT

This amusing teapot in the shape of an organ-grinder's monkey clutching a coconut dates from 1870. It is a splendid example of the japonaiserie that became popular toward the end of the 19th century. H 5in/13cm

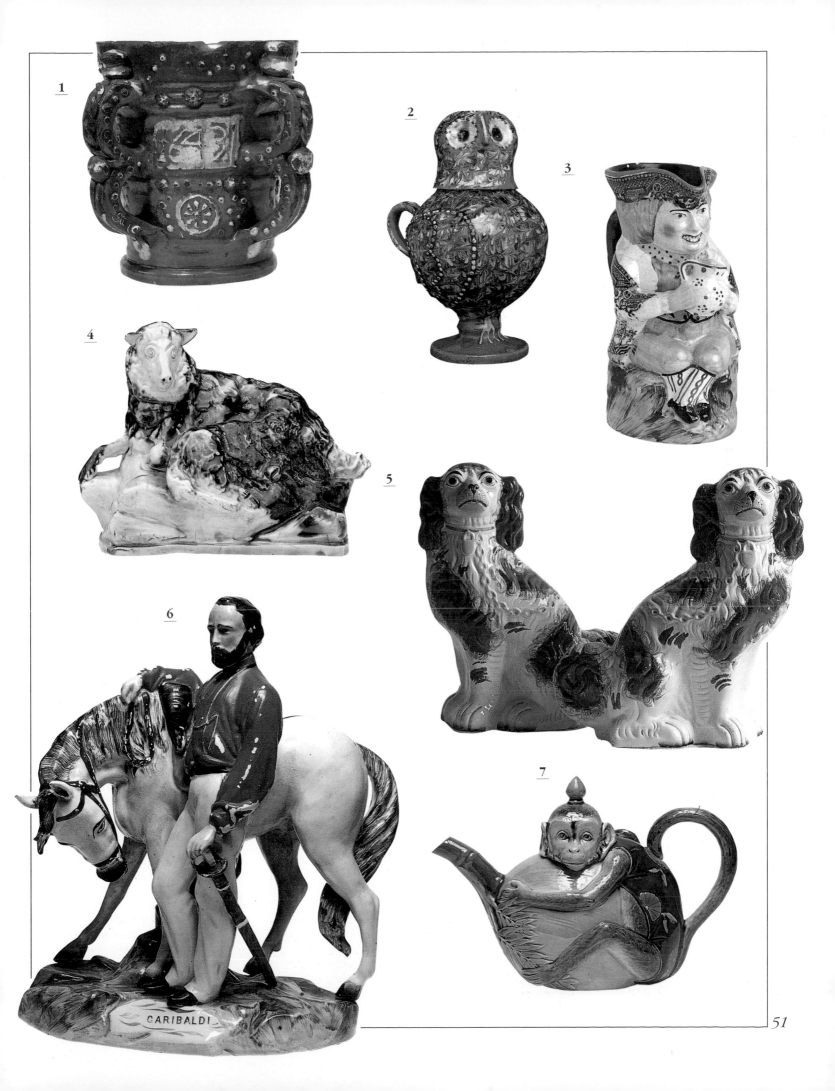

1

2

3

4

5

6

GARIBALDI

7

CREAMWARE AND PEARLWARE

A fine, creamy-white earthenware, creamware was developed from the salt-glazed stoneware made in Staffordshire, England, in the early 1700s. It was lightweight, could be thinly potted and easily decorated, and with its fine lead glaze was soon preferred to the old, heavy tin-glazed wares. Creamware was relatively cheap to produce and by the 1760s was recognized as the finest pottery in England.

Josiah Wedgwood realized its potential as an alternative to fashionable, but expensive, porcelain. He refined the body further and dubbed his pottery "Queen's Ware," after Queen Charlotte. At the height of the popularity of creamware in the 1760s to 1780s, the Wedgwood factory and its rivals, notably in Yorkshire, Derbyshire and Liverpool, flourished.

Creamware was decorated by printing, enameling and painting; plain relief molding and piercing were also used to great effect on the fine body. In 1779, Wedgwood introduced pearlware. A whiter form of creamware with a blue tint in the glaze, it was especially suitable for underglaze blue decoration.

The creamware creators

Regarded by most of his contemporaries as the greatest potting genius of his day, Thomas Whieldon (1719–95) made many fine pieces of both plain and colored creamware. Whieldon was also generous with his knowledge: Daniel and William Greatbatch (3) and Josiah Spode all worked with Whieldon before setting up their own potteries; and Josiah Wedgwood (1730–95), after being Whieldon's partner in the 1750s, went on to perfect creamware (2, 7) and produce pearlware.

Cauliflower ware

In the 1750s, when Wedgwood and Whieldon were partners, they introduced a type of creamware called "cauliflower ware" (1). All types of pieces, including tea wares, tureens and punch pots, were made in the shape of a cauliflower. The idea was later extended to melons, pineapples and corn, and copied at other potteries, most notably Chelsea and Worcester. Reproductions were made in the 19th century, but these tend to be more crudely modeled and use inferior colors and glazing.

1 CAULIFLOWER COFFEE POT

The detailed molding and rich green glaze are typical of the naturalistic forms that were much in vogue in the 1760s. Pieces in this style are known as Whieldon type, even though many factories produced similar wares. H 10in/25cm

2 WEDGWOOD TEAPOT

Enameled in pink, green, yellow and black, this David Rhodes "Chintz Pattern" teapot with an acanthus-molded spout and scroll handle was made at the Wedgwood factory in 1775. H 5½in/14cm

3 GREATBATCH OVAL TUREEN

Blue and white designs influenced by oriental porcelain decorate this elaborately molded tureen. The shape was inspired by silver shapes, and the pattern of chinoiserie figures and European flower sprays was painted in underglaze blue. Made c.1780, this tureen has been attributed to the Greatbatch factory at Burslem, Staffordshire. W 14in/36cm

4 NAVAL MUG AND JUG

Inscribed "Success to G.B. Rodney," the creamware mug was probably made in Staffordshire to mark Admiral Rodney's victory over the French at the Battle of the Saints in April 1782. Flanking the inscription and bust of Rodney is a rather crudely painted gunboat under sail. The jug was made in Liverpool (c.1790) and decorated with "An East View of Liverpool Light House & Signals on Bidston Hill." H 6½in, 7½in; H 17cm, 19cm

5 PORTRAIT PLAQUE

A relief-molded plaque of Sir Isaac Newton, with his clothes and hair picked out in bright colors, made in Yorkshire c.1800. H 5½in/14cm

6 PEARLWARE STALLION

Attributed to the pottery in Newcasile (c.1800), this handsome stallion, with the characteristic bluish tint in the glaze, is a fine example of a pearlware figure. H 17in/43cm

7 WEDGWOOD DINNER SERVICE

Simple creamware services such as this, totaling 170 items, were popular. Made c.1815, the elegantly shaped pieces are adorned with a restrained border pattern in blue enamel and a little gilding; some pieces are pierced.

◄ **FIGURE OF A SOLDIER ON HORSE**
It has been suggested that this creamware figure of a large man on a rather squat horse may represent George II at the Battle of Dettingen in 1743. Whatever the truth, this piece, made around 1760, is typical of a group of figures known as Astbury-Whieldon type.

John Astbury was a Staffordshire potter who worked in the mid-18th century. He is credited with making a great many charming figures, including cavalrymen and musicians. Their decoration, with colored glazes, is generally associated with Whieldon, hence the term Astbury-Whieldon used to describe them. H 10in/25cm

POTTERY AND PORCELAIN

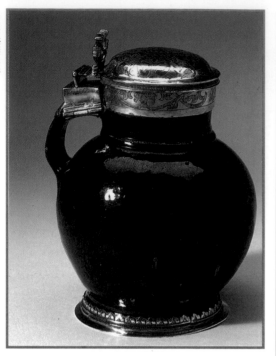

Stoneware, as its name suggests, is harder than earthenware. It is made of a type of clay that can be fired to a higher temperature, at which it vitrifies enough to become impervious to liquids even when unglazed, unlike earthenware. Toward the end of the fourteenth century, the use of salt to glaze stoneware was discovered in Germany. Salt was thrown into the hottest part of the kiln, where it vaporized and gave a shiny glaze, with a texture like orange peel, to the surface of the vessel.

The Rhineland of Germany became the heart of the production of early salt-glazed stoneware, owing to rich deposits of suitable clay in the region. The Westerwald area, Siegburg, Frechen and Cologne were among the major producers in the fifteenth and sixteenth centuries. Jugs, mugs and beakers dominated the output, often with incised, applied or molded decoration of leaves, masks and armorials.

The dull gray color of the clay of most Rhineland wares could be enlivened with a wash of color. In the late sixteenth century, a cobalt blue glaze was developed, which became characteristic of Westerwald wares; at Siegburg, a white-firing body was used.

Much German stoneware was exported from Cologne to England and other European countries. Its influence was, therefore, widespread. In England, such stoneware was made in Fulham, London, by John Dwight in the 1670s, and later by the Elers brothers in Staffordshire.

◀ **TUDOR PITCHER**
The shape of this pitcher, made c.1550, is reminiscent of that of German stoneware pitchers and of their tin-glazed English imitations known as Malling jugs (see p.46). Unlike the latter, however, the body is a red near-stoneware, and the glaze is strongly iron stained to give the dark color. The silver-gilt lid and mounts suggest that the pitcher was regarded as a valuable object. H 7½in/19cm

The Bartmannskrug

One of the most characteristic items of early German stoneware is the *Bartmannskrug* (**1**), which means, literally, "bearded man's jug." It was so-called because of the bearded face molded on the neck of the flask. In England, a similar bottle-shaped flask was known as a Bellarmine, after Cardinal Bellarmino, a Counter-Reformation leader whom the mask was thought to represent.

Böttger stonewares

The most refined of all stoneware was that produced by Johann Friedrich Böttger for Augustus the Strong at Meissen, c.1707, as a prelude to his discovery of the recipe for true porcelain (*see p.62*). Since Böttger was actually trying to make precious stones, he treated his deep red stoneware as a lapidary would, and it was cut, engraved and polished.

The combination of these techniques and the fine, hard material led to superb and unusual effects (**7**). A dark glaze was applied to some pieces, which were further decorated with gilding, and silver was often applied to spouts to protect them from chipping.

1 ARMORIAL JUG
A large Bartmannskrug, or jug, dated 1607, made in Cologne. It bears extensive decoration of coats of arms and masks and has also been embellished with splashes of brown wash and cobalt blue. H 14in/36cm

2 GERMAN JUGS
The Rhineland was the home of salt-glazed stoneware, and these jugs, all mounted in pewter, are typical of types produced in the region. Left to right: late 16th-century Bartmannskrug from Cologne or Frechen, molded with a mask and inscription; Siegburg jug with typical white body and crisp molding, dated 1601; two Westerwald jugs from the early 1700s, with cobalt blue glaze and incised decoration. H 7½in, 9in, 5in, 10in; H 19cm, 23cm, 13cm, 25cm

3 RHENISH CHARGERS
Although these stoneware chargers, dated (left to right) 1674, 1720 and 1750, were made over a period of almost 100 years, they are similarly decorated in a manner more usually associated with earthenware. Biblical subjects have been incised and colored using slip, then lead-glazed. H 23½in, 19½in, 24in; H 59cm, 49cm, 61cm

4 ANNABERG TANKARD
A stoneware tankard mounted in pewter and made in Saxony. It is molded and enameled with the head of a young woman, rosettes and seed pods, but its most unusual feature is the opaque blue ground. c.1660–80. H 5½in/14cm

5 WESTERWALD PITCHER
Finished in characteristic fashion with stamped and incised decoration, this pitcher includes a portrait medallion of Wilhelm III. It dates from c.1690 but the silver mount is a 19th-century addition.

6 TEA JAR AND TANKARD
Some of the finest stoneware was made in England by the Elers brothers in Staffordshire. They copied Chinese stonewares, and their work is usually unglazed and decorated with applied reliefs. The countersunk decoration on this tea jar from the late 17th century is unusual. H 4½in, 4in; H 12cm, 10cm

7 BÖTTGER TEAPOT
The precursor to porcelain developed at Meissen by Böttger was red stoneware, so fine and hard that it could be cut and polished like glass. This elegant and rare teapot, dating from c.1710–12, is cut overall with diamond and lozenge shapes. The silver mounts on spout and handle are linked by a chain. H 4½in/12cm

The production of stoneware in England was stimulated by large imports of German wares, and by the late 1600s, potters such as John Dwight of Fulham, London, were making stoneware with, typically, a gray-brown body and golden brown wash. There was, however, considerable development of stoneware in Staffordshire and elsewhere from the 1720s.

The addition of white Devon clay and ground flint to the body gave it whiteness and made it lighter. The resulting white, salt-glazed stoneware was used for household wares by potters in Staffordshire and elsewhere and enjoyed great popularity between 1740 and 1760.

Early examples were often decorated with stamped reliefs, and the development of slip-casting allowed the stoneware to be thinly molded, enabling much finer detail to be captured. This technique was used to create some novel forms and to achieve superb decorative effects without the use of added color.

Some white stoneware is decorated in "scratch blue." Designs incised into the body before firing were filled with cobalt blue, which was then wiped off the surface, leaving only the design colored. From c.1740, enamel colors were used for decoration, initially in Chinese style, though later examples followed European themes. Transfer printing was little used.

Pew groups

This is the name given to groups of seated figures (4) made in stoneware and earthenware c.1730–45. It is thought that they may have been produced by a single potter, perhaps Aaron Wood, although John Astbury has also been suggested (see p.52).

Characteristically, they are naive in form and have round, doll-like faces with beady brown eyes. Highlights and details are emphasized with brown slip. Sometimes the men are depicted as musicians, while other similar figures include equestrians and female figures whose dress forms a bell. Fewer than 30 genuine pew groups are currently known.

▼ **STAFFORDSHIRE SWANS**
These brilliantly enameled swans were made c.1750. They are of a more sophisticated form than most salt-glazed white stoneware, which tended to be largely domestic. The potential of this material for fine molding is clear in the crisp detail of the feathering. H 6½in/17cm

1 TWO BOTTLES
Two bottles show the influence of German stoneware in their form, though the proportions, particularly of the Bellarmine (right), suggest that they were made in London c.1685. The one on the left, attributed to John Dwight of Fulham, 1675–85, bears a thistle in relief, with other motifs and the initials CR for Charles II. H 8½in, 10½in; H 21cm, 26cm

2 PUZZLE JUG
A brown salt-glaze stoneware jug, possibly from the Vauxhall pottery, is a rare early example (c.1720). The natural color of the clay contrasts with a rich, golden brown iron-oxide wash, and the orange-peel texture typical of salt glaze can be seen. To drink from the jug, two of its three spouts had to be covered by the drinker's fingers. H 7½in/19cm

3 STAFFORDSHIRE BEAR JUG
Bear jugs with detachable heads date back to the 1500s, but were especially popular in the mid-1700s. The body of this salt-glazed example (c.1740) is covered with shredded clay to represent fur. This bear has captured the bear-baiting dog. H 9in/23cm

4 PEW GROUP
A Staffordshire salt-glazed stoneware group, dating from c.1745. The figures have the doll-like stiffness and startled faces typical of the type, with highlights and details painted in brown slip. H 6½in x W 7½in; H 17cm x W 19cm

5 STAFFORDSHIRE CAMEL TEAPOT
An example of the finely modeled forms allowed by the development of the slip-casting technique. Novelties, such as this teapot (c.1750) in the form of a camel with a relief-decorated howdah on its back, topped by a lid, were popular. H 5in/13cm

6 COFFEE POT
The technique of decorating salt-glazed stoneware with enamel colors produced some most attractive pieces. Enamels on this pale, hard body look particularly brilliant, as this example, dating from c.1755, shows.

7 TWO-HANDLED CUP
The decorative technique known as "scratch blue" is evident in this large cup, made in Staffordshire in 1756. W 12in/30cm

The name of Wedgwood is synonymous with much of the best of English pottery. Technical skill, artistry and entrepreneurial flair combined in Josiah Wedgwood, who produced a wide variety of innovative wares.

In 1759, after five years in partnership with Thomas Whieldon, Wedgwood set up his own factory at Burslem, Staffordshire. His first commercial success came with a refinement of creamware which he called Queen's Ware after Queen Charlotte.

During the 1760s and 1770s, Wedgwood developed his dry-bodied stonewares. The first, in 1767, was "black basaltes," a hard, unglazed body capable of taking fine molding and applied relief decoration. The second was Jasperware, developed in 1774. Around this time, in partnership with Thomas Bentley, Wedgwood started using his new wares to produce ornamental pieces in the neoclassical style.

Other developments included *rosso antico* (antique red), another stoneware inspired by ancient Italian pottery, and caneware, which was molded to simulate bamboo. The success of Wedgwood's wares is shown by their worldwide popularity, which continues to the present day.

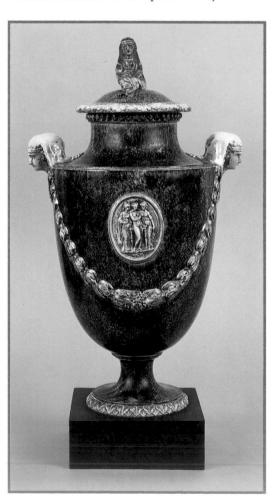

◀ **TWO-HANDLED VASE**
Handles in the shape of Egyptian heads, a Three Graces medallion, swags, and a "widow" (shrouded figure) finial complete the neoclassical decoration on this handsome urn-shaped vase. It was made c.1775 and has a gray-blue glaze that resembles porphyry – a type of rock used for sculpture. The base is marked Wedgwood & Bentley, Etruria. H 16in/41cm

WEDGWOOD MARKS
Genuine pieces are invariably marked Wedgwood (beware of misspellings). In 1860, a date-marking system was started with letters denoting the year and date.

wedgwood   WEDGWOOD

Impressed mark c.1760   Impressed mark c.1759–69

Impressed or incised on wares made in partnership with Bentley (1769–80)

Jasperware
Introduced in 1774, this hard, smooth, unglazed stoneware, which could be stained with metallic oxides – most commonly cobalt blue (**4, 6**) – is the ware most closely associated with Josiah Wedgwood. In addition to blue, jasperware colors included green, lilac, yellow and black. It was decorated with finely worked reliefs, usually in white.

After 1777, instead of staining all the clay, a layer of color might be imparted simply by dipping the body in colored slip. Jasperware was widely imitated by other potters, but these later copies are generally of inferior quality.

Wedgwood & Bentley
In a partnership that lasted from 1769 to 1780, Wedgwood and the Liverpool merchant Bentley made ornamental pieces in the neoclassical style (*left*, **1**) that swept Europe from the 1760s. Since Wedgwood's pottery could be made to resemble stone, marble or ancient pottery, it lent itself perfectly to the elegant classical forms. At the Etruria factory, Wedgwood employed some of the best artists of the day – including the sculptor John Flaxman – making copies of many ancient Greek, Roman and Egyptian designs.

1 BLACK BASALT FISH-TAIL EWER
On this extraordinary piece, an applied mask forms the spout, and an arching, scaly fish tail the handle. Marked Wedgwood & Bentley, Etruria, it has been attributed to the sculptor Flaxman, who worked for Wedgwood between 1775 and 1787. H 12in/30cm

2 CREAMWARE COFFEE POT
Black transfer prints are particularly effective decoration on pieces of creamware. This elegant 1770s coffee pot is printed with a shepherd and his flock. H 8in/20cm

3 "FROG SERVICE" PLATE
Made in 1773, this plate was part of a service numbering 972 pieces that was commissioned by Catherine the Great of Russia – probably Wedgwood's most famous commission. Each piece is painted with a different English view and bears the frog crest to denote its destination – the Grenouillère Palace in St. Petersburg (grenouille is the French for frog). Diam. 9in/23cm

4 BLUE AND WHITE JASPERWARE VASE
"Apollo and the Muses" stand in white relief above a band of musical motifs, and a white Pegasus knop finishes the decoration on this solid, not dipped, jasperware vase (c.1785). H 16in/41cm

5 BLACK BASALT PORTRAIT BUST
In the neoclassical fashion of the late 18th century, portrait busts of famous people were popular. This one depicts the English poet William Congreve wearing a smoking cap. H 7in/18cm

6 JASPERWARE CAMEO PLAQUES
On some cameo plaques, the relief work is very fine. The hand of the figure on the left has been undercut to give a three-dimensional appearance.

7 CANEWARE TEAPOT
Named for both its color and style of modeling, caneware was used for neoclassical pieces and elaborately molded game dishes. On this teapot (c.1790), the surface decoration is neoclassical, while the shape shows Chinese influence. H 3½in/9cm

8 ROSSO ANTICO POTPOURRI VASE
Wedgwood called his unglazed red pottery, most of which was made in the neoclassical style, rosso antico. This vase, made in 1815, was based on a Greek krater or bowl for mixing wine and water. H 13in/33cm

The arrival in Europe of Chinese porcelain in the late 1400s and early 1500s inspired potters in the West to attempt to make porcelain. The first successful experiments were carried out in Florence for Grand Duke Francesco I de Medici; about 60 pieces of Medici porcelain, made *c.*1575–87, have been recorded. The porcelain produced was of the soft-paste type, which incorporated powdered glass instead of the feldspathic rock of true, hard-paste porcelain.

In the late 1600s and early 1700s, the craze for all things Chinese led to renewed attempts by potters and even glassmakers all over Europe to produce porcelain. Although early experimental pieces exist from both Britain and Germany, the French were the first to establish factories making a soft-paste body. At St. Cloud, production of a creamy porcelain with a soft, glassy surface began in the early 1700s, followed in 1725 at Chantilly and 1734 at Mennecy.

This soft-paste porcelain was generally enameled, often in the Kakiemon palette (*see p.32: 3*), although some was left white, with imitation Chinese raised-prunus decoration. Initially, Japanese and Chinese shapes and decoration were dominant.

Despite these soft-paste imitations of Chinese porcelain, the quest for the true, hard-paste body continued unabated. In 1708, a formula was finally developed by the German alchemist Johann Friedrich Böttger. Soon after, the factory at Meissen was set up to exploit this achievement.

Porcelain decorators

Even in the earliest days of the Meissen factory, independent decorators known as *Hausmaler*, from the German for "house painters," would buy porcelain in white and decorate it with painting and gilding in their own workshops. Large quantities, usually of service wares, were bought at one time, so there might be a delay of some years between their manufacture and decoration. The names of several *Hausmaler* are known, among them Ignaz Preissler (**1**), the son of a famous glass decorator. He particularly favored monochrome decoration, especially in black or red.

▼ **PAIR OF MINIATURE VASES**
Although their origin is unclear, some experts hold that these experimental porcelain vases, dating from the 1660s, were made in the Duke of Buckingham's glass works in Greenwich, London. On view in The Burghley House collection, Lincolnshire, these unique vases (shown larger than life) may be an example of the earliest type of soft-paste porcelain made in England. The high-shouldered guan *shape and the decoration of putti heads, festoons and foliage painted in iron-red, puce and black on a gilt ground show a strong Chinese influence. H 1½in/4cm*

1 EARLY MEISSEN BÖTTGER TEAPOT
This square-form teapot (c.1720), an example of the first European hard-paste porcelain, was made to Böttger's formula. It was decorated with molded panels of dragons, enhanced with black-lead painting, a technique known as "Schwarzlot" (see p.94), which was fashionable among German Hausmaler, *in this instance Ignaz Preissler. H 6in/15cm*

2 ST. CLOUD BONBON DISH
Established in 1664, St. Cloud was the first factory in France to manufacture soft-paste porcelain. This small silver-mounted bonbon dish, modeled in the form of a cat, was made c.1730. Although crude, it has typical Kakiemon-style decoration and a thick, glassy glaze. L 2½in/6cm

3 LARGE WHITE MEISSEN EAGLE
Among the first figures to be produced at the Meissen factory were large white birds and animals for the Japanese palace of Augustus the Strong, Elector of Saxony. This eagle (c.1735), based on a Japanese Arita original, was modeled by J.J. Kändler (see p.62). H 22in/56cm

4 CHANTILLY KAKIEMON BOWL
Established by the Prince de Condé, a collector of Japanese Kakiemon wares, the Chantilly factory was well placed to imitate this style. The exquisite decoration on this bowl (c.1753) features two ho-o birds in the center with a diaper-pattern border. The gilt- and metal-mounted rim is a later addition. Diam. 10in/25cm

5 LOUIS XV MENNECY CANDELABRA
Figures were rarely made by the Mennecy factory, but when they were, they usually depicted oriental characters. This seated, upward-gazing figure, made in 1740, is typical of the style, as is the delicate decoration of his attire. H 10in/25cm

6 TWO FRENCH FIGURES
Two soft-paste figures (c.1750) of a man playing a guitar and a huntress of unknown French origin. Their clothing is enhanced with "indianische Blumen" (see p.62). H 7½in, 8in; H 19cm, 20cm

7 MENNECY OVAL SNUFFBOX
Enameled with brown, pink, blue and yellow, this tortoise-shaped snuff-box was made at Mennecy c.1755. It was silver-mounted by the Parisian silversmith Éloy Brichard. L 2½in/6cm

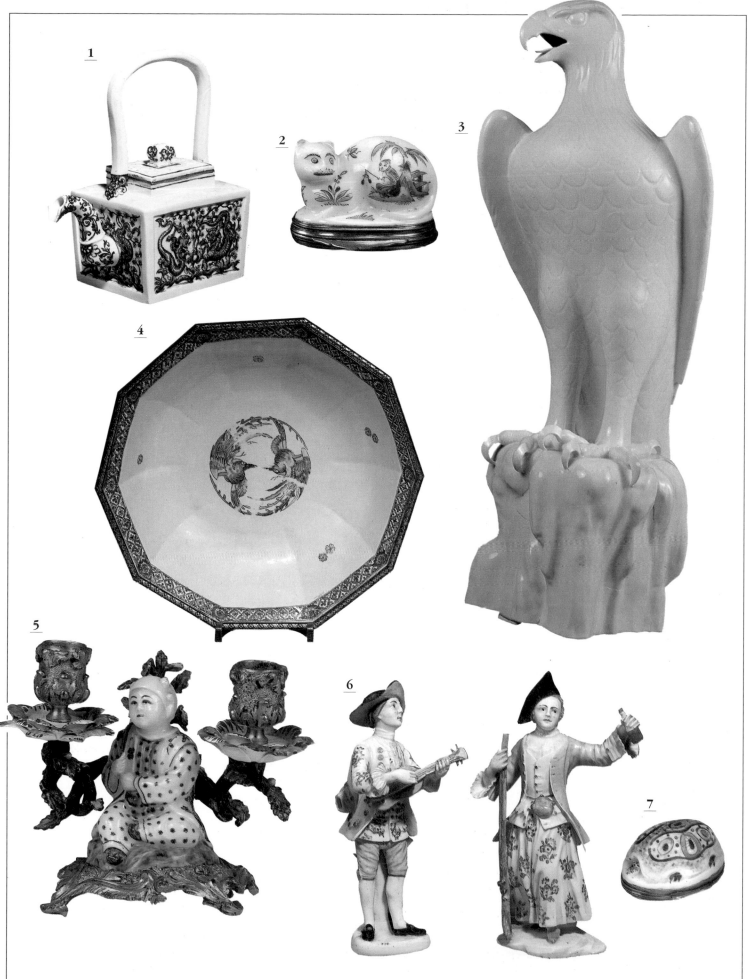

Although soft-paste porcelain had been made in Europe in the 1600s, the secret of true hard-paste remained obscure until a young alchemist named Johann Friedrich Böttger appeared. Under the patronage of Augustus the Strong, Elector of Saxony, Böttger gave up trying to make gold and developed a red stoneware which was produced at the factory in the elector's castle at Meissen. This was followed in 1713 by Europe's first hard-paste porcelain.

Decoration of Meissen porcelain took off with the arrival in 1720 of Johann Höroldt, a brilliant painter, who designed the whimsical and detailed chinoiseries typical of the 1720s–30s. Designs were also copied from Japanese Kakiemon porcelain from 1729; in the 1730s, a more European style of flower painting emerged. Rich ground colors were another specialty, with areas reserved for detailed painting against a backcloth of turquoise, yellow, green, puce or red. Meissen also developed a reputation for figures.

Meissen's great period ended with the Seven Years' War (1756–63), after which it lost its preeminence in Germany. In the late 1700s it adopted the neoclassical style, following the French lead.

◄ BALUSTER VASE

This large baluster vase with a domed cover is decorated in the brilliantly colored chinoiserie designs favored c.1730. It bears the "Augustus Rex" monogram mark, indicating it was probably meant either for royal use or as a royal gift. H 18in/45cm

SOME MEISSEN MARKS

1724–25	c.1740
1774–1814	1725–30

The famous Meissen crossed-swords mark in underglaze blue, used from 1724, is still in use today. Both this and the "Augustus Rex" mark have been extensively forged by other factories.

Meissen figures

The Meissen factory is well known for the superb porcelain figures made in the mid-18th century, which are some of its most valuable products. Johann Joachim Kändler (1706–75), who joined the factory in 1731, was the finest of the modelers, introducing a sculptural quality to his work.

In addition to making amazing large figures of animals and birds (*see p.60: 3*), he produced charming work on a modest scale such as the squirrels (7) and also figures from the *Commedia dell'Arte*, an improvised entertainment performed by traveling players that was highly popular in the 18th century.

Johann Böttger (1682–1719), whose earliest figures were made in red stoneware as well as in porcelain, was the first at Meissen to portray *Commedia dell'Arte* characters, including Harlequin, Columbine, Pulcinello (Punch) and Scaramouche.

The figures shown here (8) are by another good modeler, Peter Reinicke, who worked at the factory from 1743 until his death in 1768.

1 BÖTTGER PORCELAIN GROUP
Examples of early Meissen porcelain (c.1719) with the typical, rich creamy colored glaze. This type of gilt chinoiserie decoration was often done by artists working in studios outside the factory, in this instance Augsburg.

2 CREAM POT AND COVER
This design, originally derived from China, is known as the onion pattern, because of the strange outline which here appears on the lid. The cream pot is a rare example (c.1730) of Meissen's underglaze blue decoration, little of which was made. L 5in/13cm

3 CHINOISERIE TEAPOT
Chinoiserie designs such as those on this teapot (c.1730), with scenes of elongated figures contained by gilded scrollwork, were the inspiration of Johann Höroldt, one of Meissen's greatest painters. The dominance of iron-red and puce is typical.

4 CHOCOLATE POT AND COVER
The decoration here copies a Japanese original made at Arita, though the form is European. The ear-shaped handle is typical of the period (1740s), but a close look at the lid reveals a rare feature – a hole for the stick to stir the chocolate. H 8in/20cm

5 "INDIANISCHE BLUMEN" VASE
The decoration on this vase (c.1735) is known as "indianische Blumen," or "Indian flowers," a style introduced by Höroldt and rarely seen after 1740. It derives from both Japanese Kakiemon and Chinese famille-verte porcelain.

6 ARMORIAL TEA BOWL AND SAUCER
Much porcelain decorated with coats of arms was specially commissioned from China, but Meissen also made armorial wares. These pieces are part of a service for the Trotha family, probably to mark a marriage in 1731.

7 PAIR OF RED SQUIRRELS
These red squirrels (c.1750) show how brilliantly Kändler portrayed the vitality of animals. H 8in/20cm

8 COMMEDIA DELL'ARTE FIGURES
Modeled by Peter Reinicke, these figures show the liveliness typical of early Meissen figures (c.1743–44). They stand on simple pad bases, and the areas left white and undecorated reflect the factory's pride in the quality of its porcelain. H 5½in/14cm

1

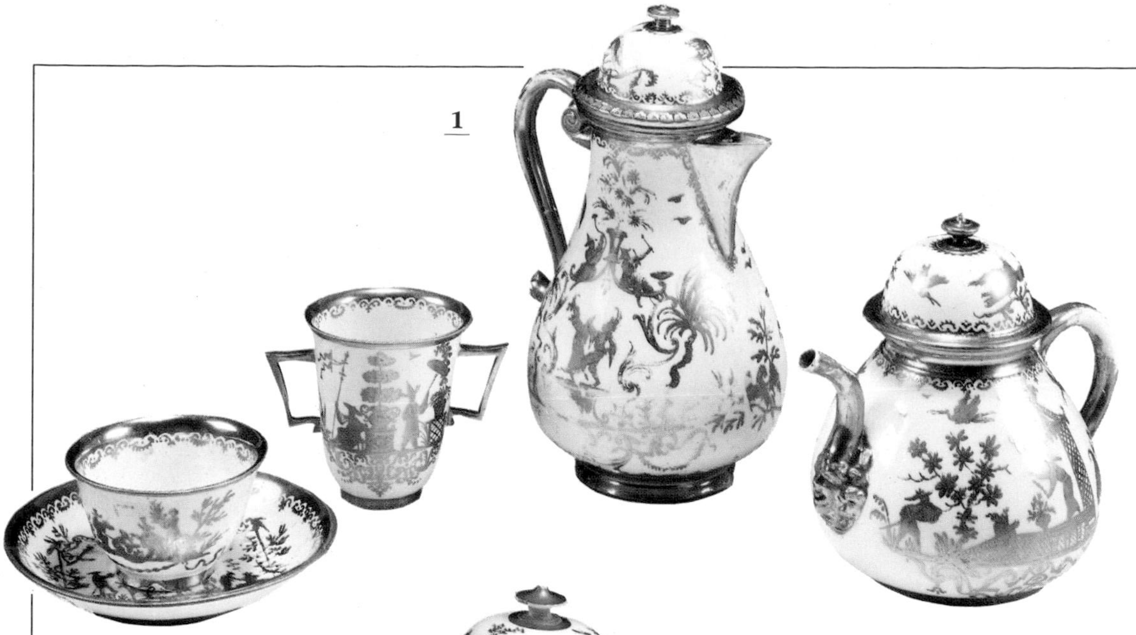

2

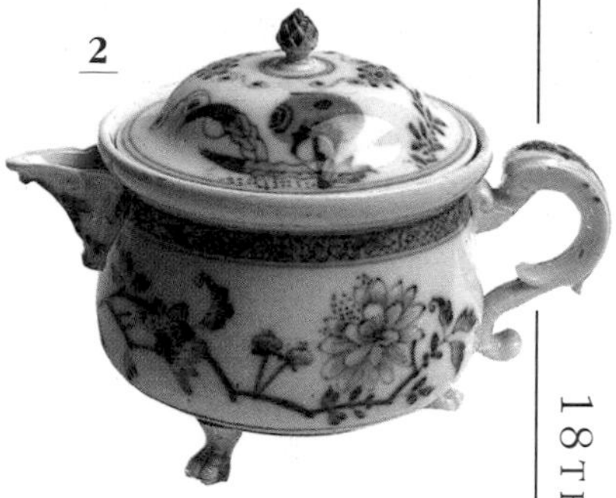

3

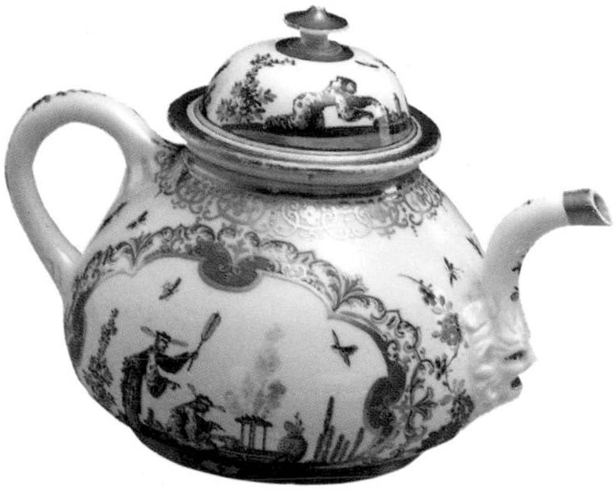

6

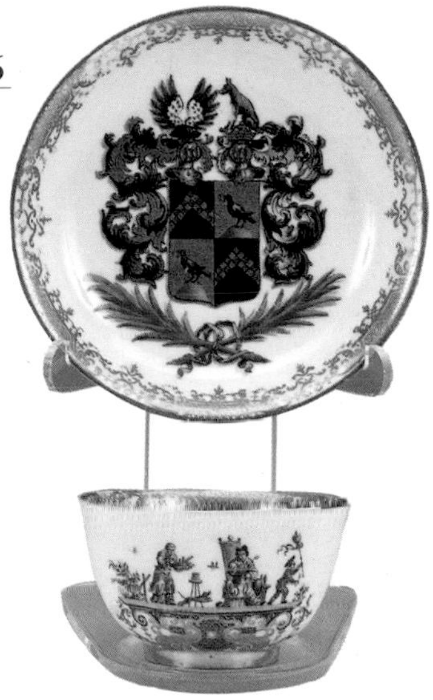

4

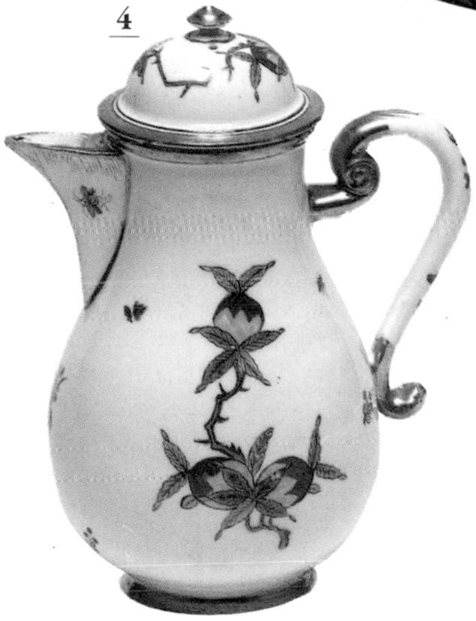

5

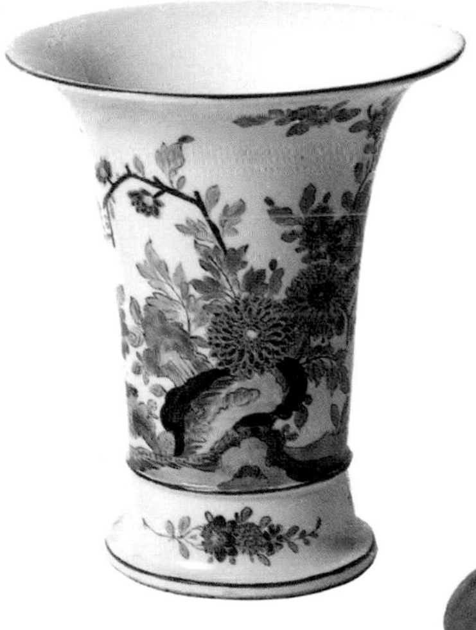

7

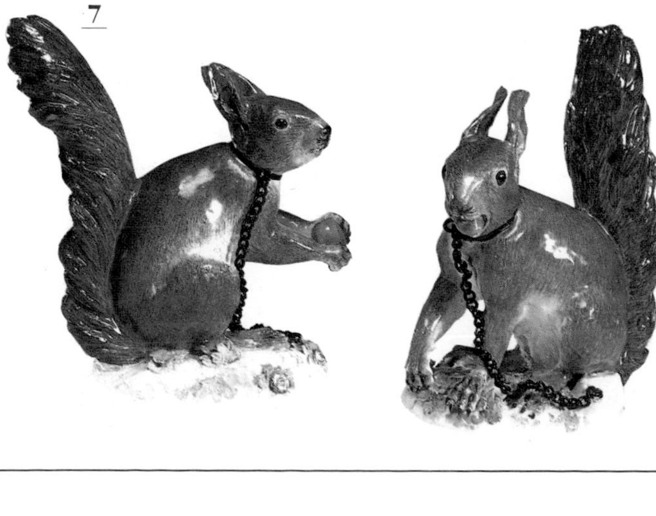

8

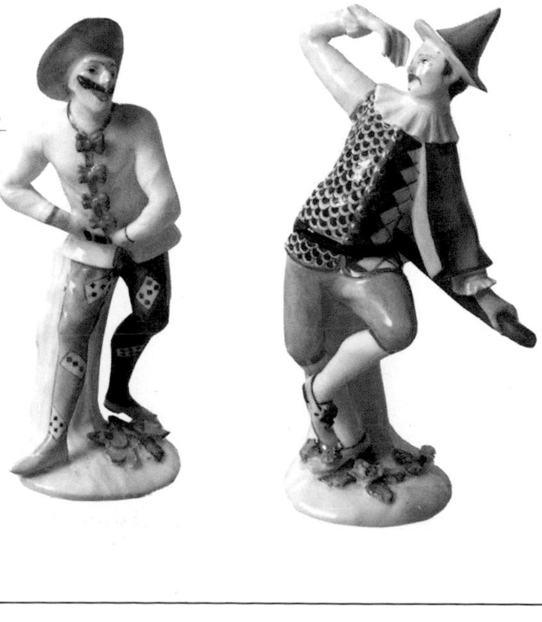

MEISSEN DERIVATIVES

With one exception, the secret of true hard-paste porcelain remained with Meissen for about 40 years, until the mid-1700s. Even then, what Meissen made, others aspired to, both in form and decoration. No other factories rivaled Meissen for creativity and originality, but they did develop their own strengths and characteristics and were not entirely imitative.

In 1719, two workers from Meissen defected to Vienna and helped Du Paquier to set up a factory, where porcelain was successfully made. The shapes produced were often original and not derived from Meissen, and between 1720 and 1740 the porcelain was decorated with chinoiserie, Imari flowers and landscapes.

It was from Vienna that the secret of porcelain ultimately spread, mostly through the journeyings of one man, J.J. Ringler, a kiln hand. He left Vienna in 1750, and in the following years took his knowledge to Nymphenburg and was later instrumental in founding other factories, including Strasbourg, Frankenthal, Ludwigsburg and Höchst. His assistants then spread the secret to Fürstenburg and Berlin.

While the demand for Meissen porcelain remained strong, these factories could best flourish by imitating its baroque style, and Oriental and European decoration. At the time of the Seven Years' War (1756–63), production at Meissen was disrupted, and the factory ceded its dominance to Sèvres.

Franz Anton Bustelli

The figure illustrated here (6) is an example of the work of the great porcelain modeler Franz Anton Bustelli. He worked at Nymphenburg from 1754 until his death in 1763 at a young age. His figures are full of life, with expressive faces and every limb in dynamic pose. He is particularly famous for his set of Italian Comedy figures, some of which were left white, while on others color was only sparingly applied.

1 VIENNA TEAPOT
An early example (c.1720) of rather freely painted porcelain from the Du Paquier factory, with typical decoration on the handle and spout. Other pieces, however, show finely painted chinoiseries. H 8½in/22cm

◀ **FRANKENTHAL FIGURES**
These figures depicting Oceanus and Thetis – characters from a ballet – were modeled c.1765 by Konrad Link, a great sculptor who worked briefly at Frankenthal as chief modeler. They are typical of his oeuvre *in having much applied decoration and being painted in strong colors. H 11½in, 9½in; 29cm, 24cm*

2 NYMPHENBURG PLATE
The factory at Nymphenburg was established in 1747, the year Prince Maximilian III of Bavaria married the granddaughter of Augustus the Strong of Saxony, who had set up the Meissen factory. The fine gilding and luscious flowers and insects on this well-decorated plate were painted by Josef Zachenberger in 1760–65. Since it is impressed with the Bavarian shield mark, the plate is likely to have come from a service that was made for the electoral court.

3 FÜRSTENBURG PLAQUE
Plaques with lavish scrolling frames such as this (c.1765) are typical of Fürstenburg's output. They were painted with Watteauesque figures and landscapes by J.H. Eisentrager, who worked at the factory 1754–68. H 4½in x W 6½in; H 12cm x W 16cm

4 HÖCHST ARBOR GROUP
The Höchst factory was renowned for fine figures and groups, especially those in rococo style. The group here, c.1760, is well composed and attractively set in a delicately modeled rococo arbor, hung with grapes. The coloring, dominated by puce and green, is typical of Höchst.

5 LUDWIGSBURG COFFEE POT
The basketweave molding around the neck and cover of this coffee pot is characteristic of the Meissen original on which it was modeled in the 1760s. Ludwigsburg porcelain tends to have a grayish, smoky hue. H 9in/23cm

6 BUSTELLI FIGURE
An example of the work of Bustelli, whose rococo figures were to Nymphenburg what the baroque figures of Kändler were to Meissen. This twisting figure of a beggar (c.1760), dressed in ragged clothes and holding out his hat, shows the great elegance, vitality and sense of movement he could impart to the clay. H 6½in/17cm

7 BERLIN DISHES
Berlin developed a reputation for tableware and was one of the biggest German factories. The porcelain has a hard, cold, bluish-white appearance, and is not particularly attractive. These dishes, decorated with birds in typical, somewhat garish, enamel colors, date from c.1770. Diam. 10in, 15½in; Diam. 25cm, 39cm

◄ **SÈVRES PLATE**
Although this plate was made in 1811, its style is 18th century. It was part of the magnificent 76-plate Egyptian service made at Sèvres to commemorate Napoleon's Egyptian campaign, a theme also found on many tea services of the period.
The center features a "Dyvan Militaire," an oriental council of state, painted by Swebach. The central figure, presumably Napoleon, is shown holding court before some Egyptians. The deep blue border was superbly gilded with Egyptian figures, deities and hieroglyphics by the gilder P.L. Micaud. Diam. 10in/25cm

2 SÈVRES VASE AND COVER
Large vases were a major part of Sèvres production during the 1760s. The rare blue ground of this piece (c.1768) has been scraped away to give space for paintings of fruit and flowers. The typically lavish gilding extends across the body in a fine "partridge-eye" pattern. H 17in/43cm

3 LARGE SÈVRES SEAU À BOUTEILLE
This fine seau à bouteille, or wine cooler, has an added value, since it bears the inscription "Ode sur le mariage de Mr. le Dauphin 16 mai 1770," commemorating the marriage of the future Louis XVI. It is painted with circular panels of cupids. H 7in/18cm

4 SÈVRES BLACK-GROUND CACHE-POT
The black ground on this flowerpot holder (c.1785) imitates oriental lacquer. The effect is enhanced by the gold and platinum chinoiserie decoration. W 5in/13cm

5 SÈVRES HARD-PASTE TEAPOT
Hard-paste porcelain was produced at Sèvres from c.1769. This classically inspired teapot, bearing the date mark for 1791, is painted with bachelor's buttons and colored bands adorned with gilt foliage. W 7in/18cm

6 TRANSITIONAL VINCENNES TRAY
Painted birds and flowers bordered by rich ground colors and heavy gilding were typical of late Vincennes pieces, although the style was only brought to prominence under Sèvres. The border of this tray (c.1752) shows an early use of the bleu céleste ground. W 11in/28cm

7 LATE VINCENNES TUREEN
Monochrome decoration, such as this, was popular at Vincennes until rich ground colors took precedence. Birds and flowers are the familiar themes of this early 1750s piece. W 8in/20cm

8 CHANTILLY ORIENTAL FIGURE
This figure (c.1730) shows many of the features of early Chantilly porcelain. The delicate painted design is outlined in black, and detail is lacking on the face and hands. H 5in/13cm

9 TOURNAI PLATES
The Tournai factory, set up in Flanders, Belgium, in 1751, was influenced strongly by both Meissen and Sèvres. These spirally molded plates (c.1765) show the quality of the factory's wares. Diam. 10in, 7in; Diam. 25cm, 18cm

In the mid-1700s the French manufactory at Sèvres provided a fresh style in porcelain which superseded the oriental and baroque influence of Meissen. The forerunner of the Sèvres factory was that at Vincennes, near Paris, which, after a faltering start in 1738, began to produce fine soft-paste porcelain. Although initially imitating Meissen wares, Vincennes quickly responded to the growing taste for rococo designs. A specialty was flowers modeled in porcelain, naturalistically painted and set on ormolu stems. Traditional wares were also made, usually painted with flowers, in either a monochrome or polychrome palette.

Under the patronage of Louis XV, the Vincennes factory moved to Sèvres in 1756. Many of the rich ground colors for which Sèvres remains famous had been developed by this time, as had the decorative style, which featured reserves – areas left free of ground color – superbly painted with birds, flowers, children and scenes, and bordered with lavish, tooled gilding.

Vincennes-Sèvres took porcelain to a level of sophistication hitherto unknown. The influence of their work can be seen in most European factories in the second half of the eighteenth century. By 1770, the more severe neoclassical style had become dominant, and hard paste had started to replace soft paste. The range of wares made by Sèvres was huge, and despite the hiatus caused by the French Revolution (1789–93), production continued into the 1800s.

Sèvres figures

The greater part of Sèvres production consisted of service and ornamental wares. Early attempts at polychrome figures like Meissen's failed; however, from *c*.1750 a new technique was pioneered using unglazed or "biscuit" porcelain. This came into its own with the rise of neoclassicism, since such figures resembled classical statuary (**1**).

Ground colors

Vincennes-Sèvres was renowned for its rich ground colors. Introduced in 1749, the dark blue, known as *bleu lapis*, was the only one to be applied under the glaze. Over the next decades, further colors were introduced, which included the yellow *jaune jonquille*, the turquoise *bleu céleste* (**6**), the green *vert pomme*, and the pink *rose* which was also known as "rose Pompadour," although this name was not used at Sèvres. Many other colors were used briefly in the 1770s and 1780s; one of the most striking was the black that imitated lacquer (**4**).

1 SÈVRES SOFT-PASTE BISCUIT GROUP
The technique of modeling in biscuit porcelain was pioneered at Sèvres. This piece (c.1764) depicts the classical tale of Leda and the Swan, attended by a naked maiden. E.T. Falconet, the greatest sculptor at Sèvres, took this theme from a painting by François Boucher. H 15in/38cm

POTTERY AND PORCELAIN

Unlike the porcelain factories of Germany, France and Italy, British factories enjoyed no royal or aristocratic patronage. As a result, they had to survive purely on their commercial success, so they explored the potential market widely, rather than making only a highly exclusive range of wares. Of the many porcelain enterprises that were set up in England at the height of the "porcelain fever" in the mid-eighteenth century, three important factories emerged to lead the market. The porcelain made at these, and at most of the early factories, was distinct from Meissen and Oriental ware, being of a soft-paste body.

Although it is still disputed, the laurels for the first porcelain of any quality made in England are usually awarded to the Chelsea factory, founded in 1745. The wares are of fine quality, superbly painted, and comprise original naturalistic designs, as well as those copied from Meissen, the Orient and, later, Sèvres. Chelsea wares are divided into four periods, according to their marks (see right).

Factories at both Worcester and Derby started around the middle of the century and became highly successful, surviving various changes of ownership. Tea wares were a specialty at Worcester, and few figures were made. By contrast, figures dominated the early wares from Derby; these were followed in the later part of the century by the lavishly painted and gilded service wares. In 1769 the Chelsea factory was taken over by Derby.

CHELSEA AND DERBY MARKS
Most Chelsea and Derby wares have some sort of mark, often wrong for the apparent period. All marks should be treated with the utmost caution.

Chelsea 1752–57 in red, 1757–69 in gold, painted

Chelsea/ Derby 1769–84 in gold

Chelsea/ Derby 1769–84 gold or color

Derby 1785–1825 painted blue

Derby 1782–1825 painted

Derby 1785–1825 blue, copy of Meissen mark

Chelsea marks
Chelsea porcelain is divided into four periods, denoted by factory marks. An incised triangle, used in 1745–49, was followed for the next three years by a raised anchor, molded in relief on a pad. The red anchor marks a period (1752–57) when many of the best-known Chelsea wares were made: animal tureens, botanical plates and early figures. The gold anchor period, 1757–69, was known for elaborate decoration with extensive gilding. All these marks have been much faked.

1 EARLY DERBY CHINOISERIE GROUP
A Derby dry-edge group (c.1752–55), so-called because the glaze has been wiped off the edge of the base. Its vitality and detail are in strong contrast to the romantic sentimentality of other English figures. H 8½in/22cm

2 CHELSEA BOTANICAL DISH
Botanical wares, as here (c.1755), with realistically painted vegetables or fruit were favored from the mid-1750s. Diam. 8in/20cm

3 CHELSEA DOVES TUREEN
Rococo tureens in the shape of birds, animals and vegetables are among the most desirable pieces of Chelsea porcelain. This tureen (c.1755) in the form of a pair of cooing doves bears the red anchor mark. W 17½in/45cm

4 HARLEQUIN AND COLUMBINE
These Chelsea Commedia dell'Arte figures (c.1760) were influenced by Meissen, but being of soft paste, they lack its brittle clarity. H 6½in/16cm

5 CHELSEA CLARET-GROUND PLATES
Porcelain with ornate floral designs, rich ground color and fine gilding inspired by Sèvres wares is typical of the gold anchor period. These plates were decorated c.1765 in James Giles's workshop. Diam. 12in/30cm

6 FIRST PERIOD WORCESTER TEAPOT
An early teapot (1765), painted in enamels and gilding, based on a contemporary Chinese famille-rose original. H 6½in/16cm

7 WORCESTER CABBAGE-LEAF PITCHER
The molded cabbage-leaf shape was popular, and pieces bore a wide range of decoration; on this pitcher (c.1768), it was inspired by Japanese Kakiemon designs. H 10½in/27cm

8 WORCESTER IMARI-PATTERN VASE
The shape and coloring of this vase (c.1770) reflect the continuing fashion for Oriental styles. The mottled green ground imitates shagreen (shark skin), while the panels are decorated with "Japan" designs. H 12in/30cm

9 WORCESTER BLUE-SCALE DISH
In imitation of Sèvres, Worcester developed a rich blue ground which was most successful when its intensity was relieved by painting scales of blue, thus creating a slightly dappled effect. About 1770. W 10½in/27cm

◀ **DERBY BOTANICAL DESSERT SERVICE**
The Derby factory became renowned for high-quality decoration on porcelain. Toward the end of the 18th century and during the Regency period, botanical painting was particularly fashionable; specimen flowers were depicted in great detail and vivid color. Here, each flower is named on the back of the piece, in both Latin and English. The painting on this dessert service, dating from c.1800, is in the style of John Brewer, one of a number of skilled artists working for the factory.

POTTERY AND PORCELAIN

In addition to the three major factories in Chelsea, Derby and Worcester, many other porcelain concerns sprang up in England in the mid-eighteenth century. In London, where Chelsea made porcelain for an exclusive market, the factory at Bow was also productive, making countless figures and tablewares. Most of Bow's decoration was of Oriental inspiration, both in blue and white and in a polychrome palette. Also operating in London in the 1750s were the Vauxhall China Works and the Limehouse factory, both acknowledged only recently.

In Staffordshire, the home of the potteries, the first porcelain factory of any significance was Longton Hall. Several factories, known by their proprietors' names – Pennington's, Chaffer's, Christian's, and Gilbody's – were set up in Liverpool. In eastern England, in Suffolk, well removed from any fashionable influence, was the factory at Lowestoft, making humble tablewares with quaint, unsophisticated versions of chinoiseries and their own designs.

In 1750 Benjamin Lund established the Bristol factory, which was bought by the proprietors of Worcester in 1752. Some 25 years later, Bristol again became significant, when Richard Champion acquired the secret of making true hard-paste porcelain. Champion's lasted from 1774 to 1781, when the formula passed to the New Hall factory in Staffordshire.

◀ **BUST OF GEORGE II**
This large and ambitious piece of porcelain sculpture (c.1755) is one of 16 known examples usually attributed to the factory of Richard Chaffer, one of the small firms extant in Liverpool at the time. Most of this factory's known products were tablewares, but figures such as this show great skill in both modeling and firing. H 13½in/34 cm

BOW AND BRISTOL MARKS

Bow 1750 Incised marks on early soft paste	Bow 1750–60 "repairer's" mark: Tebo Impressed	Bow 1760–76 "anchor and dagger" period Painted
Bristol 1770–81 Painted	Bristol 1770–81 Painted	Bristol 1770–81 Painted

Transfer printing

Though much of the finest decoration on 18th-century English porcelain was hand-painted, the technique of transfer printing was also extensively employed. This was much cheaper than hand painting, since less skilled painters were employed to color in the printed designs, and it allowed factories to extend their markets. At Bow and Worcester, outline designs were printed, while at Worcester, Caughley in Shropshire, Lowestoft (and less successfully at Bow and Derby), complete line-engraved images were printed in underglaze blue. Overglaze printing in black also enjoyed particular popularity at Worcester.

Blue and white porcelain

Although Chelsea produced very few blue and white pieces, almost all the other early English factories started by decorating their porcelain with cobalt blue painted under the glaze. Cobalt was the only color that could be fired within the glaze and so was much less expensive to use than enamel colors, for which further firings were needed. Worcester and Bow were the main specialists in this technique, though later Lowestoft and Caughley became substantial producers. Designs were largely Chinese in inspiration.

1 BOW FIGURE OF KITTY CLIVE
The factory at Bow was particularly successful at making figures. They were usually copied from Meissen or Oriental originals, but a further source of inspiration was the theatrical figures of the day, such as Kitty Clive. About 1750. H 10½in/26cm

2 BOW BOWL AND COVER
A fine example of Japanese Kakiemon-style decoration on English porcelain c.1750. The design and palette are typical and may have been taken either from a Meissen copy or from a Japanese original. W 6in/15cm

3 BRISTOL GRAVYBOAT
A rare piece (c.1751) from the first Bristol factory, established by Benjamin Lund. The shape is copied from contemporary silver, and the molded swags are picked out in enamels. L 8in/20cm

4 LONGTON HALL TUREEN AND COVER
This factory was noted for figures and tablewares of rather primitive form in vegetable, leaf and flower shapes, such as this bowl and cover in the form of stylized tulips (c.1755). W 4½in/12cm

5 BRISTOL VASE AND COVER
Hexagonal tapering vases such as this (c.1775) are unusual in 18th-century English porcelain in that they are of hard paste. This vase, one of a pair, was made by Champion and features fine gilding, for which the factory was renowned, as well as landscape painting in both polychrome and blue and white. H 18in/45cm

6 LOWESTOFT MUG
This mug (c.1790) is typical of the simply decorated commemorative and souvenir wares that were a specialty of the factory. H 4½in/12cm

7 COALPORT DISH
Among the firms making extensive services at the end of the 1700s was the Coalport factory in Shropshire. This dish is part of a sophisticated and extensively gilded "silhouette" dessert service (c.1805) in classical style.

8 NEW HALL TEA AND COFFEE SET
Colorful Oriental designs like this Imari pattern became popular for tea wares in the late 1700s. Saucers in sets such as this, of hard paste (c.1800), were shared between tea cups and coffee cans.

POTTERY AND PORCELAIN

All over Europe during the eighteenth century, porcelain factories sprang up, keen to imitate the success of Meissen. Their ability to do this depended on peripatetic workmen who, once they had learned the secret of making porcelain, were keen to sell their valuable knowledge. So, in the history of the many European factories, the same names recur frequently.

The factory at Vienna was the first after Meissen to achieve the manufacture of hard-paste porcelain. This was achieved by bribing Meissen workmen to defect and bring Böttger's formula with them. The factory had three periods: the first, the Du Paquier (1718–44) period, was followed by 40 years when rococo-style wares were made, while the later, neoclassical period ran from 1784 until well into the 1800s.

A similar sequence of events meant hard paste could be made in Venice in the 1720s, at the Vezzi factory. But it was not until the 1760s that large quantities of porcelain were made, at the Cozzi factory.

In 1759, on becoming King of Spain, Charles III, King of Naples, transplanted the staff of the Italian Capodimonte factory, which made some of the finest soft-paste porcelain, to the palace of Buen Retiro in Madrid. Capodimonte's successor, set up in 1771, was the Naples factory.

Porcelain factories were also established in more far-flung corners of Europe. In Holland, there were Amstel, Weesp and Oude Loosdrecht, while in Denmark the famous Copenhagen factory started making soft paste in 1759 and hard paste in 1771.

Itinerant workmen

The Vienna factory was founded in 1718, after its proprietor had bribed C.K. Hunger, a Meissen decorator and arcanist (the term used for a workman who knew the secret of hard-paste porcelain), to work for him. He was later joined there by another arcanist, Samuel Stolzel.

A painter from Vienna then took the formula to the German factories of Höchst, Frankenthal and Ludwigsburg in turn. Hunger went on to help start the Vezzi factory in Venice.

Knowledge of soft-paste also moved from factory to factory via workmen: one example is Chantilly to Vincennes, Vincennes to Copenhagen.

▼ DUTCH CABARET SET

Cabaret set is the term used for 18th-century porcelain tea, coffee and chocolate sets with a tray. This charmingly decorated tea set, made in hard-paste porcelain (c.1780), is an example of the work of the Dutch factory of Oude Loosdrecht. This concern had its origins at Weesp, near Amsterdam, in 1757, but was sold and moved to Oude Loosdrecht in 1771.

Although early designs were much influenced by Meissen, a softer French style has been favored here. Printed sprigs and flower garlands are wound around a purple and gilt band. The molded borders and handles are also gilded. L tray 19in/48cm

1 SPANISH SEAU CRENELÉ

The factory of Buen Retiro, which made this two-handled glass cooler (c.1765), was set up by Charles III of Spain, with the staff of the Italian Capodimonte factory. The factory continued to make fine soft paste, decorated in prevailing styles, and concentrated particularly on figures and tiles.

2 COZZI SUGAR BOWL AND COVER

Many figures, as well as service wares, were made at the Venetian Cozzi factory. This bowl, painted with scenes of ladies and gallants in parklike surroundings in typical bright colors, dates from c.1770. H 4in/10cm

3 VIENNA DINNER SERVICE

This part dinner service dates from c.1765, the period when the long-lived Vienna factory was under state control. The similarity to Meissen is clear both in the painting of the European flowers and in the palette. The molding shows strong rococo influence. L deep oval dish 15in/38cm

4 NAPLES SOUP PLATE

A replacement for the Capodimonte factory, which closed in 1759, was set up in 1771. This example of its wares, dating from c.1800, is decorated in neoclassical style. The roundel, with Pompeian-style figures, is encircled by a frieze of stylized anthemion – a device used also on furniture of the period (see p.174). Diam. 9½in/24 cm

5 OTTWEILER TUREEN AND COVER

Several German factories were set up to make porcelain in the 18th century, but the wares of this small Rhineland concern are rarely seen, especially complex examples such as this tureen (c.1770). The elaborate vegetable knop and molded feather scrolls of the border are typical of the factory's wares. L 14in/36cm

6 NAPLES SOUP TUREEN

This elaborate piece comes from the Ercolanese dinner service, which was commissioned c.1781 by Ferdinand IV, King of the Two Sicilies, who started the factory. It was inspired by the collection of antique bronzes discovered at Herculaneum. The shape was taken from a piece now in the archaeological museum in Naples, and the finial from the famous fresco showing Hercules wrestling with the Nemean lion. H 14in/36cm

1

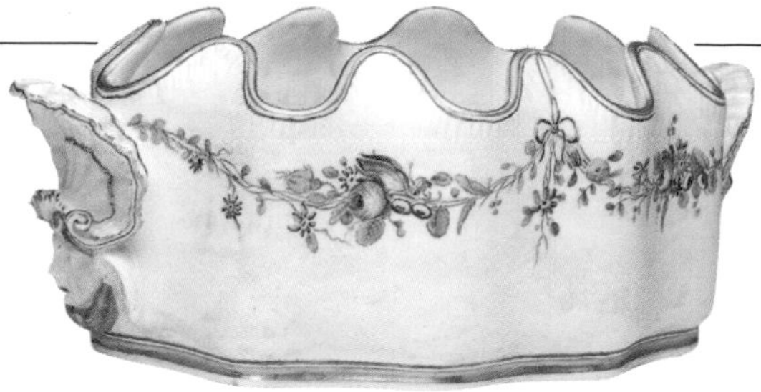

2

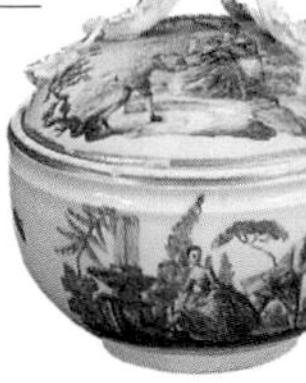

3

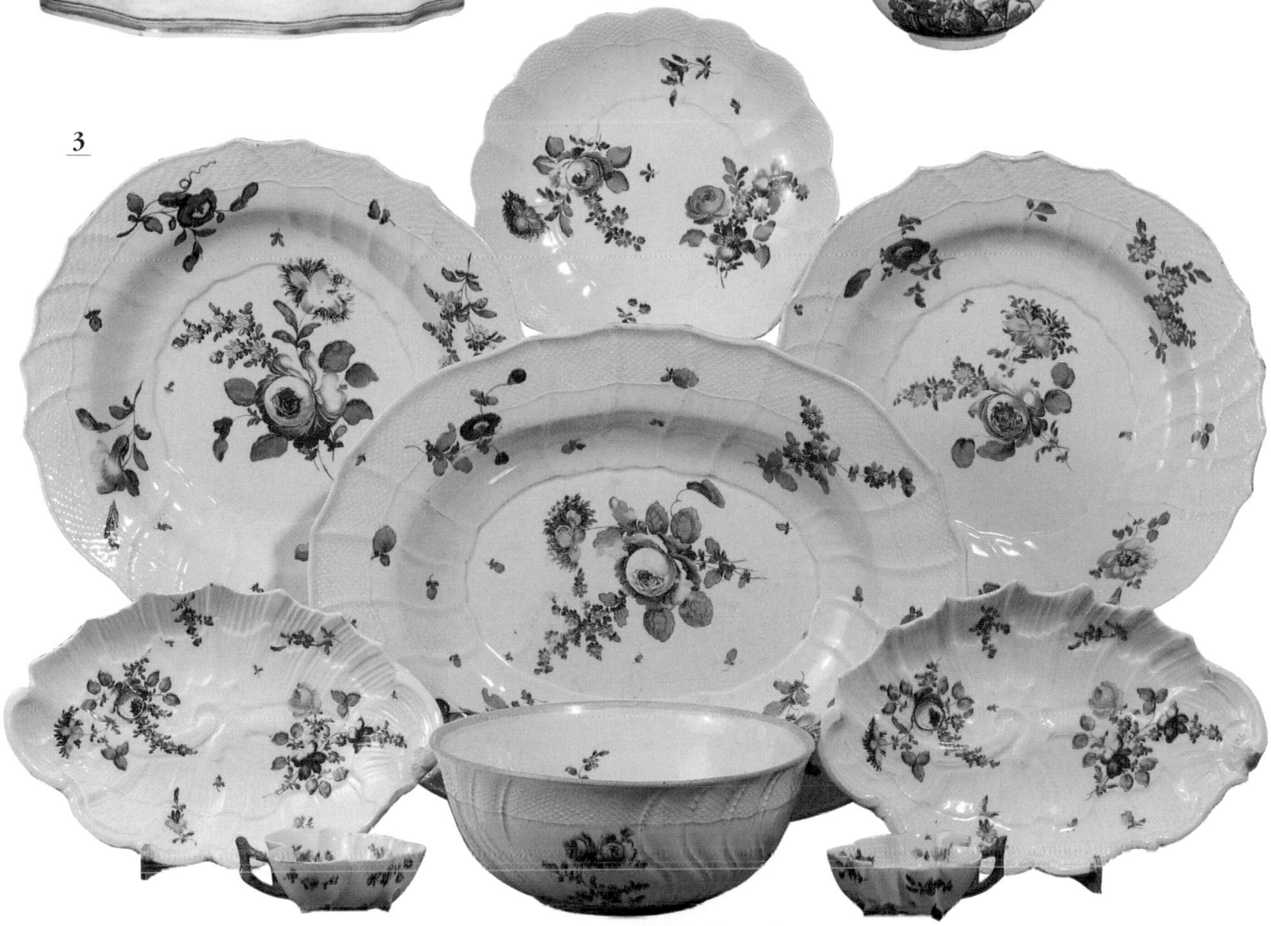

4

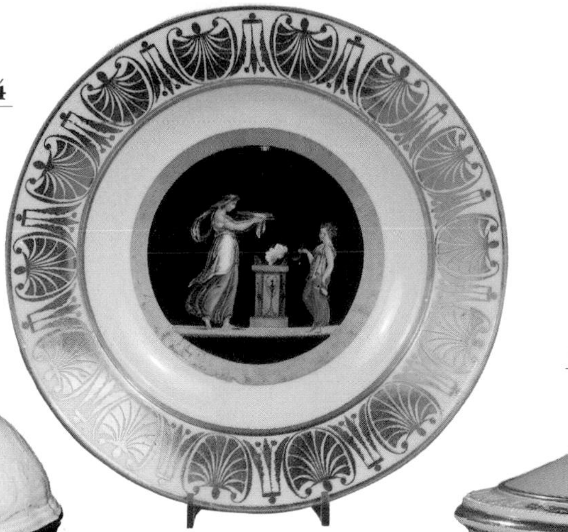

5

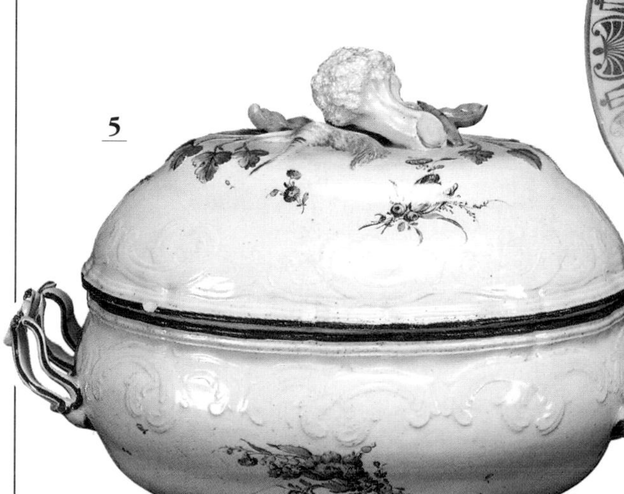

6

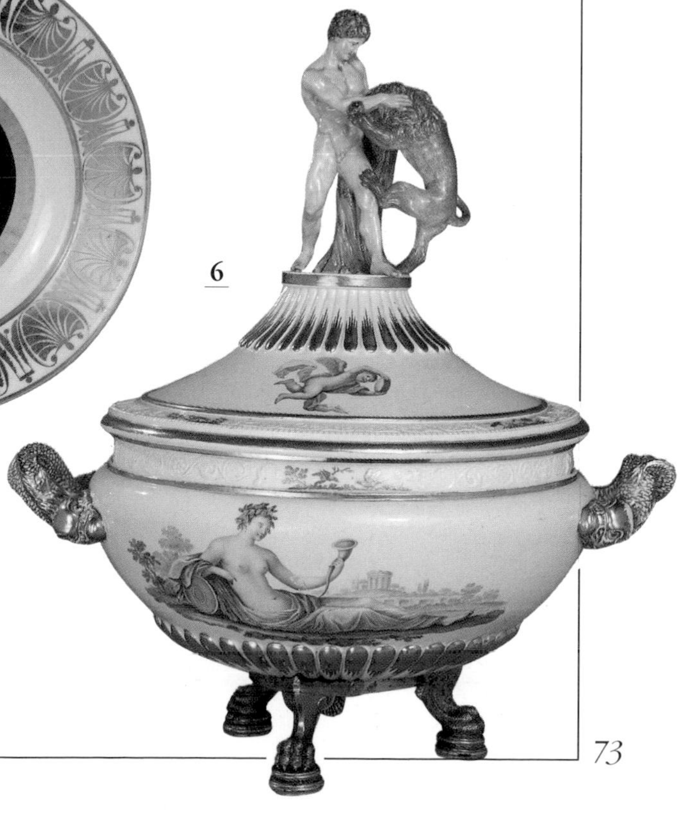

◄ NAPLES GROUP

An example of the work of the Naples factory which opened in 1771 to replace the Capodimonte factory (see p.72). Under the directorship of Domenico Venuti, hard paste was used from 1780. The factory produced fine services and classical figures as well as everyday groups such as this sleeping shepherdess being watched by two youths.

The reverse of this piece, modeled in the round, shows a boy watching the youth who is peeping over the top of the tower and a girl stroking a sheep. The group was made c.1790. H 14½in/37cm

1 FIGURE OF A PRETZEL SELLER

This figure of a pretzel seller, standing beside a tree stump, was made at the Vienna factory c.1760, a time when the factory was government-run. The modeling and decoration show the influence of Meissen. H 8in/20cm

2 DOCCIA FIGURE OF A TURK

This colorful figure of a Turk, dating from the mid-1760s, was made near Florence in Italy at the long-lived Doccia factory. The small head, large forearms and the colors of his flowing coat of puce and yellow over a flowered robe are typical of this factory. H 5½in/14cm

3 THÜRINGIAN FIGURE

In the German Thüringian states west of Saxony, many small factories were set up in the mid-18th century to make hard-paste porcelain. This scantily clad figure of Saint Jerome, shown holding two stones and with a lion at his feet, was probably made c.1765 at Volkstedt, one of the most important of these factories. H 8½in/21cm

4 LUDWIGSBURG GROUP

Figure modeling was particularly successful at the Ludwigsburg factory, as this example in the classical taste shows. It is the work of Domenica Feretti, known for his fine classical allegorical groups, and represents Mars at Vulcan's forge. Mars, in the plumed helmet, is shown directing Vulcan and his companion, while a putto looks out from beneath Mars' red cloak. Only one other example of this group, made in the mid-1760s, is known to exist. H 13in/33cm

5 ZÜRICH FIGURE OF A POSTMISTRESS

The pale color washes that decorate this hard-paste figure (c.1770), the rather static pose and the simple greenish mound on which the woman stands are all characteristic of figures from Zürich, the most important Swiss factory. H 4in/10cm

6 ANSBACH ARBOR GROUP

The fine-quality porcelain produced at the German factory of Ansbach (1758–1860) is now rare. J.C. Kändler, a relative of the famous Meissen modeler, J.J. Kändler (see p.62), was the main figure modeler at Ansbach. This group, made in the 1770s, depicts two lovers beneath a rococo flower-covered arbor. H 10in/25cm

The idea of making figures and groups in porcelain had its origin in the sugar or wax figures used to decorate German banqueting tables at this time. Once porcelain had been developed, durable versions of such figures could be made, and the Meissen factory was quick to capitalize on this fashion. Since they were made as table decorations, intended to be seen from all sides, early figures were modeled in the round. This contrasts with later examples, destined for the cabinet or mantel shelf, where little attention was paid to the back.

Great skill and ingenuity went into creating these figures, and many themes were adopted – mythological, pastoral, theatrical (such as the *Commedia dell'Arte* characters), allegorical and classical. From the outset, as in so many areas, Meissen was the dominant influence, setting standards that other factories struggled to emulate.

Throughout the 1700s, porcelain factories tried making figures, some with more success than others. The dramatic and lively movement of baroque pieces soon gave way to the softer colors and more romantic images of the rococo. Each factory developed certain characteristics – color of paste, proportions of figures, palette or facial features – which can help to distinguish its products.

Damage and restoration

Figures are so vulnerable that it is rare to find an example in mint condition. Heavy restoration, for instance that involving extensive repainting, can change the character of a piece. It is also important to know whether a figure or group is complete, since subtle amputations of damaged parts can be easily disguised.

Points to note

There are several features to consider when trying to distinguish between hard- and soft-paste porcelain. The hard-paste type is generally cold to the touch, and any chips on the surface reveal a hard, almost glassy, body to which the glaze is completely fused.

Soft-paste porcelain, in contrast, has a slightly warmer feel, and the body is more granular. The glaze itself seems softer and is liable to crazing, producing tiny cracks, and on early pieces is prone to discoloration. The differences between the pastes can only really be understood by actually handling a piece of each.

BRITISH 19TH-CENTURY PORCELAIN

Bone china, a porcelain body modified by the addition of bone ash which made it particularly white, translucent and stable, was probably the most significant development in ceramics in the early 1800s. By 1820, it was in use in most English factories.

During the first 20 years of the nineteenth century, the taste for neoclassical shapes prevailed; particularly popular were urns and vases. Decoration was extravagant, and the finest pieces combined superb painting with lavish gilding. An interest in naturalism was also evident in panels painted with shells, feathers and flowers, and landscape painting was popular. Colorful Japanese patterns in iron-red, blue and gold, with occasional splashes of green, pink and yellow, were frequently favored for the enormous tea and dinner services of the period.

By 1840, the Rococo style was enjoying a revival, and many factories, particularly in Staffordshire, obliged with exuberant shapes and floral decoration. The well-known eclecticism of the later Victorian period found expression in porcelain as in every field, and international exhibitions were filled with huge, overdecorated vases. Yet among the excesses were some fine artistic achievements: Minton's *pâte-sur-pâte* technique, Royal Worcester's novel piercing and Belleek's iridescent glaze.

◀ **LARGE MINTON VASE**
From an 18th-century-style design by the sculptor Albert Carrier de Belleuse, this vase is enriched with silver and gilding. It is lavishly decorated with sculpted pâte-sur-pâte *by Marc Louis Solon, the Frenchman who perfected the technique. In the late 1870s, when this piece was made, the Minton factory was enjoying great success, and its pieces epitomize the technical expertise and artistic mastery of the best British 19th-century porcelain makers. H 3ft/91cm*

Parian porcelain

Named for its resemblance to the marble mined on the Greek island of Paros, this type of fine white porcelain (6) was developed separately in 1846 by the Minton and Copeland factories. It was ideal for making copies, especially miniatures, of both classical and contemporary figures and busts, as well as other sculptures. The Belleek factory in Northern Ireland specialized in producing delicate parian pieces treated with a clear, pearly, or iridescent glaze (9).

Pâte-sur-pâte

This technique (*above*), translated from the French as "paste-on-paste," was developed at the Sèvres factory in the 1860s and was taken to England by Marc Louis Solon, who joined the Minton factory from Sèvres in 1870. *Pâte-sur-pâte* involved a process of gradually building up a relief design by painting layers of white or colored slip on a piece of unfired porcelain, usually parian. When the layers were carved, a remarkably translucent effect could be achieved.

1 COALPORT DINNER SERVICE
When this service was made (c.1810), the Coalport factory was producing more dinner services than any other English factory. These items, from a set of more than 100 pieces, were decorated with a bold Japanese pattern in underglaze blue and gilt with red, yellow and brown flowers and trailing honeysuckle. The tureens have gilt lion's head handles and lids with lion finials.

2 STAFFORDSHIRE PASTILLE BURNER
Household odors were banished by using vessels such as this, in which aromatic spices and resins were burned. This bone-china piece (c.1825), is shaped like a cottage. H 6in/15cm

3 CHAMBERLAIN'S WORCESTER MUG
By the early 1800s, there were three separate factories in Worcester. This claret-ground mug, an example from the Chamberlain factory, was painted and inscribed by Enoch Doe c.1840. H 5in/13cm

4 SPODE POTPOURRI VASE
With its pierced cover and lavender ground, this magnificent Spode vase, made c.1825, shows the quality of early 19th-century porcelain. The rich use of gilding reflects the Regency taste for grandeur, as do the dragon handles and finial. The superb shell painting shows the prevailing interest in natural history. H 8½in/21cm

5 SPODE EWER
Hand decorated in red and gold, this fine ewer, with a dragon handle, was made by Spode (c.1875), possibly as an exhibition piece. H 15in/38cm

6 PARIAN BUST
Designed by the sculptor Raphael Monti and made in parian by Copeland c.1860, this mother and child group features the veiled modeling characteristic of Monti's work. H 11in/28cm

7 CHINESE-STYLE MINTON JARDINIÈRE
Jardinières, or ornamental plant holders, enjoyed a particular vogue in the Victorian period. This example, made at the Minton factory c.1878, has a black-printed floral design on a rich turquoise glaze. The overall shape and lion's paw feet are inspired by Chinese styles. H 20in/51cm

8 COALPORT VASES
Although these vases appear to be similar and date from c.1895, their handles betray the fact that the large vase is not part of the set. All three are decorated with fine hand-painted landscapes, set upon cream and blue backgrounds, and are finished with raised gilding. H large vase 14in/36cm

9 IRISH BELLEEK CACHE-POT
This elaborate cache-pot (c.1900), a container used to hide a flowerpot, is decorated with finely detailed flowers and leaves. Young women with nimble fingers were employed to model such details, the edges of which can be sharp enough to cut the skin. Shells and other marine objects are more usual than flowers on Belleek pieces. H 10in/25cm

The end of the eighteenth century and the opening decades of the nineteenth saw a change in the role of porcelain, from a prestigious appurtenance of the aristocracy and royalty to part of an industry, which had to be able to turn a profit. Many factories sprang up in continental Europe to furnish demands for less-expensive porcelain from the rising middle class. Superb quality luxury items were still made, however, particularly by the long-established factories at Vienna, Sèvres and Berlin.

After a period of financial difficulty, the Vienna factory enjoyed a second flowering. The neoclassical style was embraced, with colored grounds and fine, tooled gilding, emulating that of Sèvres. Indeed, decoration became more lavish than ever, with ground color and extensive gilding in Empire style; at Vienna and Berlin, porcelain was used as a canvas for fine painting.

Sèvres emerged from the Revolutionary period as a government-owned concern and made hard-paste porcelain which allowed huge vases to be constructed; simpler wares were also produced. In Paris, many small factories sprang up making hard-paste porcelain, usually simply decorated.

Empire style

This was a late development (from about 1800) of the neoclassicism that had become fashionable following the excavation of Pompeii and Herculaneum in the mid-18th century. It employed many of the same elements, but was more elaborate. The simple shapes of 18th-century neoclassicism were replaced by more monumental Egyptian and Etruscan forms. Instead of the pure cylindrical shape, cups and pitchers with tall looped handles and everted lips (3) were typical.

At Sèvres, a technique of "jeweling" was developed, whereby drops of enamel were used as relief decoration, to imitate rare stones. The Empire style spread from France to other European countries through the influence of Napoleon.

1 BERLIN FIGURE
A late 18th-century figure of a Cossack (c.1770) after a model by Friedrich Elias Meyer, who was one of the chief modelers at the Berlin factory between 1761 and 1785. H 11½in/29cm

◀ **VIENNA CABARET SET AND CASE**
Richly colored grounds, lavish tooled gilding and painted classical scenes were all typical of the Vienna factory in the late 18th and early 19th centuries, as were cabaret sets such as this. Sometimes they are just for one, but here there are two cups, teapot, coffee pot, sugar bowl, creamer and tray.

This example was decorated later than its date of manufacture – the individual pieces bear different date codes, ranging between 1801 and 1812. Tray L 16½in/42cm

2 VIENNA COFFEE SERVICE
The unusual trompe l'oeil *decoration on this coffee set, dating from c.1790, imitates engravings of landscapes with wooden backgrounds. The technique, which is known as* faux bois, *or* fond bois, *developed c.1770 at the Niderviller factory, in Lorraine, and was widely copied.*

3 PARIS TEA AND COFFEE SERVICE
Pieces from an ornithological service made (c.1810) by Nast, one of the many factories operating in Paris in the early 19th century. The shapes are typically Empire, and the decoration of finely painted birds and bands of gilding is characteristically simpler than that on contemporary services by Sèvres and Vienna.

4 SÈVRES CUP AND SAUCER
During the Empire period, it was fashionable to decorate porcelain with portraits of Napoleon's family, in this instance Marie la Grande Duchesse de Bade, Stephanie Napoleon. The hard-paste porcelain is entirely obscured by the gilded ground. 1815.

5 SÈVRES BOTANICAL TAZZAS
Although Sèvres porcelain was usually entirely covered with decoration and ground color in the early 1800s, these tazzas (1825) show that it could be more restrained. The clear white of the new hard-paste porcelain is used to offset the finely painted orange and almond blossom. Diam. 8½in/22cm

6 BERLIN TOPOGRAPHICAL VASE
Ornately decorated and richly gilded neoclassical wares continued to be made at Berlin long after other factories had moved on to Rococo Revival. Precisely observed city views, such as this of Potsdam c.1845, were painted on vases and plates, in the 1830s and 1840s particularly. H 26in/66cm

7 AMERICAN PARIAN FIGURES
Soon after parian, an unglazed biscuit porcelain, was first made in England c.1846 (see p.76), it was introduced into America. Several factories copied English figures, and it is often difficult to distinguish between them and the English originals. These molded figures of a young man and woman, with the fruit, flowers and basket separately shaped and applied, were made in Bennington, Vermont, c.1848–58. H 9–10in/23–25cm

OTHER 19TH-CENTURY PORCELAIN: 2

Continental porcelain in the late 1800s continued to be made by the established factories – Sèvres, Berlin and Meissen – as well as by a host of newcomers, particularly in Bohemia. Empire style lingered on, but much porcelain tended to revive earlier styles, and this historicism lasted throughout the century, although new fashions arose, among them Art Nouveau and Japanese-inspired styles.

Appreciation of the porcelain itself, which meant that decoration tended to enhance rather than obscure the body, was replaced by a hunger for elaboration and technical wizardry – as is evident in the huge ornate vases displayed at great exhibitions. Heavily tooled gilding, finely wrought gilt-metal mounts and dark ground colors covered the porcelain completely. Added to these were exaggerated Rococo Revival scrolling shapes, generally alive with cherubs, resulting in a surfeit of decoration.

Artists also copied Old Masters on plates, vases and plaques, or painted portraits and romantic images, which are often of very high quality.

American porcelain

Though porcelain had been made in the U.S. in the 18th century, truly commercial production started with William Ellis Tucker, who set up a factory in Philadelphia in 1826. Other factories followed, helped by high levels of immigration in the 1840s, which provided trained workmen. Main factories included Charles Cartlidge's Pottery and the Union Porcelain Company, both in New York. Much American porcelain imitates its European counterparts, but it also includes some startlingly innovative designs.

1 SÈVRES VASE
Napoleonic scenes returned to favor during the reign of Napoleon III (1848–70), after a period of prohibition. This grand vase (c.1870), one of a pair, celebrates Napoleon's victories in a continuous frieze painting, while the monogram, eagle motif and laurels on neck, cover and base reinforce the message. H 3ft 3in/99cm

2 SÈVRES CABARET SET
In the 1800s, the Sèvres factory continued to look to the past and to repeat earlier forms of decoration. This cabaret set (c.1880), a 19th-century version of a late 18th-century idea, is suitably decorated with "jeweling" (clots of enamel) and complex gilding against a rich blue ground. Diam. plate 9in/23cm

3 MANTEL TIMEPIECE AND STAND
The German Sitzendorf factory in Thüringia made this riot of flowers, scrolls and cherubs, representing the seasons, c.1880 to house a French clock movement. The piece is representative of the extremes of decoration reached by some 19th-century porcelain makers. H 23in/58cm

4 AMERICAN VASE
A porcelain vase with painted floral decoration and handles in the form of monkeys, possibly modeled by an immigrant designer, K. Müller. It was made at the Union Porcelain Works, New York, c.1885. H 12in/30cm

5 SÈVRES-TYPE CENTERPIECE
Rather poorly executed decorative elements borrowed from the previous century, such as blue ground color and paintings of figures in 18th-century dress in romantic settings, appear on this bowl (c.1890). The addition of extravagant, gilt-metal pierced mounts comprising bases, borders and caryatid handles make it vastly more ornate. H 22½in/57cm

6 CORNUCOPIA VASE
The famous Danish factory at Copenhagen, which opened in the 1770s, enjoyed a revival in the late 19th and early 20th centuries. This unusual vase of Chinese inspiration, dating from the early 1920s, has also an air of Art Deco. H 24in/61cm

7 DRESDEN VASE
Made in the early 20th century, this very large vase is one of a pair taken from a 19th-century Meissen original. The decoration is highly ornate, with brightly colored vignettes of 18th-century figures, encrusted garlands of fruit and flowers, and cherubs perched on the shoulder and the cover. H 3ft 5in/1.04m

◄ **BERLIN PLAQUE**
During the 19th century, porcelain was frequently used at the Berlin factory merely as a vehicle for fine painting. This plaque, painted by one of the factory's best-known artists, R. Dittrich, dates from the mid-1800s and represents the biblical figure of Ruth. At this time, the subjects painted on plaques tended to be copies of Old Master paintings; later, pretty girls and nymphs became more fashionable. H 19½in x W 12in; H 49cm x W 30cm

ENGLISH ART POTTERY

In the second half of the nineteenth century, it became apparent to some that the technical excellence of ceramics had eclipsed true invention and art and had led to ostentatious vulgarity, a characteristic much in evidence at the Great Exhibition in London in 1851. The response of a growing number of potters was to develop their personal creativity, whether individually or as part of a small, close-knit team of designer, potter and painter. This involvement and freedom to follow decorative inspiration was fundamental to Art Pottery.

Around 1871 Henry Doulton set up a studio in Lambeth, London, at which students from the local College of Art were employed to make and decorate pottery by hand. It continued during the 1870s and 1880s to foster fresh talent, and the most notable decorators included Hannah Barlow, George Tinworth and Eliza Simmance. Other large potteries, including Minton and Wedgwood, opened studios devoted to making Art Pottery in order to satisfy the growing middle-class demand.

Independent potters produced some of the most imaginative and ingenious work. Among the best was William de Morgan, who opened his own pottery in 1872 and produced superb original wares, using luster finishes or Persian designs and colors. Many others, such as Burmantofts, Linthorpe, Della Robbia, Ruskin, Bretby and Moorcroft made worthwhile contributions.

The Martin brothers

From 1877 to the early 1900s, the four Martin brothers worked as a team to create some original pieces of stoneware, usually salt-glazed, which was known as Martinware. The famous, and now expensive, pieces include figures of birds (4), among others.

William Moorcroft

A designer from a potting family, William Moorcroft (1872–1946) worked for Macintyre & Co. from 1897 and in 1913 set up his own factory. He popularized the technique of slip-trailing (previously used in the 1600s), drawing fine, Art Nouveau designs on his vases. His early pieces included Florian Ware (7), and he went on to develop spectacular Flambé Ware in the 1920s.

▼ DE MORGAN POTTERY

All the pieces in this group date from De Morgan's best period: at the Fulham pottery 1888–98. They exemplify the rich blues, greens and dark reds he loved. Left to right: *Luster vase designed by Halsey Ricardo, De Morgan's partner at Fulham. Three "Iznik" vases, one with unusual serpent handles, showing typical De Morgan Persian-type designs in blues and greens. Charger, painted by Charles Passenger with a fantastic winged beast. H vases 10in, 9½in, 11½in, 15in; H 38cm, 29cm, 24cm, 25cm; Diam. dish 21in/53cm*

1 MINTON PLAQUE
This plaque was painted c.1872 by W.S. Coleman, the artistic head of Minton's Art Pottery Studio in Kensington, London, from 1871 to 1875. Diam. 23in/58cm

2 DOULTON VASE
A fine-quality faience vase painted in 1882 in typically autumnal colors by Isabel Lewis, who worked at the factory from 1876 to 1897. H 11in/28cm

3 DOULTON TINWORTH VASE
George Tinworth decorated his pots in scrolling gothic-style foliage and was the only Doulton artist to sign them on the side with his monogram. This pot dates from 1885. H 10in/25cm

4 MARTINWARE BIRD
Among the most entertaining pieces of Art Pottery are the stoneware birds, with smug, lugubrious, or leering expressions, made by Martin Brothers. Most, such as this, marked 1896, have removable heads. H 12½in/32cm

5 MINTON "SECESSIONIST" EWER
The style of decoration of this ewer (1900) was influenced by Art Nouveau and the Vienna and Glasgow schools of design. H 18in/46cm

6 DOULTON JUG
This strange, salt-glazed stoneware piece, modeled by Mark Marsham, is alive with applied, molded and incised decoration. It was made for one of the many exhibitions held in the late 1800s. H 6ft/1.8m

7 MOORCROFT FLORIAN WARE VASE
Decorated with a slip-trailed design of tulips, this vase (1904) carries Moorcroft's signature. But this is simply a mark of quality, for he was chiefly a designer working at the time for Macintyre & Co. H 12in/30cm

8 WEMYSS DRESSING-TABLE TRAY
A tray (1905) typical of the brightly painted and popular pottery introduced by the Wemyss factory in Scotland in the 1880s. L 11½in/29cm

9 RUSKIN VASES
From c.1901 to 1914 Ruskin pottery enjoyed international acclaim. Vases of simple, Chinese-inspired form such as these (c.1905–06) were typical. They were decorated in rich glaze colors, monochrome, mottled or flambé. H 7½in, 6½in; H 19cm, 16cm

EUROPEAN ART POTTERY

The first of the art potters in Europe was Theodore Deck, who set up a workshop in Paris in the mid-nineteenth century and produced pottery inspired by Middle Eastern ceramics. In addition to the rich blues and greens of his version of Iznik ware, he produced flambé glazes (streaking red and purples) and also underglaze gold. By the end of the century, many other potters, particularly in France, were developing their individual artistic styles, rather than following the mass-produced line.

Two strong influences are clear in the work of European art potters. Art Nouveau, with its sinuous shapes and soft floral designs, was high fashion at the end of the nineteenth century and is expressed in many pottery forms. The other predominant influence, particularly in France, was found in the simple forms of Japanese pottery. The oriental, mainly Chinese, glazes were especially inspirational, and many French potters, such as Ernest Chaplet and Auguste Delaherche, worked hard to perfect their own versions of flambé and other glaze techniques.

Entertaining pieces of decorative figure pottery were also made, perhaps the best-known examples being Gallé's smiling cats, which are more novelty than art. The work of Theodore Deck, however, with its brilliant coloring and well-modeled forms redresses the balance. Many of the Zsolnay pieces, from Pécs in Hungary, also have merit, with lively, inventive shapes and beautiful iridescent glazes.

A sculptor turned potter

The attractions of working with stoneware, especially when enlivened by the numerous rich glazes inspired by the Orient, extended beyond the potters to other artists. Among them was Jean Carries, a French sculptor who developed an interest in stoneware after seeing Japanese examples on display. He subsequently developed a wide range of glazes of his own.

Carries was commissioned to make an entire doorway of stoneware, using masks (possibly like that at **3**) and figures of animals as decoration. He also made various other pots and ceramic sculptures.

1 GALLÉ FAIENCE PUG DOG AND CAT
Emile Gallé is known chiefly for his work as a glass maker (see p.110), but he also made faience, including witty animal figures. Cats, such as the one here (c.1890), dressed in a peignoir, with the picture of a terrier in the locket around her neck, are best known. Many have been faked. The pug dog, dressed as a judge, dates from c.1880 and is a rarer piece. H cat 13½in/34cm; dog 12½in/32cm

◄ **ROZENBURG VASES**
The Dutch pottery of Rozenburg, established in 1883 at The Hague, produced some of the best interpretations of Art Nouveau seen in pottery, embracing not only surface decoration but also shape. These pieces, the work of the painter Sam Schellink, are typical in the use of color and the soft, flowing rendition of flowers. The vases are made of light, thinly potted "eggshell" earthenware, developed at Rozenburg in 1899. The chrysanthemum vases date from around 1900, the pitcher from c.1910. H 9in, 11½in; H 23cm, 29cm

2 ROOSTER
A brilliantly colored rooster made by Theodore Deck c.1880. It is, in fact, an egg basket, with a cavity between the wings. Deck was inspired by Persian colors and glazes, although he also drew inspiration from Chinese and Japanese pieces. H 16in/40cm

3 PORTRAIT MASK
The work of Jean Carries, this mask is an example of a sculptor working in the ceramic medium, which was not uncommon in the 1890s. The olive-green mottled glaze on the mask is just one of many glazes developed by Carries. H 11in/28cm

4 JAPANESE-STYLE VASE AND BOWL
Experimentation with glazes on stoneware was stimulated by interest in Japanese examples. These two pieces, dating from c.1900, show the effects that two French potters achieved on very simple forms. The ovoid vase, by André Methey, has a dripped and pitted white glaze, while the bowl by Auguste Delaherche has a traditional dark Japanese temmoku glaze. H vase 10in/25cm; bowl 4in/10cm

5 ZSOLNAY VASE
A piece typical of the production of the Zsolnay factory in Hungary c.1900. The life-like shape of the fish, with its open mouth forming the neck, is set off by the rich green and brown iridescent luster. H 16in/41cm

6 DALPAYRAT VASE
The rich, deep red glaze, speckled and streaked with dark green and stone, on this vase (c.1900) was perfected by the French ceramist Dalpayrat. The simple Japanese bottle shape with a twist neck is also typical of his work. H 13in/33cm

7 PORTRAIT VASE
The gilding and glamour of this vase, painted with flowers and a female portrait in Art Nouveau style reminiscent of the artist Gustav Klimt, belie its earthenware body. It was made by the Bohemian manufacturer Reissner, Stellmacher and Kessel, which traded as Amphora from 1903, and dates from around that time. H 9½in/24cm

1

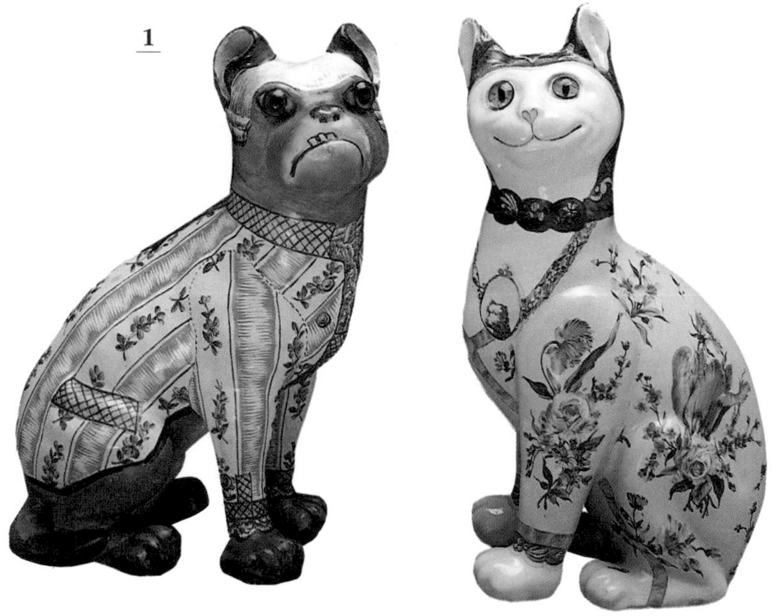

2

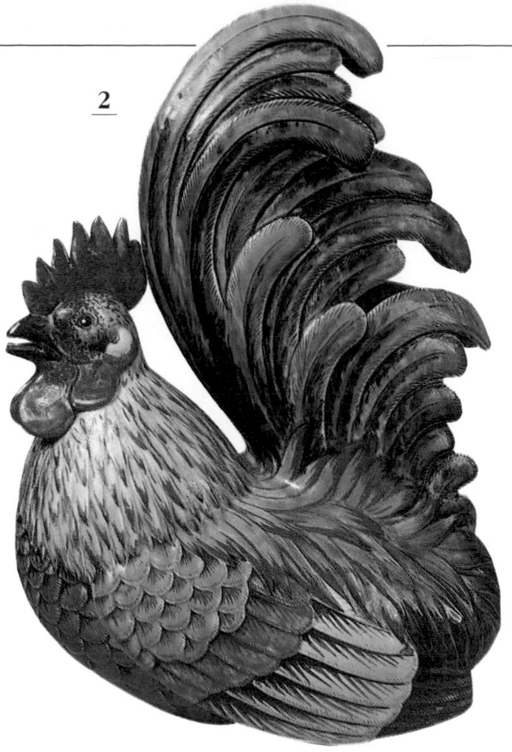

3

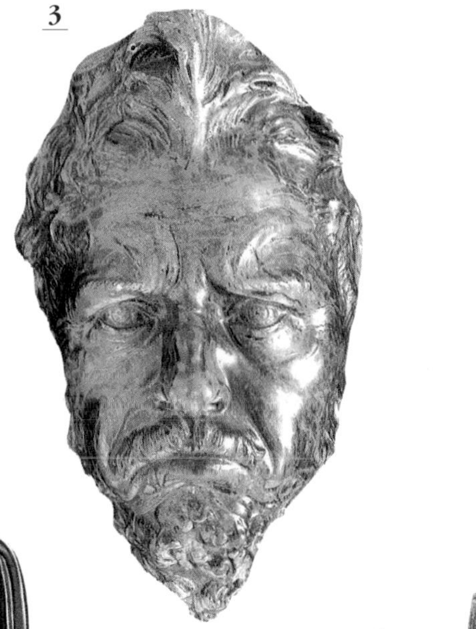

4

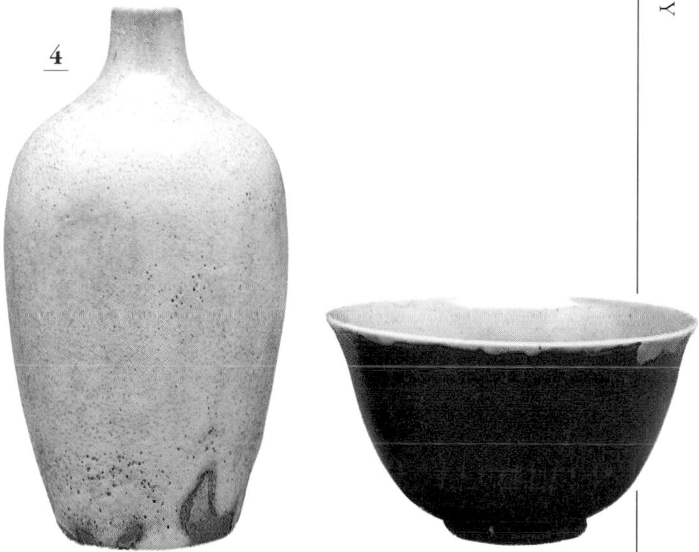

5

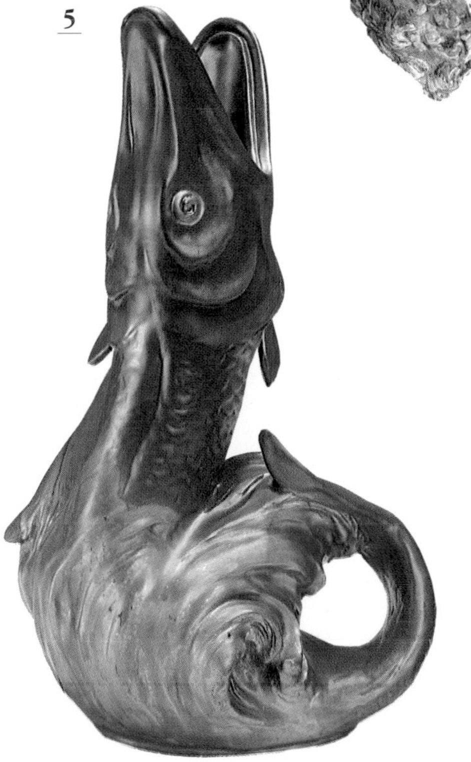

6

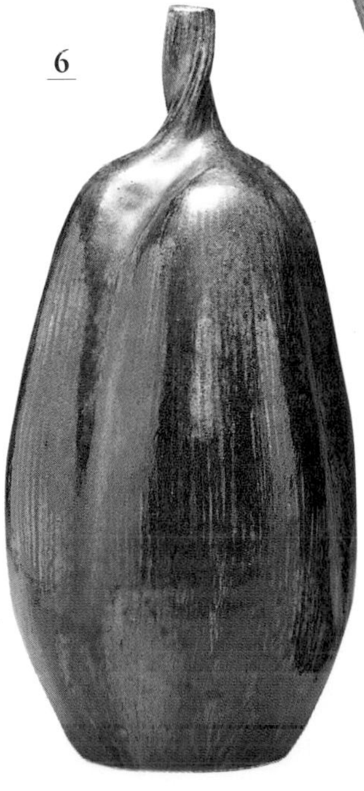

7

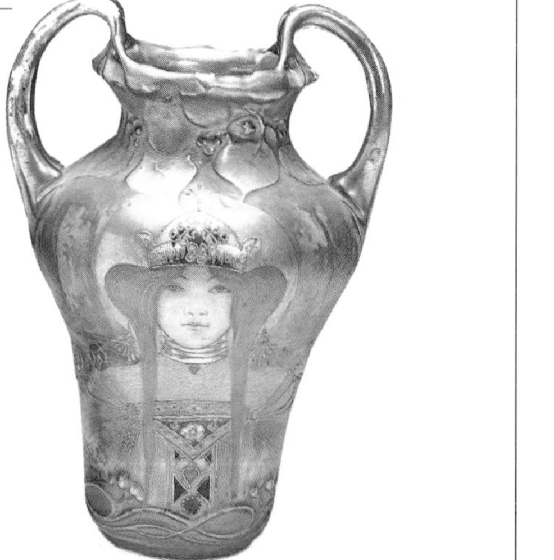

POTTERY AND PORCELAIN

The Arts and Crafts Movement in the U.S. found extensive expression in art pottery in the late nineteenth century. The center of the Art Pottery Movement was Cincinatti, Ohio, where, in 1880, Maria Longworth Nichols (later Storer) set up the Rookwood Pottery, which led the field for some 40 years. As in Europe, Japanese style had a strong influence. This was especially clearly seen in Rookwood pottery, since they had brought a Japanese craftsman to work with them. Rookwood wares typically had asymmetrical designs of flowers, in flame and amber colors, against a dark ground painted in slip under a high glaze.

Another successful pottery was the Grueby Faience Company, established in Boston, Massachusetts, in 1894. Here they specialized in wares of bold and simple form with applied botanical moldings and mottled glaze colors. The founder, William Grueby, followed the social ideology of the Arts and Crafts Movement, intending his studio to be "a happy merger of mercantile principles and the high ideals of art."

During the last decade of the nineteenth century and the early years of the twentieth, the United States became a center for the production of high-quality and original art ceramics. European artists and designers blended their skills with a new generation of American potters, who had been trained in art schools, and the results were very exciting, with an emphasis on interesting forms, often of natural inspiration, rare glaze effects and fine painting. Even some of the more commercial potteries were able to make a contribution.

An art-potter eccentric

George Ohr (1857–1918) was one of the more unusual characters in the world of artist-potters. Having worked at various trades, he settled to pottery in the 1880s in Biloxi, Mississippi. His highly original and innovative ideas were expressed in strange vessels (4), some of great size, which were very thinly potted and folded, pinched or crumpled into unexpected forms.

A showman by nature, Ohr sported a fine handlebar mustache of such proportions that it had to be tied behind his ears to avoid mishaps when he was at the potter's wheel. Perhaps the danger became too much for him for, having declared himself the world's greatest potter, in 1909 he suddenly gave up pottery and opened a Cadillac dealership in Biloxi.

1 ROOKWOOD LANDSCAPE PANEL
Vellum, the misty, translucent matte glaze used for painting landscapes on flat plaques such as this, made c.1912, was developed in 1904 at Rookwood. These plaques, which were a particular specialty of the pottery, usually featured hazy scenes of mountains or rivers painted in a delicate, almost impressionist, palette.

◄ LARGE GRUEBY JARDINIÈRE
Dating from c.1905, this piece is a typical example of wares by the Grueby Faience Company of Boston. William Grueby's company specialized in producing thrown pots to which hand-modeled botanical forms were applied in relief.

These heavily potted wares were finished with distinctive matte glazes. This "watermelon" green glaze with a mottled surface was a particular favorite, although shades of yellow, brown and blue were also produced.

2 TWO ROOKWOOD VASES
The style of the left-hand vase with its soft colors, was typical of Rookwood pottery, although the Japanese-influenced design of the other piece was more usually associated with this pottery. Both vases were made in 1895–1915. H taller vase 10in/25cm

3 FINE TIFFANY VASE
Although better known for glass, Louis Comfort Tiffany also made pottery, which he exhibited from 1904. Pieces were usually cast, rather than hand-thrown, and featured relief decoration inspired by naturalistic plant forms. Most were glazed in pale yellow, black or moss green. H 8in/20cm

4 EXPERIMENTAL GEORGE OHR POT
George Ohr was one of the most adventurous American studio potters of the early 1900s. His pieces ranged in size from miniatures to huge pots. This thinly potted vessel has been pinched together at the top. H 6in/15cm

5 EMBOSSED TILE
A boom in art tiles was a feature of the American Art Pottery Movement. In 1898, Dr. Henry Mercer established the Moravian Pottery and Tile Works in Doylestown, Pennsylvania, where this fine tile was made (c.1910). Mercer took inspiration from a wide range of sources – from classical and medieval to American Indian designs – although animal subjects, such as this rabbit, were unusual. He aimed for an old, handmade look and left some tiles unglazed to show the natural color of the clay. 6in/15cm square

6 GREEN GOBLET-SHAPED COMPOTE
This green-glazed white earthenware compote was molded in the form of a tree, with the branches shown in relief on the bowl. Its origin is uncertain, although such pieces were made in New Jersey and Ohio c.1910–20. Art Nouveau pieces such as this were in vogue in the United States about ten years later than in Europe where they originated. H 10in/25cm

7 FRANK LLOYD WRIGHT PORCELAIN
The American architect and designer Frank Lloyd Wright was associated with the Arts and Crafts Movement and had a major impact on the arts beyond his own field. He designed this service c.1917 for the Imperial Hotel in Tokyo, which was also his work. Diam. large plate 10in/25cm

1

2

3

4

5

6

7

CHAPTER TWO

GLASS

Glass is a remarkable material. Technically, it is a super-cooled liquid, but we experience it as solid and fragile, yet durable and waterproof. It transforms our lives in more ways than we can readily appreciate. It insulates us from the weather, while still letting light through. When molded and shaped, glass can be used to examine the universe at both the microscopic and macroscopic levels and to restore vision to those with imperfect sight. It has furnished our homes for more than 4,000 years, and its unique blend of beauty and utility is still appreciated today.

Until the late 1970s, glass was a relatively undeveloped field of collecting by comparison with ceramics and metalware. Various factors may have been responsible for this. Makers' marks were rare before the nineteenth century, making authentication and attribution a matter of experience and expertise. Furthermore, valuable pieces were subject to reproduction and forgery. Today, however, collectors are enthusiastic about glass. The reasons for this include the fact that more information is available about the subject, and that, for some antique glass, it is still possible to start a worthwhile collection without spending too much money.

The following pages cover all the major types of glass that may be encountered today, along with some examples of very rare or specialized pieces. Although Venetian glass is the first subject explored in detail in this section, the Venetians were not responsible for inventing glass, and it is important to put them, and all later developments, in context by briefly considering the early history of glass and the major methods of its manufacture.

The actual origins of glassmaking are obscure, but there is evidence that it was being made in western Asia as early as the middle of the third millennium B.C. This knowledge spread to northern Syria, Cyprus and the Aegean; but it is from Egypt that the best of this early glass comes. Due to the excellent conditions for glass preservation, much has survived from this industry, which flourished *c*.1500 B.C. The Egyptians produced beads, scarabs and amulets and other small items, the most memorable of which were richly colored vessels decorated with trails of contrasting colors. These fine objects were manufactured using the rod- and core-forming and casting techniques.

After a period of disruption, glassmaking was revived in the eastern Mediterranean and western Asia. By the tenth century B.C., it had spread to Mesopotamia and from there to Syria and then Assyria. As a result of trade by the Phoenicians and colonization by the Greeks, the knowledge then moved westward into the Mediterranean basin, where small bottles for holding ointments were made in vast quantities.

The development of the blowing technique in the first century B.C. profoundly affected glassmaking. The spread of this efficient process, which allowed glass vessels to be made relatively cheaply, coincided with the expansion of the Roman Empire. This fostered widespread trading links between producers and consumers, not only in Italy, but also throughout the Near East and Europe. A vast quantity of the household and decorative glass made during Roman times still survives. In the first centuries A.D., migrating workmen took their skills to France, Germany and other northern European countries and set up workshops there.

Glassmaking developed slowly in northern Europe, and glass was considered a luxury until the emergence of the bourgeoisie in the 1700s and 1800s led to a great increase in demand. Much of this glass was made by unknown workers in glass factories. It was only in the late 1800s that a reaction to the new industrial mass-production of glass led to the emergence of glass

▶ **ANCIENT SYRIAN GLASS BOWL**
In the 8th century B.C., the Etruscans established a settlement at Praeneste, a short distance north of Rome. When the princely tombs there were discovered and opened, a veritable treasure trove of gold jewelry, ivories and elaborate silver-gilt vases was found.

In one of them lay this beautiful glass bowl, probably made in Syria in the 7th century B.C. by drawing the melted glass out into a thread and winding it around a core of sand and clay. Its elegant, simple shape and vibrant color, which could have come from the studio of a modern artist, serve only to emphasize the timeless nature of glass.

AN INTRODUCTION TO GLASS

To appreciate antique glassware, it is important to understand some fundamental aspects of its composition, manufacture and decoration, all of which can help to indicate its age and origin.

Basic ingredients

The raw materials for glass are silica (sand, quartz or flint) and an alkaline flux to fuse it together at high temperature (c.2,000°F/1,100°C). Once fused, this molten mixture, known rather confusingly as "metal," can be blown, molded or cast into shape. Throughout history, glass makers have experimented with these ingredients to give their products individuality and a characteristic look of their own.

Soda glass was favored by the Egyptians, the Romans and the Venetians because it could be worked into thin, intricate forms. It was made with sodium carbonate (an alkaline flux), derived from the ash of seaweed, and had a slightly yellowish or greenish tinge. The Venetians managed to counteract this coloring by adding manganese oxide and so produced their famous cristallo glass (see p.92). Although fragile, soda glass could withstand the constant reheating needed for the elaborate tooling and pincering of Venetian dragon-stemmed glasses.

As its name suggests, the alkali contained in potash glass was potash (potassium carbonate), which was obtained by burning wood or bracken. Potash glass had a characteristic green coloring and, since it hardened more quickly than soda glass and was less malleable, favored decoration by cutting or engraving. It was produced across northern Europe in medieval times and was revived, with additional ingredients, as the basis for much modern utilitarian glassware.

Although lead oxide was added to some ancient glass, so producing lead glass, the significance of this addition was not fully realized until, in the mid-1670s, George

Ravenscroft used it in England. Lead glass produced a richer "metal" than soda glass and, although it could not be blown as thinly, was excellent for cutting because of its ability to refract light (see p.104). Flint glass is often confused with lead glass because, at about the same time as the latter was introduced, ground flint was used as the silicate. Although it was later replaced by sand, the term "flint glass" remained.

Working with glass

The processes involved in transforming glass from a liquid to a solid had an important effect on the finished article. The earliest glass vessels were made using a technique known as rod- and core-forming, in which a solid core of sand and clay was built up around a rod, then covered with molten glass and rolled into shape. When the glass cooled, the rod was removed and the core scraped out, to leave a hollow object. The rod

▲ **GLASS BLOWER AT WORK**
A worker at the Waterford factory in Ireland cutting off some glass to add a handle to the still-soft jug he has blown. To reach this point, he first gathered a ball of molten glass on the end of a long iron blowpipe, rolled it into a more manageable shape on a marver, or oiled slab, and then blew the glass freely into the air. An iron rod, or pontil, was used to press and squeeze the glass into the desired shape and to attach the handle.

◀ **STILL LIFE WITH A ROEMER**
Painted by the Dutch artist Pieter Claesz, active in the mid-1600s, this picture features a fine roemer, or rummer. The glass has a tall stem, a high-spun conical foot and prunts on the stem that have been patterned with a stamp. Such glasses were common in still-life paintings of the period, which attests to their popularity.

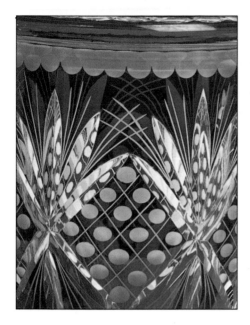

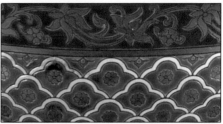

alone was also used to make small solid objects such as jewelry. Casting was another technique used in ancient times, with molten glass being treated like metal and poured into a mold, either open or closed. This technique had a relatively modern counterpart in the pressed glass of the nineteenth century (*see p.108*).

The discovery, around the first century B.C., that molten glass could be blown like a bubble was a great advance in the industry. A small "gather" of glass on the end of a long tube was blown, either into a pre-formed mold or freely into a sphere. This sphere could then be pulled out to form the required shape.

Decorative techniques

The decorative qualities of glass could be enhanced through color, form and applied decoration. Certain techniques required the glass to be molten, while others, such as cutting and engraving were carried out once the piece had cooled.

Decoration was added to early German pieces while the glass was hot and soft. Examples included "claw beakers," in which the body of the vessel was pulled down into points resembling claws. More common were prunts, little knobs of glass applied to the body or stem (*see p.94*). In ancient and medieval times, vessels were also decorated with trailing, thin threads of molten glass applied to the body. The famous Venetian technique of *filigrana* (*see p.93*) involved fusing slen-der rods of white or colored glass to clear glass, which was then blown and twisted to create the design.

Colors were produced by various impurities in the glass mixture. Although some makers eliminated these tints to produce completely clear glass, others deliber-ately added minerals to impart a color. While colored glass was favored by the Egyptians because it imitated semiprecious stones, the glass makers of seventeenth-century Bohemia elevated its use to an art form and originated some of the more spectacular shades, such as ruby red. They also specialized in techniques,

▲ **SOME DECORATIVE TECHNIQUES**
Diverse decorative effects could be achieved on glass. Clear glass was dipped into molten colored glass, or "flashed," and this layer was then cut through, in this instance (left) *with an "ear of corn" design. The engraving of a classical scene* (center) *is on clear, blown glass. Similar to cased or flashed glass, cameo glass* (right top) *involved carving or, more commonly, etching away with acid the top layer of glass to leave a pattern on the contrasting base. Enameling, a colorful translucent coating, and gilding were used on this piece* (right below).

such as flashing and casing (*see p.94*), that made the most of colored glass. The most complex use of colored glass was probably in cameo work (*see p.110*).

Glass is soft enough for designs to have been scratched on its surface since ancient times. Stipple engraving was a technique favored by the Dutch in the eighteenth century; a diamond point was tapped and stroked across the glass, using myriad dots and dashes, to create an image. Greater detail was made possible with copper-wheel engraving, which used different sizes of wheel, operated by a treadle, to abrade the surface of the glass. This type of engraving was employed extensively in Germany in the 1600s, and in England from the 1700s. In the nineteenth century, less precise designs were imparted to glass by acid-etching and sand-blasting, which gave a frosted finish.

Lead glass lends itself to being cut, the facets and prismatic effects enhancing its refractive qualities (*see p.104*); such glass is often referred to as crystal. The technique was practiced to great effect all over Europe in the late 1700s and the early 1800s.

Other decorative techniques include enameling and gilding. Enamel colors could either be cold-painted or, for a more lasting finish, given a low-temperature firing to fuse them to the glass. Gold was applied in a variety of ways: one ancient technique, revived in Bohemia in the 1600s, involved "sandwiching" a thin leaf of gold or silver between two layers of glass (*see p.94*).

VENETIAN GLASS

There was a glass industry in Venice from at least the tenth century, but it was not until the late 1400s that recognizable styles emerged. The city's position and excellent trading links contributed to the pre-eminence in Europe of the Venetian glass industry until the 1700s. A more important factor, however, was the development of a clear soda-glass, called cristallo, that imitated highly prized rock crystal. Light and thin, it could be easily manipulated and drawn into dazzling decorative effects.

Glass making was at its height in Venice in the sixteenth and seventeenth centuries. The decorative techniques employed included *filigrana* (*latticinio*), enameling, gilding, *millefiori* and ice glass. But most characteristic was the molten, trailed decoration, whereby threads of glass were woven and pincered into fantastic shapes to form the stems of drinking glasses.

Venice lost its dominance in the 1700s as lead glass was developed elsewhere and the potential it offered for new forms of decoration was realized.

Imitators of Venetian glass

Venetian glass became the height of fashion in Europe, and by the mid-16th century it was being imitated all over the continent. Much of this glass in the *façon de Venise* (style of Venice) was made by emigrant Venetian glass-workers, particularly winged glasses and other ornate embellishments, as well as *filigrana* glass. It is usually impossible to tell precisely where such pieces were made, and it can be difficult to distinguish them from true Venetian examples.

Filigrana

This characteristic form of Venetian glass involved the decoration of clear glass using threads of opaque white glass (*latticinio*) and sometimes also of colored glass. Many different designs could be created through the skillful manipulation of these threads to create patterns: crisscross (*vetro a reticello*), twisted thread (*vetro a retorti*, **3**), and spiral or helix (*vetro a fili*) among them.

1 ENGRAVED PLATE
Cristallo glass is characteristically thin, and this makes it less than ideal for engraving. There was, however, a fashion for diamond engraving around the mid-16th century, and this fine blown plate dates from that time. Diam. 9½in/24cm

2 ENAMELED DISH
Gilding and enameling usually appeared together on bowls and tazzas of Venetian glass made in the first half of the 16th century. This bowl, with a central well rising to a point, has a gilt border, embellished with colored enameled dots. Diam. 10in/25cm

3 FILIGRANA TAZZA
From the early 16th century until the 18th, glass with filigree designs such as this 17th-century tazza was made in Venice. Many different patterns could be made by manipulating threads of white (latticinio) or colored glass. This design is known as vetro a retorti. Diam. 6½in/16cm

4 ENAMELED FLASK
This brilliantly colorful flask, dating from c.1730–50, is from the studio of Osvaldo Brussa. The Brussa family of Murano was noted for the enameled decoration on its glass; flowers, birds and fruit were typical subjects. H 3½in/9cm

5 FAÇON DE VENISE GLASSES
These drinking glasses in Venetian style (façon de Venise) were made in the Low Countries during the 17th century. The serpent-stemmed goblet on the left has an elaborately coiled section enclosing entwined colored threads between pincered ornament in clear glass. It shows the same manipulation of the glass as that used on Venetian-made goblets (left). The stem of the wine glass (right), with pincered wings, encloses a turquoise thread. H 10½in, 8in; H 27cm, 20cm

6 VENINI AMPHORA
During the 1800s, only reproductions of old styles were made, but innovations in the 20th century have given new life to Venetian glass. This vase (1928) is the work of Paolo Venini, the foremost Italian designer, who had a factory on Murano from 1925. He called this richly colored opaque glass with bubbles vetro pulegoso. H 10in/25cm

◀ **DRAGON-STEM GOBLET**
This represents one of the classic types of Venetian glass that was imitated widely throughout Europe in the late 16th and early 17th centuries. The complex stem, constructed of threads of glass coiled and tooled into the form of a dragon, was worked at the lamp. The blown bowl and foot were then added at the furnace. This 17th-century example was made in Italy, probably in Venice. H 10½in/27cm

GERMAN AND BOHEMIAN GLASS

Some of the most decorative of European glass was that produced in Germany. Bohemia, the region east of Bavaria in southern Germany and now part of the Czech Republic, was particularly renowned for its glass in the 1700s and 1800s.

Early German glass, dating from c.1400 onward, was known as *Waldglas*, or forest glass. One of the ingredients was potash from burnt wood, which gave it a characteristic greenish or brownish tinge. Typical examples are robust drinking vessels decorated with prunts (decorative blobs of glass).

Venetian influence in the 1500s stimulated the adoption of more sophisticated styles and forms and inspired the development of enameling, which became highly popular and was extremely well executed.

When a more stable glass including lime was made in Bohemia late in the 1600s, engraving became popular. A technique developed in Nuremberg combined deep engraving with polishing and enhanced the sculptural quality of the relief to superb effect. Some of the finest wheel engraving was done in Germany in the 1700s and in Bohemia in the early 1800s.

Types of vessels

Beakers of various forms were made from early times. A plain, parallel-sided glass with a slightly flared base is known as a *Humpen*. Varieties include the *Passglas*, with levels marked for shared drinking, and the *Stangenglas*, a tall, narrow version. A *Roemer* was an enduring form of drinking glass, with an ovoid bowl on a flared foot. Colored glass was used, with ruby red, blue, green and opaque white (simulating porcelain) popular in the 18th century.

Flashing

In the 19th century, dramatic innovations were seen in Bohemian colored glass, and it became famous for the use of flashing (6). A clear glass object was dipped into molten glass of a different color, and this thin layer was then engraved to reveal the clear glass, with striking effect. A similar result was achieved by brushing on a yellow or ruby stain, a technique developed by Friedrich Egermann of Bohemia in the early 1800s.

Lithyalin and Hyalith

Friedrich Egermann also developed Lithyalin (7). This opaque glass, marbled in imitation of agate and other semiprecious stones, was patented in 1829. A similar, usually black or red, glass called Hyalith was produced by another maker. But by the middle of the century, the fashion for "stone" glasses had waned.

1 KRAUTSTRUNK BEAKER

The rows of prunts on the stem of this beaker give it its name, which means, literally, cabbage-stalk. Such beakers were probably made from medieval times in Germany, and this one is a rare survivor from the 15th century. It is made of Waldglas, *as its greenish hue suggests.*

◄ PUZZLE GOBLET

This green glass goblet plays a joke on the imbiber – only by closing certain holes and drinking from the deer's snout, creating a siphon effect, can anything be had from it. Such puzzle pieces were made in glass and pottery over several hundred years. This one dates from the 17th century.
H 14in/36cm

2 BOHEMIAN REICHADLERSHUMPEN

This beaker, made in Bohemia and dated 1601, is an example of a type which remained popular until the 18th century. Literally an "imperial eagle beaker," the design shows the double-headed eagle with the crests of the Holy Roman Empire displayed on its wings. H 11½in/29cm

3 BOTTLE

A rectangular bottle, dating from c.1705, from the workshop of Franz Gondelach, one of the great engravers of glass working in Germany in the early 18th century. It bears a coat of arms and, on the reverse, a bust. H 8in/20cm

4 COVERED GOBLET AND COVER

Zwischengoldglas (gold-between-glass), a technique developed in Bohemia, was popular from the 1730s to the 1750s. It involved placing a clear glass sleeve over a glass decorated with engraved gold leaf, and sealing the two together. This covered goblet demonstrates its effectiveness. H 10½in/26cm

5 SCHWARZLOT BEAKER

This beaker is decorated using a technique called Schwarzlot *(black lead). Inspired by printed engraving, pieces were painted with transparent black enamel. The technique was popular from the mid-17th to the mid-18th centuries, and designs ranged from battle scenes such as this to chinoiseries. H 11in/28cm*

6 BOHEMIAN GOBLETS AND COVERS

These Bohemian goblets, dating from c.1850–60, show the technique of flashing. Both are finely engraved with complex hunting scenes, a popular theme at the time. H 23in, 12½in; H 58cm, 32cm

7 BIEDERMEIER BEAKERS

A group of Bohemian beakers from the Biedermeier period, 1830–40, showing a variety of colors and decorative techniques. Left to right: *transparent emerald-green waisted beaker; large Lithyalin opalescent beaker; topographic scene in translucent enamel within an amber-flash cartouche; North Bohemian octagonal Lithyalin beaker with chinoiserie figures; hexagonal Lithyalin beaker marbled in mauve, blue and ocher, and embellished with gilt. H 4–6in/10–15cm*

GLASS

◀ ENGLISH RUMMER
Blue is the rarest color for English drinking glasses; it is, however, more common in other types than in rummers. This glass is decorated with both engraving and gilding, and dates from c.1797. H 5in/13cm.

Renowned enamelers
William Beilby and his sister Mary were renowned for the superb enameled work (**6, 8**) they produced between 1762 and 1778 in Newcastle-upon-Tyne. William decorated glasses with royal armorial bearings in the 1760s, later depicting rustic scenes, birds, flowers and classical ruins. Much of his work was executed in white monochrome, but he also worked in color to great effect.

Firing glasses
The glass shown in the center (**8**), is a type of dram glass known as a firing glass. Such glasses have a particularly short, stout form, with a robust foot, and were used for drinking toasts, after which they would be slammed on the table. The noise was said to be like the sound of gunfire, hence their name.

Types of stem
Baluster: solid, curvaceous stems bulging toward the foot. *c.*1685–1725
Silesian: molded and angular stem, showing Central European influence. *c.*1715–50
Balustroid: similar to baluster, but lighter and more slender. 1725–60
Air bubble: a tear-shaped bubble of air is trapped within the glass (**4, 5**). *c.*1720–40
Air twist: twisting pattern created by an enclosed bubble of air. *c.*1745–70
Opaque twist: twisting pattern created by enclosing a strand of white glass (**6, 8**). *c.*1755–80
Color twist: twisting pattern created by enclosing strands of colored glass (**7**). *c.*1755–1800

1 VERZELINI WINE GLASS
The Venetian glass maker Giacomo Verzelini worked in London in the 16th century, and the shape of this dated, mold-blown glass, with its decorated knob, shows the Venetian influence. The glass is embellished with intricate diamond-point engraving and gilt. H 8½in/21cm

2 NETHERLANDS FLUTE
The tall, slender flute was a form popular in the Low Countries and Germany in the 17th century. This example, dated 1662, is decorated in diamond-point engraving with a winged figure of Fortune standing on a globe.

3 ANGLO-VENETIAN GOBLETS
The term Anglo-Venetian is used to describe glass made in England in the 16th and 17th centuries by makers of apparently Venetian origin. These late 17th-century goblets show Venetian influence in their multi-knobbed stems and mereses (collars), and in the gadrooned bowl of the one on the left. H 9½in, 11½in; H 24cm, 29cm

4 COMMEMORATION GLASS
Glasses commemorating William III were popular long after his death in 1702, particularly with Irish Protestants. This large and superbly engraved example is probably Irish, and its plain form and tear-drop stem suggest a date of c.1720. H 10in/25cm

5 AMEN GLASS
This is a special form of Jacobite wine glass commemorating the Catholic Stuart uprising of 1745/6 against the Protestant King George II that ended in defeat at Culloden. Such glasses were engraved with the words of the Jacobite anthem, ending with "Amen," hence their name. They date from c.1746–50, and very few are known. H 7in/17cm

6 BEILBY ARMORIAL GLASS
An opaque-twist glass (c.1765) showing armorial work attributed to the great enameler William Beilby. H 6½in/16cm

7 COLOR-TWIST WINE GLASSES
Glasses with color-twist stems were a development of opaque-twist stems. Though all are rare, red, green, blue and brown are the most common colors; yellow and violet are very unusual. These date from c.1760–65. H 6½–7½in/16–19cm

8 BEILBY ENAMELED GLASSES
The funnel bowls of the opaque-twist wine glasses (left and right) are decorated in white enamel with chinoiserie and pastoral scenes respectively; the firing glass (center) has masonic decoration. All c.1770. H 6in, 4in, 6in; H 15cm, 10cm, 15cm

Encouraged by the creation of the new lead crystal glass by Ravenscroft in the late 1600s, Britain led the way in the development and diversification of drinking glasses throughout the eighteenth century. Domestic demand increased, and glasses of all types were made, from small conical ale glasses (ale was much stronger then) to cordial glasses, and from dram glasses to stout rummers (from the German *Roemer*).

The development of style and decoration was most clearly demonstrated in wine glasses. Heavy baluster-stemmed glasses in many variations were produced in the late 1600s and early 1700s. Stems could also be thick and taper smoothly from the bowl, relieved by a tear-shaped air bubble.

A move away from the baroque toward a simpler style, combined with a new tax on glass by weight in 1745/6, caused glasses to become lighter and smaller. Stems became the province for decoration by twisting and drawing out either bubbles of air or inserts of opaque glass. This resulted ultimately in highly intricate air-twist and opaque- or cotton-twist patterns. Later, color-twist glasses were also made.

The bowls of many glasses with spectacular stems were often left plain, but engraving was used, and in the late 1700s enameling became one of the major styles of glass decoration. Plain, richly colored wine glasses in green, amethyst and, more rarely, blue were also made at this time.

97

DRINKING GLASSES: 2

After about 1775, cutting as a technique for decorating glass became immensely popular in England and Ireland, and it remained so well into the nineteenth century. Drinking glasses demonstrate the popularity of the technique, with faceted stems and cutting often extending to the foot and the bowl. By the end of the century, stems on cut-glass drinking glasses were much shorter, and the increasingly elaborate cutting was often confined to the bowl and the underside of the foot.

By the mid-1700s, glass making was well established in America, and in subsequent decades, aided by immigrant workers from Europe, production flourished. Molding was the predominant technique, often embellished with engraving, but cutting was not common until about 1830.

In the 1800s, many types of colored glass were introduced, while enameling, engraving and, to a lesser extent, cutting were used for decoration. Early in the twentieth century, glasses were decorated in Art Nouveau style, particularly in Germany, and in the 1920s to 1930s the fashion for brightly painted cocktail sets spread to Europe from America.

Opaque glass

Several European glass-producing countries made opaque white glass (1) and decorated it to resemble porcelain. This was particularly widespread during the period up to the mid-18th century, before European porcelain was much in evidence. A more translucent form, known as opaline, became highly successful in Bohemia and then France in the mid-19th century. No longer imitating porcelain, but intended to show off its own qualities, this glass was made in many colors from pale green to deep blue to rich coral.

▼ **SET OF ENGLISH GLASSWARE**
By the late 1800s, extensive sets of glass were made all over Europe. These included stemmed glasses of different sizes for wines, tumblers, decanters and ewers. This set, nicely engraved with wreaths of holly, includes more than 170 pieces, including eight types of drinking glass. H ewer 12in/30cm

1 OPAQUE WHITE GLASS TUMBLER
A tumbler (c.1770) from the studio of one of London's greatest glass artists, James Giles. The flower heads, garlands and mosaic motifs in gilt are typical of his work. H 4in/10cm

2 AMERICAN ENGRAVED GOBLET
This large goblet was made at the Pennsylvania glassworks of a German immigrant, Henry Stiegel, to mark the marriage of his daughter to William Old. It was engraved by another immigrant, Lazarus Isaac from England, c.1773. H 7in/18cm

3 IRISH RUMMERS
Late 18th-century Irish glass is rarely colored, and these blue (left) and amethyst (right) rummers are most unusual. They have a type of molded foot known as a lemon-squeezer – which it resembles, viewed from beneath. The restrained gilt linked-oval border is characteristic of the period c.1800. H 5½in/14cm

4 AUSTRIAN ENAMELED BEAKER
Superb transparent enameling, usually depicting views of cities, was applied to Bohemian and Austrian beakers in the early 1800s. One of the best artists was Anton Kothgasser, who painted this example with a view of Vienna c.1815. H 4in/10cm

5 ENGRAVED TUMBLER
Among the thriving glassworks in the U.S. in the early 1800s was Bakewell's of Pittsburgh. It was the first to supply the White House. Enclosed in the base of this cut and engraved tumbler, dating from c.1824, is a sulfide, or molded portrait, of George Washington. H 3½in/9cm

6 ENGRAVED RUMMERS
The Sunderland Bridge rummer on the left is engraved with a view of the bridge and a sailing ship. The one on the right, dated 1835, is extensively engraved with Masonic symbols, which were often depicted on glass. H 5½in, 6in; H 13.5cm, 15cm

7 GERMAN WINE GLASSES
These fine early 20th-century glasses show the influence of Art Nouveau design. Left to right: cameo-cut glass by Otto Prutscher of the Wiener Werkstätte; champagne coupe with gilt and enamel by Hans Christansen; wine glass enameled in pink and green. H 8¼in, 7in, 8in; H 21cm, 18cm, 20cm

GLASS

Vessels for carrying and serving drinks have been made since ancient times. In England, jugs of stoneware were used to store wine until, late in the seventeenth century, thick, dark green molded glass bottles were developed for the purpose. These bottles, with their characteristic "shaft and globe" shape, were in widespread use in America and most European countries by the early 1700s. Bottles gradually became taller and slimmer throughout the century until, *c.*1760, the cylindrical shape still common today was achieved.

Glass decanters, developed during the 1700s, initially took their form from bottles. The shouldered shape, common by mid-century, was soon followed by the tapered shape. The distinctive, broad base of ship's decanters was developed to help maintain their stability at sea.

Colored glass decanters, usually blue, green or amethyst, were made from the 1770s onward. They were often finished with a gilded imitation label. Since decanters produced outside England were generally made of potash, rather than lead glass, they tended to be of poorer quality.

DECANTERS AND STOPPERS

These 18th-century decanter shapes were all copied in the Victorian and Edwardian periods, both in England and in Bohemia.

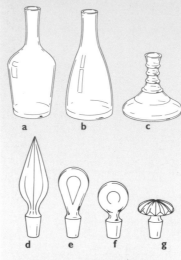

DECANTERS **a** Shouldered 1760–70. **b** Tapered 1780. **c** Ship's 1820. STOPPERS **d** Spire 1770–80. **e** Lozenge 1760–1820. **f** Target 1780–1820. **g** Mushroom 1790–1840.

Sealed bottles

A law of 1636 led to the introduction in England of embossed seals on bottles to prevent irregularities of size. Wealthy individuals, wine merchants, and publicans often had bottles made bearing their own seal and the date (4).

Points to note

Decanter stoppers were ground to fit individual decanters firmly. Small rim nicks can be ground down; larger chips and interior scratching can reduce the value of a piece.

Irish decanters

Many Irish decanters were blown into a shallow mold to imprint the vertical fluting before they were engraved. They were extensively exported to America.

◄ **RARE WILLIAMITE DECANTER**
"The glorious and immortal memory of King William" is inscribed on the shoulder of this unusually large, club-shaped decanter (c.1765). It was made in Ireland to commemorate the victory of William III over the deposed King James II at the Battle of the Boyne in 1690. The engraved spinning wheel probably refers to the spinning of flax for linen. H 17in/43cm

1 "GRAPE" FLASK
The grape-like protuberances in the glass give this type of flask its name. They were known in the Eastern Mediterranean and Syria from the early centuries A.D.; this one dates from the 5th century. The flask, with its everted rim and collar, was shaped by blowing the dark amber Roman glass into a mold. H 5in/13cm

2 NETHERLANDS SERVING BOTTLES
Made in the Netherlands in the mid- to late-17th century, these turquoise glass serving bottles are forerunners of the decanters that developed during the following century. Although made in the "shaft and globe" form, typical of bottles of the period, the thin glass and elegant gilt-metal fittings indicate that they were not mere storage vessels. H 8in/20cm

3 GERMAN AMETHYST FLASK
Although this flask, with a screw stopper, has the same shape as bottles of the 17th century, the crisp vertical molding, silver-mounted base and amethyst color suggest that it was designed for display as well as utility. H 11in/28cm

4 SEALED BOTTLE
Made for Robert Smith of Haughton Castle in 1712, this dark green bottle is of the shouldered type typical of the early 18th century. Such sealed bottles were made until the mid-19th century. H 6in/15cm

5 BOHEMIAN LIQUOR FLASKS
Dating from c.1760, these enameled and engraved flasks with their narrow necks are typically Bohemian. They may have been made to celebrate a wedding. H 9in/23cm

6 PUNCH DECANTER
As the engraving suggests, this rare, large, club-shaped engraved decanter was made for punch c.1770. The kidney-shaped cartouche, flanked by floral motifs, imitates a silver wine-label. H 16in/41cm

7 LIQUOR BOTTLES
These two bottles, made in the 1820s, demonstrate the great transition in shape that occurred in the second half of the 18th century. They are of the tapering cylinder shape that is still used today, but are adorned with beautiful hand-gilded labels. H 12in/30cm

GLASS

During the eighteenth century, English decanters were frequently decorated with cutting. This was generally confined to fluting of the base and faceting of the shoulder, but by the early 1800s cutting had become the dominant form of decoration. Horizontal steps or prisms extended from shoulder to neck, with further bands of decoration on the body.

In the 1830s, cut-glass decanters developed a cylindrical shape, sometimes with heavy vertical flutes on the body and steps on the neck. For liquor, square decanters became fashionable and often came as a set in a lockable wooden box, or tantalus.

Following the Great Exhibition in London in 1851, engraving came back into fashion. The remarkable detail and complexity of pieces from this time set them apart from eighteenth-century examples. Classical and Renaissance themes were popular and inspired not only the decoration but also the shapes of decanters. Meanwhile, glass makers in Bohemia were experimenting with new colors. To show off the deep blues, reds and golds, they developed the techniques of flashing and casing.

Although known earlier, claret pitchers only became common after the mid-nineteenth century, when tax on the wine was removed. They took many forms, from urn-shaped ewers to stylized Art Nouveau shapes, and were often decorated with patterns of grapes and vines and mounted in silver or pewter.

Mass-produced bottles

By the mid-19th century, bottles were being made not only for wine but also for mineral water (7), liquor and medicine. In 1872, Hiram Codd invented the internal glass-ball stopper which maintained the gas pressure in carbonated drinks. (The metal crown stopper was developed 20 years later.) This led to glass bottles for drinks such as beer and lemonade.

Industrialization triggered a huge increase in production so that by the end of the century, automated machines could churn out 50,000 bottles per day. Many late 19th-century examples were embossed with the manufacturer's name, while some bottles for household products have words such as "Poison" or "Not to be taken" on them.

▼ **BOXED LIQUEUR SET**
Bohemian cased glass was much copied in France, Britain and America, and this traveling set (c.1850) in an elaborately fitted and inlaid ebonized wooden case, could be Bohemian or French. This set is typical of the large sets of decanters and glasses popular in the 1800s. It includes four square decanters and nine liqueur glasses, all overlaid in opaque white and blue and enameled with floral sprigs. H decanters 8in/20cm

1 GLASS PITCHER AND FLASK
The pale green glass pitcher of simple blown form and the more refined cream flask with latticinio effect are both typical of the Nailsea works, near Bristol, England. They date from the early 19th century. H flask 6in/15cm

2 GROUP OF SHIP'S DECANTERS
All these English decanters, dating from c.1800, have wide bases for stability, rings around their necks to afford a secure grip and bull's-eye stoppers. The pair at the back, with star-cut bases and faceted sides, are of magnum size – they hold two quarts (2.2 litres). H 10–11in/25–28cm

3 ENGRAVED DECANTER AND COOLER
The shape and decoration of this decanter indicate that it dates from c.1860 and may be from the works of John Ford in Edinburgh. It is engraved with bust portraits of the Dukes of Wellington and Cumberland.

Beside it is a wine-glass cooler with typical opposing lips. This dates from the early 19th century and is decorated with close diamond cutting in lozenges. H decanter 12in/30cm

4 GERMAN ENGRAVED CLARET PITCHER
Classical and Renaissance motifs adorn this elegant claret pitcher (c.1860). The fine engraving may be by Hermann Müller of Hamburg, who also made glasses that were mistaken for early Venetian wares. H 17in/44cm

5 SILVER-MOUNTED CLARET PITCHER
Mounted in silver, this English claret pitcher is engraved with vines – a theme picked up on the silver mount. It has the flared base and parallel sides that were fashionable in the late 19th century. H 14in/36cm

6 AMERICAN FLAGON
Although the shape is ancient, this American flagon, mounted with a pierced and engraved silver casing in delicate decorative style, dates from the early 20th century. The silver work was by the firm of Gorham & Co. of Providence, Rhode Island, well known for this type of work. H 7½in/19cm

7 CARBONATED DRINKS BOTTLES
By the late 1800s, machine-made bottles such as these were being made for carbonated drinks. The bottle on the left would have been sealed with a glass ball stopper held in place by the pressure of the gas. H 8½–9in/21–23cm

CUT AND ENGRAVED GLASS

The technique of cutting glass, known from Roman times, was eclipsed for centuries by the exploitation of the plastic properties of glass, so superbly achieved by Venetian makers. Although cutting was employed in Germany and Bohemia in the seventeenth and eighteenth centuries, it was Irish and English makers, working with strong lead glass, who made cutting the height of fashion from the late 1700s to the mid-1800s. By cutting a design of straight lines and facets, light could be caused to bounce off the glass and be refracted through it, to maximum sparkling effect.

Cutting was achieved using a revolving wheel with a shaped edge – flat, rounded or pointed – that determined the groove. After the mid-1700s, facet cutting on the stems of drinking glasses was soon joined by cutting in diamond, fan and star designs. In the early 1800s, cutting became deeper, and heavy prismatic designs and fluting were widely used.

Glass was also decorated by engraving with a sharp tool (diamond point) or a wheel. In Britain, early engravers used diamond-point engraving, but with the invention of lead glass, wheel-engraving took over. This technique, practiced in Germany and Bohemia to great effect, allowed finer detail and could be used to create designs in both high relief and intaglio (cut into the surface).

A later form of engraving, used in the late 1800s, was acid-etching, whereby acid was used to eat into the surface of the glass in carefully marked areas to leave a frosted, or matte, design on the clear glass.

▲ IRISH CUT GLASS

Cutting in the early 1800s carved up the surface of the glass into bands of facets and diamonds. Star cutting can be seen on the underside of the mallet-shaped decanter. The covered bowl (center) has an unusual lace-like edge, known as a vandyke rim. The butter dish (left) is a typically Irish form. H decanter 10in/26cm

Candelabra

Nothing sets off cut glass better than unsteady light, and superb chandeliers and candelabra (4), dripping with glass pendants to glitter in candlelight, were a natural development of the British glass industry in the 1700s. Elsewhere in Europe, glass drops were added to metal or porcelain candelabra; in Britain they were made almost entirely of cut glass. They progressed from the delicate, whimsical rococo structures of the mid-18th century to the lavish Regency examples with long drops, and then to the heavy, colored-glass lusters of the Victorian period.

Irish glass

The glass industry flourished in Ireland from *c.*1770 until *c.*1825, when a new excise duty damaged its viability. At first, English styles were followed, and the decorative techniques employed, using lead glass, were mainly cutting and engraving. Certain typically Irish forms were later introduced, including canoe-shaped bowls, bowls with deeply everted rims, butter-coolers and piggins – imitations of wooden pails with short vertical handles.

1 SILESIAN BOWL

Some of the finest engraving was done in Silesia during the 1600s and 1700s. This small bowl, dating from c.1700, is said to be from the workshop of Friedrich Winter, one of the great engravers, and combines simple cut ornament with figurative engraving. Diam. 4in/10cm

2 DUTCH ENGRAVED ARMORIAL GLASS

Stippling is a form of diamond-point engraving in which the design is rendered in tiny dots and dashes by tapping on the surface of the glass. It was developed most notably by the Dutch in the 18th century. This piece dates from c.1745. H 7½in/19cm

3 ENGRAVED DISH

This is an example of top-quality engraving from the Austrian company Lobmeyr in 1878–81. Engraved by Karl Pietsch, one of the leading craftsmen at the time, with a design inspired by a classical frieze, it shows the three-dimensional effect that can be achieved. Diam. 17in/43cm

4 REGENCY CANDELABRUM

One of a pair of gilt-brass and glass candelabra dating from 1825. The delicacy of the glass echoes the 18th century, while the gilded chains and winged cherubs are more typical of the Regency period. H 13in/33cm

5 VICTORIAN LEMONADE SET

A frosted effect can be achieved by acid-etching the surface of glass. It has been used here to complement the simple cut decoration. H jug 10in/26cm

6 BOHEMIAN OVERLAY DECANTER

This ship's decanter (see p.100) is an example of cut overlay, or cased, glass. The technique involves blowing one or more layers of colored glass into an outer casing; the layers are heated to fuse them, then cut or engraved to reveal the contrasting glass beneath. The cutting on this 1920s piece is inferior to earlier work. H 9in/23cm

7 ENGLISH CUT RUBY GLASS

Dramatic decorative effects can be achieved by cutting through a layer of colored glass to reveal clear glass beneath, as this sideboard set (c.1910) of covered vase, wine and liquor decanters shows. Although widely used in Bohemia in the 1700s, the technique spread to Britain and France only in the mid-1800s. H vase 19in/48cm

DOMESTIC GLASS

The proliferation of glass for use in the home that began in the eighteenth century continued apace throughout the nineteenth. In a well-equipped household, a wide variety of articles might be made of glass, such as extensive sets for use in the dining room, with glasses, pitchers, bowls and plates for every eventuality. In other rooms there were washstand sets, vases, perfume bottles and desk accessories. Many decorative techniques, including cutting, etching, engraving and enameling, were lavished upon this good-quality glass.

At the other end of the scale, a vast quantity of objects for mass consumption was made by the basic technique of blowing glass into a mold. This was effective and inexpensive and allowed imitation of more costly techniques such as cutting. Plain blown and molded glass was also used as a base for further cutting or applied decoration.

In the 1820s, the process of mechanically pressing glass into a mold was developed in the U.S. This brought true mass production to glass making, and it was swiftly taken up in Europe. Complex patterns in relief then appeared on all types of molded household glass, either in clear glass or a wide range of colors, which were sometimes mixed together.

Friggers

Objects made by glass workers in their own time, using leftover glass, are known as "friggers" (3) or "end-of-day" glass. They are usually purely decorative, and common examples include glass walking canes, rolling pins, pipes and bells. Some of the most amusing are virtuoso displays of the glassmaker's skill – delicate birds and animals with details carefully wrought with pincered trails of glass.

Ice glass

The technique of treating glass to give it the appearance of cracked ice (*below*), which originated with the Venetian makers of the Renaissance, was "rediscovered" during the 19th century. The best effect was achieved by plunging a white-hot vessel into cold water and then rewarming it to seal the fractures. Later variations involved encrusting the hot glass with crushed glass fragments. Several European manufacturers made ice glass, and the firm of Clichy, near Paris, was among the best.

1 ROLLING PIN

Decalcomania is the name given to the decorative technique by which printed pictures are transferred to the hollow interior of a glass piece and then sealed, using a paint or plaster wash. This rolling pin was made near Wolverhampton or at Nailsea, near Bristol, England, in the 1880s. L 12in/30cm

2 CELERY VASE

Celery vases have been made in England since the late 18th century, and this 19th-century American example (1840–55), with a flaring body on a short stem and flat base, is of typical form. Faceted design is common; here it has been achieved by cutting. H 10½in/27cm

3 CANDLESTICKS

Although true friggers have no useful purpose and are purely ornamental trifles, these multicolored candlesticks of simple form may be "friggers," made by mixing together small quantities of leftover glass. 1860–80. H 8½in/22cm

4 WASHSTAND SET

Made by the famous French firm of Baccarat in 1880, this good-quality washstand set is complete with soap and powder boxes. The ruby glass overlay has been cut away in fan shapes to reveal the clear glass beneath. H pitcher 12in/30cm

5 PRESSED GLASS BOWL

Opaque white pressed glass, often called "milk glass," was particularly popular in the United States in the late 1800s. This bowl was made in the northeast of England in 1870–90. H 5in/13cm

6 AMERICAN CRUET SET

Made by the Mount Washington Glass Company, Massachusetts, (1885–1900), this mold-blown set has "Burmese" glass inserts. In this process, gold and uranium are added to the molten metal, giving the glass a soft yellow color, which shades to salmon pink on reheating. H (max) 9in/23cm

7 ENGLISH CRUET SET

A flashed ruby-glass cruet set in a pierced and engraved silver-plated stand (c.1910–20). Cruet sets with variously shaped glass bottles and silver or wooden stands were made from the late 17th century onward. H 13in/33cm

◄ DESSERT SERVICE
At first glance, this strikingly decorated service could be mistaken for porcelain. It is, in fact, made from apple-green "ice glass," with fine enameling of flowers on a white ground. The dolphin-shaped supports to the tazzas (large flat or slightly dished plates on stems) suggest that the service probably came from the Clichy factory in France c.1870.

The set contains more than 150 pieces, including 6 different types of drinking glass, as well as plates, fruit bowls, covered compotes, tazzas, decanters and pitchers. H tazza 11½in/28.5cm; pitcher 12½in/32cm

MOLDED GLASS

The technique of blowing glass into a mold was developed in the first century A.D. and was widely used throughout the Roman Empire. It allowed glass to be not only shaped but also decorated at the moment of manufacture, and molds ranged from simple geometric designs to complex patterns of figures and faces. Reproductions of such pieces have been made in the Middle East, although these are heavier than the originals.

In more recent times, mold-blowing has been used to form the stems and feet of some drinking vessels (**1**) and also to pre-form vessels that might subsequently be further embellished with engraving or cutting. In the nineteenth century, mold-blowing was employed as an inexpensive way to imitate cutting, particularly in the United States.

A new technique for molding glass was patented in the U.S. in 1828 by Deming Jarvis and taken up in Europe in the following decade. Known as press-molding, it involved molten glass being pressed into a metal mold by machine. The outer surface took the impression of the mold, while the inner surface remained smooth, in contrast to blown-molding where the interior, as well as the exterior, follows the mold shape. For the first time, mechanized mass production of glass was possible, making it affordable in every home. Designs imitated traditional types of decoration, particularly cutting, although later in the century patterns became shallower and less like hand work.

"Lacy glass"

Among the most collectible of pressed glass is the early American type known as "lacy glass" (**4**); pieces made before 1840 are particularly in demand. Decoration included flowers, leaves, scrolls, diamonds and rosettes, and the entire background was close-stippled, ensuring that any blemishes in the molding were obscured. The overall effect was sparkling.

Slag glass

This term is generally applied to a type of marbled, mottled glass (**6**) which derived its streakiness from waste material included in the metal, or glass body. Colors included bright blue and black, but the most common was purple. Slag glass was press-molded into ordinary domestic wares by several English factories in the late 1800s, including Sowerby and Davidson of Gateshead, and Greener of Sunderland, who all marked their wares.

Carnival glass

Made in imitation of the fashionable and expensive works of Tiffany (*see p.112*), Carnival glass (**8**) was brightly colored pressed glass coated with metallic salts which when refired gave it an iridescence. It was mass-produced in the early 1900s by several American makers. The name "Carnival" glass derives from the fact that it was given as prizes at fairgrounds and carnivals, and it is also known as "Taffeta" or "Nancy" glass. It was copied in England by Sowerby and other makers.

1 ENGLISH RUMMER
In the late 1700s and early 1800s, English rummers often had stout molded feet. In this example, the bowl, too, was molded before being cut to enhance the brilliance of its decoration. H 5in/13cm

2 PAIR OF CANDLESTICKS
The great popularity of cut glass in the U.S. in the early 1800s made the production of cheaper imitations inevitable. These blown and pattern-molded candlesticks were made in Pittsburgh in 1830–40. H 13½in/32cm

3 AMERICAN FLASK
Liquor flasks such as this, made by the Union Glass Works in 1826–30 in Philadelphia, were produced in large numbers in the early 1800s. Mold-blown in colored glass, they depict historical figures and patriotic emblems – here it is the American eagle and, on the reverse, Columbia, regarded as a symbol of the United States. H 7½in/19cm

4 "LACY GLASS" TRAY
This is an example of early American pressed glass of the highly decorative form known as "lacy glass." The entire surface is covered in decoration, and the lacy effect is increased by the openwork rim. c.1830–45. L 12in x W 8in; L 30cm x W 20cm

5 MOLDED GLASS DOG
The brilliant green of this dog is the result of adding uranium to the metal. This piece, made c.1860 by John Derbyshire of Manchester, England, was probably inspired by Staffordshire pottery figures.

6 SLAG GLASS JUG AND SUGAR BOWL
Opaque streaky glass such as this is known as slag glass. It is generally press-molded and was popular in Britain and the U.S. in the late 1800s. H bowl 4in/10cm

7 COMMEMORATIVE PITCHER
This piece, with the words "Peace and Plenty," decorated with grapes, wheat and fruits, was made in 1888 by Henry Greener. H 5in/13cm

8 GLASS DISHES
Iridescent glass such as this (c.1910) was known as Carnival glass. As the glass was still malleable after pressing, rims of dishes and pitchers were often molded or crimped. W 5½in/14cm

◄ **ANCIENT BOWL**
This bowl, made in the Eastern Mediterranean region, probably in the 4th century A.D., is an example of glass blown into a patterned mold. The technique was commonly employed by glassmakers throughout the Roman Empire. H 3in/8cm

The term Art Glass is loosely used to describe innovative forms of decorative glass that appeared *c*.1850 and continued into the early years of the twentieth century. Such glass is generally characterized by specially developed surface textures, colors or designs, which, at least initially, were inspired more by art than commerce. These techniques were often patented by their inventors.

The Victorian market had an unquenchable thirst for the novel, and glass makers looked particularly to color as a way of satisfying it. In the United States in the 1880s, many new colors were developed, (to modern eyes, the more lurid the better), with one color cleverly shading into another. These were given attractive names, such as Burmese, Peachblow (which imitated Chinese porcelain), Amberina and Pomona, and enjoyed enough success to be copied by other factories.

The cameo technique, known in the ancient world and in China, was revived in England in the mid-1800s. Superb pieces were made in Stourbridge, by Thomas Webb and other companies which, by the 1880s, were satisfying a great demand. Cameo glass was made elsewhere in Europe. In France, it was the base from which the influential and innovative Emile Gallé (1846–1904) developed his interpretations of Art Nouveau on glass vases, bowls and lamps, all adorned with naturalistic forms such as flowers, birds and insects.

Cameo technique

A blank is formed of two or more layers of different-colored glass fused together. The design is sketched on the surface, and the superfluous outer layer removed (2). Initially this was done by hand, but by the 1880s, for commercial expediency, acid was applied to background areas. Copper-wheel carving was used on the remaining raised areas to give depth and detail to the design. Superb three-dimensional effects could be achieved by the best artists. The work of George and Thomas Woodall at Thomas Webb's is among the most remarkable.

▼ **VICTORIAN ART GLASS**
This collection of drinking vessels shows many of the different colors and techniques developed by American glass makers in the late 1800s. Left to right: *Pomona lemonade glass, Joseph Locke, New England Glass Co., 1885; Peachblow punch cup, Hobbs Brockunier, 1885–90; Plated Amberina tumbler, New England Glass Co., 1886–88; Burmese goblet, made under licence by Thomas Webb, Stourbridge, 1886–90; Wild Rose punch cup, the New England Glass Co.'s name for their peachblow coloring, 1886–88; Agata tumbler, a type of Wild Rose with a glossy, mottled surface, New England Glass Co., 1887–88; Crown Milano cup and saucer in white opal glass, Mount Washington Glass Co., 1890–95.*

1 FRENCH ENAMELED BOWL
Islamic art was one of many influences on European glass makers in the late 19th century, and Philippe-Joseph Brocard revived the art of enameling on glass in Islamic style. This signed example was made for the London International Exhibition of 1871. Diam. 12½in/31cm

2 FRENCH CAMEO GLASS VASE
Cameo glass was not limited to English makers. This late 19th-century carved and etched vase, on which the white base is overlaid in blue flowering clematis, is signed by Désiré Christian of Meisenthal in Lorraine. H 16½in/42cm

3 GALLÉ VASE
This striking vase (c.1900) was formed by mold blowing, double overlay and acid etching. Designed and signed by the great glass artist Emile Gallé, it demonstrates the heights to which the cameo technique could be taken. The translucent yellow glass is overlaid in red and amber and carved with calla lilies. H 14½in/37cm

4 GALLÉ LAMP
Superb naturalistic designs of irises in amber overlay on the stand of this lamp, and bats in deep amethyst overlay on the shade, are beautifully set off by electric light. High-quality work by Gallé, such as this signed piece, dating from c.1900, is extremely valuable. Gallé's signature appeared on pieces he himself made, but also on those made to his designs, even after his death. Gallé also designed furniture (see p.230). H 23in/50cm

5 ENGLISH CAMEO GLASS VASES
Cameo glass became increasingly commercial in England from the 1880s onward. Bright background colors were introduced, and floral designs replaced classical figures. These examples from Thomas Webb's factory in Stourbridge, Staffordshire, date from about 1885. H 16½in, 12½in; H 41cm, 31cm

6 LATE CAMEO GLASS VASE
The design and decoration of this vase, made in the 1920s by the French glass maker Barg, have a Middle Eastern theme. In the early 1920s, under the influence of films such as The Sheik, *starring Rudolf Valentino, Arabian subjects became popular in Europe and the U.S. H 15in/38cm*

GLASS

The final years of the 1800s saw continued enthusiasm for innovation in art glass. In the U.S., Louis Comfort Tiffany became highly influential and developed new styles in glass in the Art Nouveau manner, two of which were particularly notable.

Tiffany-designed lamps, with umbrella- or mushroom-shaped shades of stained glass on naturalistic metal bases, were produced c.1895–1928 for the luxury market in New York. His other great success was Favrile glass, the name given to a type of hand-blown art glass with an iridescent surface, developed c.1892. It was widely imitated in the U.S., especially by the Steuben glass works, which were so successful with their Aurene glass that Tiffany sued them. In Europe, it was copied by the Loetz factory of Austria, among others, and inspired a widespread fashion for iridescent glass.

A move away from figurative design toward the abstract, often accompanied by technical developments, can be seen in glass of the period. Daum Frères, an important French maker, used acid etching to create a range of textured surface effects, and even combined glass and metal by blowing glass into a metal armature. Form took on a particular significance, and many vases and bowls were strangely sinuous, often asymmetric, in shape.

Pâte de verre

This technique, known in ancient times, was revived in France and found favor with those working at the end of the 19th and in the early 20th centuries. It involved molding a paste made of ground glass and allowed figures to be made which could be further refined by carving.

A major exponent of the technique was René Lalique, who made car mascots and pendants from *pâte de verre*. Gabriel Argy-Rousseau (5) developed a particularly translucent form of *pâte de verre* called *pâte de cristalle*, which he used for lamps and vases.

Loetz glass

The Loetz factory (3, 7), started in Bohemia in 1840, became particularly successful with its art glass at the end of the century. It produced affordable iridescent glass in the Tiffany manner, which, although made in vast quantity, was of good quality. Decoration was nearly always abstract and color intense – often blues and greens heightened by iridescence. Many of these pieces were not signed.

1 CLUTHA VASE
Designed by the innovative designer Christopher Dresser, this vase (c.1895) is made in Clutha glass. The word, meaning cloudy, aptly describes the striated, marbled appearance of the glass, patented by the maker James Couper of Glasgow. Dresser's simple, uncluttered designs show the influence of Japanese art. H 14in/36cm

2 DAUM POPPY VASE
The carved glass flowers on this vase (c.1900) have been applied to the body using a technique developed by Gallé known as marqueterie-sur-verre. The stems are etched and the ground carved. H 8in/20cm

3 LOETZ VASE
A strangely shaped goosenecked vase, of cobalt Papillon iridescent glass. It was made in 1900, possibly by Max Ritter von Spaun, a top designer at the Loetz factory. H 10in/25cm

4 TIFFANY FAVRILE GLASS VASE
The green and silvery pink iridescent feather pattern on this Favrile glass vase (c.1900) was achieved by using vaporized metals on the molten glass. H 13in/33cm

5 PÂTE DE VERRE LIQUEUR SERVICE
Gabriel Argy-Rousseau was an outstanding French glass designer of the Art Deco period (1920s–1930s). In this example of his work in pâte de verre, the Art Deco influence is apparent in the angular design and decoration. L tray 16in/40cm

6 STEUBEN VASE
This vase, designed c.1910 by an Englishman Frederick Carder, is of Aurene glass, an iridescent type he developed for Steuben. It is blown, with tooled decoration and swirled ribbing. H 11½in/17cm

7 LOETZ BOWL
This etched and overlaid bowl was designed by Josef Hoffman and made by Loetz for the Wiener Werkstätte cooperative in 1915. H 4½in/12cm

8 THREE DAUM VASES
These examples from the 1920s show a variety of techniques. Left to right: deep-red glass with foil inclusions, blown into a wrought-iron mount; amethyst glass with etched design; acid-etched mauve glass. H 10½in, 6½in, 11½in; H 26cm, 17cm, 29cm

◀ TIFFANY LAMP
Lamps such as this, in a design called "Cabbage Rose," were made by the Tiffany workshops c.1900. The shade is composed of small pieces of glass of many colors, held in place by leading in the same way that a stained glass window is assembled. The stand is of cast metal, in this instance with a Japanese flavor, though often a more naturalistic effect was adopted. H 28in/71cm

PAPERWEIGHTS AND PERFUME BOTTLES

The use of glass for paperweights began in the 1800s on the island of Murano, near Venice, and in Bohemia. It was, however, the French firms that became famous for their spectacular examples. Baccarat was making paperweights from 1846 to 1849, St. Louis from 1845 to 1860, and Clichy from 1846 to 1870. Glass paperweights were also made in Britain and America, and are still being produced.

Most frequently found are the *millefiori* (thousand flowers) designs, made using canes of colored glass melted, stretched, sliced across to resemble flowerheads, and then encased in a solid, clear-glass sphere. Many different arrangements of canes created a variety of patterns, and each factory had its own cane designs, some of which show the factory name and the date. Figure subjects, including people and animals, were made by hand before being encased in clear glass, which might be given a star-cut base. Paperweights with figure subjects are rare and valuable.

It became fashionable in the 1700s to use perfume, and perfume bottles from that time are among the finest. In England, small faceted bottles of colored glass were enameled or gilded and fitted with gold covers. Colored glass was favored, since it helped to preserve perfume from the detrimental effects of light, and during the 1800s notable perfume bottles were made in English cameo glass, French opaline and Bohemian colored glass.

Chinese snuff bottles

It became fashionable in China in the late 18th century to take snuff, and small glass bottles (*below*, 7) were made in which to carry it. Most are flat-sided oval flasks with short necks and glass-topped cork stoppers. A wide variety of decorative techniques was used on these bottles, including enameling, cameo carving and interior painting.

Cameo glass

The Beijing glass snuff bottle (*below*) and the English cameo glass perfume bottle (6) are examples of cameo cutting from East and West respectively. Chinese versions usually involved much brighter colors and higher relief than the 19th-century English technique, in which delicate naturalistic designs were carved into the white glass overlay. Thomas Webb and Sons of Stourbridge was one of the leading exponents of this technique (*see p.110*).

1 GROUP OF FRENCH PAPERWEIGHTS
The rare, large central "Newel Post" weight from Baccarat shows close millefiori *canes with silhouette canes including animals, plants, stars and whorls (H 10in/25cm). In front of it is a miniature Clichy weight on a foot, while to the right are other* millefiori *designs and a "Mushroom" weight from St. Louis. The pink snake and the butterfly and clematis in the weights on the left are examples of lamp-made figure subjects from Baccarat. All mid-19th century. Diam. 1½–3in/4–8cm*

◄ **BEIJING GLASS SNUFF BOTTLE**
Snuff was carried in this type of glass bottle in China. The fine example here, with typical carved decoration complemented by colorful enameling, was made c.1770–1850 for use in the Imperial Palace. H 2½in/6cm

2 FRENCH PAPERWEIGHTS
Examples of paperweights from the three best makers. Left to right, 1st row: weight by Clichy; St. Louis Crown weight. *2nd row:* pink overlay bouquet weight by St. Louis; Baccarat butterfly weight. *3rd row:* two Baccarat weights with star-cut bases, a "Marriage Bouquet" and a "Thousand-petaled Rose" weight. Mid-19th century. Diam. 2½–3½in/6–8cm*

3 ENGLISH PERFUME BOTTLES
These small, faceted glass perfume bottles, c.1760–65, reflect the precious nature of their contents. The decoration of the one on the left is probably the work of James Giles, a noted gilder of the period, while that on the right has a stamped gold cap and colored enamel decoration. H both 3½in/8cm

4 FRENCH OPALINE GLASSWARE
Opaline glass was made in many colors by the great 19th-century French glass factories. The iridescent pinkish-blue color of this perfume bottle and fluted toilette jar, part of a dresser set dating from c.1825, is known as "Gorge de Pigeon" because it is reminiscent of a pigeon's neck feathers. It is set off by gilding and ormolu mounts. H jar 6½in/16cm

5 HANDBAG BOTTLES
These colored glass perfume bottles, dating from c.1850–60, were intended for evening use. The green bottle with elaborate gilt-metal mounting is French. The English double-ended, hexagonal blue bottle is divided so that it could contain both smelling salts and perfume. H 4–5in/10–13cm

6 CAMEO GLASS PERFUME BOTTLE
An English perfume bottle, made in 1885–87, of deep blue glass, overlaid with white glass that has been carved with a design of stylized apple blossom. The floral motif is repeated on the silver cover, which is fitted with an atomizer. H 8in/20cm

7 CHINESE SNUFF BOTTLE
Using a fine brush applied through the neck, the renowned artist Ding Erzhong painted the design on the interior surface of this bottle in 1905. It is a splendid example of one of the intricate techniques employed in decorating Chinese snuff bottles, the making of which has continued into recent times. H 2½in/6cm

SILVER

The history of silver wares can be traced back over 5,000 years, but it is in the third millennium B.C. that wrought silverware in the modern sense was first made, in Mesopotamia and Anatolia. From there, the knowledge of silversmithing spread east to Persia and west to Europe, where by the time of the ancient Greeks and Romans, it had already reached a high level of sophistication. Many of the techniques practiced in early times, such as casting, embossing and chasing, are still used today.

This brief survey looks at the styles and influences that particularly affected English and American silver. Although the Christian religion was formally recognized within the Roman Empire in A.D. 313, it was not until the fifth century that specifically Christian requirements overtook classical styles in silver ware. Within a short time, the demand by the Church for silver objects for use during the liturgy meant that it became the chief patron of silversmiths.

Continental styles have long been a major source of influence for English craftsmen, and the story of English silver proves no exception, although it is nearly always simpler than its European models. In the Middle Ages, French silversmiths led the field in both design and skill, producing magnificent articles in the gothic style that were often decorated with enamels or jewels. In the 1500s, English silversmiths modeled their work on contemporary German silver. During the English Civil Wars (1642–51), much early plate (a term traditionally used to describe items of sterling silver, not silver-plated items) was melted down for coinage. The new silver made after the restoration of the English monarchy in 1660 was strongly influenced by Dutch styles, and much was made with repoussé (embossed) decoration featuring flowers, fruit, masks and cherubs.

By the 1690s, the Dutch influence had waned in favor of French styles. The introduction of the Britannia standard in 1697 (see p.146), with its higher silver content, meant that the metal was softer and more difficult to work, so both forms and decoration became simpler. Even after the sterling standard was reintroduced in 1720, although more elaborate silver became popular, plainer shapes were still made. Much silver was produced in the mid-1700s in French-inspired rococo style, decorated with flowers and

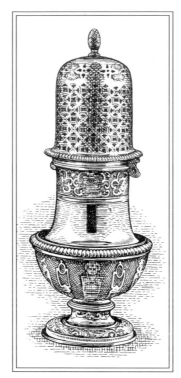

swags, marine motifs, chinoiserie and figures. From the 1760s onward, silver decoration reflected the growing interest in neoclassical forms and style, which by the end of the century emerged as a simpler version of the classical style. After 1810, silver became more massive, and its decoration was taken from French Empire and Egyptian motifs as well as from the earlier rococo styles.

By c.1850, silver was being produced in several styles, including Rococo Revival and Gothic Revival. This eclecticism continued through to the end of the century, but there were some interesting additions, such as the introduction of Japanese-style decoration c.1880 and designs inspired by the Arts and Crafts Movement. The latter designs, together with those influenced by Art Nouveau styles, were popular until the outbreak of World War I.

The history of American silver is interwoven with that of Britain although, as with other decorative arts, the equivalent styles do not generally run concurrently. Boston, Philadelphia and New York were great centers for silvermaking during the eighteenth century; Dutch influences were particularly strong in New York, which had formerly been a Dutch settlement. American silver was usually quite simply decorated when compared to its British models, since a greater emphasis was placed on shape. The War of Independence (1775–83) brought a halt to the manufacture of American silver, and it was only after the American economy had recovered c.1790 that silver was made once more in any quantity.

British silver was still the dominating influence at this time, but after the War of 1812 between the United States and Great Britain, American silversmiths turned to France for their models. This Empire-style silver remained popular until the 1830s; thereafter, in America as elsewhere, a mixture of styles prevailed.

▶ **SOUP TUREEN WITH COVER AND STAND**
Paul Storr, one of the foremost English silversmiths, made this elegant neoclassical tureen in 1819. It is simple in shape and is embellished with many of the decorative features of the style: chased fluting, gadrooned borders, lion's masks, lion's paw feet and, on the tureen itself, shell and scroll feet. L stand 20½in/52cm; tureen 18in/46cm

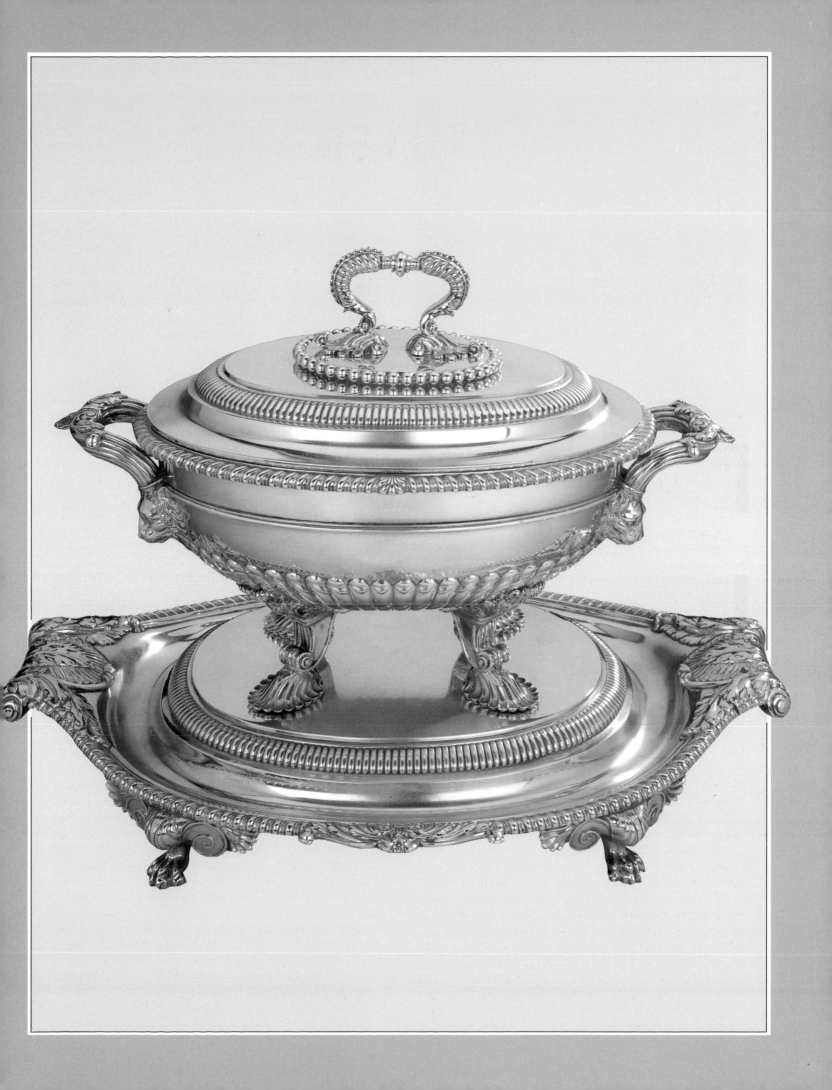

▲ **DANISH PARCEL-GILT TANKARD**
*Made by Christen Jensen in 1700, this tankard has a detachable sleeve
with a repoussé classical scene; the knop on the lid, the handle and
the bands on the body have been parcel-gilded. H 10in/25cm*

In order to understand more about silver and to
know whether a piece is entirely of its original
period, it is necessary for the collector not only to have
an appreciation of silver styles, but also to know a little
about the techniques used in making silver objects.

Working with silver

Silver items were usually made by one of two processes
or by a combination of both. In the first, known as
raising, a silver ingot was hammered or rolled into a
flat sheet of equal gauge. The silversmith cut out a
piece of metal to the required size for the article he
was making and then hammered it into shape. During
this process, the structure of the metal changed and it
became brittle. To counteract this, the silver was peri-
odically strengthened, or annealed, by being heated
and then cooled to make it malleable again.

The second process was casting, which used more
silver than the raising process, but resulted in a
stronger piece. Some candlesticks were cast, but the
process was generally used to make stems, handles,
spouts, feet and finials. In order to cast a piece, a
model of it was made, and an impression of it was
molded in a sand casting-box. The model was then
removed and the sand allowed to dry before molten

silver was poured into the mold. Once the silver had
solidified and cooled, the cast piece was soldered to
the main object.

While today a heavy piece of silver seems attractive
to the user, the weight of the silver used in the manufacture of objects has varied over the years. In the late
seventeenth century, silver was quite scarce on occasion, so items made at this time are usually lighter than
their eighteenth-century counterparts. In the Regency
period, silver objects were fairly massive and weight
was regarded as an indication of a piece's quality.

Some silver objects have the original weight
scratched on the bottom. This "scratch weight" should
be a little higher than the current weight of the piece,
since some silver will have been lost through
polishing. If there is a large loss or gain, the piece has
probably been adapted at some stage.

Decorative techniques

Silver was generally decorated by engraving or by
chasing. In engraving, the design was cut into the surface with a sharp tool, so removing a small amount of
the metal; in chasing, the metal was not lost, but rather
repositioned by hammering on the reverse (*see p.142*).
Chased designs could be refined by flat chasing or by
repoussé work, in which some of the raised detail
could be pushed back to give modeling to the design.
Both of these processes were carried out from the
front of the piece. Other types of decoration, such as
cut-card work (*see p.152*) and piercing (*see p.134*),
were also fashionable from time to time.

As with furniture, an important part of the decorative effect of antique silver is its patina, the blue-silver
sheen that normal use and polishing build up on the
surface. (Items with a good patina should not be
machine-polished, for the patina will be lost, to the
detriment of the piece.)

When the decoration was completed, the piece was
sometimes gilded: a thin layer of gold was applied to
the surface of the silver. This could cover either the
entire surface of the piece, when it was known as
"silver-gilt," or only certain areas, when it was described
as "parcel-gilt."

One method of applying gold was fire gilding, in
which an item was coated with a mixture of gold and
mercury and then heated so that the mercury evapo-
rated, leaving a layer of gold fused to the silver. This
process was eventually abandoned because of the risk
to workmen from the poisonous mercury fumes. The
other method of gilding was by gold plating, using the
electroplating technique. The major part of a gilded
item is silver, and it is therefore hallmarked as such.

Sheffield plate

In Britain, the growth of a prosperous middle class in
the 1700s led to a demand for a cheaper alternative to
silver, which was the preserve of the very wealthy. This
demand was partially satisfied in the 1740s by the
discovery of a method of fusing silver to a copper base

to make what became known as Sheffield plate. In the 1830s, a variation – British plate – was made, using an alloy in place of silver. Both these forms were superseded in the 1840s by the introduction of electroplating.

The chief proponent of this technique, which involved coating a base metal, first copper and later nickel, with silver by electrolysis, was the firm of Elkington in Birmingham, England. The process was employed to make a wide range of household and ornamental pieces, many of which bear the stamp "EPNS" for electroplated nickel silver.

A joining seam was always present on hollow items of Sheffield plate; if one is not visible, it is likely that the item has been replated. Lead solder was used in the construction of Sheffield plate, and it is normal to find evidence of this underneath and inside pieces; where solder has been used on the outside, the item has probably been repaired. The edges of Sheffield plate were bordered with silver wire, which was lead-soldered to it. It is usually acceptable for some lead to be visible here, as a result of wear, as is a little "bleeding," or wearing away, of the silver to reveal the copper below.

Decoration on Sheffield plate was always flat-chased, since engraving would remove the silver and reveal the copper. The only exception is coats-of-arms. In the late eighteenth century, a more heavily plated shield, which could be engraved, was let into the piece; by the early nineteenth century it had been replaced by a pure silver disk. If a piece is stamped "Sheffield plate", it has been electroplated; the genuine article is rarely marked.

Repairs and alterations

The desirability of a piece can be affected by its condition. If hallmarks are only just discernible, it is likely to be in a poor state. There should be no pinholes, cracks or splits in the body of hollow pieces, such as pitchers or teapots, and handles and spouts should be intact. Pierced decoration is easily damaged.

If a piece feels thin at the center, it may be because a coat-of-arms or inscription has been erased, either totally or to make way for a new one. Sometimes worn areas were covered up by patching them; such repairs are usually visible from the inside or underside of the object. If carried out using silver solder, these repairs are acceptable, but in some instances they have been crudely done using unsightly lead solder.

Silver objects have often been subject to alteration. This can range from the addition, in the 1800s, of chased decoration on plain, earlier pieces to make them more attractive to Victorian taste, to the replacement of the original borders on salvers by more fashionable ones. Among examples of adaptations to change the function of a piece are liners which have been converted into tureens or punch bowls, and tankards that have been made into coffee pots or pitchers. Reproductions are quite acceptable, since the hallmarks will clearly indicate the date of manufacture.

◄ **GADROONING**
Silver was decorated in various ways. One of the most common was with gadrooning, a continuous, usually curving, pattern of bosses applied as a border, often on the edge of a piece – at the foot or around the lid, for instance.

◄ **CAST CANDLESTICK**
A candlestick made by Ebenezer Coke in 1760. It was cast in several pieces, which were then soldered together and decorated with chased flutes, foliage and shells. On the socket, a crest has been engraved, and there is a band of gadrooning around the base of the nozzle. H12½in/32cm

▶ **EMBOSSED DESIGN**
The scrolling design here has been chased in low relief, or embossed, and the background matted, or stippled, with a punch to set off the raised design.

BRITISH HALLMARKS

The practice of marking silver began in England in 1300, but even earlier, the purity of gold and silver was controlled. Silver testers, known as Touch Wardens, carried out their duties in goldsmiths' workshops. But true "hallmarking" did not start until 1478, when testing and marking began to be carried out at the Goldsmith's Hall in the City of London.

Today, all silver weighing more than 7.78g must carry four official marks from an assay office, which guarantee authenticity. Those always found are the **town mark**; the **standard** (quality) **mark**, usually indicated by the lion passant (sterling), although there are variations; the **date letter** and **maker's marks**.

Between 1697 and 1719 the purity standard of silver was raised from 92.5% ("sterling") to 95.8% silver. The figure of Britannia and the lion's head in profile, or "erased," indicated the new standard, which replaced the combination of the lion passant and leopard's head.

In 1720 the "sterling" standard was revived, although Britannia continued to be used for higher-quality silver. From 1784 to 1890, a fifth mark, the sovereign's head, was generally present on silver and indicated that the tax had been paid.

Hallmark for Birmingham, 1851

| Sovereign's head | Lion's head (erased) | Britannia | Lion rampant (Scotland) | Thistle (Scotland) |

LONDON HALLMARKS

These marks were established by the mid-1500s. The **leopard's head**, originally a standard mark introduced in 1300, was retained as London's town mark when the lion passant was introduced.

The **maker's mark** is usually the maker's initials, although symbols were used for early marks, and was required by law from 1363.

The **date letter,** a letter of the alphabet, has been used since 1478 to indicate the year. The **lion passant,** showing the sterling lion walking to the left, was introduced in 1544 to show royal control of the assay office.

Although these four marks have been used together in London for 400 years, it is quite easy to identify a precise year from various alterations to the style of the marks (*see right*).

| 1479 | 1592 | 1647 | 1724 | 1836 |

SCOTTISH HALLMARKS

The town mark for Edinburgh, the only Scottish city still marking, is a castle. Date letters were used from 1681 onward. Prior to this, silver was struck with the marks of the town, the maker and the deacon. In 1681–1759 the assay master's mark replaced the deacon's mark; in 1759 the thistle replaced the assay master's mark and was itself replaced by the lion rampant in 1975.

The hallmark for Glasgow (1819–1964) was a tree, with a bird and a bell in its branches and a fish at the base. Until 1914, when the thistle was added, the marks used were the tree, the lion rampant, the date letter and the maker's mark.

| Edinburgh 1485–present | Glasgow 1819–1914 | Glasgow 1914–1964 |

IRISH HALLMARKS

Dublin is, and has always been, Ireland's only official assay office. Marking started in the 1600s, with three marks – the standard mark of a crowned harp, date letter and maker's mark – being used between 1638 and 1730. In 1731 the figure of Hibernia was added as a fourth mark. The sovereign's head was used for the first time in 1807 and continued to be used as in the rest of the United Kingdom until 1890. Irish provincial marks can be found from Cork and Limerick. Both used the word "sterling," albeit with various spellings and abbreviations, together with the maker's mark.

OTHER ENGLISH TOWN MARKS

The assay offices at Sheffield and Birmingham resulted from petitions to Parliament in 1773. Their marks, a crown and an anchor respectively, were inspired by a meeting of the petitioners at the Crown and Anchor public house in Westminster.

Now defunct, but important in their day, were assay offices in Chester (closed 1962), Exeter (1992), Newcastle (1884) and York (1858). Several other towns and cities also had their own marks – Norwich, Bristol and Hull, for example, though few items bearing their marks are found today. In general, from 1701 all towns and cities used systems similar to London's, adding their town mark to the four "London-style" marks. In most instances, they eventually dropped the leopard's head.

| Birmingham 1773–present | Chester 1686–1962 | Exeter 1701–1882 | Sheffield 1773–present | Newcastle 1423–1884 | York 1423–1700 | York 1701–1858 |

| Dublin 1638–present | Hibernia mark 1810–20 |

HALLMARK DATE CHARTS

Since 1478, all silver made in England has been legally required to carry hallmarks guaranteeing authenticity. However, few items made before the late 17th century have survived, since most were melted down to make coins to pay the army during the Commonwealth period (1649–60).

Four marks were usually struck on items of silver, but a fifth was sometimes added to commemorate a special, usually royal, occasion. Shown here are some of the marks used by the most important British assay offices.

It is quite easy to identify a precise year from the date letter, its style and the shape of the shield enclosing it. Each had its own unique style of alphabet which changed at the end of every cycle. In London this cycle was 20 years; the letters j, v, w, x, y and z were omitted. Other assay offices often used the full alphabet. In one cycle, the style might be gothic, for example, and in the next Arabic or Roman. Town and standard marks also changed style from time to time.

BIRMINGHAM

Year	Year
1798 — a	1849 — A
1824 — Q	1875 — ⓐ
1834 — ℒ	1900 — a

Hallmark for Sheffield, 1907, clearly showing the lion passant and the crown.

LONDON

Year	Year
1799 — D	1840 — ⓔ
1816 — a	1856 — ⑧
1822 — g	1876 — A
1836 — ℨ	1896 — a

Hallmark for London, 1699, with Britannia standard and lion's head erased.

CHESTER

Year	Year
1799 — ⓒ	1864 — ⓐ
1818 — A	1884 — A
1834 — Q	1901 — ⓐ

EXETER

Year	Year
1800 — D	1837 — ⓐ
1805 — I	1857 — A
1817 — a	1877 — A

SHEFFIELD

Year	Year
1799 — E	1868 — A
1824 — a	1893 — ⓐ
1844 — A	1918 — a

EDINBURGH

Year	Year
1799 — T	1832 — Ⓐ
1806 — a	1857 — A
1820 — O	1882 — ⓐ
1824 — S	1890 — ⓘ

DUBLIN

Year	Year
1800 — D	1838 — S
1810 — OO	1846 — a
1821 — A	1861 — Q
1832 — M	1896 — ⓐ

UNITED STATES

Unlike Britain, America has never had an organized method of marking silver. Although unmarked pieces exist, most silversmiths stamped a maker's mark on their work. These were usually either a monogram or a full last name.

NEW YORK

Most early American silversmiths followed the English styles although those working in New York, where the Dutch influence was strong, often combined both English and Dutch taste. In addition to the maker's mark, some New York silver bears extra marks, which can be regarded as pseudo-hallmarks. They were, possibly, added after some regulatory checking, but this is not known for certain. New York's most famous silversmiths include Bartholomew Le Roux II and Myer Myers in the 18th century, and the Tiffany company in the 19th century.

Daniel C. Fueter
1754

Bartholomew Le Roux
1738

Myer Myers
1745

TIFFANY YOUNG & ELLIS
J. C. M
20
Tiffany & Co
1850–52

TIFFANY & CO.
295
ENGLISH STERLING
925 – 1000
•
550 BROADWAY
Tiffany & Co
1854–70

TIFFANY & CO
14786 MAKERS 5885
STERLING SILVER
925~1000
C

Tiffany & Co
since 1902

BOSTON

The first American silversmiths worked in Boston in the 1630s. In 1660, a town ordinance stated that no one was allowed to open a shop trading in silver until he was 21 years of age and had completed an eight-year apprenticeship.

John Coney
1676

Jeremiah Dummer
1666

Jacob Hurd
1723

Nathaniel Morse
1709

Paul Revere
1725

Paul Revere, Jr.
1757

PROVIDENCE, RHODE ISLAND

Providence was an important early port. Jabez Gorham, founder of the Gorham Corporation, was the town's most famous silversmith.

Jabez Gorham
1815

Jabez Gorham & Son
1842

Bartholomew Le Roux II's mark (B and joined LR) lies beneath the engraver Ledell's name.

PHILADELPHIA

The first capital of the United States, Philadelphia was for many years the richest city in North America and, as such, was a centre for silver work. Although less important than Boston or New York, it still produced important makers.

Joseph Richardson, Jr.
1773

Philip Syng
1714

Philip Syng, Jr.
1726

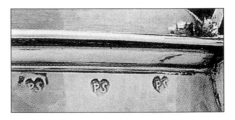

This mark, PS within a heart, belonged to Philip Syng, Sr., of Philadelphia.

HOLLAND

Until they were abolished in 1798, town guilds were responsible for hallmarking. In 1807 the French gained control of Holland and imposed their marking system. Upon independence, in 1814, the Dutch set up their own system which kept many of the French features.

	Marks in use from 1814 to 1953
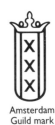 Amsterdam Guild mark 18th C	934 833 Large wares Standard marks
The Hague Guild mark 18th C	833 Small wares Standard mark Assay Office mark

BELGIUM

In 1814, national silver standards were established that lasted until 1868. After this date, however, some silver was still tested and marked, but only at the discretion of the seller or purchaser.

Brussels
Guild mark
Early 18th C

Belgium
800 Standard mark
18th C

Antwerp
Guild mark
Early 18th C

FRANCE

The French have controlled the quality of their silver since the 1200s. However, the diversity of the marks, which include those for the maker, town, standard and guarantee, can be confusing.

Paris
Guild mark
1724–25

Paris
Guild mark
Mid-18th C.

Paris
Guarantee mark
early 19th C

F.T. Germain
Maker's mark
Paris, 18th C

Marks in use from 1798 to 1809

Marks in use since 1838

950

A maker's mark

Guarantee marks

800
Standard mark

950   800
Large wares

Guarantee mark

800

H. Swiering
Maker's mark
Amsterdam
18th C

800
Small wares

Date letter

GERMANIC COUNTRIES

As with most European countries, individual town guilds controlled all local silversmiths and set their own marks. In the 19th century, some countries introduced national standard marks.

Berlin
Guild mark
Late 18th C

Cologne
Guild mark
Late 17th C

Munich
Guild mark
Early 18th C

Nuremberg
Guild mark
18th C

Austria
950 Standard mark
Mid-19th C

Vienna
Guild mark
Mid-18th C

Budapest
Guild mark
18th C

Zurich
Guild mark
17th C–18th C

Geneva
Guild mark
18th C

SPAIN AND PORTUGAL

In both Spain and Portugal, guilds in major towns and cities controlled the standard of the silverware produced. Between 1881 and 1934, however, Spanish silver was free of all controls.

Madrid
Guild mark
18th C

Madrid
Guild mark
1797

Cordoba
Guild mark
19th C

Lisbon
Guild mark
17th C–18th C

Oporto
Guild mark
1836–43

BALTIC COUNTRIES

Across this region, the standard of silver in each area was controlled by a local guild. Marks from the guild in Bergen, Norway, go back to 1580, and those from the Moscow guild date from the 1600s.

Sweden
Control mark
Mid-18th C

Stockholm
Guild mark
18th C–mid-19th C

Västerås
Guild mark
18th C

Orebrö
Guild mark
18th C

Oslo
Guild mark
Mid-17th C–mid-19th C

Bergen
Guild mark
1815

Copenhagen
Guild mark
17th C

Moscow
Guild mark
Early 18th C

St Petersburg
Guild mark
1775

ITALY

Town guilds, such as those in Milan, Bologna and Florence, imposed their own standards and marks. Between 1872 and 1934, when a national system was introduced, production was free from control and assaying was optional.

Italy
950 Standard mark
c.1870–1930

Rome
Guild mark
Late 17th C

Florence
Guild mark
17th C–18th C

FLATWARE: 1

Spoons were first made in Roman times and then declined in popularity and were not produced again in Europe in significant quantities until the Middle Ages. Most surviving English spoons were made after *c.*1500 and can usually be dated by their hallmarks. Early spoons had a curved, fig-shaped bowl and a thin hexagonal stem, usually surmounted by a decorated finial or knop, which was often gilded and from which particular types of spoon derived their names.

Spoons were not made in sets until the end of the seventeenth century, with one exception, Apostle spoons. These came in sets of thirteen, their finials depicting the Master and the 12 apostles, who can be recognized by the emblems they hold.

The hexagonal stems gradually became flatter, with rounded, rather than faceted, sides. By the end of the 1600s, a rib, or "rattail," to give additional strength, ran from the end of the stem to halfway under the bowl, which at this date was of elongated shape.

Prior to 1760, spoon handles had an up-turned end, which meant that they sat steadily when displayed with the bowl facing downward, as was the custom of the time. Spoons from this period are, therefore, always decorated on the back of the bowl and handle. After 1760, it became customary to set spoons with the bowl upward, so the ends were down-turned, with any decoration on the front of the handle. The bowls were then made in the egg shape that is still used today.

▼ AMERICAN SUCKET FORK
These forks, which were used for sweetmeats, are most often of American origin and combine a two- or three-tine fork with a rattail spoon. This example, which is engraved with floral designs on both sides of the shaft and fork, was made by Jesse Kip (c.1682–1722). The son of immigrants from Holland, Kip was born in New York, where he lived and worked throughout his life. By the late 1700s, he had become a notable silversmith.

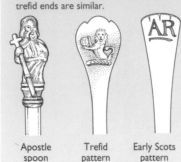

EARLY BRITISH SPOONS
Apostle spoons, with a figure of Christ or an apostle, date from the late 1400s. In the late 1600s, the Trefid pattern, with three distinct points at the end, became popular. Early Scottish spoon ends and trefid ends are similar.

Apostle spoon   Trefid pattern   Early Scots pattern

Other early spoon types
Disk end: These spoons have a flat circular disk finial and were made in 16th-century Scandinavia and in Scotland from the late 1500s to the mid-1600s.
Berry: Spoons with this finial were made from the early 15th century and were popular in Holland and Germany.
Hoof: Although some English examples exist, these spoons with a leaf-shaped bowl and a stem with a hoof finial are chiefly of Italian and Swiss origin.
Seal top: Made from the 15th century through to the mid-17th century, these spoons have a flat seal top which became more ornate in the later period.

1 ENGLISH SLIP-TOP SPOONS
From the 14th century onward, spoons without finials were made in France and England, where they remained popular until the 1640s. The central spoon here dates from 1596, the pair from 1638. L all 6½in/17cm

2 CHARLES I APOSTLE SPOONS
These late examples, made in London c.1641, depict (left to right) Saint John, Saint Matthew and the Master. Most Apostle spoons have a halo, or nimbus, around the head which, from the late 1500s, was solid and engraved with the Dove of the Holy Spirit. L 6½in, 7½in, 6½in; L 17cm, 19cm, 17cm

3 TWO SILVER-GILT SPOONS
The smaller of these spoons, made in Cologne in 1650–70, bears the silversmith's mark of Peter Kaff, (or Petrus Kaft). Like many early spoons, these were probably given as tokens of appreciation or christening presents. L 7½in, 7in; L 19cm, 18cm

4 TREFID SPOONS
The emergence of the Dognose pattern can be seen in these three trefid spoons which date from between 1701 and 1720. The earliest spoon, on the bottom, is typical in its decoration, while the bowls show the uneven transition from the fig-shaped bowl to a more elongated one.

5 SILVER-GILT SPOONS
A silver-gilt dessert spoon and sugar sifter, the handles single struck with sprays of flowers and bunches of grapes in early 19th-century Rococo Revival style. They were part of a large set made in London in 1810–14 by Eley Fearn and Chawner.

6 SHELL-SHAPED LADLE
This fluted soup ladle (c.1770) is in the rare Onslow pattern, named after a famous Speaker of the British House of Commons. L 14in/36cm

7 STRAINING SPOON
The finely pierced bowl of this spoon is unusual because of its slightly square shape. It bears a faint mark for the London maker George Smith and the date letter for 1778. L 10in/25cm

8 VICTORIAN SPOONS
Spoons with pierced bowls, such as this late example (top) dating from 1900, were used for sifting sugar over fruit. The fruit spoon for serving compotes (bottom) is a plain tablespoon of 1800 which was embellished in the 1860s by embossing and gilding – a common practice in Victorian times. L 6in, 9in; L 15cm, 23cm

1

2

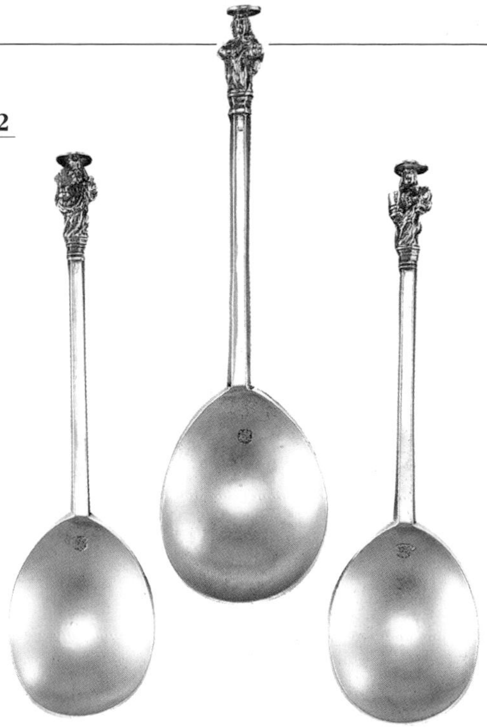

3

4

5

6

7

8

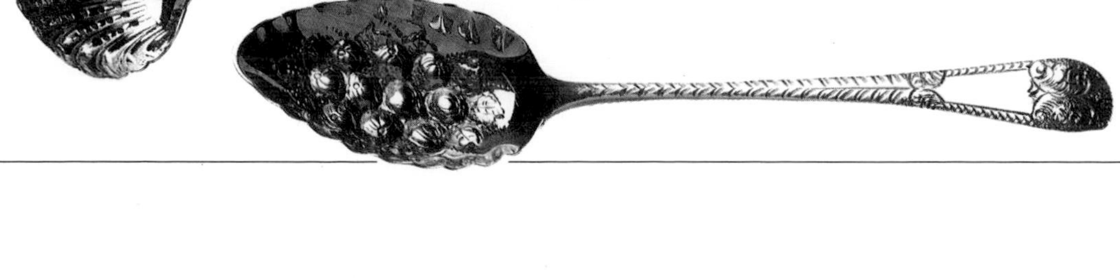

SILVER

Forks were rarely used in England before the Restoration of the Monarchy in 1660, and it was customary for guests at a banquet to bring their own spoons and knives with them. Charles II brought European ideas of dining back with him, including the use of forks, and it soon became the norm to have a matching set of spoons and forks for table settings. Knives of a similar pattern were later added to form a service.

The earliest design was the Trefid pattern, introduced from France, with decorative notches at the top of the handle. By 1700, silversmiths were omitting the notches, and the resulting pointed shape became known as the Dognose pattern. This remained in favor until the reign of George I (1714–27), when the Hanoverian pattern took over.

After 1760, forks were made with four tines instead of three, as can be seen in examples of the Old English pattern that evolved at this time. In the early 1800s, the Fiddle pattern, based on eighteenth-century French designs, became the most common style. Later, the Hourglass pattern, again derived from French flatware, was favored, as were the King's and Queen's patterns; all three are still produced.

Single or double struck
The raised decoration found on flatware is produced by stamping it with a steel die. If only the front is decorated, as is often the case with Scottish flatware, it is "single struck." However, if both the back and front are decorated, it is said to be "double struck," and such pieces are considered to be more attractive.

Knives
It is rare for knives dating from the 18th century or earlier to have survived in a usable state. The handles were made from sheet silver and filled with pitch for solidity and to give them balance. When the knives were washed in hot water, the pitch expanded and many knife handles were damaged or destroyed in this manner. It is considered acceptable, however, to use reproduction knives of the same pattern with original services.

1 FORK STYLES
This grouping shows the development and variation of styles from the early 1700s to the mid-1800s: (a) Dognose, (b) Hanoverian, (c–g) various styles of Old English, (h–k) Fiddle Pattern, (l) Hourglass, (m) King's and (n) Queen's patterns.

2 GEORGE II SPOON AND FORK
Part of a set of 12 Hanoverian tablespoons (1735) and forks (1736) made by John Jacob. The spoons no longer had the rattail at this time, but were still set bowl downward so that the backs, decorated here with a coat-of-arms, could be seen.

3 GEORGE II DESSERT SPOONS
These silver-gilt spoons by Paul de Lamerie bear the royal cypher, Garter motto and monogram of King George II. They were part of a large commission executed over some 10 years and date from c.1740, eight years after de Lamerie had registered his sterling standard mark.

4 OLD ENGLISH PATTERN
These spoons and fork show the plain style from the 1760s as well as its variations. (a) Old English; (b) Feather Edge; (c) Old English Bead; (d) Old English Thread and (e) Old English Bright-cut. All were produced in the 1800s and are still made today.

5 GEORGE III DESSERT SERVICE
A silver-gilt service of 12 spoons (1789) and forks in Hanoverian pattern and 12 knives with pistol-grip handles engraved with the royal crest and Garter motto. They are stored in an 18th-century knifebox.

6 FIDDLE PATTERN AND VARIATIONS
The name derives from the violin-shaped handle. (a) Plain Fiddle pattern (1800–1920); (b) Fiddle Thread (1810 onward); (c) Fiddle Thread and Shell (1815 onward) – the King's pattern derives from this; (d) Fiddle Husk (1820 onward). These patterns fell out of fashion after the 1920s, but are enjoying a revival.

7 BACCHANALIAN PATTERN
The handles of these spoons and forks, part of a composite dessert service, are chased with a drinking scene and vine leaves. They are good examples of the florid late Regency (1825) taste in silver, which anticipates the eclectic styles of the Victorian period.

◄ **VICTORIAN GAME PATTERN SERVICE**
A representative selection of items from a rare table service containing 384 pieces, most of which were made in 1871 by Hunt and Roskell. The cast and chased handles have beaded edges and are ornately decorated with fish or hanging pheasants. The 82 pieces comprising the dessert service are of silver-gilt.

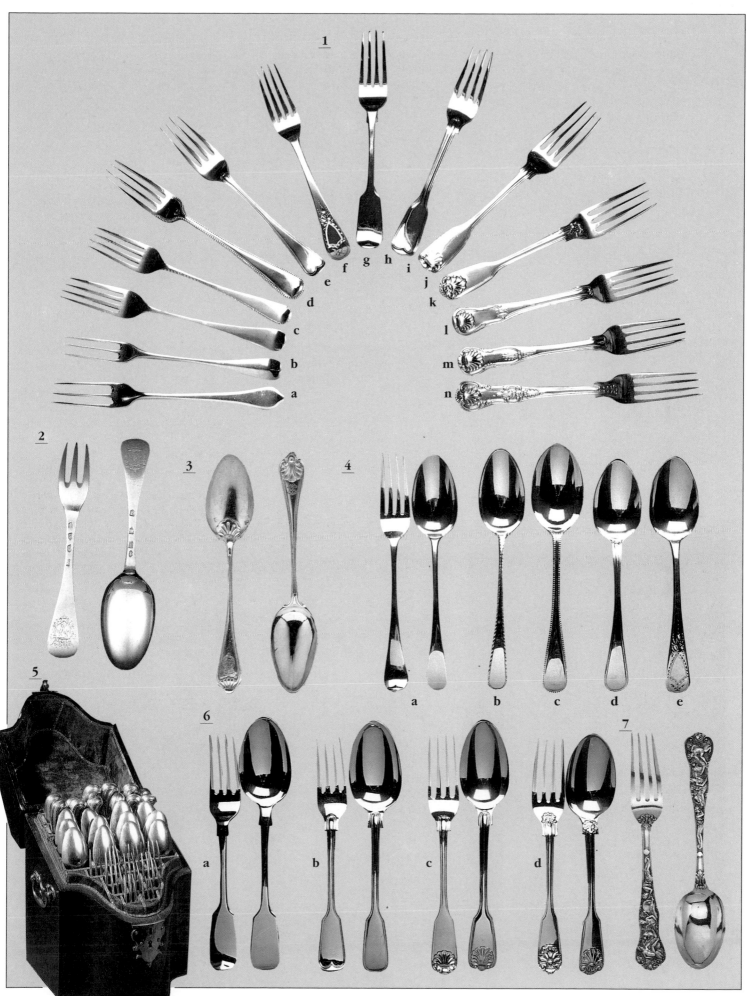

SALTS, CRUETS AND CASTERS

In Roman times salt, or in Latin, *sal*, was part of the payment to the Imperial soldiers, and from this the word salary derives. By the Middle Ages, salt formed an important element in trade, since it was used both for flavoring and as a preservative for meat. The value placed on salt meant that until well into the 1600s, salt cellars were often elaborate status symbols, set on the table near high-ranking diners.

Casters, or sifters, originated in France in the mid-1600s; their use had spread to England by the 1670s and reached America in the 1690s. They were normally made in sets of three, with the largest used for sugar, the others for pepper and dry mustard. The earliest casters resembled a lighthouse, but from c.1700 they were pear-shaped and the covers had baluster finials. In Britain, from the 1770s, sugar casters were gradually replaced by sugar bowls, while in mainland Europe both forms were used.

Cruets, derived from the frames used to hold the wine and water bottles during Mass, were used in England from c.1720. At first, they held only bottles for oil and vinegar, but by 1750 they contained several bottles and casters, which after 1770 were made of glass. In Victorian times sets could have as many as eight pieces.

Paul Storr

One of the most eminent silversmiths in 19th-century London was Paul Storr (1771–1844). He worked from 1807 until 1819 for the retailing firm of Rundell, Bridge & Rundell, the Royal Goldsmiths, and it was during this 12-year period that he produced a large part of the ornamental plate for which he is famous.

Much of this was made to other people's designs, since Storr does not appear to have been a particularly original designer himself. For instance, William Theed RA is thought to have produced the design for the set of salts shown here (**5**).

In 1822 Storr set up his own firm, in partnership with John Mortimer, and continued making silver until his retirement in 1838. He produced a large number of superb pieces, stamped "PS," which still appear in auction rooms occasionally.

1 WILLIAM AND MARY CASTERS
Set of three plain cylindrical casters, dating from 1694, in the lighthouse shape that was common at the time. Each caster has a fluted, spreading circular foot and bayonet fitting for the partly fluted pierced domed cover. The largest caster would have been used for sugar, the smaller ones for pepper and spices. H 7in, 5½in; H 18cm, 14cm

◄ **ELIZABETH I BELL SALT**
Bell-shaped salts were an English form, made from c.1580 to 1620; this example in silver-gilt bears the date 1599. They are usually plain or have chased strapwork decoration on a matted ground, as in this rare and important piece. It is unusual in that it was made in three tiers. The lower section stands on three ball feet, and the upper domed section, with a detachable finial, forms a caster for either spice or sugar. H 8½in/22cm

2 FRENCH SUGAR CASTER
The molded rib around the broadest part of the body is the unusual feature of this caster, made in Paris in 1732–33 by Nicholas Bertin. It is decorated in the Régence style, with strapwork, female busts, birds and baskets of fruit, and the pierced cover is topped with an artichoke. H 10in/25cm

3 GEORGE II SALT CELLARS
Made by Frederick Kandler in 1741 for the Fourth Earl of Stafford. These four silver-gilt salts, of standard circular shape, have been transformed into fine examples of English Rococo style by the application of shells and mermaids, whose twin tails form the feet.

4 WARWICK CRUET
The first cruet in a frame, such as this, was made c.1725 for the Earl of Warwick, hence the name. This rococo example by John Wood, with three pear-shaped casters and two silver-mounted glass bottles, dates from 1744–45. H 9in/23cm

5 SILVER-GILT SALTS
The design for these salt cellars, two of a set of four made in 1811–13 by Paul Storr, is probably based on silver made in the 1740s by Nicholas Sprimont for Frederick, Prince of Wales. They are cast and chased as waves through which tritons tow the shell salts. L 4½in/12cm

6 VICTORIAN SALT CELLARS
Made in 1852 by John Hunt and Robert Roskell, successors to Storr & Mortimer, these salt cellars are cast in the form of shells, which rest on the backs of eagles standing on ducal coronets. The gilt lining to the shells prevents corrosion. H 7in/18cm

7 VICTORIAN CONDIMENT SET
These parcel-gilt chimpanzees with toffee-colored glass eyes, made by Edward Charles Brown in 1868, are a good example of the novelty shapes that amused the Victorians. The monkey mustard pot has a matching spoon; its terminal forms the plume for the hat. H mustard pot 4in/10cm

8 ELECTROPLATED CRUET
Cruet with cups and cut-glass bottles; designed by Christopher Dresser in 1878 for the makers Hukin & Heath. Influenced by Japanese style, Dresser sought to minimize decoration and emphasize form in his designs.

GRAVYBOATS AND SAUCE TUREENS

In the early eighteenth century, in France, gravyboats were double-lipped with a molded rim and stood on a base. Although this design continued to be used in continental Europe, it was not popular when it was introduced into England c.1715, and by 1725 British silversmiths were making gravyboats with a lip at one end and a scrolled handle at the other.

These early gravyboats were often plainly finished, but by the mid-eighteenth century, the molded base was replaced by either three or four feet and, influenced by the work of Huguenot silversmiths, some gravyboats began to be decorated in the flamboyant rococo style that had become paramount in France. Designs included swags and festoons, as well as handles in the shape of human or animal figures, and were comparable to the French examples upon which they were modeled.

While gravyboats in the prevailing taste of the day were still made between 1760 and 1820, sauce tureens also became fashionable. These often matched soup tureens, although they were generally less ornate than their larger counterparts. In the early nineteenth century, gravyboats were once again rather elaborately decorated, but as the century progressed, many were made in traditional styles, and earlier examples were often copied precisely.

A master of the Rococo

The Huguenot silversmith Paul Crespin (1694–1770), who worked in London in the early to mid-18th century, was one of the greatest exponents of the elaborate rococo style. Relatively little of his work survives, but the pieces that exist (**2**) rival those of Paul de Lamerie (see p.152), England's other famous maker of rococo silver. The rivalry seems to have been friendly, since Crespin and de Lamerie sometimes worked on the same commissions.

Points to note
Hallmarks

Gravyboats with legs are usually marked in a straight line on the underside, although from the late 18th century onward, some have the hallmarks below the lip. On a gravyboat with a central foot and on a sauce tureen, look for the hallmarks under the rim or under the foot; the lid of a tureen will also be marked.

Damage

The rims, handles and feet of gravyboats are prone to damage, and they should be examined carefully for any flaws or signs of repair.

1 GEORGE II GRAVYBOAT
Made by the Huguenot silversmith Peter Archambo, this double-lipped gravyboat (1729) is a fine example of the style that was introduced into England from France c.1715. Although later displaced in England, the form remained popular in the rest of Europe.

2 ROCOCO GRAVYBOAT
One of a set of four gravyboats made in 1735 by Paul Crespin. The decoration incorporates floral and fruit swags, paw feet and lion masks that were popular at this time, and there are fish-head terminals on the handles.

3 FLUTED GRAVYBOAT
This English rococo gravyboat, one of a pair, was made by Frederick Kandler in 1747. The shell and scroll decoration featured on the oval cast foot is repeated on the scalloped rim. The scroll handle is leaf-capped.

4 MID-GEORGIAN GRAVYBOAT
This gravyboat, on three shell and scroll feet, was made by Edward Wakelin in 1758. It is a good example of the shape that was favored in England from 1725, since it was easier to pour from than the earlier, double-lipped form.

5 GEORGE III GRAVYBOAT
The neoclassical design of this two-handled boat-shaped gravyboat – one of a set of six – has been attributed to Sir William Chambers. The gravyboats formed part of a large order for silver placed by the Fourth Duke of Marlborough with the firm of Parker and Wakelin in 1768–69.

6 GEORGE III SAUCE TUREEN
Paul Storr's interpretation of the neoclassical style is evident in this elegant tureen and cover (one of four) dating from 1800. The tureen stands on a pedestal foot and has drop-ring handles; the cover has a simple loop handle. Decoration is restricted to a gadrooned border on both stand and cover.

7 REGENCY SAUCE TUREEN
This tureen and cover (1821) show how styles moved away from the classical toward a more ornate style in the early 1800s. It is richly decorated with bold shell and foliate feet, sprays of oak leaves trailing from branch handles and a gadrooned rim.

◀ **GEORGE II GRAVYBOATS**
A good example of English Rococo, this pair of gravyboats with stands and ladles was made by Nicholas Sprimont in 1746. Sprimont came to England from Belgium and worked in London as a silversmith between 1743 and 1748 before becoming director of the Chelsea porcelain works (see p.68).

SOUP TUREENS

Silver soup tureens were French in origin and were introduced to England through Huguenot silversmiths who settled in the country at the end of the seventeenth and beginning of the eighteenth centuries. Although the earliest tureens appear to date from *c.*1715–20, they were costly items and remained the province of the wealthy. It was only *c.*1760 that they became more common; initially, most had stands, which have sometimes been lost.

While elaborate rococo examples were made in Britain, it was in France, Germany and Italy that this style really flourished. Such tureens were adorned with an often incongruous mixture of animal and human figures, marine life, fruit and vegetables, and the impression of movement was an essential ingredient of rococo style.

From the early 1760s, classical influences can be seen in the shape of tureens, which emulated that of urns, and in their decoration, which followed the neo-classical trend toward simplicity and symmetry and employed many of the same motifs used on furniture, such as anthemion or stylized honeysuckle.

Soup tureens were not common in eighteenth-century America; however, in the early 1800s, some were made based on French Empire examples, although they were simpler in execution. Soup tureens were produced throughout the 1800s both in Britain and continental Europe, with the decoration of some grand Regency ones emulating that of the previous century.

Coats-of-arms and crests

Silver was often used to symbolize an owner's wealth, and many items of silver, especially large pieces such as tureens and salvers, were engraved with either coats-of-arms or crests. Full coats-of-arms easily help to identify the family or institution to which the silver belonged.

The same cannot be said of crests, which are usually not specific to one family. Often crests have a motto, which in Scotland is placed above the crest, while in England it is placed below it.

Armorials should be contemporary with the piece of silver on which they appear, but often they have been added later, or even erased and replaced as pieces changed ownership. Such alterations affect both the historical and market value of silverware.

▼ **GEORGE II SOUP TUREEN**
Made by Paul de Lamerie and hallmarked for London in 1741, this shaped oval tureen with a cover stands on four feet, as was customary at this date. It is a good example of English rococo, with its use of wheat sprays, berried foliage, lions' heads and grotesque masks for decoration. The handle on the cover is formed from shells and foliage, and the rim of the tureen and the cover have gadrooned borders. W 18in/46cm

1 OVAL SOUP TUREEN AND STAND
One of a pair made by Thomas Pitts in 1772, perhaps to a design by the architect Sir William Chambers. The decoration was strongly influenced by that of the noted 18th-century French silversmith Thomas Germain. The stand (1a) is chased with bands of flutes, tied laurel swags and shells. H 13in/33cm; L stand 23½in/59cm

2 OVAL SOUP TUREEN AND STAND
An urn-shaped tureen made in 1774 by John Carter for Sir Watkin Williams-Wynn to a design by Robert Adam, who built Sir Watkin's house in St. James's Square, London, and designed the silver for it. The classical decoration – swags, beading and anthemion – is typical of Adam's oeuvre. The tureen is supported by a central pedestal as was usual in c.1770–1800. L stand 16in/41cm

3 OVAL SOUP TUREEN AND COVER
The noted silversmith Paul Storr made this fluted tureen in 1809 for presentation to University College, Oxford, by the retiring Master, and it bears the coats-of-arms of both. Shells, scrolls and foliage decorate the handles, which end in lions' masks, and an entwined snake forms the handle. L 17½in/44cm

4 CIRCULAR TUREEN AND COVER
This unusual tureen and cover, which looks back to the previous century in its decoration, was made by Robert Garrard over a period of 18 years: the cover in 1814, the tureen in 1832 and turtle finial in 1830. Diam. 16½in/42cm

5 SOUP TUREEN AND GRAVYBOAT
It was fashionable in the early 1800s to have matching soup and gravy tureens. This soup tureen is one of a pair, the matching gravyboat one of four, which were made by Richard Sibley in 1815 and 1817. The lion's-paw feet were common at this date. L 18½in, 10in; L 47cm, 25cm

6 GEORGE IV SOUP TUREEN
Made in 1827–29 by Robert Garrard & Brothers, this tureen with stand is an example of the "massive" style that was popular in the first part of the 19th century. The marine motifs used in its decoration include simulated waves on the stand, handles in the form of a mermaid and a triton, four dolphins supporting the bowl, shells and crustaceans.

BOWLS AND BASKETS

In Europe, silver vessels to hold food and drink and for display were known from c.2000 B.C. As the metal became less rare and expensive, bowls began to be made for more humdrum uses, such as holding sugar or candy and even for the toilette.

Oval bowls, with a half-moon section cut from the rim so that they fitted against the neck, were used for shaving. They were decorated simply, with a coat-of-arms or gadrooned rim. Bowls for powder and lotions were made for toilette sets and remained popular until the 1910s, when glass bowls with silver or plated lids were still being made for the purpose.

Another derivative of the basic bowl is the shallow, single-handled bleeding bowl, or porringer as it is known in America. English porringers differ from American bowls of the same name and were used for drinks and mixtures such as caudle (see p.46). They were deeper, with two handles, a lid and occasionally a spout.

Baskets were made as early as the sixteenth century, but did not become popular until the 1730s. They were used on the dining or tea table to hold bread, cake, fruit and sweetmeats. Early baskets were round, but in the late 1720s this was superseded by the oval shape. Sometimes these baskets, usually with scalloped edges, pierced sides and swing handles, were made to resemble woven work.

After the 1750s, baskets were made with feet rather than a rim, and they became shallower, with simpler decoration. By the early nineteenth century, when mass production took off, baskets were generally either oblong or circular.

Monteith

The name for these scallop-edged bowls (below), used to suspend wine glasses in iced water to cool them, is said to have come from a 17th-century Scotsman named Monteith who had a cloak with a scalloped edge. Early monteiths, which appeared in the late 1600s and were generally smaller than punch bowls, were characterized by gadrooning, drop handles and a detachable rim so that they could be used either for cooling glasses or for serving punch. A full set of hallmarks should be found both on the side of the monteith and on the detachable rim if it has one.

Pierced decoration

Before industrialization, the pierced decoration (2, 5) that was particularly popular on 18th-century baskets had to be chiseled or sawn out by the silversmith. By the end of the century, simple and repetitive designs could be die-stamped – punched out using a steam-driven hammer – although more intricate work was still done by hand. Pierced baskets with thin, delicate work are prone to damage and should be checked carefully for solder repairs.

1 IRISH GEORGE II CIRCULAR BOWL
Standing on a spreading foot, this fine silver bowl, by Robert Calderwood of Dublin (1732), is chased with deep flutes and has a fluted everted lip. It is engraved with a crest and an earl's coronet above. Diam. 7½in/19cm

◄ **JAMES II MONTEITH**
Known as "The Basingstoke Trophy," this silver monteith was made in 1688 to celebrate a win at the Basingstoke Races by a horse belonging to Edward Chute, a local landowner. It is divided into ten large panels decorated with a fanciful version of the race and separated by smaller panels of exotic plants. The monteith has a detachable rim that matches the rest of the piece. H 9in/23cm

2 GEORGE II OVAL BREAD BASKET
This bread basket, made by Paul de Lamerie in 1747, is decorated with pierced lattice-work sides that resemble a woven basket. This style is echoed in the chased lattice-work of the base. The everted rim is decorated with cast wheatears, flowers, scrolls and ribbon motifs, and the handle is a rope-twist. L 14in/36cm

3 GEORGE III DESSERT BASKETS
Delicate reeded lattice-work forms the sides of these silver-gilt baskets (c.1765). The applied trailing vine decoration and the overall shape have led to suggestions that they may be an early form of bottle stand or wine coaster. Diam. 7in/18cm

4 LOUIS XVI SILVER-GILT VERRIÈRE
Like the monteith, the verrière had a lobed rim and was used for cooling glasses. This oval example, one of a pair, is chased with leaves and a central patera. It was made in 1782 by Robert-Joseph Auguste for his "Moscow" service. One of the leading French silversmiths of that time, Auguste worked for the Russian court among other patrons. L 11½in/29cm

5 GEORGE III SILVER-GILT BASKET
Made by Thomas Arden in 1805, this basket is unusual because it was made without a handle. Its spreading foot is pierced and chased with palmettes and anthemia, while the sides have applied decoration of vine tendrils, grapes and leaves. L 13in/30cm

6 EARLY REGENCY BREAD BASKET
Chased with waved fluting and edged with a gadrooned shell and foliage border, this basket was made by Paul Storr in 1812. Baskets were shallower in the Regency period, as this example illustrates. L 13in/33cm

7 FRENCH SILVER-GILT OVAL BASIN
Made by Marc-Augustine Lebrun between 1821 and 1838, this basin is decorated with applied marine and classical motifs. L 15in/38cm

8 VICTORIAN SILVER ROSE BOWL
This rose bowl, one of a pair, is dominated by chased decoration depicting battle scenes. The interior is gilt, and the spreading base is adorned with floral festoons. The pair was made by James Barclay Hennell in 1886 for Robert Hennell & Sons, London. Diam. 13in/33cm

SILVER

CANDLESTICKS

Tallow or wax candles set in candlesticks were used in Europe for lighting from the tenth century. But in England, very few examples have survived from before the English Civil Wars in the mid-1600s, when much of England's silver was melted down for coinage. Examples of candlesticks from later in the century, in a chunky, angular style, do, however, exist.

By the last quarter of the seventeenth century, silver candlesticks were made by casting, usually in three pieces – sconce, stem and base – which were then soldered together. Because a large quantity of metal was used, they were heavy and solid in appearance. This process was common until the late eighteenth century, when it became customary to make candlesticks of fine rolled sheet silver, often reinforced with a metal rod and with a central core of pitch and plaster of Paris to give stability.

In the early 1700s, candlesticks were usually about 7in/18cm in height, rising to some 12in/30cm by 1800; in Victorian times they were slightly shorter: 10in/25cm. The invention of Sheffield plate in the 1740s, followed by electroplating in 1840, meant that silver candlesticks could be produced that the middle classes could afford, and they were made in quantity.

Points to note

Nozzles
After 1740, most candlesticks had a nozzle – a saucer-shaped fitting at the top of the column which held the candle and prevented wax from running down the stem. The decoration and shape usually followed that of the base.

Hallmarks
Marks on candlesticks and candelabra vary according to both the date and style of the stick. Each part, including the nozzle, should bear the lion passant at least, and the maker's mark.

1 CHARLES II CANDLESTICKS
Made in 1667 by Jacob Bodendick, who came from Germany, this pair of candlesticks is of sheet silver which has been raised by hand. They have the square bases and fluted columns typical of the period. H 9in/23cm

2 AMERICAN CANDLESTICKS
Candlesticks produced in America in the 18th century are rare. These two, made c.1710–30 in Boston by Nathaniel Morse, depend upon their decorative shape for their appeal and show how English designs influenced American makers. H 6in/15cm

3 TAPERSTICKS
These miniature candlesticks held the tapers used to melt the wax used when sealing letters. The two outer pieces date from 1698 (right) and 1702 (left), the more elaborate central taperstick from 1754. H 4in, 4½in, 4in; H 10cm, 11cm, 10cm

4 GEORGE I CANDLESTICKS
A pair of cast silver-gilt candlesticks made in 1717 by Pierre Platel, to whom Paul de Lamerie (see p.152) was apprenticed. The decoration of stylized shells and lambrequins on these beautiful candlesticks is derived from French designs. H 7in/18cm

5 GERMAN CANDLESTICKS
These two silver-gilt candlesticks were made in Dresden c.1750 for Augustus III, Elector of Saxony, by Christian Heinrich Ingermann. The high domed bases and ornate chased and embossed decoration are typical of the German interpretation of the rococo style. H 10in/25cm

6 GEORGE III CANDLESTICKS
Two of a set of four made by Daniel Smith and Robert Sharp in 1761. The rectangular bases, baluster stems and gadrooned decoration mark the start of the transition from rococo forms to more classical styles. H 10½in/27cm

7 TRAVELING CHAMBERSTICKS
Made by William Stroud in 1809–10, these plain chambersticks with typical dished saucers bear the cypher for Queen Charlotte. Diam. 5½in/14cm

8 SHEFFIELD PLATE CANDLESTICKS
Cast candlesticks with shell and foliate borders dating from the 1830s. The style proved popular and was widely copied in the last 25 years of the 19th century. H 9in/23cm

9 DUTCH WALL SCONCES
Although sconces were made earlier, none survive from before the mid-1600s. This pair of sconces, made at The Hague c.1710, follows the European fashion of using a human arm to hold the candle.

10 CANDLE SNUFFERS AND STAND
Scissor-type snuffers, used to trim the candle wick, were placed in the stand when they were not in use. Such pieces were common between 1680 and the 1720s; this one was made by John Laughton in 1691. H 8in/20cm

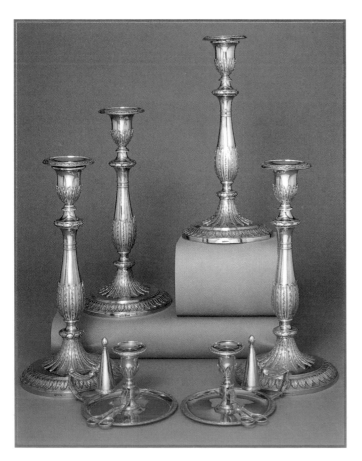

◄ GEORGE III CANDLE- AND CHAMBERSTICKS
These four silver-gilt candlesticks show the classical baluster stem, vase-shaped socket and acanthus-leaf decoration favored in the late 18th century. The similarly decorated silver-gilt chambersticks are fitted with their own conical extinguishers and snuffers. All the pieces were made by John Scofield in 1791–92. H candlesticks 14in/36cm

CENTERPIECES AND CANDELABRA

Made to catch the attention of the diner, centerpieces have been produced for many centuries, and while some centerpieces were purely ornamental, others had some practical use. Early instances include the great salts of the English Middle Ages and the nefs (wine or salt containers in the shape of fully rigged ships) of France and Germany. One later example, known as an epergne, was a stand with one central basket and several smaller ones used for serving crystallized fruit or sweetmeats.

From the rococo period onward, French and German silversmiths began to specialize in creating elaborate centerpieces of both a decorative and practical nature. These pieces were often placed on a plateau, or raised, mirrored platform, which, by the early 1800s, ran almost the length of a table; and some incorporated a candelabrum into the design. In Britain in the nineteenth century, rosebowls and vases became fashionable as centerpieces.

Candelabra, candlesticks with arms, were first produced in the late seventeenth century and remained popular into the nineteenth century, when the introduction of gas lighting reduced their importance. Until the 1770s, candelabra generally had two branches, but after this date many were made with three or more. Victorian examples were often of quite massive proportions with as many as 15 branches.

Epergnes

These elaborate stands (2, 3) originated in France and were first seen in England around the beginning of King George I's reign (1714). They included a large central basket or glass dish and several smaller ones and were designed to save diners the trouble of passing dishes around the table, hence the name epergne from the French, *épargner*, meaning to save.

Point to note

In the Regency and Victorian periods, many pieces were made as testimonials and inscribed with suitable words for the recipient (8). Such contemporary inscriptions do not detract from the collectability of items; in fact, the value of pieces made to honor an historic figure is generally increased by an inscription.

▼ GEORGE III TABLE GARNITURE

Made toward the end of the 18th century, this fine epergne, with lion's paw and foliage feet, has four detachable leaf-capped branches each ending in a cut-glass circular dish. Flanked by four smaller dessert stands, each with a matching glass dish, the whole set is reflected in a mirrored plateau in three sections. H epergne 12in/30cm; W plateau 4ft 6in/1.37m

1 PARCEL-GILT TABLE FOUNTAIN

The figures of Neptune and Bacchus, among others, adorn this ornate fountain. It was made by Melchior Gelb I in 1625–30 in Augsburg, the center of German silvermaking, and is a fine example of the elaborate pieces made in the area during the 16th and 17th centuries. H 25in/64cm

2 GEORGE III FIVE-BASKET EPERGNE

Thomas Pitts, a specialist in epergnes, made this elaborate piece in 1763. With its pierced decoration and swags of trailing flowers, it is a good example of late rococo silverwork. H 13in x W 18in; H 33cm x W 46cm

3 LATE GEORGIAN EPERGNE

This epergne, made in 1808 by William Pitts, the son of Thomas (see 2), has a "lighter" appearance than earlier examples. A late neoclassical piece, its decorative motifs include cherubs, flaming lamps, musical trophies and a detachable bull's-head crest below the central bowl. H 17in/43cm

4 LARGE GERMAN CENTERPIECE

An oak tree forms the central element of this elaborate parcel-gilt piece. The sides of the triangular base show enameled coats-of-arms and views of Washington, D.C., Frankfurt-am-Main and London. Above them are figures representing Charity, Industry and Maternity. Made by Lazarus Posen of Frankfurt (c.1890), it was used as a family tree – each acorn is engraved with the name and dates of a family member. H 31in/79cm

5 GEORGE III CANDELABRUM

A large candelabrum, by Paul Storr (1816), decorated with features from baroque and rococo designs including owl masks, dolphins, dragons and lions. H 27in/69cm

6 EARLY VICTORIAN CANDELABRUM

A fine oak-tree candelabrum, made by Richard Sawyer of Dublin in 1843. It stands on a mirrored plateau and has five detachable arms with acorn sockets and petal drip-pans. The figures on the triangular base represent agriculture. H 25in/64cm

7 CANDELABRUM-CENTERPIECE

Fighting animals, including bears, tigers and hounds, are the theme of this piece, one of a set of four made by Robert Garrard (1845). The branches can be replaced with pierced baskets, so transforming the candelabrum into a centerpiece. H 33in/84cm

8 THE TWEEDDALE TESTIMONIAL

A massive 13-light candelabrum depicting a scene from the Tweeddale family history. It was presented in 1848 to the Eighth Marquess when he was Governor of Madras, as "a Token of Respect and Esteem." H 4ft/1.2m

Salvers, flat platters measuring more than 10in/25cm across, first appeared in England during the Restoration period. Made of silver or silver-gilt, they were used for formally offering food, drinks, letters or visiting cards, although some elaborately decorated examples were just for display.

Early salvers were generally left undecorated; they stood on a central foot and were usually circular with a broad embossed rim. By the start of George I's reign, salvers were being made in a variety of shapes with narrower rims and three or four small feet on the underside of the rim. As the eighteenth century progressed, the plain molded borders became more elaborate, and flat surfaces were covered with chased, or engraved, decoration. Shell-shapes, gadrooning and piercing were all common on rococo examples, while later pieces often had beaded edges.

Smaller versions of salvers, known as waiters, were also made, often in matching sets. Neither had handles, and it was not until the 1750s that silver trays – salvers with handles – first appeared. These were normally oval, with the squarer forms only emerging in the early 1800s. Trays with a gallery developed in Victorian times.

Silver plates gradually became fashionable from the mid-sixteenth century onward, although most surviving examples date from the eighteenth century or later. They were made in varying sizes and in sets of at least a dozen. Their design has remained fairly constant, although early plates with molded rims have given way to those with shaped gadrooned edges.

Early Huguenot silversmiths

Louis XIV's revocation of the Edict of Nantes in 1685 meant that France's Protestants, known as Huguenots, were deprived of their religious and civil freedom. The persecution that followed led to their mass emigration. Although a fair number were already established in England, it was the accession of William and Mary in 1688, which secured the Protestant Succession, that led to the great influx of Huguenots.

Many were silversmiths of great skill, whose arrival was at first deeply resented by their English counterparts. Pierre Harache I (*below*), who arrived in London before the revocation, worked mostly for the aristocracy and was the first Huguenot to be made a freeman of the Goldsmith's Company. Augustine Courtauld (**1**) founded a dynasty of silversmiths, as did David Willaume I, whose firm included his son David (**2**), daughter Ann Tanqueray, the foremost woman goldsmith, and son-in-law David Tanqueray. Paul de Lamerie (*see p.152*), probably the greatest of them all, was apprenticed to another famous Huguenot silversmith, Pierre Platel.

1 EARLY GEORGIAN OCTAFOIL SALVER
Made by Augustine Courtauld in 1714, this finely engraved salver with its plain molded border stands on four cast bracket feet. At the time, this type of support was an innovation, and many silversmiths were still using a central foot. Diam. 14in/36cm

◀ **WILLIAM & MARY STANDING SALVER**
Engraved with the coat-of-arms of Charles Seymour, Fourth Duke of Somerset, and his wife Elizabeth Percy, this fine salver was made by Pierre Harache I. Since it was made in 1689, the year of the coronation of William and Mary, and Seymour was a favorite at court, it is possible that the salver was used in the ceremony, perhaps to bear a crown. At the time, it was customary for those involved in such ceremonies to claim a piece of plate, such as this salver, as their fee. Diam. 7in/18cm

2 GEORGE II DISHES
A selection of dishes from a service (1731) by David Willaume II. The oval centers of the dishes on the left indicate that they are for meat, while those with round centers are for the second course. All the plates have a gadrooned border and are engraved with a coat-of-arms within a rococo cartouche. W 14in, 13in; W 36cm, 33cm

3 MID-GEORGIAN IRISH SALVER
This square salver is by the Dublin silversmith John Hamilton (1736). It is finely engraved with a coat-of-arms in a baroque-style cartouche inside a strapwork border and is decorated with crests and scrolls. W 9in/23cm

4 ROCOCO OVAL TRAY
A pierced and upcurved border, with gadrooning and foliate decoration, finishes this unusual tray (1749) by Paul Crespin, one of the finest rococo silversmiths in England. This piece must have been made to support a centerpiece or soup tureen, since trays were not made in their own right until later in the century. W 23in/58cm

5 GEORGE III SILVER-GILT TRAY
The upcurved border, with its quilted and gadrooned decorations, conceals four carrying handles for this large tray by James Young. The ground is engraved with neoclassical motifs, while the center has the coat-of-arms of John James Hamilton, Ninth Earl of Abercorn. W 29in/74cm

6 SET OF REGENCY DINNER PLATES
Part of a set of 12, these plates were made by Robert Garrard in 1815. They are engraved with an earl's coronet and coat-of-arms and have the shaped edge and gadrooned rim typical of the period. Diam. 10in/25cm

7 LATE REGENCY SALVER AND WAITER
Elaborately decorated with flowers, shells and scrolls on a matted ground, and with a similar molded border, these pieces, made by Paul Storr in 1826–29, illustrate the naturalistic style that was emerging at the time. Diam. 17in, 7in; Diam. 43cm, 18cm

8 EARLY VICTORIAN SILVER-GILT TRAY
This large presentation tray, with heavily worked borders and handles and embellished with bold cartouches, scrolls, acanthus leaves and other motifs, was made in 1837 as a gift from Queen Victoria. W 33in/84cm

DRINKING VESSELS

Vessels specially for drinking have been made since ancient times. Early examples were generally large and were often used as ceremonial cups, such as loving cups, which were passed from person to person, and many were lidded.

Beakers have been used throughout Europe since the Middle Ages. Their shape, derived from the straight section of a drinking horn, remained constant until their decline during the 1800s. The only exceptions were British eighteenth-century examples which were shorter and had narrower bases. Silver wine goblets were widely used until the mid-1700s, when they were ousted by wine glasses.

Tankards were common from the 1500s, but few examples remain from that time. In the late 1700s, more wine and liquor were drunk than ale, and the tankard's popularity declined until Victorian times, when they were widely reproduced. Mugs, or tankards without lids, were made after c.1680 and were more popular in America and Britain than in the rest of Europe. Early shapes were taken from contemporary pottery, and in the eighteenth century tankards and mugs were plain or carried a simple inscription or coat-of-arms; by the 1800s, both were elaborately ornamented.

▼ THE BROWNLOW TANKARDS
Made for the Brownlow family, these magnificent James II tankards (1686) are of slightly tapered form, with molded borders and lobed scroll thumbpieces. They are chased with chinoiserie themes, including birds, trees, warriors and buildings, which were probably executed in a workshop to which makers sent their pieces for decoration. H 8½in/22cm

Types of decoration
The term "chasing" refers to the decoration of silver using punches, with no silver being lost in the process (*below*, **4, 8**). Large-scale relief shapes are achieved by embossing (**1**), a method that involves hammering on the reverse of the piece of silver. Two methods of chasing could be used for adding detail to the embossed shapes.

Repoussé (French for "pushed back") chasing adds intricate detail by selectively pushing back some of the silver raised during embossing. This technique was widely used in the late 17th- to mid-18th centuries and was revived in 19th-century Britain.

Flat chasing, also worked from the front, uses either punches or small hammers to produce low-relief patterns that resemble engraving. However, tell-tale imprints on the reverse of a chased piece mean that it can always be distinguished from one that has been engraved.

Chinoiserie silver
The influence of China is evident in the form and decoration of many silver items. In late 17th-century Britain, flat-chased chinoiserie engraving was used to decorate a variety of items from tankards (*below*) to toilette sets. By the mid-18th century, the Chinese theme had spread to items associated with tea drinking, such as teapots and sugar bowls, and some silver candlesticks were made in the form of Chinese men. In the Regency period, there was a revival of interest in the Orient that led to the chinoiserie style of applied ornamentation being used on a wide variety of silver pieces.

1 GERMAN SILVER-GILT TANKARDS
Embossed narrative decoration is typical on German tankards from the late 1500s and early 1600s. The smaller one, made in Nuremberg in 1594, has roundels depicting acts of mercy, while the other (c.1625), from Augsburg, shows a mythological scene. H 7in, 10in; H 18cm, 25cm

2 PAIR OF CHARLES I GOBLETS
Made by Walter Shute of London in 1627, the goblets have the vase-shaped bowls and baluster stems usual at this date. Normally they were either plain or engraved with a coat-of-arms and inscription. H 11in/28cm

3 SMALL CHARLES I SILVER TANKARD
A tankard with a tapering shape made in 1647. It has a double-lobed thumbpiece and, as was customary, a hinge on the top of the handle. The coats-of-arms reflect the marriages of the first owner's family. H 10in/25cm

4 TWO WILLIAM III TANKARDS
Although these fine cylinder tankards (1699) are by different makers, the decoration is similar. The swirling flutes and foliate motifs are typical of the late 17th century. H 7in/18cm

5 18TH-CENTURY SWEDISH BEAKERS
Beakers were particularly popular in Scandinavian countries. The plain one by Modin of Örebrö dates from 1735, while the other, decorated with stylized flowers, was made by Bengt Biorn of Västerås in 1726. H 3½in/9cm

6 GEORGE II BALUSTER TANKARD
A baluster-shaped tankard with a slightly domed lid by Richard Bayley (1740). Even during the rococo period of English silver, the decoration of tankards was restrained. H 9in/23cm

7 AMERICAN ENGRAVED CANN
This cann, or mug, was made c.1750 by the New York maker Bartholomew Le Roux II, and engraved by Joseph Leddel with six inscriptions and biblical scenes from the life of Joseph. H 4½in/11cm

8 WILLIAM IV SILVER-GILT TANKARD
Known as the "King's Cup," this fine tankard was made by George Bridge in 1830 as a gift from the British king to the winner of a yacht race. It is cast and chased with foliage, paddling putti and a central plaque of Britannia. H 13in/33cm

DRINKING ACCESSORIES

Most early silver pitchers, made from c.1660, had silver handles without any insulation, which suggests that they were meant for cool liquids, and until the end of George I's reign in 1727, some were found with covers. The shape of pitchers followed the prevailing style: in the eighteenth century, they were either oval, baluster- or pear-shaped. Claret pitchers, made either entirely of silver or of glass with silver mounts, appeared in the early 1800s.

Wines and liquor were decanted before serving, so as the variety increased during the 1700s, it became necessary to identify a decanter's contents. In the 1730s, engraved silver labels, or bottle tickets, cut from sheet silver were introduced to replace earlier parchment labels. Early silver labels were generally cartouche-shaped and had only a maker's mark, since they weighed less than the minimum for full hallmarking.

Wine funnels, used to decant wine from the bottle, appeared during the late seventeenth century. At first they were plain and made in one piece, but by the middle of the century, most had two sections, so that the stem and bowl could be taken apart for cleaning. Later funnels vary in both shape and decoration.

Hip flasks were designed to fit snugly into a pocket, and most date from the late nineteenth century. Earlier examples do exist, but they were made of glass with silver mounts and few have survived. Some flasks were made in the United States during Prohibition (1919–33) and are occasionally engraved with wry comments.

Points to note

Tankards have a full set of marks on the side or base of the body and also on the lid. The marks on early examples are across the top of the lid, while on later pieces they are usually grouped on the inside. The body of a British beer or wine pitcher generally has a full set of marks, while the lid, if it has one, shows only the maker's mark and lion passant. If a lid has a full set of marks, it is likely that it is a converted tankard.

Wine coolers have full hallmarks on the base or the side. The liner and rim should have the same marks, but often without the town mark. Coasters are usually hallmarked on the rim base, but some from the late 18th and early 19th centuries are marked on the side.

The Warwick Vase

This 6ft/1.8m high white marble vase, dating from the 2nd century A.D., was found in pieces near Rome in 1770, bought by the Earl of Warwick and set up at Warwick Castle in 1774. Its beautiful classical shape was widely copied by silversmiths for ice buckets, (4), tureens and centerpieces.

▼ **MID-VICTORIAN LIQUEUR SET**
A parcel-gilt mounted pitcher in the form of a raven with a detachable head, dating from 1871–72, is surrounded by 12 glasses in parcel-gilt oak-leaf and acorn-cup holders. The oak tree motif is repeated in the silver mounts and handles of the oak tray.
H pitcher 8½in/21cm; L tray 19in/48cm

1 PAIR OF GEORGE II BEER PITCHERS
Pear-shaped bodies were common on pitchers of the first half of the 18th century. These beer pitchers (1733) have scroll handles, a short curved spout and a hinged, domed cover and are engraved with a contemporary coat-of-arms within a rococo cartouche. H 10½in/26cm

2 WINE LABELS
Although it is earlier (1790), the label on the right is, unusually, of a simple oblong shape. The cartouche-shaped label dates from 1820. W 1½in/4cm

3 GEORGE III WINE COASTERS
Bottles or decanters were placed on coasters to prevent furniture from being marked by wine stains. This set, with lobed sides and gadroon and shell rims, was made by Paul Storr in 1810 when he worked for Rundell, Bridge & Rundell. Diam. 7in/18cm

4 WARWICK VASE ICE BUCKET
Made by Paul Storr in 1814, this magnificent ice bucket has a detachable circular dish inside and stands on a square base. The body is cast silver-gilt applied with masks, lions' pelts, trailing vines and other foliage. The handles, too, are vines, a theme continued on the dish. H 10in/25cm

5 REGENCY WINE FUNNEL
Many funnels had pierced bowls for removing pieces of cork, and some had a detachable rim to hold a piece of cheesecloth to filter sediment. This funnel, made by William Bateman in 1815, has a broken stem. H 6in/15cm

6 VICTORIAN PARCEL-GILT CLARET JUG
Vine tendrils decorate the handle and base of this unusual hexagonal jug by Joseph Angell (1856). The detachable trellis of vines on the body is adorned with bacchante, followers of the wine god Bacchus, who are harvesting the grapes for wine-making. H 10in/25cm

7 EDWARDIAN SILVER HIP FLASK
This flask is slightly curved so that it sits better next to the body. The lid is hinged, although many flasks had a screw cap, or even a detachable cup, to make drinking easier. H 6in/15cm

8 SILVER-MOUNTED WOODEN MAZER
A maple bowl with silver rim and foot mounts, made by Omar Ramsden in 1931 in the style of a medieval mazer, or drinking bowl. Diam. 9in/23cm

TEA SETS

Introduced into Europe in 1610 by the Dutch East India Company, tea was an expensive commodity which gained favor only gradually. The earliest surviving teapots, dating from the 1670s, were small.

As tea drinking grew in popularity, larger teapots, whose shapes followed the current fashion, were made. Pear-shaped teapots were common until the octagonal form came into vogue, c.1720; it was soon followed by the globular, or bullet, shape. The drum shape was fashionable from 1770 until it gave way to the oval shape, which was, in turn, superseded by the square shape in the early 1800s.

During the 1700s, tea sets were built up piecemeal, and it was not until late in the century, when tea had become cheaper, that the demand grew for full tea sets, including cream pitchers, sugar bowls, hot water kettles and tea caddies. In Victorian times, ornate silver tea sets were regarded as highly desirable, and they were copied in both silver plate and Britannia metal.

▼ **EARLY GERMAN SILVER-GILT TEAPOT**
Just as tea came from China, so the inspiration for teapots came from Chinese hexagonal wine pots. Made c.1690 in Augsburg by Matthäus Baur II, this teapot is one of the earliest examples. The exotic nature of tea, and the preoccupation at the time with all things Turkish, explain the engraving on the teapot. This shows three Turkish sultans alternating with three "winged Hussars," horsemen who had helped end the Turkish siege of Vienna in 1683. H 18in/46cm

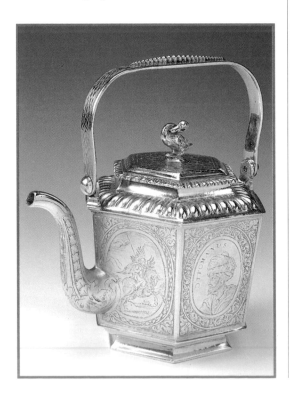

SAMOVARS AND URNS

Vessels to heat water were a necessity in houses where the kitchen and formal rooms were some distance apart. Russian samovars used hot charcoal dropped down the open funnel to heat the water, while urns, more popular in Britain, used a heated iron core or alcohol burner.

Typical Russian samovar
early 19th century

Globular urn with alcohol burner
early 19th century

Globular urn with iron ring
early 19th century

Pear-shaped rococo-style urn
mid-19th century

Britannia standard
A standard silver content of 95.8%, known as the Britannia standard (**1**), was made compulsory on silverware produced in Britain between 1697 and 1720. It was introduced to deter silversmiths from melting down coins to make household silver.

Britannia metal
An alloy of copper, tin and antimony that resembles pewter, Britannia metal was developed c.1770 in Sheffield. From the 1840s onward, it was used as a base for some electroplated pieces that were mass produced in both Britain and America. Marked EPBM (electroplated Britannia metal), these items were intended for the lower end of the market and were softer than pieces with a nickel base, called EPNS (electroplated nickel silver).

Bright-cut engraving
A form of engraved decoration – usually festoons, husks and flowers – in vogue in the late 1700s in Britain, America (**5**) and Scandinavia. The pattern was gouged out with a double-edged tool, or graver, which burnished the silver on one side of the incision as it cut, making the pattern stand out.

1 GEORGE I OCTAGONAL TEAPOT
With a spreading molded foot, faceted curved spout and domed cover with baluster finial, this teapot by Peter Archambo is a good example of a style popular in 1710–25. The Britannia standard mark guarantees the purity of the silver. H 6in/15cm

2 GEORGE II SCOTTISH TEA SERVICE
Rounder than English versions, this globular teapot has an angular spout and spreading domed foot. Included in the tea service, by William Aytoum of Edinburgh (1733), is a circular stand, sugar bowl and helmet-shaped cream pitcher. H teapot 6½in/16cm

3 TEA KETTLE, STAND AND TRAY
Similar in outline to contemporary teapots, this ornate kettle (1738) is decorated in the early rococo style. Resting on a four-legged stand and incorporating a burner to keep the water hot, it sits on its own shaped triangular tray with three leaf-capped scroll feet. H 14in/36cm

4 FINE AMERICAN TEAPOT
Marked "S:J", this teapot was made c.1765 in New York by Samuel Johnson, a member of the Gold and Silversmiths' Society. The inverted pear-shape was popular in America in the mid-18th century. L 10in/25cm

5 AMERICAN TEAPOT AND STAND
This fluted oval teapot with bright-cut decoration was made in Boston by Paul Revere, Jr., c.1790. The shape and decoration are similar to those found in England at the same date. H 6in x L 7½in; H 15cm x L 19cm

6 PART OF A GEORGE III TEA SET
Each piece of this set is decorated in neoclassical style with fluted corners, reeded borders and bands of vermicule engraving (a mass of worm-like lines). The set was made during the 1790s by Peter and Ann Bateman. H teapot 9in/23cm

7 EDWARDIAN TEA SET
Elegant chased decoration of this type is typical of pieces from the early 20th century. Both teapot and hot water pitcher have carved ebonized handles.

8 IRISH ROCOCO REVIVAL TEA SET
This tea set (1915) reproduces an exuberant style popular in Victorian times, although the decoration here is rather overdone. H teapot 6in/15cm

COFFEE SETS

Like tea, coffee came to England in the seventeenth century. The first coffee house had opened in London by c.1652 and in the American colonies, in Boston, by 1670.

Coffee pots were always taller than those used for tea, since it was necessary for the spout to be clear of the coffee grounds at the bottom of the pot. Early eighteenth-century English pots were cylindrical in shape, although the octagonal form was also favored. The lids on these early coffee pots were usually quite high-domed, but by c.1725 a flattened dome shape had become more general. After c.1730, the baluster-shaped coffee pot became popular, and it remained so until late in the century, when it was replaced by the more classical vase shape.

Continental coffee pots had straight wooden handles set at a right angle to the spout. Their pouring lips were smaller and more suited to the thicker Turkish coffee that was commonly drunk. In the 1700s, most continental coffee pots were pear-shaped and stood on three legs, and many dating from the middle of the eighteenth century have spirally fluted decoration around the body.

English coffee pots in the early nineteenth century were squatter, but by the 1840s the pear shape had returned, and they were often made *en suite* with tea sets, when they could be used either for coffee or as hot-water pitchers. Such sets remained popular as presentation pieces into the twentieth century.

Sheffield plate

A cheaper alternative to silver, Sheffield plate (7) was discovered by a cutler, Thomas Bolsover, c.1742, but it was not developed commercially until the 1760s.

Sheffield plate was produced by fusing a sheet of silver to a copper ingot with heat. When cool, the ingot was rolled out into a sheet and the metal used in the same way as silver to make articles of all types, but far more cheaply since less silver was used. After 1770, for making objects such as bowls, where the interior was visible, the copper was sandwiched between two sheets of silver, and silver wire was soldered over the exposed edge to conceal the copper.

Sheffield plate became popular, and many fine objects, including tureens, candlesticks, epergnes and coffee pots, were made and stamped with hallmarks similar to those on silver. Quality declined after the 1830s, and in the late 1840s, Sheffield plate was gradually ousted by electroplated silver.

▼ TIFFANY TEA AND COFFEE SET
An elaborate eight-piece set, made c.1852 by John Moore of Tiffany & Co. for Mrs. William Astor, Jr., a leading New York socialite. The body and domed covers are flamboyantly decorated with repoussé and chased grape vines in the prevailing Rococo Revival style, and the handles and spouts are also in the form of vines. H kettle on stand 17in/43cm

1 QUEEN ANNE COFFEE POT
The octagonal shape was popular for English coffee pots c.1710–25. This tapering pot with a domed hinged cover was made by John Read in 1711. The swan-neck handle is set at a right angle to the spout, a feature that had disappeared in Britain by 1730. H 7in/18cm

2 GEORGE I COFFEE POT
The handle on this pot by John Bache (1724) is, conventionally, opposite the spout, which has a duck's-head terminal, a device introduced c.1710. The coat-of-arms is a later addition. H 11in/28cm

3 BELGIAN COFFEE POT
A pear-shaped body with chased spiral fluting was popular in the rococo period. The domed hinged cover of this typical coffee pot, made in 1753 in Mons, is detachable, which suggests that it might have been used for chocolate as well. H 12in/30cm

4 FRENCH COFFEE POT
Made by the great French silversmith François-Thomas Germain in 1756, this rococo coffee pot has a typically European straight-sided handle. The decoration includes coffee berries and leaves on the spout, handle and finial.

5 GEORGE II COFFEE POT
Although this pot was made by John Swift in London (1758), it could at first glance be Irish because the cast and chased decoration covers the entire pear-shaped body. English pots of this date were normally decorated only at top and bottom. H 12in/30cm

6 COFFEE AND TEA SET
The Rococo Revival style of this set, made by Benoni Stephens between 1835 and 1839, was popular in the early 19th century. H kettle on stand 18in/48cm

7 SHEFFIELD PLATE COFFEE POT
This baluster-form coffee pot (c.1775), with rococo-style cast spout, clearly shows the roll-over edge construction both inside the lid and on the underside of the base. H 11in/28cm

8 DANISH COFFEE SET
A three-piece set with ivory handles, made c.1930 by Georg Jensen to a 1906 design. It epitomizes the simple, uncluttered lines favored by Jensen. H coffee pot 6½in/17cm

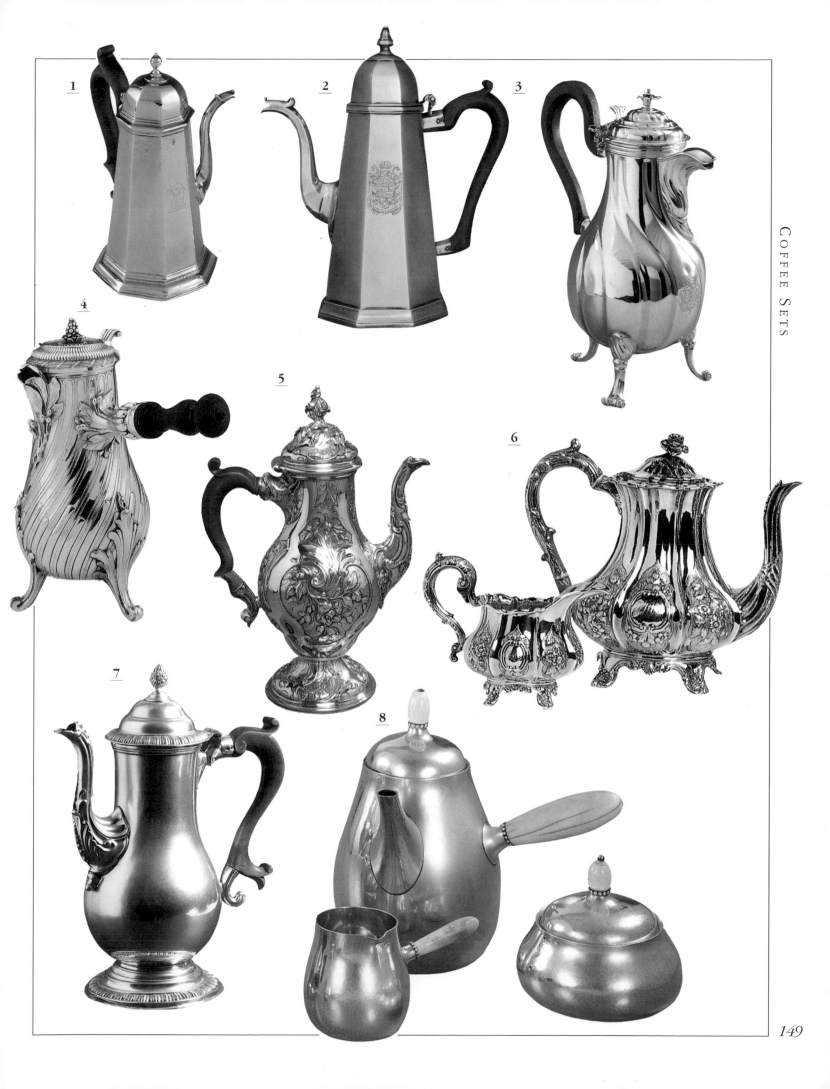

CHOCOLATE POTS AND TEA ACCESSORIES

Just as the drinking of tea and coffee developed during the seventeenth century, so did the drinking of chocolate. Seventeenth- and eighteenth-century chocolate and coffee pots were similar in both form and decoration, but with one major difference. The finial on the lids of chocolate pots was either removable or was part of a small hinged cover that formed part of the main lid. This was designed so that a rod, or molinet, could be inserted into the pot to stir the chocolate, so that it was evenly distributed before pouring.

Tea was expensive when introduced in the early 1600s and so was used sparingly. It was kept in caddies, a name derived from *kati*, the Malaysian word for the containers, holding just over 1lb/550g, in which tea was first shipped. In the early 1700s, caddies had a sliding top or bottom allowing a lead liner to be fitted, which kept the tea fresh.

Since both black and green tea were used in the 1700s, caddies were usually made in pairs or threes, sometimes with a matching box or covered bowl for storing sugar. These sets were often kept in special wooden boxes and might also have included a caddy spoon, sugar tongs, or nips, and teaspoons. After the 1750s, as tea became cheaper, larger tea caddies were made, and by the century's end, pairs had been replaced by single, often oval, caddies. In the 1800s, caddies were made in silver and a variety of other materials.

CADDY SPOONS

Introduced in the mid-18th century, caddy spoons and shovels were ornately decorated and made in many shapes. Early examples had a shell-shaped bowl, probably because shells were included in tea chests to enable buyers to sample the tea, while the bowls of later pieces include those shaped like an acorn, a leaf, a horse's hoof or an eagle's head.

▼ SET OF GEORGE III TEA CADDIES AND BOX

Based on a 1751 design by Paul de Lamerie and made by Frederick Vonham in 1763, the three caddies are decorated with chinoiserie scenes of tea-picking enclosed in shell and scroll borders with lions' masks and topped with flower finials. The original silver-mounted shagreen box also contains 12 teaspoons, with leaf-shaped bowls, and a pair of matching sugar tongs.

1 QUEEN ANNE CHOCOLATE POT
Made by Gabriel Sleath in 1709, this tapering cylindrical pot is typical of the period. It has a detachable domed cover in the lid, and the handle is set at a right angle to the spout. H 10in/25cm

2 PROVINCIAL CHOCOLATE POT
Probably made by the Plymouth silversmith John Boutet, this chocolate pot (1741) has the bell-shaped finial removed from the hinged lid to show where the stirring rod would have been inserted. H 9½in/24cm

3 GEORGE I SUGAR BOX
Sugar boxes were first used in the 17th century. This 1716 example is in the octagonal shape favored by many silversmiths in the Queen Anne and early Georgian periods. L 5in/13cm

4 THREE GEORGIAN SUGAR BOWLS
The sugar bowl on the left, of Irish manufacture, dates from 1717. The English bowls on the right are from 1728 (front) and 1730. The cover was used as a tray for teaspoons when tea was taken. H 3½–4in/9–10cm

5 "TEA-CHEST" STYLE TEA CADDY
A rare caddy (1778) with lock and key, engraved with chinoiserie scenes based on the designs of Jean Pillement, a French engraver. H 3½in/9cm

6 SUGAR TONGS
Early sugar tongs were scissor-shaped and derived from fire tongs. The spring-style handles of these U-shaped tongs indicate they were made after 1775.

7 CADDY SPOONS
These large-bowled spoons (1830–39) show the King's (top) and Queen's flatware patterns. Most caddy spoons had short handles so they could be kept in the caddy. L 4in, 5in; L 10cm, 12cm

8 TEA INFUSERS
Forerunners of the tea bag on a string, infusers on chains and infusing spoons were common from c.1890. They were usually egg-shaped, although some were made in the shape of a teapot.

9 VICTORIAN TEA STRAINER
Spoon strainers were used during the 18th century, but they were small and clogged up quickly. In the late 1800s, the tea strainer as it is known today began to be made in the Netherlands and Germany. This strainer and stand are in the Rococo Revival style.

DISPLAY SILVER

Silver has always been regarded as a sign of affluence, and from medieval times it became customary for the wealthy to possess ornamental silver objects purely for display. Among such items were large decorated circular or oval dishes which, although their popularity waned in the early eighteenth century, came back into fashion during the nineteenth.

Vases were introduced into England from the Netherlands in the 1660s. They were usually made in sets, or garnitures, for the mantelpiece resembling contemporary porcelain models, which included ginger jars with covers, as well as flower vases. Reproductions of these sets were made in the 1800s. Two-handled cups, which evolved from the porringer and cover in the late 1600s and were often quite large, were found in Britain until the mid-1800s.

From the middle of the seventeenth century, all over Europe, the fashionable gift to a bride from her groom was a toilette set, which might consist of up to 30 items, including a mirror on an easel frame. Many such sets have been broken up over the years, but occasionally a full one is found. Dressing-table sets, as they are known today, first appeared in the mid-1800s.

Cut-card work
This name is given to a form of decoration often used by Huguenot silversmiths in the late 17th and early 18th centuries. Thin, flat sheets of silver were cut out in simple patterns, usually of foliage or scrollwork, and then soldered onto the surface they were to decorate. Examples of such cut-card work can be seen around the lower body and neck of Pilgrim bottles (7).

Paul de Lamerie
A famous silversmith of Huguenot origin, Paul de Lamerie (1688–1751) was apprenticed to Pierre Platel, another renowned Huguenot silversmith. In 1713 de Lamerie registered his maker's mark. His early work (3) was in Queen Anne and *Régence* style, and until 1733 he worked in the Britannia standard. He is well known for his rococo silver with beautiful cast decoration (*see pp.132, 134*).

◀ **CHARLES II TOILETTE SET**
The covers of the chest and boxes in this magnificent toilette set are chased in high relief with scenes depicting the classical ideal of Love.

Cupid is shown gazing at his reflection in a pool of water, and Paris appears both with Diana and at his first meeting with Helen. On the perfume flasks, hairbrush and pincushion there are other classical motifs – putti, scrolling foliage, acanthus leaves and swags of fruit – while the cresting on the mirror shows the courtship of the goddess Pomona.

With the exception of the pincushion, which dates from 1698, all the pieces were made in 1675 and 1676 by Jacob Bodendick and Robert Cooper. H mirror 29½in/75cm; L chest 9½in/24cm

1 CHARLES II SILVER-GILT VASES
A pair of baluster vases (c.1670), with waisted necks and domed covers, chased with acanthus leaves, fruit and ribbons. They would probably have been part of a garniture for a mantelpiece. H 13in/33cm

2 TOILETTE BOWLS AND EWER
Originally part of a toilette service, these pieces, (c.1700) can be attributed to a Huguenot silversmith, probably Pierre Harache. The bowls and covers are particularly French in style, and the strapwork and engraving on the ewer are similar to that found on silver bearing his mark. H ewer 7in/18cm; H bowls 4½in/11cm

3 TWO-HANDLED CUP AND COVER
This piece, dated 1717, was made by Paul de Lamerie. The inverted bell-shaped body and domed cover with a baluster finial are typical of English silver in the early 18th century. The engraved coat-of-arms is set within a baroque cartouche. H 12½in/32cm

4 SILVER-GILT CUP AND COVER
A cup and cover in campana, or inverted bell, shape made by Robert Garrard as a yachting trophy. It was awarded to Joseph Weld, one of the greatest yachtsmen of the early 19th century, by Britain's Royal Yacht Club for racing successes in 1826. The nautical decoration includes sailors, dolphins and corals. H 15in/38cm

5 EARLY VICTORIAN DISH
This large dish, with a central plaque of a Muse and a lioness within borders of flowers and acanthus leaves, dates from 1839. It is a good example of the type of dish displayed on sideboards. Diam. 20½in/52cm

6 VICTORIAN GARNITURE
This set of a ginger jar and matching vases, from 1856, is a 19th-century reproduction of the garnitures found in the late 17th century. It copies their decoration of fruit swags and acanthus leaves. H jar 28in/71cm

7 LATE VICTORIAN PILGRIM BOTTLE
Large silver Pilgrim bottles were made from the mid-1500s to the early 1700s as decorative pieces. One of a pair, this reproduction flask was made in 1893 and given to Prince Alexander of Teck on his marriage in 1904. The name derives from the flasks carried by medieval pilgrims. H 21in/54cm

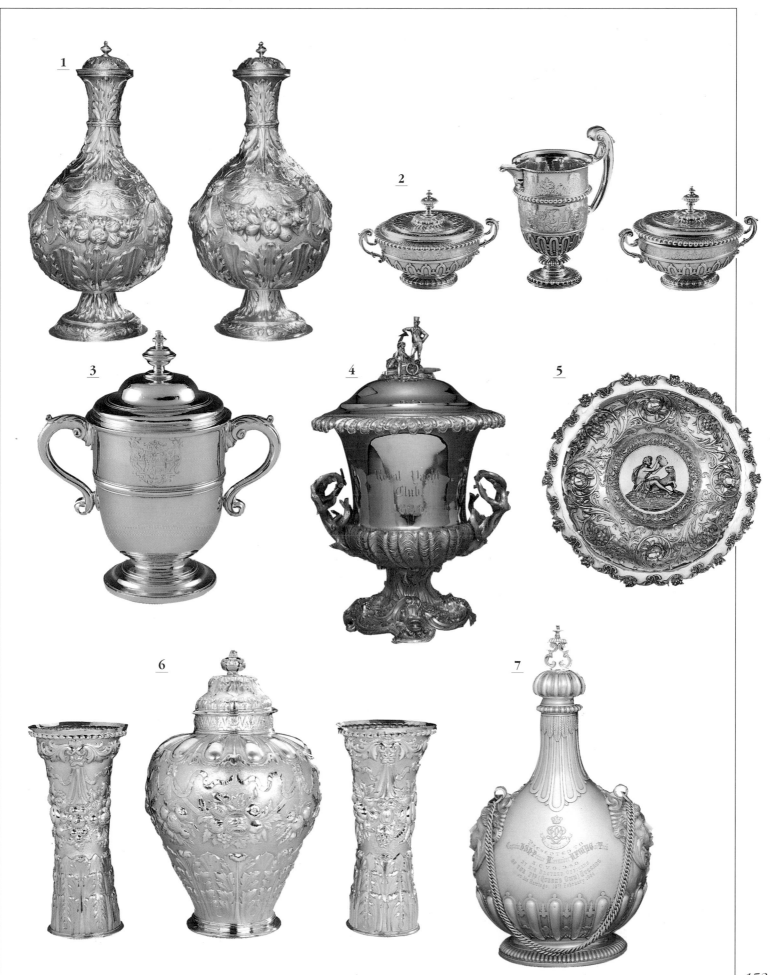

◄ **GEORGE III COMMUNION SET**
Made in 1786 by William Pitts for the Governor of Bermuda, this set includes two flagons with domed hinged lids, bell-shaped chalice, paten (receptacle for the priest's wafer), and tazza, each of which is engraved with the sacred monogram IHS. The flagons also bear the royal arms on the lids. The pieces are in fine condition, with marks of burnishing tools clearly visible. H flagon 11½in/29cm

Church plate has been made since Christianity became the official religion of the Roman Empire under Constantine the Great. Throughout the Middle Ages, articles for religious use were the mainstay of the silversmith's craft. The leading designers from c.1200 to c.1400 were French silversmiths, much of whose work was inspired by the great abbeys and churches that were being built in the gothic style. And architectural elements, such as spires, tracery or the figures of saints, were incorporated in their designs, whether for a reliquary, pyx, or bishop's crozier.

Silver objects were often decorated with enamels, depicting religious scenes, and jewels. In thanksgiving for answered prayers, it was customary for the wealthy to give gifts of jewelry, which was melted down and made into religious pieces in which the jewels were set. Much church plate and many a saint's shrine were thus enriched.

After the Reformation, plate suitable for the new forms of service was produced in England, often by local silversmiths. Communion cups were made with larger bowls than those of Catholic chalices, and by Victorian times, silversmiths were making Gothic Revival communion sets to match the fashionable church architectural style of the day. The Reformed Church in Scotland, America and Scandinavia sometimes used silver beakers for communion wine.

Although nothing survives from before the Middle Ages, Jewish religious objects have been made since Old Testament times, for ceremonies both at home and in the synagogue.

IHS

This sacred monogram (*above*), found on religious plate, is normally understood to represent the first three letters of Jesus' name in Greek. It can, however, also be interpreted as standing for the Latin phrase *In Hoc Signo Vinces*, "With this sign you shall conquer."

Gothic Revival

In 19th-century Britain, there was a renewed interest in gothic art, and most churches built from the 1830s onward were built in this style. A.W.N. Pugin (*see p.178*) produced designs for church plate, as did the architect and designer William Burges (1827–81) later in the century. While some church plate shows a genuine attempt to reproduce medieval originals, other pieces were a typical Victorian concoction of gothic details and decoration.

1 ELIZABETHAN CHALICE AND PATEN
When inverted, the domed lid of this communion cup forms a paten; the tapering cylindrical body is typical of cups made after the Reformation. The ornamentation consists only of an engraved band of arabesques on both cup and cover: sacred monograms or symbols were not used at this time. H 8in/20cm

2 SICILIAN CHALICE
The chased and applied decoration on the foot, stem and lower part of the bowl of this chalice (c.1700) is in the typical baroque style of the period. Similar examples can be found in other Latin countries. H 10½in/26cm

3 GERMAN COMMUNION PLATE
This silver-gilt communion plate, made in Berlin by Otto Männlich c.1710, was given to the Evangelical Reformed Church of Neubolland by Frederick I of Prussia and bears his cypher. H 9½in/24cm

4 PORTUGUESE SANCTUARY LAMP
Sanctuary lamps, such as this (c.1880), are found in Catholic churches all over Europe; when lit, they denote the presence of the consecrated Sacrament in the Tabernacle. H 4ft/1.2m

5 HANUKKAH LAMP
The main feature of the Jewish festival of Hanukkah, which commemorates the rededication of the Temple after its recapture from the Syrians c.164 B.C., is the lighting of a lamp each day until eight are lit. On this European example (c.1900), lions with hinged heads form the lamps. The oil jug and "servant" light, from which the others are lit, are detachable. H 11½in/29cm

6 SILVER KIDDUSH CUPS
In Jewish homes, it is customary for the head of the household to say a prayer or "kiddush" over a cup of wine at the start of the Sabbath. Both of these cups are of typical octagonal form and bear Hebrew inscriptions. Left: *cup made in Augsburg by Hieronymous Mittnacht, in 1761–65*; right: *cup made in Nuremberg in the mid-1800s.* H 4½in, 5in; H 11cm, 13cm

7 ENAMELLED SILVER-GILT PYX
A pyx is used to carry consecrated wafers to the sick. The body and hinged lid of this pyx, made in London in 1910 by the firm of Barkentine & Krall, is decorated in the gothic style with ropework and foliage scrolls on a deep blue enamel ground. L 5½in/14cm

8 SILVER-GILT CIBORIUM
This ciborium (1911), used to hold communion wafers, is from the same set as the pyx (7). The chased and enameled base, with inset turquoise, coral, amethysts and other semi-precious stones, was inspired by William Burges's designs. H 11in/28cm

SMALL SILVER

In addition to their use for grand, important pieces, silver was also employed to make small everyday items and gifts. Children's rattles with coral or ivory teethers, for instance, proved popular as christening gifts from the sixteenth century onward, and their design changed little until the beginning of the twentieth century, when teething rings became more common. Another type of gift, favored from the seventeenth century, was the silver box, often engraved with initials, inscriptions or historic scenes.

In the late 1600s, in an attempt by men and women of quality to combat the stench of filthy streets and open sewers, vinaigrettes were introduced. These were small containers of precious metal, usually silver, in which a small piece of sponge soaked in spiced vinegar was kept behind a pierced cover. Early examples were flask-shaped, but by the beginning of the 1800s, the shape had changed to a small box with a flip-up lid. Vinaigrettes had become less fashionable by the middle of the century and were replaced by a double-ended flask with a perfume container at one end and a vinaigrette at the other.

Match cases, which first appeared in the 1830s, were designed to hold the small matches known as vestas. They became a fashionable accouterment for gentlemen and were made in a variety of shapes, including many novelty ones.

Points to note

On rattles, the hallmark is usually found where the teether and rattle join, with the maker's mark beneath the whistle. On vinaigrettes the lid, grill and base should all be marked.

Matting

The term describes the punching of the surface of silver with dots or circles to produce a dull, or matte, background, so providing a contrast to the polished areas on a piece. Matting was also used to form a background to other forms of ornamentation, such as stamped decoration (3). This form of embellishment was frequently found in both England and Germany during the 17th century.

1 GEORGE III HONEYPOT AND COVER
One of a pair made by Paul Storr in 1797 in the form of a bee skep, or wicker beehive, with a clear glass liner. The stand has a neoclassical type reed-and-tie border. H 4½in/11cm

2 CHILD'S SILVER-GILT RATTLE
Although the shape of this rattle (1860), with a whistle, bells and coral teether, is traditional, such rattles were usually made in silver and were considerably smaller. Mother-of-pearl and ivory were more commonly used for teethers in the early 20th century. L 7in/18cm

3 TRINKET BOX
This little box, dating from 1895, would have been made as part of a dressing-table set. It has stamped rococo-style swags and scrollwork decoration on a matted ground and a gilded interior. L 3½in/9cm

4 FRENCH CIGARETTE BOX
Cigarette boxes in silver and gold, often inset with semiprecious stones, were popular in fashionable society in the interwar years. This box, in silver, lapis lazuli and glass was made by Cartier in 1930. L 7in/18cm

5 AGATE VINAIGRETTE
Made from 25 pieces of variously colored agate and mounted with silver-gilt, this 19th-century vinaigrette is probably of Scottish origin. H 3in/8cm

6 PERFUME BOTTLE WITH VINAIGRETTE
Made in 1871, this ruby glass perfume bottle, mounted in silver-gilt, has a base that hinges open to reveal a vinaigrette. Such bottles were fitted with a loop and could be hung from a lady's belt. L 4½in/11cm

7 "NELSON" VINAIGRETTE
A rare, silver-gilt example celebrating Admiral Nelson's victory at Trafalgar in 1805. The cover is engraved with a bust of Nelson, and the cast and pierced grill inside depicts Nelson's ship, HMS Victory. L 1½in/4cm

8 19TH-CENTURY VINAIGRETTES
This group shows how the decoration of box-shaped vinaigrettes became more elaborate as the century progressed. Left to right: Silver-gilt box embossed with grapes and vine leaves (1814); silver example by the renowned maker Nathaniel Mills (1848), with a scene of London engraved on the lid and a silver-gilt grill; engraved box with an inset cameo of a country scene (1853). L 1½–2in/3–5cm

9 LATE 19TH-CENTURY MATCH CASES
The ornate bright-cut engraving is typical of the period (1860–1910). All three have a ridged striker on the base and a small hole at the top left corner to hold a lighted match for melting sealing wax. L 1½–2in/3–5cm

10 SILVER PINCUSHION
Pigs are a popular animal design; this silver pincushion, made in 1909 in Birmingham, has a velvet back in which to stick the pins. H 1½in/3cm

◀ **DUTCH MARRIAGE CASKET**
Silver boxes have been perennially popular as love tokens. Among the earliest such boxes are the rather rare little Dutch marriage caskets made in the 16th and 17th centuries. As on this example, dating from 1630, they are often engraved with scrolling foliage and cartouches containing pictures of courting couples and romantic scenes. L 3in/8cm

CHAPTER FOUR

FURNITURE

Over many centuries, furniture has evolved as a decorative art form. Its development provides a social history, for changes in living patterns have led to the demand for new types of furniture, the chest of drawers or the bureau, for instance, in the 1700s, the golden age of letter writing. The style and decoration reflected the age in which furniture was made, and apart from the more grandiose pieces designed for palaces and great houses, most followed the precepts of designer George Hepplewhite, who wrote in 1788 that furniture should "unite elegance and utility and blend the useful with the agreeable."

Many of the examples of the different types of furniture discussed in this chapter are of British origin. There are several valid reasons for this. When compared with mainland Europe, England has, since its Civil Wars of 1642–51, enjoyed political stability, with no revolutions or land wars on its soil to destroy homes and their contents.

In the seventeenth and eighteenth centuries, the growth of the middle class, as a result of economic prosperity, led to a demand for the fashionable furniture of the day. This meant that large quantities of furniture were produced, much of which survives. The English aristocracy did not appreciate the lackluster courts of the Hanoverian Georges and so lived on their estates in great style, often refurbishing their houses in the prevailing fashion. In this way, new concepts in furniture design reached the countryside from the city, and country furniture was produced in simplified versions of these styles.

English designs, as well as furniture that was exported, were popular in many other European countries. Even France, whose styles strongly influenced furniture design throughout Europe in the eighteenth century, followed the English taste during the time of Louis XVI (1774–93). European craftsmen, such as Abraham Roentgen (1711–93), whose son David was cabinetmaker to the French and Russian courts, and Georg Haupt, the leading Swedish cabinetmaker during the late 1700s, came to England to work for a time before returning to their own countries. Such migration was not unusual: many of the most prominent cabinetmakers in Paris in the eighteenth century were of foreign extraction.

The English influence spread also to Britain's colonies, notably America, where cabinetmakers used English designs throughout the eighteenth century, although they also looked to France for inspiration during the Federal period, in the late eighteenth and early nineteenth centuries.

Antique furniture is popular with collectors because it is functional and because, with reasonable care, it is sturdy enough for everyday use. These pages are devoted largely to furniture made from the mid-seventeenth century on, since these pieces are most likely to be found on the market today, and the way in which styles have developed and influenced succeeding styles is considered. The basics of construction, and the various characteristics of the different periods, are discussed both in the introductory pages and when considering individual examples of furniture types. These factors need to be understood for a true appreciation of antique furniture, and the knowledge will enhance the enjoyment to be gained from studying and collecting the furniture of our forebears.

▶ **CHIPPENDALE BREAKFRONT LIBRARY BOOKCASE**
Known as the Messer bookcase, after its one-time owner Samuel Messer, this mahogany bookcase is a masterpiece of the neoclassical style that became fashionable in Europe from the 1760s. It is attributed to Thomas Chippendale, and both the design and construction testify to the quality of his work.

The entire piece is inlaid with ebony, from the elegant scrolled pediment with a central plinth for a bust or vase, through the foliate scrolls at the corners of the glazed doors, to the four long drawers and side cabinets. The top drawer is fitted with a baize-lined sloping easel or bookrest, which is raised by a double ratchet. H 8ft 3in x W 6ft 7in; H 2.51m x W 2m

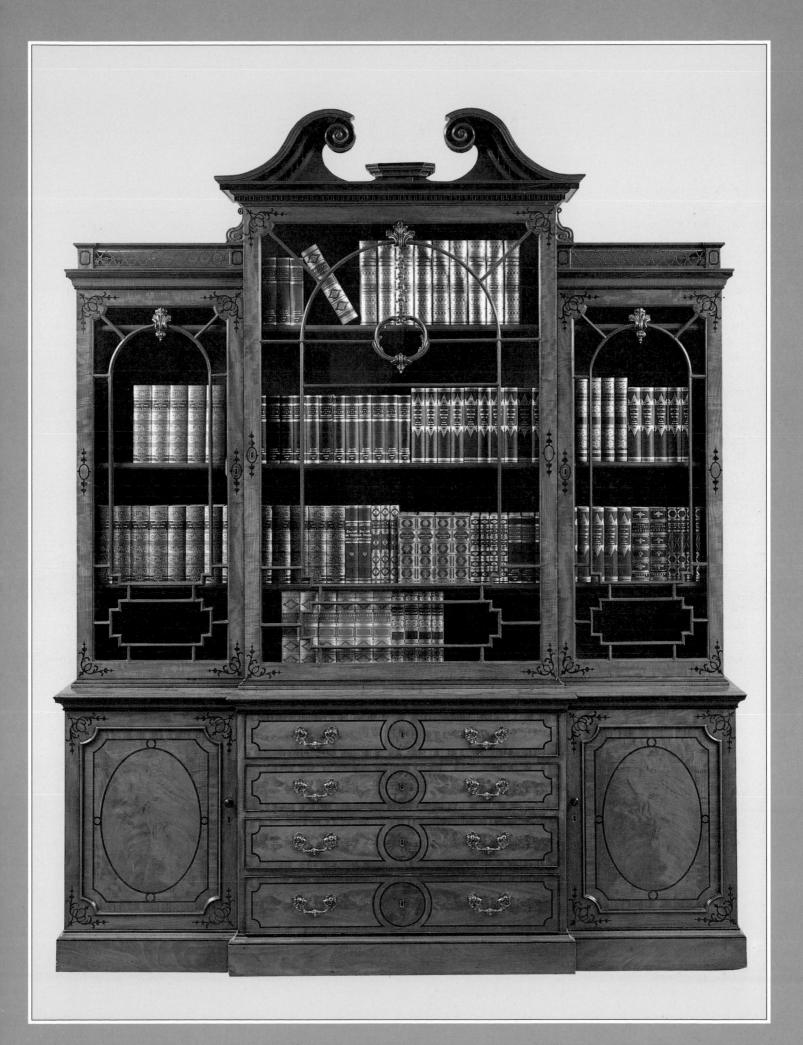

Cabinetmakers and Designers

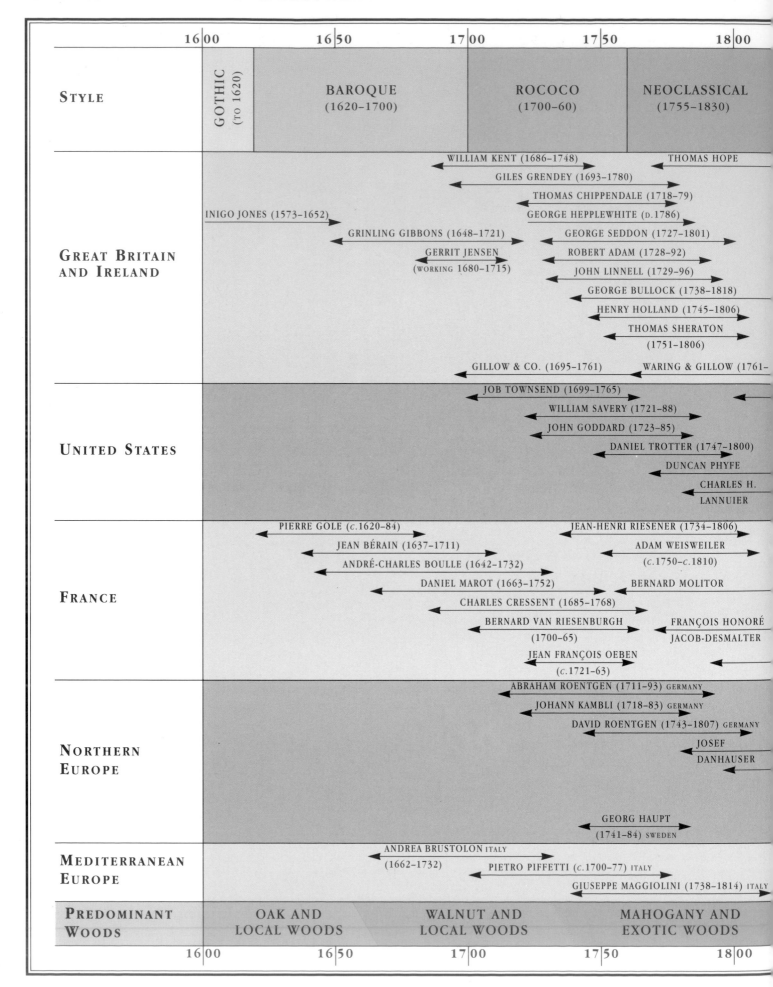

	16|00	16|50	17|00	17|50	18|00
Style	GOTHIC (TO 1620)	BAROQUE (1620–1700)		ROCOCO (1700–60)	NEOCLASSICAL (1755–1830)

Great Britain and Ireland

WILLIAM KENT (1686–1748)
THOMAS HOPE
GILES GRENDEY (1693–1780)
THOMAS CHIPPENDALE (1718–79)
INIGO JONES (1573–1652)
GEORGE HEPPLEWHITE (D.1786)
GRINLING GIBBONS (1648–1721)
GEORGE SEDDON (1727–1801)
GERRIT JENSEN
ROBERT ADAM (1728–92)
(WORKING 1680–1715)
JOHN LINNELL (1729–96)
GEORGE BULLOCK (1738–1818)
HENRY HOLLAND (1745–1806)
THOMAS SHERATON (1751–1806)
GILLOW & CO. (1695–1761)
WARING & GILLOW (1761–

United States

JOB TOWNSEND (1699–1765)
WILLIAM SAVERY (1721–88)
JOHN GODDARD (1723–85)
DANIEL TROTTER (1747–1800)
DUNCAN PHYFE
CHARLES H. LANNUIER

France

PIERRE GOLE (c.1620–84)
JEAN-HENRI RIESENER (1734–1806)
JEAN BÉRAIN (1637–1711)
ADAM WEISWEILER
ANDRÉ-CHARLES BOULLE (1642–1732)
(c.1750–c.1810)
DANIEL MAROT (1663–1752)
BERNARD MOLITOR
CHARLES CRESSENT (1685–1768)
BERNARD VAN RIESENBURGH
FRANÇOIS HONORÉ
(1700–65)
JACOB-DESMALTER
JEAN FRANÇOIS OEBEN
(c.1721–63)

Northern Europe

ABRAHAM ROENTGEN (1711–93) GERMANY
JOHANN KAMBLI (1718–83) GERMANY
DAVID ROENTGEN (1743–1807) GERMANY
JOSEF DANHAUSER
GEORG HAUPT (1741–84) SWEDEN

Mediterranean Europe

ANDREA BRUSTOLON ITALY
(1662–1732)
PIETRO PIFFETTI (c.1700–77) ITALY
GIUSEPPE MAGGIOLINI (1738–1814) ITALY

Predominant Woods	OAK AND LOCAL WOODS		WALNUT AND LOCAL WOODS		MAHOGANY AND EXOTIC WOODS

	16|00	16|50	17|00	17|50	18|00

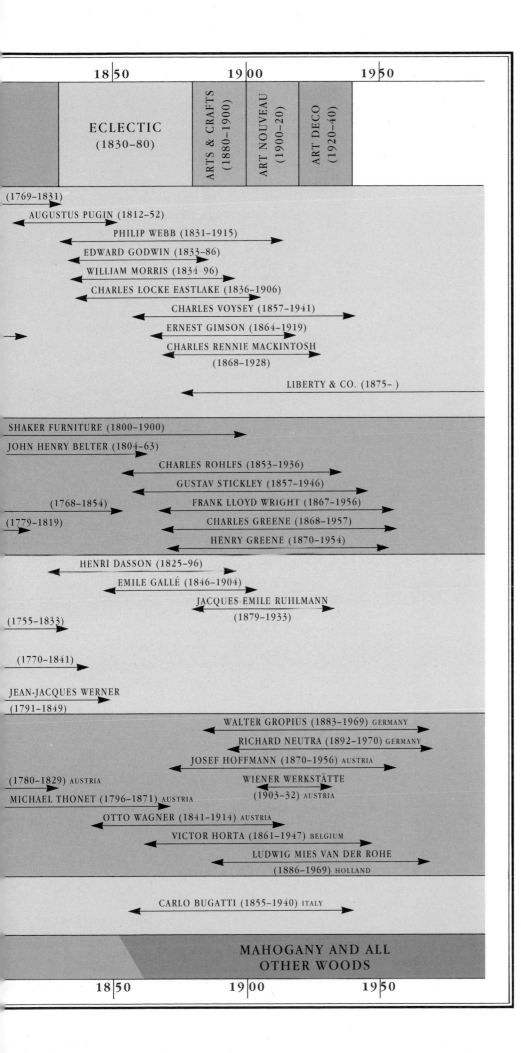

The names of the major furniture makers and designers of Europe and the United States, and the styles predominant at the time they were working, are combined on this chart. It may be useful to compare this chart of the makers with the general Periods and Styles chart (*see pp.10–11*), which gives more detail about particular countries and regions.

The color bands for the styles, including baroque, rococo and neoclassical, allow those people who dominated the design and manufacture of furniture to be placed within an historical and stylistic context.

The band at the bottom, which shows the woods favored at different periods, demonstrates that the changeover between the use of wood was a fairly gradual process which varied from country to country.

Evidence of furniture styles in ancient Egypt, Greece and Rome can be gleaned from excavated funerary objects, pottery, sculpture and wall paintings. Some of these styles have continued over the ages or have been resurrected from time to time. The X-shaped folding stool from Egypt, for instance, spread to ancient Greece and Rome, appeared in medieval times and was translated into the X-shaped chair. Later, Renaissance and neo-classical styles, in particular, drew on early models.

Medieval style

The medieval court and its nobles led fairly itinerant lives, so most furniture had to be portable. Some cup-boards were, however, built in, and seating was some-times incorporated into the paneling of a room. Most large tables were of trestle form, which could be dismantled and stored or transported. Chairs were few and their use denoted rank; they ranged from plank-constructed bench-types to X-shapes and turned-wood constructions.

Sideboards with stepped shelves were used to display silver in great houses, while food and drink were served from simpler pieces. Chests for storage were important items. Flat-topped chests with stile feet usually formed part of the permanent furnishing of a castle or manor house, while the domed-lid variety, without feet and often strengthened and decorated with iron, were taken from one residence to another. Richly decorated cupboards, or *armoires*, were also used for storage. Beds were status symbols, and were later canopied and hung with rich materials.

Renaissance style

This style, which originated in Italy in the thirteenth and fourteenth centuries, marked a re-emergence of classical design. Most furniture was elaborately carved, often with architectural features, and ornament incor-porated mythological creatures, cherubs, urns and the acanthus scroll. This period saw the emergence of joined furniture in northern Europe (*see p.170*).

With the rise of the printed book, new designs spread into France and also Spain – which followed its own local traditions as well. One typically Spanish piece to evolve in the 1500s was the *vargueño*, or chest-on-stand. Renaissance ideas were incorporated into cabinets in Germany and the Low Countries, and from there reached England. Marble-topped tables were popular in England, but otherwise there was no great flowering of renaissance style, although some decorative motifs appeared in carving.

Baroque style

The heavy baroque style also originated in Italy, and by the 1620s was spreading northward through Europe. Baroque furniture had an architectural quality: great wall mirrors were designed with elaborate carved and scrolling frames, and below them would be matching console tables incorporating cherubs, mythical figures or birds in their ornamentation.

Cabinets were decorated with mosaics, *pietra dura*, columns, painted panels or lacquer and stood on highly ornate carved stands; everywhere, the cabinet-on-stand was used to display the owner's valued possessions.

Although inspired by Italian design, furniture in France at the time of Louis XIV (1643–1715) was of a more classical nature, and these French styles began to influence other European countries such as Holland. In 1660, with the Restoration of Charles II, who intro-duced Dutch craftsmen, European influences began to reach England. French designs affected English furniture only after 1685, when the revocation of the Edict of Nantes brought an influx of Huguenot craftsmen.

The destruction of houses and their oak furniture in the Great Fire of London in 1666 created a market for the styles fashionable in continental Europe: glazed bookcases, wing chairs, sofas, daybeds and desks evolved to keep pace with popular demand. In country places, items of furniture developed that were to remain popular and practical forms for the following 200 years or so. Trade and exploration introduced new woods and techniques, including caning, lacquering and japanning; veneering became common and reached great heights of excellence.

▼ **QUEEN ANNE WALNUT CHAIR AND FOOTSTOOL**
This fine spoon-backed chair, with carved cabriole legs, stands in a bedroom at Packwood House, Warwickshire, England, which dates from the early 1600s and has been restored to its original state.

Rococo style

A reaction to the exuberance of the Baroque became evident in France in the late 1600s and evolved during the *Régence* period (1710–30). The full-blown Louis XV style that emerged in the 1730s spread to Italy and Germany, which made their own modifications, with a tendency toward exaggeration. In England, the simple and elegant Queen Anne furniture of the early 1700s was followed by a short-lived expression of the Rococo in Chippendale's asymmetrical carvings.

The early settlers in America took furniture with them from England. Gradually, however, the eastern states built up their own style, based on English styles, but often incorporating features that owed their origins to the ethnic mix of the early settlers.

Neoclassical style

In the 1750s, styles returned to those of Greece and Rome, with geometrical forms replacing bombé shapes and with strictly classical ornamentation, such as paterae, urns and rams' heads. In France, this move was epitomized by Transitional, Louis XVI and Directoire styles, and their influence spread throughout Europe and to America. In England, Robert Adam's neoclassical designs covered every aspect of interiors, including furniture. Chippendale and Ince and Mayhew made furniture in this style, while in the late eighteenth century, Hepplewhite and Sheraton introduced a lighter style.

▲ **VICTORIAN DRAWING ROOM**
Pieter Wonder's painting evokes the atmosphere of a typical early Victorian room, with its balloon-back chairs, table with an ornately carved pedestal, pole screen to shield the ladies' faces from the fire, and objects from around the world, such as the Chinese blue and white jar.

Nineteenth-century styles

In England, Regency styles remained largely neoclassical, but chinoiserie, French and gothic influences were also evident. Napoleon's ascendancy meant that across Europe the Empire style was copied, and American furniture of the Federal period incorporated both French Empire and English Regency motifs. In the 1840s, the Biedermeier style was popular in Austria and Germany, and in France, a simplified Empire style emerged, using light-colored woods such as maple.

One of the main features of the 1800s was the revival of older styles, among them rococo, Greek and gothic. This hodgepodge, and the growing use of machinery in furniture making, led some designers and craftsmen toward more traditional methods of construction and purer design. The Arts and Crafts Movement, which emerged in Britain and America in the late 1800s, was typical. Later, the Aesthetic Movement was influenced by Japanese design, while Art Nouveau, fashionable from the 1880s to 1914, looked to the past for inspiration or produced forward-looking styles such as those of Charles Rennie Mackintosh and the Wiener Werkstätte.

AN INTRODUCTION TO FURNITURE

To appreciate antique furniture properly, it is necessary to understand some of the fundamental aspects of its manufacture and decoration, which can also be useful indicators of age and origin.

Woods

Identifying which wood was used in the construction of a piece of furniture can be difficult, since distinguishing between types of wood is a matter of practice, and there is no real alternative to seeing and examining the woods themselves. Wood from coniferous trees is known as softwood, while that taken from deciduous trees is called hardwood.

In addition to the more common woods (*see below*), many exotic types have been used over the centuries. Some of the most popular for veneering and inlay were amboyna, a light brown East Indian wood with a speckled grain; kingwood, a purplish South American wood; and satinwood, grown in both the West and East Indies. The satinwood from the East Indies, which tended to have a less dense grain and was a slightly paler yellow, was especially favored in the late eighteenth century by English cabinetmakers.

Ash, a more common wood that resembles oak, was often used for country furniture. Softwood pine was, until the early 1900s, used for making cheaper pieces and the frames, or carcasses, of furniture.

The term "patina" describes the layers of polish, dirt and grease that build up naturally on furniture over the years, particularly in carved decoration and crevices, and give it a rich look. Patina cannot be reproduced, so if a piece of furniture has been heavily treated with wax polish and has no sign of patina, it may not be genuine.

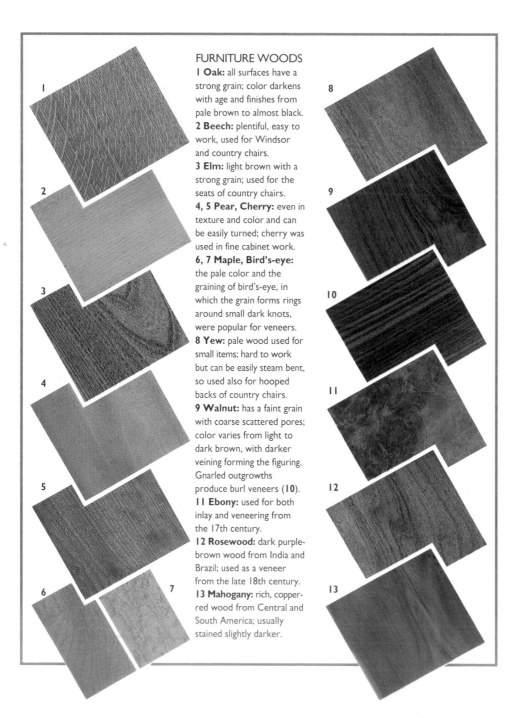

FURNITURE WOODS

1 Oak: all surfaces have a strong grain; color darkens with age and finishes from pale brown to almost black.

2 Beech: plentiful, easy to work, used for Windsor and country chairs.

3 Elm: light brown with a strong grain; used for the seats of country chairs.

4, 5 Pear, Cherry: even in texture and color and can be easily turned; cherry was used in fine cabinet work.

6, 7 Maple, Bird's-eye: the pale color and the graining of bird's-eye, in which the grain forms rings around small dark knots, were popular for veneers.

8 Yew: pale wood used for small items; hard to work but can be easily steam bent, so used also for hooped backs of country chairs.

9 Walnut: has a faint grain with coarse scattered pores; color varies from light to dark brown, with darker veining forming the figuring. Gnarled outgrowths produce burl veneers (10).

11 Ebony: used for both inlay and veneering from the 17th century.

12 Rosewood: dark purple-brown wood from India and Brazil; used as a veneer from the late 18th century.

13 Mahogany: rich, copper-red wood from Central and South America; usually stained slightly darker.

RECOGNIZING GRAIN PATTERN

Grain pattern depends on the part of the tree from which the plank is cut and the angle of the cut.

1 Quarter-sawn boards display straight-line figuring.
2 Flat-sawn lumber produces a classic contour pattern.
3 Irregular figuring is produced by the growth pattern of branches and angle cutting of the lumber.
4 Curl patterns are cut from a "Y" intersection between the trunk and a main branch.
5 Beautiful veneers can be cut from outgrowths on the main trunk.

◀ **MARQUETRY**
A highly decorative form of veneering which involved making a pattern with different colored woods. Much of the best marquetry was done by the Dutch, as this magnificent floral panel from the door of a mid-18th century bureau cabinet demonstrates.

Marquetry began to replace inlay in the early 17th century, first in Germany, then in the Low Countries and, from c.1675, in Britain and France.

The art of veneering, attaching a thin sheet of an expensive wood to a cheaper carcass, was known from the fifteenth century. Early hand-cut veneers were about ⅛in/3mm thick, but during the eighteenth century, new techniques meant that they could be cut to half that thickness. The introduction of mechanical saws in the nineteenth century allowed cheaper, paper-thin veneers to be produced. All the sheets of veneer for an item of furniture were taken from a single piece of lumber so that they matched. There was occasionally some variation in thickness, but often this was caused by shrinkage or by ordinary wear and tear.

Sheets of veneer were arranged in a variety of patterns to produce different effects, for instance butterfly or oyster veneers (*see p.214*). Thin strips of veneer were also used to trim drawers and writing desks, a technique known as banding (*see below*).

Marquetry is the art of using contrasting woods, or other materials such as ivory or bone, to make decorative patterns in a veneer. There are several styles (*see p.200*), which include swirling seaweed marquetry, floral marquetry (*see left*), and parquetry, in which the inlay is in a geometric pattern (*see p.210*). Boulle is a type of marquetry that uses brass and tortoiseshell instead of contrasting woods (*see p.218*).

To protect a piece of furniture, it was finished either with an oil polish, which turned the wood darker with oxidization, or with a mixture of beeswax and turpentine, in which the wax acted as a sealant. In the 1820s, French polish, a form of lacquer which gave a harder, shinier finish than beeswax, was introduced, and many earlier pieces were stripped and French polished.

Types of decoration

Inlay is the name given to the decorative process whereby some wood in a piece of furniture is replaced with a pattern either in wood of a contrasting color, or in metal, ivory or bone. Its most elaborate form was intarsia, an inlay of woods, usually forming a picture, displayed as part of the decoration of a door or paneling. It was popular from the Renaissance into the sixteenth century and was revived in the mid-nineteenth century to some extent.

Lacquering, gilding and painting

The influx of oriental lacquer cabinets to the West led to the widespread use of both oriental lacquering and japanning, the European imitative process, for decorating furniture (*see p.194*). Two methods were employed for gilding furniture: oil gilding and water gilding. Oil gilding, the more durable of the two processes, used a sticky, oil-based, gold size which gave a flat finish. Water gilding was the only method that allowed the gold to be burnished; but because it was produced by floating the gold leaf on water onto the receiving surface, the gold was prone to flaking and remained soluble in water. The other main type of decoration was by painting (*see p.256*), which has occurred throughout the history of furniture making.

BANDING

From the early 18th century, it was customary to apply banding to desks, drawers, panels and the edges of tables. The major types include straight banding, in which the strips of veneer follow the grain of the wood, and cross banding, which uses sections across the grain. Banding is often used as a guide to the age of a piece, but because both types were common at the same time, it is necessary to take other dating factors into account.

Herringbone banding (**1**) was created by applying two bands of veneer at an angle to each other (before 1710). It is thought that straight banding (**2**) may have been used earlier (after 1710) than crossbanding (**3**) (after 1740).

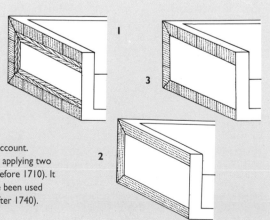

INLAY
Decorative inlay was frequently used in conjunction with banding.

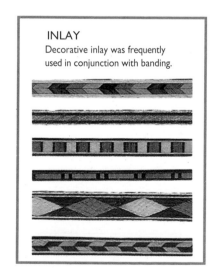

Aids to Dating Furniture

   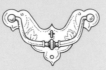

HANDLES

The style of handles and pulls followed the fashion of the time, but pieces of furniture have often been updated by replacing the handles with those currently in vogue. The earliest handles were made of iron, which was superseded by brass in the late 1600s. The finest brass handles were gilded, and traces of this may still remain.

Iron inverted heart-shaped drop handle, early 17th century

Three brass pendant handles, late 17th–early 18th century

Cast brass loop handle with engraved backplate, early 18th century

Cast brass loop handle, early 18th century

Cast brass loop handle with backplate, early 18th century

Cast brass loop handle with pierced backplate, mid-18th century

Cast brass loop handle with octagonal roses, French style, c.1750–c.1800

Decoratively cast and chased brass loop handle, late 18th century

Simple swan-neck handle of cast brass, neoclassical period c.1770–c.1780

Loop handle with stamped backplate, late 18th century

Stamped brass knob, late 18th century

Two drop handles in cast brass, 1750–75, 1775–1800

Regency period star knob, early 19th century

In Victorian times, turned wooden knobs of ebony, walnut, rosewood or mahogany were popular. They were often decorated.

The construction techniques and the accessories used on pieces of furniture can be essential when dating an item and deciding upon its authenticity.

Chairs

Early chairs were made using frame and panel construction until, in the mid-1500s, joined construction appeared. Eighteenth-century chairs tended to have a central back splat, which is fitted into a shoe brace – a bar attached to the back seat rail, not to the splat.

From the mid-1600s, upholstered chairs became a more common feature in homes. The most usual forms of upholstery in the eighteenth and early nineteenth centuries were the drop-in seat and the stuffed form of upholstery (see p.182). On drop-in seats, the seat rail was rabbeted (cut back) and small blocks were glued across the corners to provide additional strength. With stuffed upholstery, there were usually braces in the two front corners of the seat rail to cope with the strain exerted by the webbing on the side rails. These corner braces were glued in the 1700s; the combination of glue and screws was used only in the 1800s. Metal brackets and wooden blocks are an indication that a chair has been repaired.

Case furniture and tables

Often quite crude in construction, carcasses were the frames of case furniture and were generally made of cheaper woods, such as pine, covered with a veneer (see p.164). In order to examine a carcass properly, the drawers need to be removed. Both the underside and interior of the carcass should look "dry and untouched," a term used by dealers to signify that a piece has not been tampered with. The backs of early pieces were not highly finished and may be composed of three or four boards secured with the irregularly shaped nails of the period. More care was taken after the 1750s, and a paneled construction was occasionally used.

Most chests were made using mortise-and-tenon joints held together with pegs and dowels rather than screws and glue. This type of joined construction was common until the late seventeenth century. The earlier the piece, the cruder were the pegs. Screws, first made in the early 1700s, can also give strong clues about the date of a piece (see top right).

The dovetails used to join the parts of a drawer together were, at first, quite crude in shape, but became more regular during the eighteenth century. The number of dovetails used on a drawer increased from two in the 1600s and early 1700s to four or more later.

Early drawers pulled straight out and rubbed against the carcass, but by the 1650s, grooves were made in the sides of drawers that ran on runners attached to the carcass. In the 1700s, the sides of drawers projected below the drawer bottom and acted as runners. Drawer linings, usually of pine or oak, were at first fairly thick, but they became progressively thinner during the eighteenth and nineteenth centuries. The insides of drawers were not usually highly finished. Drawer bottoms were made from two or three pieces of wood, with the grain running from front to back until c.1770, after which the grain ran from side to side; shrinkage over the years has meant that sometimes a gap has opened up in the bottom of the drawer. In the Victorian period, bottom boards were usually made of a single piece of wood.

Moldings are lengths of shaped wood attached to pieces of case furniture. In the early eighteenth century, a thin molded edge, known as cockbeading, was applied to drawer edges to prevent damage to the veneer. Between c.1720 and c.1780 it was considered fashionable to have moldings that overhung the drawer.

Chest tops were usually made of more than one plank of wood, and shrinkage has often caused gaps to

ESCUTCHEONS

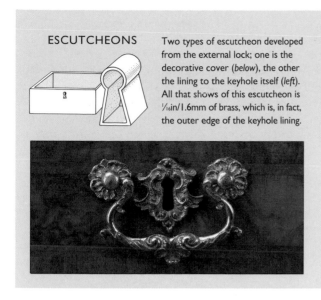

Two types of escutcheon developed from the external lock; one is the decorative cover (*below*), the other the lining to the keyhole itself (*left*). All that shows of this escutcheon is ¹⁄₁₆in/1.6mm of brass, which is, in fact, the outer edge of the keyhole lining.

BRAMAH LOCK

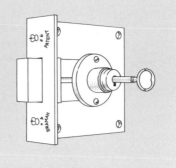

In 1784 Joseph Bramah, a British locksmith, patented this lock, which he believed was so secure that he offered a reward of 200 guineas ($350) to anybody who could pick one; the prize was not claimed for 67 years.

DATING WOOD SCREWS

The hand-made screw (1720–1830) has an uncentered driver slot, a filed top and uneven thread; the machine-made screw (mid-1800s) has a centered driver slot, a lathe-finished top and milled thread.

---

appear between these planks, splitting the veneer. Until *c*.1700, these tops were attached by pegs, as were table tops; after this date, they were normally screwed in from underneath. This can be spotted since a gouge was used to produce a circular screw hole.

It is important to check that the table top and base belong to each other. Table edges should show the signs typical of many years' use. The underside of the tops of gateleg tables should show marks caused by the legs being opened, and there should also be marks to show where the top has rested.

Legs and feet

A good way to gauge the age of a piece of furniture is by examining its feet, and its legs (*see p.188*) if it has them. Although earlier styles have frequently been reproduced during the last two centuries, it is usually possible to tell an original from a copy. Eighteenth-century cabriole legs, for example, were generally more finely carved than those on later reproductions, which took a more exaggerated form. The "earpieces" at the top of the leg were always made separately and glued to the main part. It is fairly easy to tell where replacements have been fitted by comparing the color and the quality of the carving with the rest of the leg.

Feet can be a most useful indicator of period, although there can be pitfalls since, like handles, feet were sometimes altered to reflect the prevailing fashion (*see p.208*). Bun feet were the norm in the late seventeenth century; but, due to wear, it is rare to find a piece of this date with its original feet.

Bracket feet were popular throughout the eighteenth century, while ogee feet and, later, splay bracket feet were fashionable after the mid-eighteenth century. Ball and claw feet, which were in vogue until the 1760s, re-emerged in the 1800s; on later examples, however, the claw does not seem to grip the ball as strongly as it does on earlier pieces. Feet should always match; replacements are only acceptable where they closely resemble the originals.

Furniture accessories

Other dating information can be gleaned from the use of accessories such as escutcheons and locks (*see above*) and from handles (*see far left*). The main problem is that, as furniture fashions changed, handles and other accessories were sometimes replaced with more up-to-date examples. It is, however, fairly easy to tell whether handles have been changed by examining the inside of drawer fronts for the holes made by different handles. While it is preferable to find a piece with its original handles, replacements may be acceptable as long as they remain sympathetic to the piece.

▼ **FINE MAHOGANY BERGÈRE**
The front legs of this chair, made c.1900, are carved in the form of lion monopodia – a lion's head, leg and paw foot – faced with shields.

STOOLS

Since ancient times, the stool has been a ubiquitous form of seating. During the Middle Ages, the three-legged stick stool was most often found in rural houses and kitchens, while in public places, stools of a simple trestle construction predominated. By the mid-sixteenth century, however, the better-made joined, or joint, stool had become more common, while the chair was a rare luxury reserved for the head of the house.

Upholstered stools were in general use by the 1670s, and their styles became progressively more elaborate until, early in the Georgian period, the stool was relegated to the role of accessory by the already fashionable, and now more affordable, chair. Indeed, Chippendale in his 1762 *Director* makes no mention of stools.

Despite the rise of the chair, stools continued to be made, although in far smaller numbers and usually as part of a suite of furniture. In addition to footstools, there were stools designed to stand against a wall or in front of a window, and some could be opened to form library steps; in the late 1700s, music stools with adjustable seats appeared.

During the Regency and Victorian periods, many shapes and types of stool were produced, ranging from extravagant Egyptian-revival styles to those covered in beadwork or Berlin woolwork.

▼ ITALIAN GILTWOOD STOOLS
The design of these mid-18th century giltwood stools, with rails carved with shell motifs, C-scrolls and cabriole legs, was influenced by the Louis XV style. As with other Italian furniture of this time, they are richer in decoration than their French models, but of inferior quality. H 19in/48cm

"Coffin stools"
Reproduction joint stools (1) were popular in the 19th century, and it was probably at this time that they became known as coffin stools. A source for this term may be Samuel Pepys's *Diary* of July 1661, in which he describes his uncle's coffin as resting on "joynt-stools in the chimney in the hall."

Stools at court
In court life, strict rules governed who was entitled to sit on a stool. The court of James I, in 17th-century England, provided low upholstered stools known as *tabourets* (3) on which favored women could sit in the presence of the king. At Louis XIV's French court at Versailles, a similar etiquette applied.

Liberty style
Established in London in 1875, Arthur Liberty's company strongly influenced style in the late 19th and early 20th centuries. The company commissioned furniture (4), pottery, silver and fabrics from designers of the Art Nouveau and Arts and Crafts movements, and imported Moorish and Oriental goods.

A needlework craze
Upholstery reflected the craze for Berlin woolwork that gripped Europe and the United States during the 1850s–1860s. It started in the 1830s when Berlin yarn manufacturers began selling pattern charts along with their colorful wool yarn. These charts meant that the designs could easily be copied onto canvas and worked at home. Brightly colored flowers (5) were common on upholstery, while pictorial subjects tended to be mounted as firescreen panels or framed.

1 OAK JOINT STOOL
Joint stools, so called because they were made by skilled "joiners" using the mortise-and-tenon technique, tend to be of better quality than stools made by turners or carpenters. This solid oak stool, with turned legs and block feet, is part of a set of six. Such 17th-century sets are rare, since they normally become dispersed over time. W 18in/46cm

2 CHIPPENDALE-STYLE STOOL
Dating from around 1765, this mahogany stool is in the Gothic Chippendale style. The straight pierced legs are linked by curved brackets reminiscent of the ribs of a vaulted roof. The upholstery is not original. H 14in x W 24in; H 36cm x W 61cm

3 EMPIRE TABOURET
This X-shaped giltwood tabouret is decorated with stems, anthemia and, at the intersection of the supports, a lotus. It is upholstered in close-nailed blue silk. H 18in x W 26in; H 46cm x W 66cm

4 THEBES STOOL
Introduced by Liberty & Co. of London in 1884, this stool is evidence of the interest aroused by archeological excavations in Egypt in the 1880s. The design, based on stools found during these digs, has a square leather seat supported by a rosewood and ebonized mahogany frame inlaid with ivory. H 15in/38cm

5 VICTORIAN ROSEWOOD STOOL
Although the Berlin woolwork on this large 1850s rosewood stool is worn, stools of this type, with a scrolled frieze, cabriole legs and woolwork upholstery, are popular with collectors. The value of this stool would be enhanced if the woolwork were properly restored. W 4ft/1.22m

6 GILLOWS MUSIC STOOL
The revolving top of this mid-Victorian walnut and parcel-gilt music stool has hidden in the pillar a metal thread which allows the height to be adjusted. Made by Gillows, the well-known London and Lancaster furniture-making firm, the stool is covered with its original gilt-tooled leather upholstery on square tripod legs. Diam. 15in/38cm

EARLY DINING CHAIRS

Most people sat on benches or stools in medieval times, for the chair was a symbol of rank and position reserved for the master of the house and his wife. It was not until the sixteenth century that chairs became more common. At first they were of boxed construction, but by the second half of the century, they had lost the box panels under the arms and seats and were known as joined chairs.

In the early seventeenth century, the back stool evolved. This was literally a stool with a half back (the Puritan chair, 1, is an example of this type) and was far more portable than earlier chairs. The Restoration of the monarchy in 1660 brought continental influences to England, especially from France and Holland where Charles II had spent many years in exile. And in 1685, as a result of the revocation of the Edict of Nantes which had allowed French Protestants freedom of worship, a flood of Huguenot craftsmen, among them cabinetmakers, came to England.

American Brewster and Carver chairs are named after chairs, now in Pilgrim Hall, Plymouth, Massachusetts, believed to have belonged to William Brewster (1567–1644) and Governor John Carver (d.1621). The originals were copied from chairs which the Pilgrim Fathers brought with them.

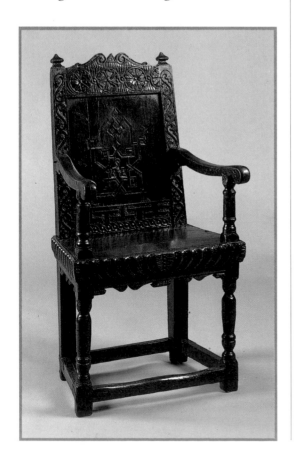

◄ JAMES I OAK ARMCHAIR
Chairs such as this open armchair were of joined construction, using mortise-and-tenon joints. The raked back panel is inlaid with bog-oak and holly, and the stylized carving and scrolled cresting on the top rail is typical of the period. Often a loose pillow would be added for comfort.

Woods in use

Almost all early chairs were made from locally available woods, such as oak and beech. The elaborate styles introduced into England from continental Europe toward the end of the 17th century were most often found in fashionable walnut, a highly figured and stable wood which was suitable for carving since it did not crack or split.

Spotting a fake

On a genuine early oak or walnut chair, the front stretcher where people's feet have rested should be worn. Heavy wear on the side or back stretchers suggests that they have been artificially worn and that the chair is probably a copy.

Cane

Introduced into Europe soon after 1660, cane (3) was obtained from Malaya through the Dutch and English East India companies. It was used initially for woven chair backs, but later for seats as well, and by the end of the century the canework had become finer and very skillful. Cane remained popular until the early 18th century after which, with few exceptions, it was not used again until the 1800s.

Methods of jointing

From the end of the 15th century until well into the 17th, most joints in chairs and other furniture were of the mortise-and-tenon type: a projecting tongue in one piece of wood is slotted into a cut-out section of the same size and shape in the second piece, and the two are pinned together with wooden pegs.

In dovetail joints (as with drawer corners) where the end grain of wood is joined to the side grain, slightly fan-shaped projections in one piece of wood are fitted into matching slots in the other. Until 1700, two large, rather rough dovetails were usually present; after that date, dovetails became more precise and numerous.

1 PURITAN CHAIR

This chair, dating from c.1655, epitomizes the simplicity of style favored in England after the Civil Wars of 1642–51. The chair has a half back and seat covered in leather attached with brass nails. Decoration is limited to the knob turning on the legs and front stretcher.

2 PORTUGUESE CHAIR

A late 17th-century chair of stained chestnut from Portugal. The high arched back has brass finials and, like the seat, is covered with embossed and incised leather held by brass nails. Leather deteriorates with age, and as a result such chairs are rarely found.

3 CHARLES II WALNUT CHAIR

After the Restoration, styles became lighter and chair backs higher to support the sitter's head. The carving of the cresting, side panels and wide front stretcher on this English chair show the increasingly baroque influence from Europe. The "new" technique of caning has been used for the seat.

4 BREWSTER ARMCHAIR

This mid-17th century turned armchair was made in Massachusetts. The back has a double row of spindles, with further rows beneath the seat and arm rails. Carver chairs have spindles only in the back.

5 BANISTER-BACK ARMCHAIR

The name of this type of early 18th-century American chair derives from the turned uprights of the back, which copy staircase banisters of the period. This example, with a rush seat, is made from local woods – ash and maple.

6 DUTCH WALNUT CHAIR

The style of Daniel Marot (1663–1752), a French-born architect and designer who worked in Holland and later in England, is evident in this piece. Characteristic of his style are the elaborately carved, high pierced back flanked by baluster stiles and the scrolling carving of foliage and fruit. Marot was architect to William of Orange (later William III of England) and was probably the first to create complete room interiors (furniture, fittings and upholstery). His baroque style had a profound influence on designers such as William Kent (1684–1748).

1

2

3

4

5

6

18th-Century Dining Chairs

By the eighteenth century, English chairs had become less dependent on European influences and had begun to develop their own strong stylistic characteristics. The early 1700s saw the introduction of the Queen Anne chair, with bold curved lines, a back with a solid, vase-shaped splat running from the crest to the seat rail, arms set back onto the sides of the seat rail, and curved cabriole legs.

Early American chairs were closely based on English examples, but local craftsmen were soon adding their own details, reflecting the amalgam of European cultures that existed there. New York styles, for instance, owed something to the Dutch settlers. The Queen Anne style was popular from the 1720s until the mid-1760s, after which Chippendale's designs became the dominant influence for the following 20 years or so.

Throughout Europe during this time the influence of the neoclassical style had been growing, and the furniture designs of Robert Adam, George Hepplewhite and Thomas Sheraton show a steady increase of surface ornament, based on antique decorative motifs, and painting, in place of heavy carving. The War of Independence (1775–83) meant that these designs did not become the source for what is now known in North America as Federal style until the late 1780s.

Chippendale's designs

The most famous and skilled of England's master cabinet makers was Thomas Chippendale (1718–79), who published the first catalogue of furniture designs, *The Gentleman and Cabinet-Maker's Director*, in 1754.

He showed chairs with backs up to 3ft 2in/97cm high in different styles: French Rococo, with curved lines and natural motifs; Gothic, based on the pointed arches and trefoils of medieval architecture; and chinoiserie, with blind fretwork and pagoda-like crest rails. Rococo-style chairs had cabriole legs and claw and ball or scrolled feet, whereas gothic and Chinese designs had straight legs and stretchers.

The move to Classicism

Interest aroused by excavations at Pompeii and the influence of architect-designers such as Robert Adam caused a shift back to the classical style by the 1770s. Chair backs, seats and legs became straighter; the backs were oval, rectangular, or shield-shaped, with the splats pierced with lyres and urns. Hepplewhite gave these classical forms slenderer frames and supports, making them more "feminine" and decorative.

1 GEORGE III SIDE CHAIR
A mahogany Chippendale-style chair dating from c.1760 with cabriole legs and ball and claw feet. The shaped uprights, bow-shaped crest rail and splat pierced with bold C-scrolls and lozenges are characteristic features of mid-18th century rococo styling.

2 CHINESE CHIPPENDALE CHAIR
Despite the lattice-work sides and back, this Chinese-style mahogany armchair, one of a set of eight, reveals its English origins by its square chamfered legs and drop-in seat. In the 18th century, such lattice work was known as Chinese railing.

3 GOTHIC-STYLE CHAIR
The pierced and carved back of this armchair, one of a set of eight, resembles the tracery in a gothic window. Rather than the more usual straight legs, it has carved cabriole legs ending in finely carved ball and claw feet.

4 HEPPLEWHITE SHIELD-BACK CHAIR
The design for this rosewood shield-back armchair can be attributed to Hepplewhite, since it appears in his Cabinet-Maker and Upholsterer's Guide, published in 1794, eight years after his death. The value of the chair, one of eight, is therefore considerable.

The arched shield back and vase-shaped molded splat are finely carved with Prince of Wales plumes, acanthus and long leaves, and the square tapering legs have spade feet and oval patera headings.

5 AMERICAN SHERATON-STYLE CHAIR
Made in New York, this chair is a fine example of Federal period furniture (1790–1820) with its tapering legs and painted back splat in the shape of a flower-filled vase.

6 REGENCY ARMCHAIR
One of a fine set of eight chairs decorated in the style of Henry Holland (1745–1806) in parcel gilt and blue paint and with an ormolu splat in the form of a laurel wreath. Holland, an English architect who also designed his own interiors, was inspired by the contemporary French neoclassical style. His most famous patron was the trend-setting Prince Regent.

◀ **QUEEN ANNE BURL WALNUT SIDE CHAIR**
The curved back with its vase-shaped splat, cabriole legs with carved knees and pad feet, and shaped drop-in seat with its original brocade upholstery are precisely what is expected in a chair of this period. The carved shell motif, too, is typical and is frequently found on furniture made in America. H 3ft 2in x W 21in; H 97cm x W 53cm

FURNITURE

◄ **LATE REGENCY CHAIRS**
This fine mahogany armchair and side chair, 2 of a set of 14, show clearly how styles became heavier-looking as the century progressed. Although the back uprights no longer flow into the seat rail, the chairs still have saber legs, and there is carved anthemion decoration on the solid, overhanging top rail.

Chair styles varied considerably during the early nineteenth century. Although the French influence was still strong, and Chinese and gothic designs were again becoming popular, the neoclassical look remained dominant. Styles were, however, less delicate than those of Hepplewhite and Sheraton at the end of the 1700s and leaned toward the more robust forms of ancient Greece, Rome and Egypt.

Regency dining chairs, with their curved top rails, saber legs and scrolled arms, were an elegant form of seating. Carving was restrained and limited to the top rail and splat, with motifs usually derived from Greek architectural decoration; frames were often simply reeded. In the late Regency and William IV periods, chairs had overhanging top rails and straight legs, but over the next 20 years a new form evolved in which the top rail became continuous with the upright supports to form a curved oval back, and legs became cabriole in shape once more. This new form of chair, known as the balloon back, was most popular between 1850 and 1870 both in Britain and the United States.

Design in the nineteenth century was a potpourri of different influences: Gothic, Grecian, Elizabethan and Rococo Revival (a combination of Louis XIV and Louis XV styles). In Britain, as in the rest of Europe, in the late nineteenth and early twentieth centuries, disheartened by the eclecticism of mainstream design, "reformers" in the Arts and Crafts, Art Nouveau and Wiener Werkstätte movements, attempted to achieve a purer style.

Upholstered seats

The smell of food lingering in an 18th- or early 19th-century dining room was considered abhorrent, and the drop-in or stuffed seats of dining chairs were, therefore, upholstered in either leather or horsehair rather than fabric, which would have retained the odor. The British architect and designer Robert Adam carried this even further and decreed that there should be no wall hangings or curtains in a dining room, a belief he put into practice at Syon House near London.

Gadrooning

The decoration of Regency and Victorian chairs was influenced by the room for which they were designed, those for the drawing room being more ornate. A popular form of decoration was gadrooning (**2**), carved molding consisting of either reeds or flutes, which was found on chair rails, chests and bed posts and on the edges of tables.

1 REGENCY DINING CHAIR
The curved, veneered top rail, lyre-shaped motif on the horizontal back splat, down-scrolled arms and saber legs with rounded knees are typical features of this type of chair. It is known as a Trafalgar chair, since it dates from c.1805. H 33in/84cm

*The commonly found anthemion, or stylized honeysuckle, motif (**1a**) first appeared on English furniture in the late 18th century.*

2 WILLIAM IV CHAIR
The lyre-shaped back of this chair shows the beginnings of the balloon back. The saber legs are replaced by tapering turned legs, and the foliate carving and gadrooning of the top rail has lost the earlier lightness. The heavily upholstered seat is coil sprung.

3 AMERICAN BALLOON-BACK CHAIR
This chair of carved walnut and pine was made in Rococo Revival style, c.1840–70, in the eastern or mid-western states. Such chairs were popular for most of the century after their introduction in the 1840s.

4 ROSEWOOD CHAIR
The revival of French Rococo during the 1840s is well illustrated by the deeply curving cresting, splat and legs of this chair, one of a set of six. The design appears in George Smith's 1828 Guide for cabinetmakers, which included one for an entire "Louis Quatorze" room. H 33in/84cm

5 WIENER WERKSTÄTTE CHAIR
Josef Hoffmann (1870–1956) was a founder of the Wiener Werkstätte (Vienna Workshops), a movement that paralleled the Arts and Crafts Movement in Britain. Hoffmann's aim of providing functional furniture of pure decorative form is amply illustrated by these black-stained pickled oak dining chairs, 1907–09.

6 BENTWOOD CHAIR
This type of chair, invented by the Austrian Michael Thonet (1796–1871) in the 1840s, derives its name from the way the frame is shaped by steam. The chairs were turned out in their millions, with styles changing slightly to suit current trends. This Art Nouveau example in ash and beech was made c.1900 for the American market.

7 EDWARDIAN CHAIR
Elegance and lightness are typical of much Edwardian furniture. The cresting rail of this mahogany chair from the early 1900s has a boxwood and ivory inlaid roundel, whose design includes grotesques and foliage. H 3ft 5in/1.04m

FURNITURE

Apart from dining chairs and upholstered chairs, many other types were made which are categorized as occasional chairs. These include turned chairs, so called because they were made by turners rather than joiners or carpenters.

An early form dating from at least medieval times, turned chairs were still being made in the seventeenth century and were already regarded as collectors' pieces by mid-eighteenth century adherents of the "Gothick" style.

Sets of upholstered-seat furniture were made from the early 1600s onward, and although there are few survivors from this time, many fine examples exist from late in the century through to Victorian times.

First found during the reign of Britain's King George II, hall seats, as their name implies, were made for the entrance halls and corridors of fine houses where people sat and chatted or visitors waited. They are also sometimes referred to as rout seats since they were used to rest on during routs (dances). Chippendale (in the 1762 edition of the *Director*), Sheraton and Hepplewhite all feature this type of chair among their designs.

Normally made in sets, at first usually of mahogany and then later oak, hall seats were still in demand in the early 1800s, but their popularity gradually diminished as the century progressed.

Drawing-room furniture sets

Many makers produced sets of furniture, most often as a special commission for wealthy clients. It is difficult now to find complete sets, but when they do exist they are usually worth more than the sum of their parts.

An early 18th-century set, consisting of a daybed, 6 armchairs, 20 single chairs (2) and various other pieces, was made for the Duke of Infantado's castle at Lazcano in Spain and remained in the family's possession for 200 years before being dispersed. The set can be safely attributed to the English maker Giles Grendey (1693–1780), since his trade label was found under the seat rail of one of the chairs.

A new material

Papier-mâché (5), made from layers of paper pulp molded or pressed into shape and then lacquered, originated in the Orient. The manufacture of papier-mâché wares in the West started in the United States, but Britain and France became the most important centers of production.

There was a considerable vogue for papier-mâché in Victorian times. It was first used for small items, but by 1850 improved pressing and molding machinery made it possible to make chairs and tables. The panels of these larger pieces were molded on a wooden or metal frame.

1 TURNED ARMCHAIR
These chairs were sometimes called "thrown" chairs after the early term for turning. This fine example in ash (c.1650), has a baluster-turned back splat, ring-turned toprail with button finials and bobbin-turned spindles.

2 SIDE CHAIR
A Chinese-style single chair by Giles Grendey in bright scarlet lacquer with gold and silver, made c.1730. The apron is decorated with a carved shell, and the cabriole legs end in paw feet.

3 GEORGE III HALL CHAIR
The back of this hall chair, with a typical solid seat, is pierced, but often backs were painted with the owner's crest. H 4ft/1.22m

4 REGENCY ARMCHAIR
One of a pair, this ebonized chair has parcel gilt and painted decoration. The top rail and oval panel in the finely caned back are painted en grisaille (gray monochrome) with classical figures. The front seat rail is decorated with a Greek key pattern in gilt. Turned columns connect the tapering front legs to the arms.

5 X-FRAME CHAIR
A walnut and mahogany X-frame chair (1875–80) made from West African timber. It is based on the "curule" chair, a Regency design adapted from the sella curulis, or stool, on which the senators of ancient Rome used to sit; the X-frame was also often used for stools. H 35in/89cm

6 PAPIER-MÂCHÉ CHAIR
Black japanning, mother-of-pearl inlay and gilding decorate this mid-19th century papier-mâché chair.

7 VICTORIAN HALL CHAIR
Best described as being in French Baroque style, this mahogany chair made in the 1860s displays a typically 19th-century mélange of earlier styles. H 4ft/1.22m

8 CHINESE EXPORT CHAIR
In the late 19th century, furniture such as this huang hua li chair was manufactured in large quantities in China for the European market to designs based on those of the 18th century. It was probably exported to Europe via Canton. H 3ft 4in/1.01m

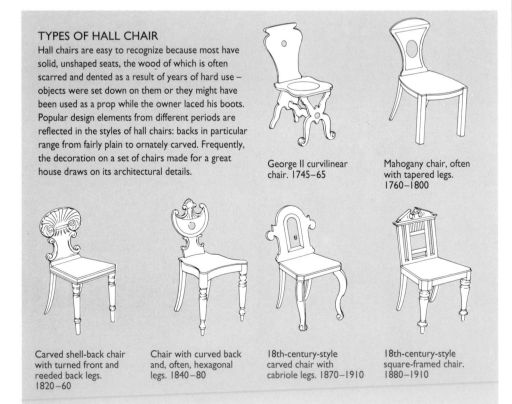

TYPES OF HALL CHAIR

Hall chairs are easy to recognize because most have solid, unshaped seats, the wood of which is often scarred and dented as a result of years of hard use – objects were set down on them or they might have been used as a prop while the owner laced his boots. Popular design elements from different periods are reflected in the styles of hall chairs: backs in particular range from fairly plain to ornately carved. Frequently, the decoration on a set of chairs made for a great house draws on its architectural details.

George II curvilinear chair. 1745–65

Mahogany chair, often with tapered legs. 1760–1800

Carved shell-back chair with turned front and reeded back legs. 1820–60

Chair with curved back and, often, hexagonal legs. 1840–80

18th-century-style carved chair with cabriole legs. 1870–1910

18th-century-style square-framed chair. 1880–1910

FURNITURE

The reign of Louis XIV had a profound effect not only on France, but also on the other European countries. The influences of French design were felt throughout the continent and, after 1660 when the monarchy was restored with Charles II, they reached Britain where, among other items, they affected chair design.

In France, chairs were an important part of the furnishing of a room. Some were designed to stand against the walls and were known as *meublant*, while smaller chairs for use in the center of a room were known as *courant*. Inspired by the discovery of the ruins of Pompeii and Herculaneum in 1757, European design changed from rococo to more classical styles, a taste which lasted into the 1800s.

Several new types of chair appeared during the eighteenth century, among them the corner chair, which probably derived from Burgomaster chairs found in the Dutch East Indies. No one is quite sure what their original purpose was, but they may have been used as writing chairs: in France, similarly shaped chairs are known as *fauteuils de bureau*.

As with other furniture, European and American chair design was subject to the revival of many styles and to varying outside influences during the nineteenth century, including, in the 1880s, the art and culture of Japan, a taste which pervaded all aspects of design.

Points to note
À chassis (4) is used to describe the upholstery on some 18th-century French chairs. The back, seat and armrests of these chairs are removable so that the upholstery can be changed. It was customary in grand houses to have a set of covers for winter (*meuble d'hiver*) and a different one for summer (*meuble d'été*).

Menuisier (4), particularly used in 18th-century France, describes makers who specialized in carved wood furniture, such as chairs, sofas and console tables, but excludes those who made veneered furniture, the *ébénistes*.

À la reine (4) is the term used to describe large, flat-backed 18th-century French armchairs. They acquired their name by association with Marie Leczynska, the wife of Louis XV, who particularly liked them.

The Gothic Revival
The armchair (6) is a typical example of the Gothic Revival style. The leading advocate of this movement toward medievalism during the 1840s was the English architect, designer and writer Augustus Welby Northmore Pugin (1812–52).

His influence extended well into the 1880s, and although inferior copies of his work were often made during this time, his designs and principles were the inspiration for many of the cabinet makers of the Arts and Crafts Movement. Pugin used oak, a wood rarely seen since the Restoration, polished to a yellowish brown, and he never allowed the carving to obscure the structure of his furniture.

◀ **REGENCY BERGÈRE**
This simulated bronze and parcel-gilt bergère *(armchair with upholstered sides), with a Medusa mask on the top rail, leopard-mask terminals, wings and paw feet, is based on a design by George Smith printed in 1804 – it differs only in the stars on the seat rails.*

The design was probably plagiarized from the Greco-Egyptian furniture in the Breakfast Parlour of the London home of the designer and collector Thomas Hope, which had been opened to the public in the same year. Hope had a marked influence on contemporary taste. H 3ft/91cm

1 WILLIAM AND MARY ARMCHAIR
The design of this walnut chair, with high rectangular back, scrolled arms and turned stretchers, is similar to that of French chairs of the time. The needlework upholstery dates from a later period.

2 AMERICAN CORNER CHAIR
Corner chairs were popular in America. This one, with a high comb back and the scrolled splats typical of Newport furniture, dates from 1735–50. It is made of walnut, cherry and pine and has cabriole legs ending in Queen Anne pad feet.
H 3ft 9in/1.14m

3 EARLY GEORGIAN OPEN ARMCHAIR
Made from walnut, this chair has a padded, waisted back and bowed seat upholstered in ivory silk. There is shell carving on the shaped arms, and the cabriole legs end in scroll feet.

4 LOUIS XV ARMCHAIR
This chair, one of a pair of giltwood fauteuils à la reine, *is stamped by the* menuisier Bauve. *Upholstered* à chassis, *the molded frame has carved decoration of foliage, C-scrolls and clasp cresting.*

5 LOUIS XVI BERGÈRE
One of a pair, this bergère *has a white-painted and parcel-gilt frame. The arched rectangular back has beaded ball and spool decoration; there are fluted seat rails around the serpentine seat and circular fluted tapering legs beaded by paterae.*

6 EARLY VICTORIAN ARMCHAIR
The designer A.W.N. Pugin disliked the furniture styles of his day and attempted to "reform" them by looking back to the gothic style. This chair in oak with restrained carving and detail, made after one of his designs, exemplifies the high standard of craftsmanship he insisted upon.

SETTEES, SOFAS AND DAYBEDS

The wooden settle of the Middle Ages, similar to some church pews of today, was the first form of seating with a back to accommodate two or more people. By the mid-seventeenth century, more comfortable types of seating were found; some early examples, such as large Puritan chairs and the wing chairs of the William and Mary period, still exist.

In the early 1700s, the "chair-back" settee with two or more chair backs and a long upholstered seat developed. It remained a popular form, and examples in all the different period styles exist. Just as more fully upholstered chairs with carved show frames evolved, so too did sofas, or seats on which to recline, and, as the eighteenth century progressed, many styles emerged, including the French neoclassical *canapé* with some of the wooden frame exposed and a padded seat, back and arms. This design proved so popular in Britain that it endured to the end of the Victorian era.

The daybed, a long upholstered seat with an adjustable inclined end, has been popular since the seventeenth century. By the mid-1700s, daybeds were common on both sides of the Atlantic, and like the sofa, their styles followed the fashion of the day. Perhaps the best-known descendant of the daybed is the *chaise longue* – French for "long chair" – which had scroll ends and a partial, fixed upholstered back. First in vogue during the Regency, *chaises longues* remained popular throughout the 1800s.

After the 1830s, sofas or settees (the names are now virtually interchangeable) in a wide range of styles were usually made as part of a set and were always included in furniture-makers' designs.

Point to note

Original upholstery always enhances the value of a sofa, while unsympathetic covering can dramatically reduce the value of a piece. As a rough guide, silk damasks or fine tapestries should be used on 18th-century sofas; velvets and brocades are better for pieces from the 19th century.

An American innovator

One of New York's foremost furniture designers, John Henry Belter (1804–63), was born and trained in Württemberg, Germany. A leading exponent of Rococo Revival style, his elaborate lacy pieces (6) were made using laminated rosewood panels. This laminating technique, which he patented, involved gluing together a number of wafer-thin panels, each time alternating the direction of the grain of the wood. The panels were then steamed in molds and shaped. His style was so popular that for years all elaborate laminated pieces were said to be in "Belter" style.

▼ GEORGE II SETTEE

This elegant settee, with outscrolling arms and serpentine padded back, was part of a set of 4 settees and 25 armchairs commissioned in the 1750s by the fourth Earl of Shaftesbury.

The front rail is richly carved with a band of acanthus leaves, garlanded with fruit and flowers. This theme continues on the square legs and pierced scrolling brackets, and more acanthus foliage emerges from the rosettes on the arms. The original upholstery was green damask, not the yellow floral damask seen today. H 3ft 3in x L 7ft 4in; H 99cm x L 2.24m

1 AMERICAN MAPLE DAYBED

The style of this early 18th-century daybed is a simpler interpretation of those from the earlier English William and Mary period. In the U.S., furniture of this style was still being made in the first 25 years of the 18th century. This example has a rush seat and backrest, which is adjusted by using a wrought-iron chain.

2 CHAIR-BACK SETTEE

Made of walnut and burl walnut, this early Georgian settee (1714–27) has the decorative details, such as shells, lion's masks and paw feet, typical of a chair of this period. Although in the correct style, the outscrolled arms with their eagle heads are later replacements. L 4ft 9in/1.45m

3 LOUIS XV BEECHWOOD CANAPÉ

Upholstered in gros and petit point, the shaped back of this sofa (1723–74) depicts landscapes with figures, while the seat shows landscapes with animals. The cabriole legs are topped by flower heads. L 6ft 10in/2.08m

4 REGENCY DAYBED

A brass-inlaid mahogany, ebony and parcel-gilt daybed, recalling a design for a Franco-Greco chair by the London furniture maker George Smith. A sofa illustrated in Smith's Designs for Household Furniture and Interior Designs of 1808 shows the same scroll ends, panther feet and projecting ram's-head shafts seen here. H 3ft 3in x L 7ft 2in; H 99cm x L 2.18m

5 MID-VICTORIAN SOCIABLE

Each end of this buttonback sofa swivels so that the occupants can face each other for intimate conversation. It is upholstered in silk damask, with a long tasseled fringe. L 6ft/1.83m

6 BELTER SOFA

An exuberant triple-back sofa made in 1850–60 from laminated rosewood by John Henry Belter in the American Rococo Revival style. The elaborate cresting was carved from solid wood and attached to the frame.

7 ART NOUVEAU SOFA

This Italian satinwood sofa, made c.1905 in Palermo, Sicily, combines Art Nouveau motifs with rustic elements. Upholstered in silver and white brocade, it has outscrolled arms and a pierced foliate top rail above a divided back. L 5ft 4in/1.63m

1

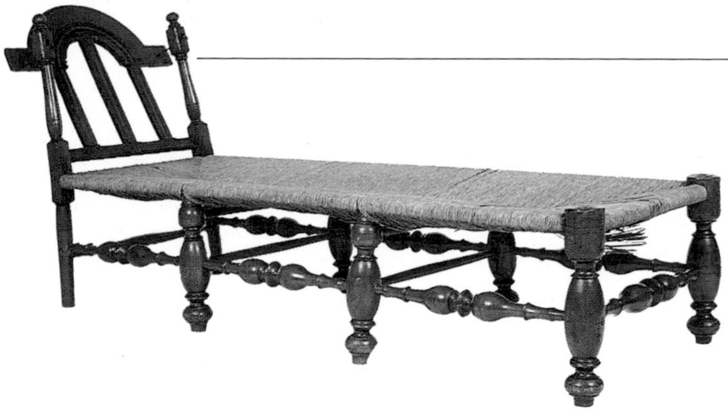

2

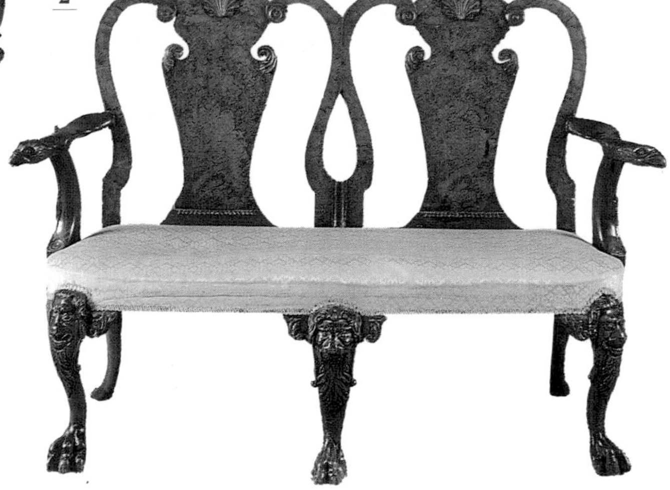

3

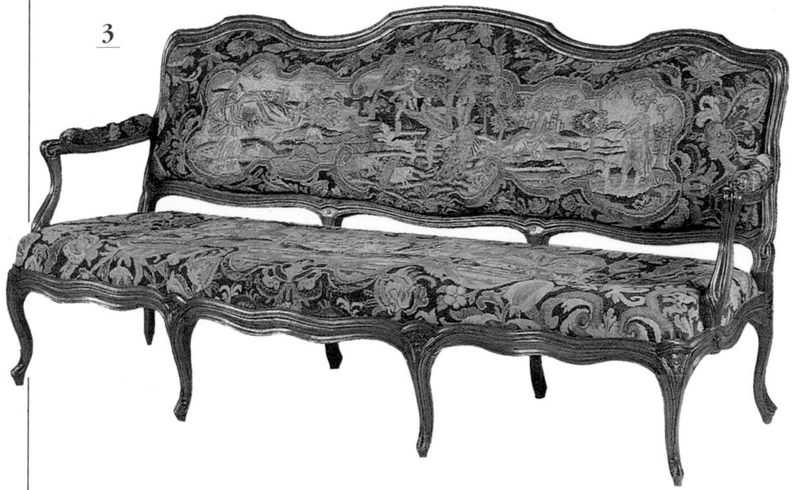

4

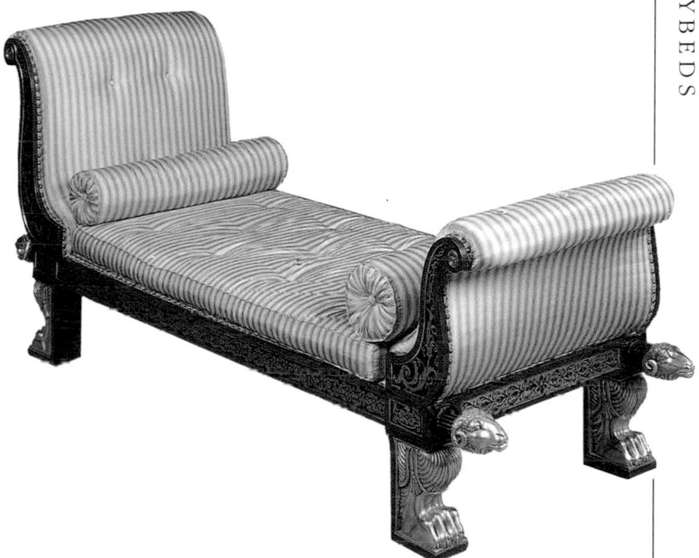

5

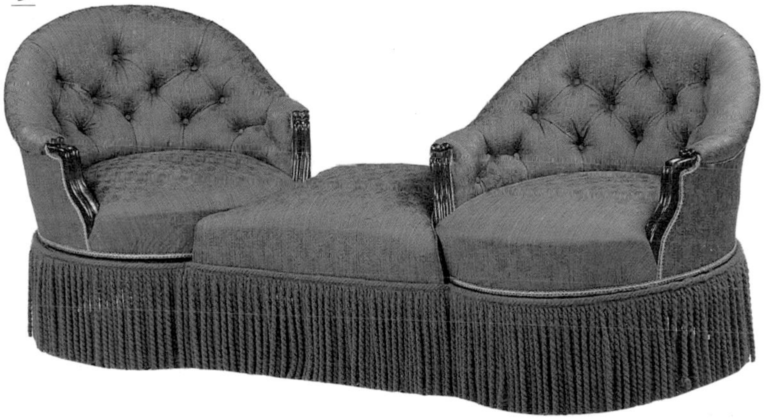

6

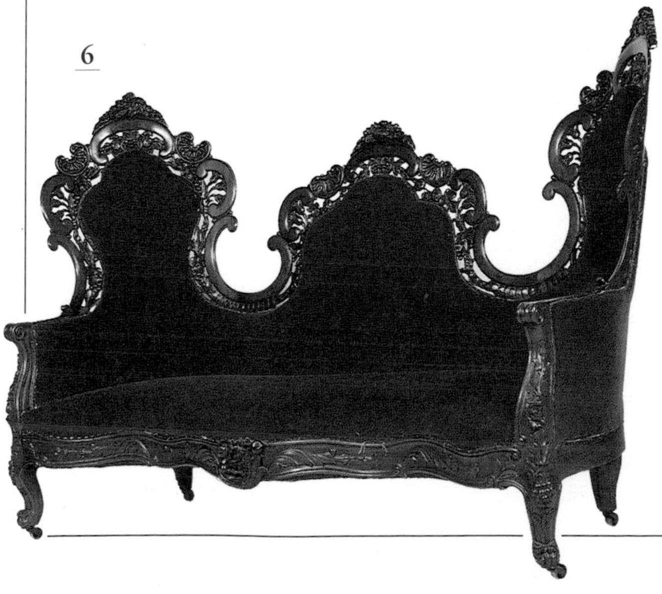

7

FURNITURE

Pillows stuffed with anything from wool to straw were used to provide a sort of upholstered comfort on the oak chairs of the sixteenth century. The return of King Charles II from exile in continental Europe meant an influx of new styles into England, but only in the early seventeenth century were fully upholstered chairs found.

In the reign of William and Mary, in the late 1600s, the loose pillow was replaced by a Dutch innovation, the drop-in seat. This consisted of a horsehair or wool cushion attached to a webbing base, covered in fabric and tacked onto a wooden seat frame which rested on brackets in the angles between the legs and the seat rail.

The overstuffed, or fully upholstered, chair was introduced in the time of Queen Anne (1702–14). The stuffing was made of horsehair on a base of webbing, with a narrow bar down the center of the back and seat for support and a roll of horsehair along the front edge of the seat.

The introduction of coiled springs in 1828 made chairs considerably more comfortable, and coiled springing was quickly adopted by commercial furniture makers.

Points to note

Although they have often been replaced, castors can be used to give a rough date for a chair. Introduced in the late 17th century, castors were made of wood and were fixed, so furniture could only be moved in a line backward or forward. Furniture became fully "mobile" when pins were developed that allowed the castors to pivot around an axle.

The leather castors (6) of the mid-18th century were soon superseded by brass castors of the square-toe or cup variety. In the Regency period, the brass lion's paw castor was popular, while porcelain castors were common in Victorian times.

▼ FLEMISH OPEN ARMCHAIRS
The padded backs and seats of these late 17th-century walnut armchairs are covered in close-nailed Flemish verdure tapestry. The tapestry on the left-hand chair depicts a lake, that on the right a building with flowers. The supports for the scrolling arms are turned, as are the H-shaped stretchers; the bun feet are later additions.

1 WALNUT WING CHAIR
This beautifully proportioned Queen Anne chair has cabriole front legs with shaped lappets and club feet. The gros and petit-point needlepoint upholstery is contemporary.

2 MID-GEORGIAN WALNUT ARMCHAIR
The curvaceous shape of this chair, one of a set of six, suggests that it is of Portuguese origin. The ornate molded frame is decorated with leaf and grape cresting flanked by tendrils. The chair is upholstered in crimson velvet.

3 GEORGE II LIBRARY ARMCHAIR
Upholstered in close-nailed tan leather, the back of this mahogany armchair is arched to match the serpentine seat. The chair, with its cabriole legs and pad feet, has padded arms with rounded ends and downswept supports.

4 GEORGIAN GILTWOOD ARMCHAIR
One of a pair of giltwood chairs from c.1770. The oval buttoned back and serpentine-shaped seat are typical of the neoclassical style fashionable at the time. The back has a ribbon-tied cresting, and the fluted seat rail is centered by ribbon-tied patera. Each fluted tapering front leg is headed by lotus leaves.

5 GEORGE III ARMCHAIR
A large English upholstered open armchair in mahogany, dating from c.1770, with later tapestry upholstery. The legs and stretchers are square and the front legs and arms well carved; the castors are brass.

6 GEORGE III LIBRARY ARMCHAIR
Originally known as a French chair, this type of open-sided upholstered chair is now popularly called a Gainsborough chair, probably because the artist often placed his models in one. The frame, true to style, is quite sparingly carved, and later porcelain castors have replaced leather ones. The upholstery would originally have been either leather or damask.

7 FRENCH ARMCHAIR
An upholstered mahogany open armchair, with a curved top rail and seat rail and serpentine arms, dating from the Restauration period, c.1820. It has cabriole legs, with carving on the knees, and scroll feet.

FURNITURE

As upholstery techniques changed, so too did the materials for covering. In addition to leather, there was turkey work, a knotted pile fabric with stylized floral patterns based on those of rugs imported from Turkey. This type of upholstery was common in England from the sixteenth century and remained popular until the 1750s.

Fine velvets and silks decorated with elaborate fringes became fashionable in the seventeenth century. Later, damasks, patterned velvets and *gros* and *petit-point* needlework were used, and they retained their popularity until late in the eighteenth century, when brocaded satin, watered silk and materials of silk mixture, often with medallion or striped patterns, gained favor. During everyday use, the fine fabrics were generally protected by slipcovers of serge or linen, which were removed when there were important guests.

Increasing wealth and rapid population growth in the nineteenth century created a demand for upholstered furniture by all classes, not just the rich. Coiled spring seating and buttoned upholstery provided additional comfort: the button back was especially popular because of the way it fitted the sitter's contours. Fabrics became cheaper, and a variety of worsteds, velvets and damasks, brocatelle and Berlin wool-work were used.

Later, designers in groups such as the Arts and Crafts Movement produced their own upholstery fabrics to suit the style of their furniture, and many of their designs are still in production.

Reading chairs

Cock-fighting chair is a misnomer used to describe a particular type of reading chair (1). The name probably arose because these chairs are sometimes found in pictures of cock fights. They are also known as horseman's chairs, because of the similarity of the sitter's position to that when riding a horse.

The Arts and Crafts Movement

The main inspiration behind the Arts and Crafts Movement, William Morris (1834–96) was an artist-craftsman who believed in simple, honest designs and a return to true craftsmanship (*see below*). Morris appears to have left the design of furniture largely to his colleague Philip Webb (*see p.194*), while he concentrated on other crafts, especially fabric and wallpaper design and book printing.

In 1861, he formed the company Morris, Marshall, Faulkner & Co. The company's furniture designs tended toward two distinct styles: on one hand early simple, utilitarian pieces; and on the other, extremely ornate and highly decorated items.

◀ **WILLIAM MORRIS CHAIR**
Commonly known as a Morris chair, this type of easy chair with an adjustable back was first produced by William Morris's company in 1865 and remained a popular style for many years. Made of finely turned ebonized wood, this particular chair retains its original "Birds" design woolen upholstery, which allows it to be dated to 1878.

1 GEORGE IV READING CHAIR
Leather-covered mahogany reading chairs were commonly found in 18th- and 19th-century libraries. The reader sat astride the chair, facing the back so that his coat-tails would not get creased, rested his book upon the hinged adjustable book rest on the top rail, and used the chair's arms for support. Many chairs had a small box which swung out to the side to hold pencils. This fine example is attributed to Morgan & Saunders, who were well-known makers of "mechanical furniture."

2 REGENCY MAHOGANY BERGÈRE
Striking reeded saber front legs, with foliate brass caps and castors, and reeded scroll arms complement the rectangular padded back and cane-paneled sides of this chair. Bergère is a French term used to describe such deep chairs with enclosed sides.

3 BIEDERMEIER ARMCHAIR
One of a pair of fine ashwood armchairs, dating from c.1825, which were made in Hungary. There is a rosewood inlay on the scrolling arm supports (3a), front rail and legs.

4 TWO DUTCH CHAIRS
Suites of "parlor" furniture were common in the 19th century. These two plush-covered chairs, in ornate Louis XVI style, are part of a Dutch mahogany suite made in the 1840s. The set includes a settee, two armchairs, four side chairs, and a table; the seats of the side chairs are higher than those of the other seating. English sets do not usually include a table; in French sets, the seats are all the same height. H armchair 3ft 6in/ 1.06m; side chair 3ft 3in/99cm

5 VICTORIAN BUTTON-BACK CHAIR
The high quality of this button-back upholstered chair, dating from the 1860s, is evident in the finely carved rosewood frame with its scroll arms, baluster legs and serpentine-fronted seat. H 3ft/91cm

6 BEVAN CHAIR
This rare adjustable chair in the Gothic Reformist style of the 1860s is by the architect Charles Bevan. The design was patented, and the chairs were made exclusively by Marsh, Jones & Cribb of Leeds and London. The detail (6a) shows the adjusting mechanism on the frame of the back.

1

2

3

3a

4

5

6

6a

Great halls were the setting for meals in medieval times in Europe. Although the lord's table was usually on a dais, he and his family and the servants all ate at trestle tables – large planks of wood supported by trestles. Such tables could be easily dismantled so that the hall could be used for dancing and other popular entertainments.

By the fifteenth century, the lord and his family began to dine in a separate room rather than the great hall. This resulted in the emergence of a "fixed table" of the type now commonly known as a refectory table, since this sort of table was used in monasteries, where the monks gathered in the refectory to eat together.

As the number of smaller houses increased in the mid-seventeenth century, folding tables became popular, and gate-leg tables were commonly used for dining. At the beginning of this period, tables were often as much as 8–10ft/2.4–2.7m long, but in time, since it was fashionable for the company to eat at several small tables rather than one large one, their size decreased. By the eighteenth century, advances in construction meant that the stretchers joining the legs of the gate-leg were no longer needed, and so the drop-leaf table emerged.

At first, large drop-leaf tables had six legs but later only four, for design modifications allowed two of the corner legs to swing out to an angle of 90 degrees to support the leaves.

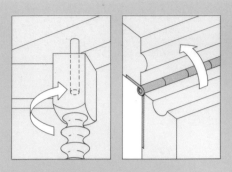

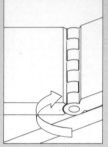

GATE-LEG DETAILS

Simple in-built wooden dowels at both ends of the fixed legs allow the gate legs to pivot outward (*far left*).

The rule joint hinge is often used on gate-leg tables; when it is, the hinged edge on the upper surface of the table shows a typical beaded profile (*left*).

DROP-LEAF DETAILS

A more refined knuckle joint is used on drop-leaf tables. This is the hinge on which the strut and leg swing out to provide firm support for the folding leaf when it is raised (*right*).

The classically molded edge of the table top conceals the hinge, giving a more elegant appearance when the leaf is dropped (*far right*).

1 SPANISH TRESTLE TABLE

This early 17th-century walnut table is of the traditional trestle type, but here the turned trestle legs are joined by ornamental wrought-iron stretchers – a characteristic also of tables that were made later in the century in Europe and Spanish America. L 4ft 2in/1.27m

2 OAK REFECTORY TABLE

This table dates from c.1660–80, and is typical of the type, with a plank top above a carved frieze rail supported by six legs united by stretchers. In this instance, the legs are of modified baluster form; in Elizabethan times they would probably have been cup and cover in style. Refectory tables are usually made of oak, but walnut and yew tables are also found. L 9ft x W 30in; L 2.74m x W 76cm

3 OAK GATE-LEG TABLE

The central section of the top of this oval table, which dates from c.1700, is supported by four fixed legs joined by stretchers at the bottom. When raised, the drop leaves are supported by hinged "gates" which swing out. In the case of large tables, there are double gates for each leaf. Diam. 4ft 2in/1.27m

4 DROP-LEAF TABLE

A descendant of the gate-leg table, this oval mahogany George II drop-leaf table of typical form has a shaped frieze. There are six tapering turned legs, ending in pad feet, two of which swing out to support the leaves. There were often drawers at each end of such tables. L 4ft/1.22m

THE CHANGING SHAPE OF THE ENGLISH DINING TABLE

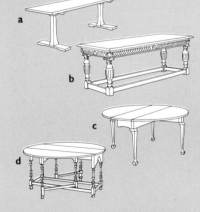

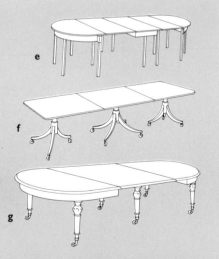

a Pre-Elizabethan dining table with early-style standard ends. b Elizabethan oak table, often made to extend, and varying in length from 4ft/1.2m to 10ft/3m. 1590. c Late 17th-century gate-leg table. d George II oval mahogany drop-leaf table, with cabriole legs and ball and claw feet. e Early George III mahogany D-ended table with extending leaves. 1770–1810. f Classic three-pedestal table with extending leaves. 1775. g Victorian mahogany table which could extend up to 20ft/6m.

FURNITURE

▲ **GEORGE II DINING TABLES**

This pair of mahogany drop-leaf tables, dating from 1745, can be used singly, or as side tables, or placed end to end to form one long table, thus illustrating the mobility of function typical of the period. The tapering turned legs terminate in ball and claw feet. Each table: H 28in x L 3ft 8in; H 71cm x L 1.12m

In great houses such as Osterley, near London in England, it remained uncommon in the middle of the eighteenth century to keep a large fixed table in the dining room and it was customary to bring in folding tables as required. By the end of the century, however, formal dining rooms were in vogue, and it had again become fashionable to eat at a large central table.

Tables with rectangular or D-ends on either pedestal or tapering legs, to which additional leaves could be added, were popular. They had the advantage of flexibility, since the two end sections could be stood against the wall as side tables or put together to make a table for six or eight.

When it was necessary to increase the size of the table, additional leaves could be added. A single extra leaf between two well-supported ends would be attached to them by means of locks – metal straps slotted into brackets on the underside of the top; where several extra leaves were added, each was supported by its own pedestal or legs.

Large rectangular, oval, or round tables on a single pedestal base, and with a hinged top that folded up vertically so that the table could be stood against a wall when not in use, were also favored. They are distinguished from similar tea tables by their size – they generally measured about 4ft/1.2m across – and were used when six or eight people sat down to eat, and for informal meals. For this reason, they became known as breakfast tables.

STYLES OF TABLE LEG

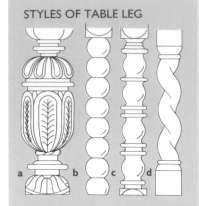

a Elizabethan cup and cover turned leg. 1580–1690
b Restoration period bobbin-turned baluster leg. 1630–75
c Restoration period reel-turned leg. 1640–75
d Restoration period barley-sugar twist-turned leg. 1660–1710

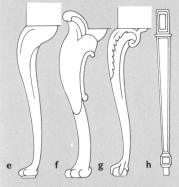

e Simple cabriole leg with pad foot. 1720–70
f Cabriole leg with carved knee and foot. 1715–45
g Cabriole leg with leaf carving and ball and claw foot. 1725–70
h Hepplewhite period classical tapering leg with carved decoration. Late 18th century

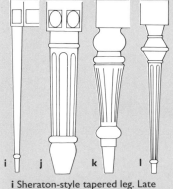

i Sheraton-style tapered leg. Late 18th century
j Turned and fluted leg. Mid-19th century
k Victorian "Tudor" leg. Late 19th century
l Reeded leg. Late 19th century

1 TILT-TOP PEDESTAL TABLE
This large center table dating from 1775 is, unusually, made of oak; at this period mahogany would have been more common. It has a simple "gun-barrel" central pedestal and a four-splay base. The downswept legs are molded, and the feet retain their original brass castors. Diam. 4ft 3in/1.3m

*The underside of the table (**1a**) shows clearly how the top is made up of several planks, with inset dovetail keys to hold the joints together.*

2 REGENCY PEDESTAL TABLE
A fine example of a popular form, this large circular table is veneered in streaky calamander wood from Sri Lanka with black and yellow coromandel crossbanding. It has a brass edge around the top and at the bottom of the frieze, and the splayed legs have brass lion's paw castors.

3 THREE-PEDESTAL TABLE
An early George III (1790s) mahogany dining table with D-ends supported by tripod pedestals, and a more traditional four-splay pedestal in the middle. Additional pedestals could be added to this type of table as support for extra leaves when it was necessary to extend it. L extended 13ft 10in/4.22m

4 MAHOGANY EXTENDING TABLE
This type of extending table, an alternative to the pedestal table, was also popular, and the designs ran concurrently from the 1760s. In this example from the 1790s, the leaves are supported by tapering legs. Often the additional supports were set slightly back from the table edge for the comfort of the diners. L extended 12ft/3.66m

FURNITURE

Throughout the eighteenth century, all-purpose tables, such as drop-leaf or tilt-top tables which could be pushed against the wall when not in use, were those most frequently found. By the beginning of the nineteenth century, round or oval tables that were often intended to remain in the center of the room were gaining favor. As long as these tables have a central pedestal and are more than 4ft/1.2m across, they are known as center tables. Most are dining tables, but the term can also refer to other types such as library or breakfast tables.

In the early years of the century, tables were made of dark mahogany or rosewood. Later, attractively figured burl walnut was more favored, and tables were often elaborately decorated with veneers, marquetry and inlays of brass, mother-of-pearl, tortoiseshell, ebony or other exotic woods. Just as tops became more elaborate, so too did the supporting column and legs. These were often heavily carved, especially as machine carving became more widespread.

The novelty of the nineteenth century was the circular or rectangular table that used mechanical action to extend it, allowing extra leaves to be inserted, and several designs for such tables appeared. The leaves rested on bearers under the table, so there was no need for extra legs.

As with other furniture, styles for dining tables were largely derivative: Elizabethan, Classical, a kind of French Rococo – the style known as *tous les Louis* – and Gothic. But some of the early commercially made furniture, designed to satisfy the demands of a moneyed middle class for comfort and the display of opulence, followed exuberant curving lines and was embellished with naturalistic carving. By mid-century, these were beginning to be replaced by crisper, more severe styles, and a simpler type of "reformist" furniture developed in parallel with the mass-produced pieces.

Modern copies

Poor copies of Victorian tables are widely produced, so be wary of a table's authenticity. Points that betray such copies are thin machine-cut veneers or marquetry and brass fittings of inferior quality compared to the original. Dirt and dust, which builds up unevenly over the years, is also often applied.

"Reformers" of style

Alongside the ornate, eclectic styles of most British furniture, including dining tables, in the 19th century those developed by various "reforming" movements are to be found. In the early years, the designs of A.W.N. Pugin (1812–52) reinterpreted the gothic style (3).

The architect and designer Charles Eastlake (1836–1906), in the middle of the century, advocated a return to simple construction and plain surfaces without polish or varnish. His ideas were seized upon by both the Arts and Crafts and the Aesthetic movements, and his influence, especially in the United States, was immense.

Philip Webb (1831–1915) was the main designer of furniture within the Arts and Crafts Movement, whose figurehead William Morris (1834–96) introduced the idea of simple, "honestly made" domestic artefacts (see pp.184, 194, 244).

In the 1870s, E.W. Godwin (1833–86), a disciple of the Aesthetic Movement, in common with designers all over Europe, began to incorporate elements of Japanese style into his otherwise European furniture designs.

By the end of the century, this trend evolved into Art Nouveau, another pan-European and American movement, one of whose most inventive exponents in Britain was Charles Rennie Mackintosh (1868–1928), founder of the Glasgow School of design (see p.200).

1 WILLIAM IV ROSEWOOD TABLE

Dating from c.1830, this large rosewood table has a nulled, or knurled, edge to the top; this was a popular decorative device between 1820 and 1870. The supporting lobed and turned column and quatrefoil base with scrolled feet are all much heavier than was the case with similar tables in the late 18th century. Diam. 4ft 6in/1.37m

2 DUTCH MAHOGANY TABLE

This large ornate table from c.1840 has a shaped apron, carved and turned pedestal and richly carved splay legs. Such exuberance, in what is generally thought of as peculiarly British and American "Victorian" style, was in fact widespread in Europe in this period. Diam. 4ft 3in/1.3m

3 REFORMED GOTHIC TABLE

An oak table in Gothic Revival style, designed by A.W.N. Pugin in 1838. The table expresses the revolutionary philosophy of avant-garde Victorian designers with its emphasis on home-grown woods, revealed structure and constructional details, and traditional pre-18th century style. L 6ft 6in/1.98m

4 SIXTEEN-SIDED TABLE

The edge of this rosewood table (c.1840) is deeply carved with spiral lobes and leaf motifs, which are repeated at the base of the pedestal. Nulling can be seen on the lower edges of the apron and pedestal base. The large trefoil platform is supported by carved animal feet and brass castors. Diam. 4ft 4in/1.32m

5 WIND-UP DINING TABLE

The date of the mahogany table shown here is established by the massive legs with bulging cabochons and by the wind-up mechanism, the first designs for which were published in 1865. (The operating handle is visible at the right-hand side of the table.) This mechanism meant that as many as six extra leaves could be added, allowing the table to be extended from 5ft/1.5m to 17ft/5.1m. The design proved popular in upper-middle-class Victorian households with big families or where large dinner parties were held.

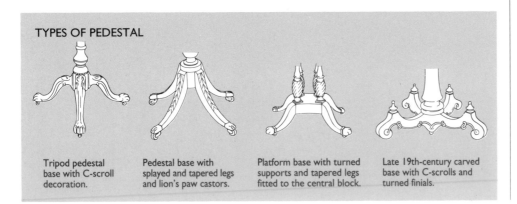

TYPES OF PEDESTAL

Tripod pedestal base with C-scroll decoration.

Pedestal base with splayed and tapered legs and lion's paw castors.

Platform base with turned supports and tapered legs fitted to the central block.

Late 19th-century carved base with C-scrolls and turned finials.

1

2

3

4

5

PEMBROKE, SUTHERLAND AND SOFA TABLES

As England prospered in the eighteenth century, a new merchant and professional class arose. Although these people lived in relatively small houses, they still required all the trappings of an earlier and grander age. Furniture had to suit a variety of needs, and so there was a growth in the number of tables for occasional use.

One such small table was the Pembroke table, named either after the Earl of Pembroke (1693–1751), a keen amateur architect or, more probably, after his wife, the Countess of Pembroke. Usually rectangular or oval in shape, Pembroke tables were frequently made of mahogany, with a single drawer in the center and a drop leaf hinged to each side. They were usually kept against a wall and simply pulled forward when needed for meals, needlework, writing or drawing.

The Sutherland table, a gate-leg table with a very narrow central portion and deep flaps, was popular in Victorian times because it folded away easily, but gave a useful surface when needed. It was named after the Duchess of Sutherland, a Mistress of the Robes to Queen Victoria.

First produced in the late eighteenth century, the sofa table became widespread only in Regency times. It was designed to be drawn up in front of a sofa, providing the lady of the house with a surface on which to read, write or draw. A development of the Pembroke table, the sofa table is longer and usually has drawers on both sides. Since they occupied a prominent place in the room, sofa tables were often elaborately decorated and were sometimes inlaid with brass or ebony.

Sheraton's definition

In *The Cabinet Dictionary* (1803) Thomas Sheraton (1751–1806) described the sofa table as "used before a sofa, and . . . generally made between 5 and 6 feet long and from 22 inches to 2 feet broad." Cheaper examples, factory-made after about 1815, tend to be smaller. No furniture made by Sheraton is known, and his fame rests on his published works.

Dummy drawers

Pembroke tables usually have a true drawer at one end with a dummy at the other to preserve the symmetry; sofa tables generally have two drawers each side, one of which is a sham.

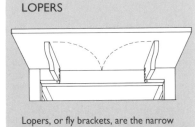

LOPERS

Lopers, or fly brackets, are the narrow strips of wood that either fold out to support the leaves of a Pembroke table, or pull out to carry the flap of a desk.

▼ **REGENCY SOFA TABLE**
This rosewood sofa table has rounded flaps with crossbanding and, typically, two frieze drawers. The lyre-shaped trestle end supports, derived from contemporary French designs and with splayed brass feet, are joined by turned stretchers. L open 4ft 9in/1.45m

1 GEORGIAN PEMBROKE table
Made in mahogany and pearwood, this George III Pembroke table has square tapering legs. H 28in x L open 3ft 5in; H 71cm x L open 1.04m

2 OVAL PEMBROKE table
Intricate marquetry and elaborate tulipwood crossbanding decorate this satinwood George III Pembroke table. H 28in x L open 3ft 6in; H 71cm x L open 1.07m

3 REGENCY ROSEWOOD SOFA TABLE
Decorated throughout with ebony stringing, this handsome sofa table (c.1810) rests on a tapering central pedestal. At each corner of the platform is a splayed leg with a stepped knee. H 29in x L open 4ft 7in; H 74cm x L open 1.4m

4 AMERICAN PEMBROKE TABLE
Attributed to John Townsend, a cabinetmaker from Newport, Rhode Island, this Chippendale-style mahogany Pembroke table has square fluted legs and diagonal stretchers. Furniture styles in North America lagged about a decade behind those in Britain, so the "Chippendale" period ran between 1760 and 1790.

5 SHERATON-PERIOD SOFA TABLE
Identifying rosewood is usually easy because of its characteristic dark purple-brown color, which does not seem to fade; here it has been inlaid with boxwood and ebony. The X-form legs are more often found on writing tables of this period. H 29in x L open 4ft 9in; H 74cm x L open 1.45m

6 PAINTED PEMBROKE TABLE
Originally, this 1780s table was plain satinwood. The decoration was added sometime after 1860 when painted furniture became fashionable, but the rather severe neoclassical motifs seem too formal for the table. L open 4ft 2in/1.27m

7 SUTHERLAND TABLE
When the gate-legs are folded away and the large flaps put down, this Sutherland table, dating from c.1860, takes up very little space (7a), making it ideally suited to the smaller rooms in many Victorian and modern houses. L open 3ft 6in/1.07m

1

2

3

4

5

6

7a   7

SIDE TABLES

These tables, intended to stand against the wall of a room, have been made since the fifteenth century and were a development of the chest. They were useful as an additional surface at mealtimes or for holding ornaments. The real importance of side tables, as part of a grand scheme of decoration or set of furniture or merely as small useful tables, grew between the seventeenth and nineteenth centuries. But no matter how elaborately decorated the front and sides of these tables became, the back was only roughly finished off.

From the 1700s, two particular types of side table emerged. Console tables, introduced from France, were fixed to the wall and often had only two front legs. They were frequently given exuberantly carved supports, backed with mirror glass to give the appearance of four legs, and topped with marble. Pier tables, as the name suggests, were designed to stand in the pier, the space between two windows. They were sometimes used to hold a candelabrum, whose light was reflected into the room by a pier glass, or mirror, hung just above the table.

▼ SIDE TABLE BY PHILIP WEBB

This oak side table has turned legs and stretchers and a single drawer with brass drop handles. Philip Webb (1831–1915) designed the table for William Morris, his associate and leader of the Arts and Crafts Movement. The table was probably inspired by Japanese temple architecture, reflecting the craze for japonaiserie (Japanese style) that swept through all areas of design from 1870–1900. H 29in x L 5ft 6in; H 74cm x L 1.68m

Gesso

A thin paste, gesso (**2**) is made by mixing size (a substance used to glaze or stiffen parchment), powdered chalk and a few drops of linseed oil. It has been favored for thousands of years as a base for tempera painting and was widely used as a base for furniture decoration until the 1730s.

Several layers of paste are spread over a piece of furniture and left to harden. When set, it can be carved, molded and used as a base for painting, gilding, molding and low-relief carving. This flexibility made gesso a popular medium with cabinetmakers producing ornate rococo pieces.

Japanning: imitation lacquer

In the second part of the 17th century, all oriental lacquer was known as japan, whatever its country of origin, so the name given to the imitative process was japanning. The fashion for chinoiserie (**8**), in the mid-18th century meant that japanning became a popular pastime for ladies, with the consequence that some rather mediocre amateur pieces exist.

The raw material for japanning is shellac, a varnish made from the secretions of lac insects. Several coats of shellac were applied to the wood. The finish was then heated to dry and harden it ready for decoration either with gilt or paint. Black was the most common background, but other colors such as red and green were used to great decorative effect.

1 RESTORATION-PERIOD OAK TABLE

The joined frame and bobbin turning of this side table, with a single drawer, show an extremely high standard of craftsmanship. L 30in/76cm

2 QUEEN ANNE SIDE TABLE

Elaborate carving and gilding decorate this fine gesso side table, one of a pair. H and L 28in/71cm

3 COLONIAL SIDE TABLE

Rather unusual because of its fifth leg, this Dutch or Portuguese rosewood side table, with fine ring-turned legs and a curved X-stretcher, demonstrates the high quality of some colonial furniture. H 30in x L 3ft 6in; H 76cm x L 1.07m

4 GEORGIAN MAHOGANY SIDE TABLE

Several features make this table typical of the period (c.1750). They are the overhanging top with a molded edge supported on a rectangular frame, the single drawer, and the tapering turned legs ending in pad feet. L 30in/76cm

5 GEORGE III SIDE TABLE

The simple lines of this mahogany table are enlivened by egg and dart carving on the apron and by pierced angle brackets between the apron and the square, chamfered legs. H 27in x L 32in; H 69cm x L 81cm

6 LATE GEORGIAN SIDE TABLE

By the late 1700s, styles had become much lighter as evidenced by this satinwood and marquetry side table – one of a pair attributed to the influential cabinetmaker George Seddon (1727–1801). It was made as part of a suite of drawing room furniture for Mersham-Le-Hatch, Kent. H 29in x L 3ft; H 74cm x L 91cm

7 GEORGE II CONSOLE TABLE

This imposing giltwood console table in baroque style, with a blue-veined marble top, is dominated by an eagle with wings outstretched, symbolizing the might of ancient Rome. H and L 3ft 1in/94cm

8 CHINOISERIE SIDE TABLE

This black and gilt japanned side table with a serpentine front dates from the late 18th century. It shows that the interest in Chinese style remained even after its heyday, from 1745–60, had passed. H 33in x L 4ft 6in; H 84cm x L 1.37m

1

2

3

4

5

6

7

8

CARD AND GAMES TABLES

Although card playing had long been popular, the first tables made specifically for this pastime appeared only in the late 1600s. They had folding tops lined with baize or felt which, when open, were supported by gate-legs. But such tables were uncomfortable to sit at, for the stretchers and legs got in the players' way.

Advances in construction in Queen Anne's reign meant that tables could be fitted with a single hinged back leg that swung out to support the top. An accordion-fold mechanism was introduced in the mid-1700s to extend the back legs and frame. Open tops had dish recesses for candlesticks and wells for counters or coins.

The advent of neoclassicism led to a change in style. Card tables were now often semicircular and decorated with marquetry or crossbanding. Many Regency tables were fitted with a well for backgammon and a reversible sliding top. A hinge and swivel mechanism was developed whereby the top swiveled around an off-center pivot, then opened out to be supported by the table frame. Also popular were fold-over tables on a central column which, by mid-century, became quite ornate.

▼ ANGLO-INDIAN GAMES TABLE
This fine early 19th-century ebony and ivory games table, with an inlaid chessboard, has an elaborate pierced border and scrolled tripod base ornamented with stylized lions. H 32in x L 3ft 7in; H 81cm x L 1.09m

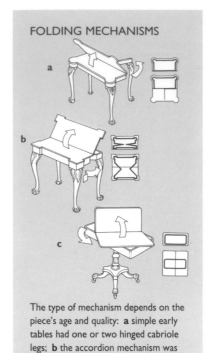

FOLDING MECHANISMS

The type of mechanism depends on the piece's age and quality: **a** simple early tables had one or two hinged cabriole legs; **b** the accordion mechanism was more complex and costly; **c** the hinge and swivel is a 19th-century innovation.

1 DUTCH GAMES TABLE
Two lifting panels in the inlaid top of this walnut and marquetry games table can be reversed to show, on one side, a backgammon board and, on the other, a chessboard. The spiral-turned legs, X-shape stretcher and bun feet are in the 17th-century style, but are later than the top. L 3ft 9in/1.14m

2 MID-18TH CENTURY GERMAN TABLE
Candles were placed at each corner of this walnut and marquetry card table with its two frieze drawers, elegant tapering cabriole legs and accordion-fold mechanism. The fine marquetry top depicts a horseman, with vases of flowers on each side and foliate strapwork. L 35in/89cm

3 GEORGE III SATINWOOD CARD TABLE
The marquetry top of this demi-lune (half-moon) satinwood card table depicts a musical trophy and part of a score by Mozart within a beaded frame and scrolling foliage and swags. The frieze, decorated with foliage scrolls and an anthemion in the center, is divided by classical urns. The square-section tapering legs are also inlaid. H 30in x L 29in; H 76cm x L 74cm

4 REGENCY ROSEWOOD GAMES TABLE
The top of this ormolu-mounted rosewood games table opens to reveal a backgammon board. A chessboard slides out beneath it, and originally there would have been a sewing basket hanging below that. D-shaped end compartments hold the games pieces. H 30in x L 29in; H 76cm x L 74cm

5 BRASS-INLAID GAMES TABLE
On this Regency rosewood games table, the reversible sliding central section, which has leather on one side and a checkerboard on the other, lifts to reveal a backgammon board. The D-shaped end sections have hinged lids, and the plain end supports are joined by a shaped stretcher. H 29in x L 4ft 7in; H 74cm x L 1.4m

6 AMERICAN CARD TABLE
Although this American mid-19 century mahogany card table still shows classical styling, it has more than a hint of the Rococo Revival style that would soon become dominant. A distinctive feature is the wooden castors which in England would have been made of brass or porcelain. L 24in/61cm

7 VICTORIAN CARD TABLE
A variation on the more usual table with a central pedestal, this 1850s card table, veneered in highly figured walnut, has exuberant curved scrolls supporting the serpentine-shaped fold-over top. The base, too, is curvilinear, with an exaggerated central finial and cabriole legs. H 31in/79cm.

Tea Tables and Stands

From the late seventeenth century, tea drinking was fashionable in Britain, but by 1727, when George II came to the throne, London's tea gardens were no longer popular with the *beau monde,* and it became customary to entertain friends to tea at home, often outdoors. A variety of tables developed, with the most popular form the tripod table: three-legged tables stand more steadily on an uneven surface than their four-legged counterparts.

Three-legged tables date back to Roman times, but they were generally used as lantern or candle stands, and it was not until the 1730s that the familiar tripod table with a single column and three curving, splayed legs evolved. Some were used for wine glasses or teacups, others as stands on which a silver kettle and its burner could be placed. These were low enough to fit beneath tea tables and often had dished tops to prevent cups or glasses from being knocked off.

Tripod tables with plain tops and rounded edges would have been covered with a cloth, and many had carved and decorated columns and bases, since only those parts were seen. Some tables had tilt-tops so they could be pushed out of the way against the wall after use. Rectangular tea tables with fold-over tops were also popular in the eighteenth and early nineteenth centuries. They were similar to card tables but had a wooden rather than a baize-covered surface on the opened flap.

◀ **CERAMIC-TOPPED TABLE**
The top of this tea table – dating from c.1890, the time of the Arts and Crafts Movement – is an octagonal Minton ceramic tray with Japanese-inspired blue and white decoration. The tray is supported by three turned legs united by a stretcher in the shape of a ship's wheel with spindles forming the spokes.

BIRDCAGE MECHANISM

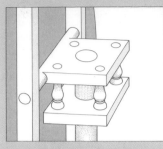

The main column passes through a central hole in two blocks under the top of the table. It is held in place (while being free to rotate) by the four small columns. To allow the table to tilt, two corners of the top block extend to form lugs which connect to runners under the table top.

Manxman tables
Tripod tables with the legs carved to represent those of a man (**4**) are known as "Manxman tables" after the inhabitants of the Isle of Man, whose flag bears a three-legged device.

Tripod tables
The heyday of the tripod table was the Georgian period (1714–1811), when craftsmen such as Chippendale were producing quality pieces in mahogany. Although the block at the base of the column became obsolete by the 1750s, and different styles of leg were used, the basic design did not change.

The main variations were in the embellishment. The edge profile of table tops varies from a plain rounded edge, through the dished edge, to the carved, scalloped edge known as a "pie crust," which was particularly popular in America. Some tables have fretwork or turned galleries around the top; on others, known as supper tables, the top has recesses for dishes or plates.

When examining a tripod table, it is customary to check that top and bottom belong together, since many tables have been constructed from firescreen bases with table tops added.

1 MID-GEORGIAN URN TABLE
This little mahogany table, made to hold a tea urn, has a pull-out shelf just large enough to hold a tea bowl or cup. With its shaped gallery and pierced corner frets, it has all the signs of a good Chippendale piece dating from the 1750s. H 30in/76cm

2 KETTLE STAND
Dating from about 1745, this small table, on which a kettle and burner would have stood, has a dished top, baluster stem and downswept legs ending in pad feet. Such tables are also known as wine tables. H 24in/61cm

3 OAK TRIPOD TABLE
Although the column on this table (c.1740) is finely detailed, the top and birdcage mechanism are rather crude, indicating that it was probably made by a country craftsman copying the work of a London cabinetmaker. The legs are joined directly to the column rather than to the more usual three-sided block base. H 30in/76cm

4 MANXMAN TABLE
*The legs of this mahogany tea table (c.1750) are carved to represent that of an 18th-century gentleman wearing buckled shoes, stockings, buttoned breeches and elaborately tasseled garters (**4a**). In this example, the legs are joined to a block with three concave and three flat faces. H 28in/71cm*

5 GEORGE III FOLD-OVER TABLE
Carved rosettes edge the fold-over top of this mahogany tea table. Vines and flowerheads on the shaped frieze, with its central crisp foliate clasp, are echoed on the square front legs, which have gadrooned edges. H 29in x L 3ft; H 74cm x L 91cm

6 REGENCY ROSEWOOD TABLES
The U-shaped and pierced spherical support are an unusual but attractive feature of these rosewood tea tables, inlaid with boxwood stringing. The downswept legs end in brass lion's paw feet and castors. H 30in x L 3ft; H 76cm x L 91cm

OCCASIONAL TABLES

▲ **ART NOUVEAU TABLE**
Designed by the Scot Charles Rennie Mackintosh (1868–1928), this lacquered oval table was possibly made for the Moscow Exhibition of 1903 arranged by the impresario Diaghilev. The leaded glass inserts are a feature found in other Mackintosh furniture.

Versatile small tables made for general use are known as occasional tables. In the late 1600s, such tables for both the center and side of the room showed the influence of Dutch design. They had rectangular tops and, often, spirally turned legs united by shaped stretchers. More ornate tables have either parquetry or marquetry tops.

In the eighteenth century, tables were often made for a particular use or room. One example is the "china" table, or tea table. Chippendale described such tables in his *Director* as being "for holding each a Set of China or may be used as Tea Tables." Similarly, in France, a plethora of small tables for various purposes such as writing and needlework and for taking coffee or tea can be found.

A feature of the English library in the late eighteenth century and Regency period was the drum table. Often such tables had revolving tops, and in the frieze there was a series of drawers or partitions for books. The frieze drawers in larger versions are sometimes lettered, and these would have been used as rent tables.

Tables with stone tops inlaid with patterns either of different types of marble alone or with *pietra dura* – a mixture of semiprecious stones and marble – were popular in the nineteenth century. The tops were normally of Italian origin, but sometimes native hardstones were used.

Marquetry and parquetry

The application of decorative veneers, ivory, tortoiseshell, mother-of-pearl and semiprecious stones, either as a pattern, picture or the representation of naturalistic forms, such as flowers or shells, is known as marquetry (1, 6). From the time of its introduction in the early 17th century, marquetry has been an enduringly popular form of decoration for furniture, especially smaller items such as occasional tables.

Parquetry (3) is the term used to describe geometric patterns made up of small pieces of veneer chosen for their grain and color.

Pietra dura

Of Florentine origin, *pietra dura* describes the use of semiprecious stones combined with marble as inlay on tables (7) and cabinets. The motifs included birds, flowers and butterflies. It was very expensive, and in late 18th-century France, *ébénistes* incorporated *pietra dura* panels from earlier, Louis XIV cabinets in their work.

Transitional style

In furniture terminology, the word Transitional is used to describe furniture made in France between approximately 1750 and 1760 (3). It marks a move away from the Rococo Louis XV style toward the more classical style of the Louis XVI period. During this time, furniture design became more restrained and combined elements of both styles.

Lambrequin

The French word *lambrequin,* meaning valance or fringe, was originally used to describe a lady's sash or mantle. Applied to the ornamentation of furniture (6), it describes a piece of wood carved to simulate swags of drapery with elaborately carved, and often gilded, tassels "hanging down."

1 DUTCH CENTER TABLE
The marquetry top of this Dutch oyster-veneered walnut center table includes the use of ivory and ebony to depict a star medallion flanked by four compass roses. The heavy, spiral-turned legs and stretchers and bun feet are typical of the late 1600s. L 3ft 10in/1.17m

2 "CHINA" TABLE
Mid-18th century mahogany tables such as this are known either as "china" or tea tables, or silver tables. Pierced fretwork is often a feature of the gallery around the top, but here it is used virtually all over with great effect. H 30in x L 28in; H 76cm x L 71cm

3 TRANSITIONAL FRENCH TABLE
This mid-18th century oval French table is in the Transitional style. The top of trellis parquetry has a pierced ormolu gallery. There is a frieze drawer and the cabriole legs are united by a concave-fronted platform stretcher, also decorated with trellis parquetry. H 29in x L 24in; H 74cm x L 61cm

4 SHERATON DRUM TABLE
The top of this small mahogany drum table from about 1790 is covered in green leather and crossbanded with rosewood. Often some of the drawers in the frieze are false, but the four drawers here all function and are lined with mahogany and crossbanded with tulipwood. The turned shaft and downswept tripod base are typical of the late Georgian period. H 29in x Diam. 24in; H 74cm x Diam. 61cm

5 REGENCY QUARTETTO TABLES
As the name implies, this is a set of four tables of varying height and width which can be stored one under the other. They are made from amboyna and rosewood with an ebony beaded rim and twin column supports. L of largest table 19in/48cm

6 WILLIAM IV TILT-TOP TABLE
This satinwood and ebony table has an elaborate marquetry top and a shaped apron decorated with lambrequins. The central column, with a parcel-gilt base, rests on a triangular platform with carved and gilded paw feet. H and Diam. 30in/76cm

7 FLORENTINE PIETRA DURA TABLE
The black marble and pietra dura top of this center table (c.1860) is signed G. Montelatici and bears three of his trade labels with his address in Florence. Swagged drapery adorns the giltwood central column, and typically ornate carved dragons and scrolls are a feature of the tripod base. H 32in x Diam. 33in; H 81cm x Diam. 84cm

1

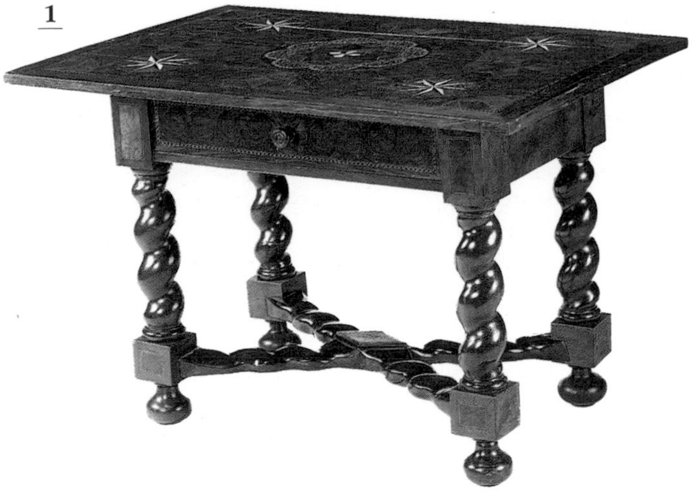

2

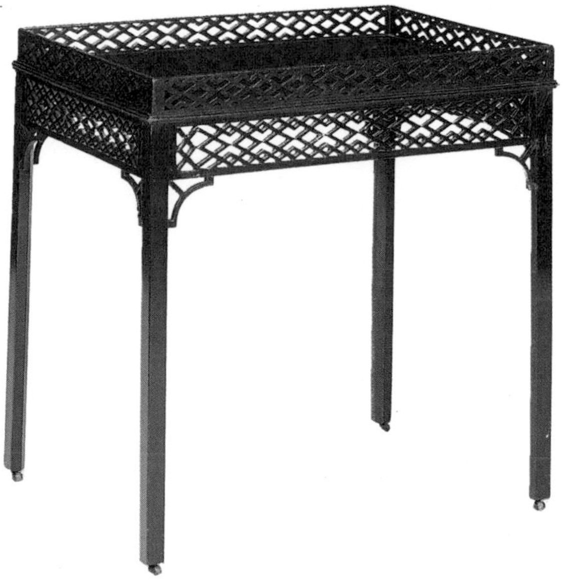

3

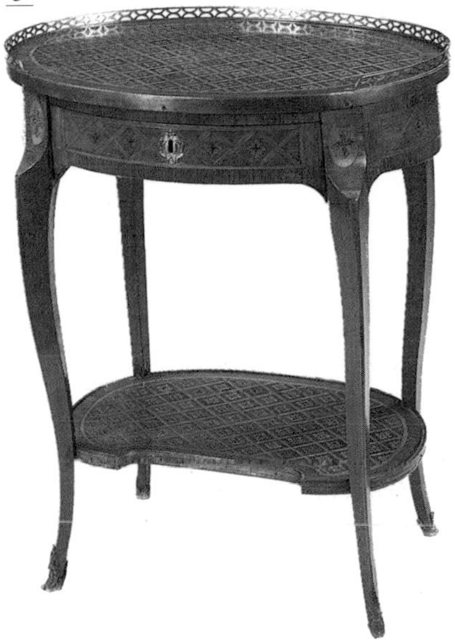

4

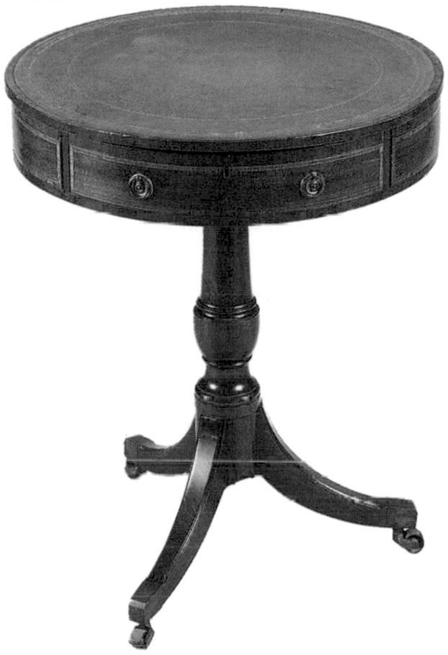

5

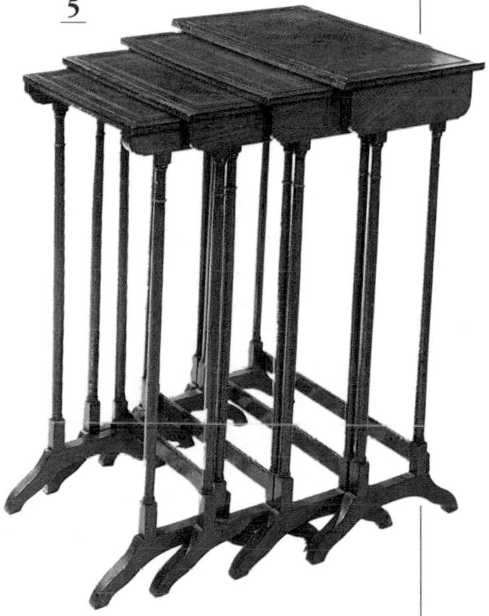

6

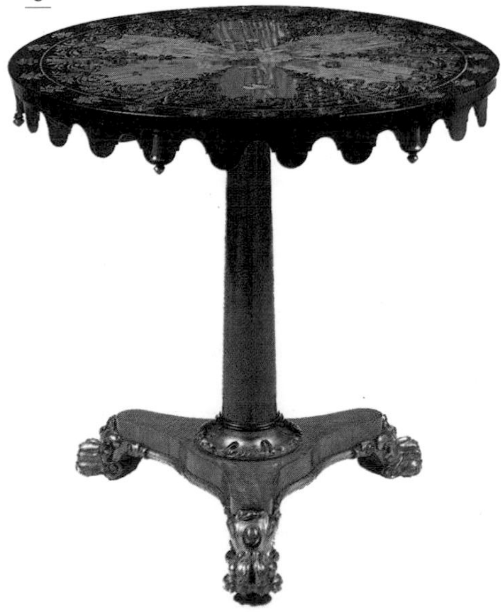

7

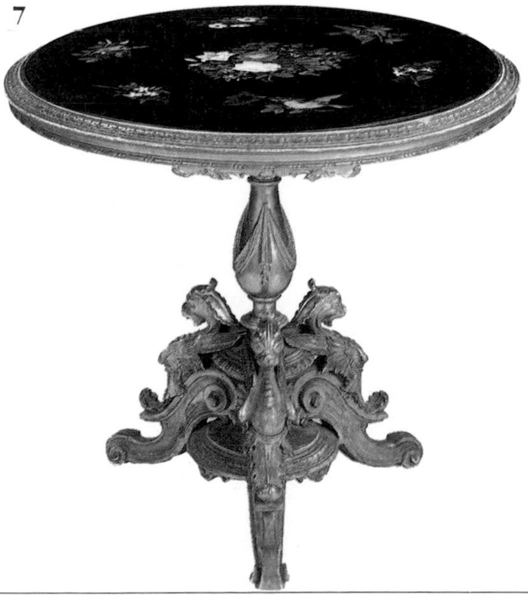

FURNITURE

Both hutches (or "dressers") and sideboards developed from side tables which, in medieval times, were used for preparing or "dressing" food. By the end of the seventeenth century, craftsmen had begun to make hutches with drawers below the board. Further storage and display room was added in the 1690s, when a low backboard was introduced with shelves and cupboards fitted above. Some continued to be made without the upper rack and were known as low dressers.

Gradually the base and upper rack with shelves became separate components. Many of the hutches seen today have a later rack sitting on an older base; since this is very common, however, it only slightly reduces the value of the piece. During the eighteenth century, hutches began to feature a tall shelved upper portion, sometimes with a backboard and often with a shaped cornice frieze and matching apron below shelves or drawers.

Hutches were essentially pieces of country furniture, made from local woods and showing regional characteristics. By the early nineteenth century, they had become unfashionable and survived only in country kitchens. It was the craftsmen of the British Arts and Crafts Movement, who, in the late 1800s, briefly revived production of hutches and spread their ideas to the U.S. and other European countries.

Woods used

Local woods were used for hutches, as for most country pieces. Oak was the most popular, but they were occasionally made from ash, elm, chestnut and even fruitwoods. In the 19th century, pine became the most common wood. In France, hutches were only made in the provinces and generally from chestnut.

Regional characteristics

Many regional variations are found among British hutches: the best known Welsh "dressers," are almost always made of oak and have geometric inlays of colored woods; South Wales (or Glamorgan) hutches have a shelf at floor level called a pot board. Hutches from Yorkshire have a central clock on the shelf section and as many as 12 drawers below, while Devon hutches usually have doors enclosing the upper shelves, and Suffolk hutches are known for their elaborate decoration.

Guides to dating

The date of a hutch can be roughly gauged by looking at the shape of its front legs – the back legs are always plain. From the 1750s the baluster leg was popular, although the spirally turned leg and flat-fronted silhouette leg were introduced in the 1670s. In the 18th century and well into the 19th century, the cabriole leg was common.

◄ WALNUT BUFFET
Elaborate marquetry decoration adorns this mid-18th century ebonized walnut buffet of South German origin. Directly below the arched top, which shows a hunting scene, is a cupboard flanked by two sets of drawers. The cupboard door, showing a man holding a church, opens to reveal five more drawers. The recessed central door on the buffet base is decorated with a hunter and hounds, while the two side cupboards each conceal another five drawers. H 7ft 4in x W 7ft; H 2.24m x W 2.13m

1 OAK COURT CUPBOARD
Dating from early in the 17th century, this oak court cupboard has open shelves for displaying plate, and a drawer in each of the two ribbed convex friezes, which are supported by elaborately carved winged beasts. The name court cupboard comes not from any connection with royalty, but because of the cupboard's low height, from the French word court meaning short. W 3ft 8in/1.12m

2 EARLY PRESS CUPBOARD
On this James I oak and parquetry press cupboard, the upper part has been enclosed by a paneled central section and two matching doors. The front of this portion rests on two carved baluster supports. The doors of the lower section are decorated with geometric designs. H 5ft 6in x W 4ft 9in; H 1.68m x W 1.45m

3 MID-GEORGIAN OAK BUFFET
The distinctive sinuous pierced frieze relieves the squareness of this large mahogany-crossbanded Shropshire oak buffet. H and W 7ft 6in/2.29m

4 VICTORIAN SIDEBOARD
With its heavily carved panels depicting scenes from Daniel Defoe's Robinson Crusoe, this English sideboard is a fine example of high Victorian taste. Made by Tweedy and Robinson of Newcastle-upon-Tyne and completed in 1872, it was probably machine carved. H 7ft 2in x W 9ft 1in; H 2.18m x W 2.77m

5 AESTHETIC MOVEMENT BUFFET
This late 19th-century Aesthetic Movement buffet, with its characteristic green staining, has an architectural gable roof above two divided shelves. The front panels of the base are decorated with intaglio peacock feathers. H 6ft 4in x W 4ft; H 1.93m x W 1.22m

6 AUSTRIAN BUFFET
This early 20th-century Austrian walnut and rosewood buffet with stylized carvings of berries is by August Ungethum. It is an example of Wiener Werkstätte (Vienna Workshops) furniture. Established in 1903, this group, influenced by both the Arts and Crafts and Art Nouveau movements, sought to re-establish good, simple design and craftsmanship. H 6ft 4in x W 6ft; H 1.93m x W 1.83m

1

2

3

4

5

6

FURNITURE

Just as the hutch developed from a side table, so too did the sideboard. In upper- and middle-class homes in the mid-1700s, side tables, or serving tables, were used in the dining room. Later, pedestals on each side of the serving table were introduced to create extra storage space or to hold wine bottles or plates; they were probably first featured in the designs for dining-room furniture by Robert Adam (1728–92).

This arrangement was not practical in smaller middle-class houses, so the pedestals became incorporated into the serving table – and the sideboard was born. Sideboards usually had six legs and could be straight-, bow-, or serpentine-fronted. They had a shallow central drawer to hold silverware and at each end was a cupboard or deep drawer which, when lined with lead and partitioned to hold wine bottles, is known as a cellaret.

From the 1790s to the 1820s, sideboards often had a brass rod fitted along the back. Curtains were hung from the rod to prevent food from being splashed on the wall when meals were served.

Sideboards with pedestal ends remained popular throughout the Victorian period; in many instances a low backboard was added, which in time became higher, and mirrors were often incorporated into the design. Eventually the space between pedestals was fully enclosed to provide additional storage space.

▼ GEORGE III SERVING TABLE

This serving table has a mahogany bowed breakfront top above a white-painted frieze on eight turned legs. Parcel-gilt feathers, leaves and paterae are used to great effect to decorate the legs and frieze. The plaque features a scene showing the marriage of Cupid and Psyche, taken from a cameo known as the Marlborough gem. H 3ft 1in x W 9ft 5in; H 94cm x W 2.87m

The *console desserte*

The 18th-century French equivalent of a sideboard was the *console desserte*. It first appeared in the reign of Louis XVI (1774–93) and probably evolved from the earlier *commode en console*.

Points to note

The styles of 18th-century sideboards were widely copied in the 19th century. More valuable early examples can be distinguished from later copies by examining the construction method. Pieces made in the 19th century tend to be clumsier and have a back panel of mahogany rather than pine, as is usual on earlier pieces.

Occasionally, large 18th-century sideboards have been made narrower to fit into smaller rooms. A simple way to check this is to pull out a couple of drawers and make sure that the grooves for the drawer runners stop short of the backboard and that the dovetails on the drawers are all of the same quality.

A piece of furniture which has been properly and sympathetically restored can, however, be worth more than a damaged item. This is particularly true of furniture such as hutches and sideboards, which will have received hard and constant use.

1 LOW OAK HUTCH
This low hutch with turned front legs is an example of the form to which cupboards, shelves and backboards were added. The mahogany cross-banding is typical of hutches from this period (c.1740). H 34in/86cm

2 BOW-FRONTED SIDEBOARD
A George III bow-fronted mahogany sideboard with rosewood banding; the tapering legs end in spade feet. The central drawer is flanked by an inlaid cupboard door to the left and a cellaret to the right. The handles are not original. H 3ft x W 5ft; H 91cm x W 1.52m

3 SERPENTINE SERVING TABLE
Probably of Scottish origin, this late Georgian serving table is inlaid with boxwood. The square tapering legs, which end in spade feet, have inlaid paterae heads and pendant bell husks. The brass rail is topped with urn finials. W 6ft 3in/1.91m

4 AMERICAN SERPENTINE SIDEBOARD
Inlaid satinwood and brass handles decorate this mahogany Hepplewhite-style serpentine sideboard. This type, with a recessed central cupboard and inlaid legs, was very popular in New England in the late 18th century.

5 LOUIS XVI CONSOLE DESSERTE
The designer of this amboyna console desserte, Adam Weisweiler (c.1750–c.1810), often incorporated a ceramic plaque in his designs; here it is one from the Wedgwood factory. The frieze has ormolu decoration of berried foliage and flutes, and the rail around the undershelf, pierced-heart decoration. The three drawers are spring operated. Although German, Weisweiler lived in Paris and became cabinetmaker to Marie Antoinette and other members of the French Court. W 5ft 6in/1.68m

6 EGYPTIAN-STYLE SIDEBOARD
Originally, this Regency mahogany pedestal sideboard in the Egyptian style would have had a gallery. Both pedestals have cupboards below and are surmounted by knifeboxes, but differ in their central sections. The one on the left has a deep drawer, while on the right a door opens to reveal three bottle recesses. There are two drawers in the central frieze, one of which has lost its handles. H 5ft 3in x W 9ft 1in; H 1.6m x W 2.77m

1

2

3

4

5

6

FURNITURE

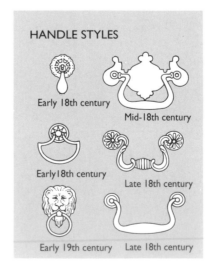

◄ HADLEY CHEST

Dower, or hope, chests such as this one in carved oak, with drawers below and a pine top attached by iron hinges, were made c.1690–1740 along the Connecticut River. They were named after Hadley, Massachusetts, by a collector who bought a fine chest there in the 1800s. Designs, which can include tulips, leaves, vines, sunflowers, pinwheels, hearts and the owner's initials (as here), were often picked out in colored stains.

The rectangular, top-opening coffer, or chest, is the earliest known type of furniture, and examples from ancient Egypt have been found. The earliest existing European chests, dating from the thirteenth century, are made of planks joined by nails; since they were designed to be portable, some have handles and are banded with iron for strength. By the fifteenth century, chests were of paneled construction, with mortise-and-tenon joints held by dowels.

But large coffers are impractical – it is difficult to reach things stored at the bottom – and to overcome this inconvenience, some fifteenth-century chests were made with a fitted drawer in the base. By the late sixteenth century, drawers had become a common feature of furniture, and by 1650 the chest of drawers as we know it had evolved.

At about the time of the Restoration in England, the old method of panel and frame construction was replaced by case construction, introduced by European craftsmen. Flat panels of cheaper woods, such as oak and pine, were dovetailed together to form the carcass of a piece of furniture, which was then veneered with high-quality wood to make it look richer.

Carving was the earliest form of embellishment. In the early eighteenth century, the use of matching figured walnut veneers and oyster veneering for decorative effect was added to parquetry and marquetry, which were popular in the late 1600s. Chests often had decorative inlays and crossbanding on tops and drawer fronts as well.

Points to note

In Victorian times, brass handles on chests were often replaced by wooden knobs, which were then fashionable. Indeed, they were the only handle style introduced by the Victorians.

In more recent times, wooden knobs have themselves often been replaced with brass handles, to give a Victorian chest the appearance of being of an earlier date.

On a chest of drawers, check that the style of the handles is contemporary with the piece and that there are no signs of their having been changed, such as old holes on the inside of the drawer which have been filled. If such evidence of handles having been replaced appears on the inside, but not on the outside, of the drawers, the fronts may have been reveneered.

HANDLE STYLES

Early 18th century

Mid-18th century

Early 18th century

Late 18th century

Early 19th century

Late 18th century

1 SPANISH CHESTNUT COFFER

Chests were an important item of furniture in Spanish homes, and much care was expended on their carving, as is shown by the flowering sunburst roundels, flowerheads and hunting scenes on this late 16th-century coffer with a hinged lid. W 5ft/1.52m

2 CHIP-CARVED PANELED CHEST

The carved geometric decoration on this 17th-century chest was "chipped out," using a round punch and half-round chisel with the aid of a ruler and compasses. The chest, which retains its iron hinges, would have stood at the end of a bed and been used for storing blankets. W 4ft/1.22m

3 EARLY 17TH-CENTURY OAK CHEST

A good early example of a chest of drawers of paneled construction; note how the side-paneling and drawer frames match up. The carving on the drawer fronts could be as early as c.1620, but the stile feet and handles are not original. H 3ft 3in/99cm

4 OAK CHEST OF DRAWERS

The chest, dating from c.1675, stands on a separate and slightly later base. The molded edges of the carcass and drawers and overhanging plank top are, however, all typical features of the period. W 34in/86cm

5 WILLIAM AND MARY CHEST

This oyster-veneered walnut chest, crossbanded with fruitwood, would originally have stood on bun feet. But possibly because of damage or 18th-century attempts to make it look more up to date, they have been replaced by oak and mahogany bracket feet. H 34in x W 3ft 1in; H 86cm x W 94cm

6 QUEEN ANNE WALNUT CHEST

The arrangement of four graduated long drawers is typical for the date (1710) of this small chest, which also has a brushing slide (see p.208). The bracket feet are of a later date. W 27in/69cm

FURNITURE

▲ **MAHOGANY EMPIRE SEMAINIER**
The name of tall chests like this comes from the French for week (semaine). Fresh linen was kept in the seven drawers, one for each day of the week. This chest has a black marble top. H 4ft 9in x L 3ft 2in; H 1.45m x L 97cm

The chest of drawers was a most useful piece of storage furniture, and after the mid-1700s, there was usually one in every room, which may explain why so many can be found today. In the early eighteenth century, chests of drawers were still rectangular; but toward the middle of the century, the ascendancy of the French Rococo style led to the adoption of the serpentine shape elsewhere in Europe. The bow-fronted chest did not emerge until the 1770s, when it became popular, and it remained so well into the 1800s. Some Regency bow-fronted chests have spirally reeded columns at the front corners.

Rectangular chests did not, however, entirely lose their appeal, and several variations emerged; among them, in the late 1700s, was the campaign chest. The Napoleonic Wars led to a demand from officers for some practical form of furniture that would make life in the field a little more comfortable, and a variety of items, including chests, was made.

Designs altered little during the 1800s, but mahogany was generally used for chests made for the wealthy and pine for those of the less well off.

Brushing slide

This is the name given to the sliding shelf found between the top and the first drawer of a chest of drawers (1, 2). It could be pulled out so clothes could be laid out on it to be brushed.

Campaign chests

Intended for use by army officers on active service, the campaign, or military, chest had to be strong, compact and versatile. It was usually made of teak or mahogany, often with brass-bound corners and recessed handles that were unlikely to be torn off by rough treatment when the chest was in transit. Many chests contained a mirror, washbasin, and writing fall or shelf, as well as drawers.

Not all campaign chests saw active service, however. The style became popular with the young men of the Regency and early Victorian periods, and many of these chests were made for purely domestic use; generally speaking, it is these which have survived.

Drawer types

The drawers of early chests pulled straight out, scraping the sides. By the late 17th century, runners were fixed to the sides of the chests which, together with corresponding grooves, or rabbets, running front to back a third of the way up the drawer sides, made drawers run more smoothly.

After 1710, a different type became the norm: the sides of the drawer were continued below the drawer bottom to act as runners. Although this form of construction puts considerable strain on the carcass, it remained popular until the present century, when side runners once more became the vogue.

TYPES OF FEET

Bracket foot
1720–80

Bracket foot
1720–80

Turned foot
1850

Ogee foot
1740–75

Splay foot
1780–1810

Turned foot
1870

1 GEORGE III MAHOGANY CHEST

A typical arrangement of two short and three long drawers is found on this simple chest (c.1775). Between the drawers and the molded top are two knobs for pulling out the brushing slide. H 33in/84cm

2 GEORGE III SERPENTINE CHEST

There are four graduated drawers and a brushing slide below the eared top of this mahogany chest (c.1765). The canted angles feature cluster columns, a fairly common feature on bow-fronted chests also. On some such chests, the top drawer is fitted as a dressing table, with a mirror and lidded compartments. H 33in x W 3ft 2in; H 84cm x W 97cm

3 AMERICAN KNEEHOLE CHEST

The kneehole chest of drawers was seldom produced in America outside Rhode Island. This fine example in mahogany, ash and tulipwood, with a typical rounded block front and stylized shell carving, dates from c.1765–75 and is attributed to the Townsend-Goddard School in Newport. H 34in x W 3ft 2in; H 86cm x W 97cm

4 MILITARY CHEST

Made of walnut with brass-bound corners and flush handles, this chest, dating from 1836, is in two sections for ease of transportation. The bottom section has two drawers, while the top has one wide drawer, with four smaller drawers and a central fall-front secretaire drawer above. H 3ft 6in/1.07m

5 BURL WALNUT WELLINGTON CHEST

First made in the early 19th century, such chests are known as Wellington chests in the first Duke's honor; this one dates from c.1845. The left- and right-hand columns are hinged and lockable, and the chest would have been used to hold coins, medals or specimens. H 4ft/1.22m

6 KILMARNOCK CHEST OF DRAWERS

A mid-19th century mahogany chest from Scotland with a slim cushion-molded top drawer. Below are two deep and two shallow drawers and three deep full-width drawers. The flanking barley-sugar twist columns are free-standing. H 4ft/1.22m

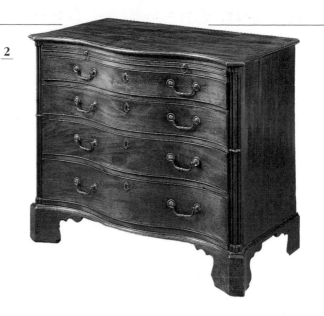

1

2

3

4

5

6

COMMODES

In Victorian England the term "commode" described a bedside cupboard or chair holding a chamber pot, but it is more correctly used to describe a lavishly decorated chest of drawers. Of early eighteenth century French origin, the commode became arguably the most important piece of furniture in a great house. It was usually found in the salon, or drawing room, and great attention was paid to the ornamentation on this symbol of an owner's wealth and taste.

From the 1740s, commodes became a feature in English houses, where they were known as "French commodes." At first, they were of bombé or serpentine shape; later, many had bow fronts. By the early 1800s they were rectangular. Decoration included marquetry and gilt-metal mounts; painted ornament became a feature around 1870. Some commodes had drawers, others doors as ornate as the top, behind which drawers were concealed. Commodes retained their popularity throughout the 1800s. Their form and decoration were often a revival of earlier styles, although some were copied exactly from eighteenth-century examples.

▼ LOUIS XV KINGWOOD COMMODE
The use of darker wood to emphasize the magnificent gilt-bronze mounts of this chest (1735), in the style of Charles Cressent, demonstrates the skill of the French ébéniste. Gilt-bronze bands linking the front corner mounts with the foliate hoof feet (sabots) protect the edges. H 3ft x W 4ft 8in; H 91cm x W 1.42m

Marble tops
Many European commodes had shaped marble tops, whereas in England they usually had wooden tops. Although some commodes retain the original marble top, from the 18th century onward this will, in many instances, have been replaced because of accidental damage or because the commode was moved to a different room and the top was changed to match the marble of the new fireplace. The fact that the top has been replaced does not necessarily alter the value of the piece.

Guide to quality
An approximate idea of the quality of a commode may be gained by examining the ormolu mounts. The best pieces have bold and heavy mounts with finely embossed detail, while those of lower quality tend to be lighter and less well finished.

1 GERMAN MARQUETRY COMMODE
Known as a commode à la Régence, this type with three drawers was popular throughout the 18th century. This early piece in walnut, yewwood and satinwood is inlaid with flowers and foliage and has a gray marble top; the block feet are later. H 33in x W 3ft 11in; H 84cm x W 1.19m

2 GEORGE III MAHOGANY COMMODE
A good example of a "French commode" c.1770, this piece is attributed to Thomas Chippendale. The design is an interpretation of those by Jean Bérain (1637–1711), one of the originators of the Louis XIV style, combined with the up-to-the-minute decoration of ebony key-pattern lines. The doors conceal pigeon holes and drawers. H 35in x W 5ft 2in; H 89cm x W 1.57m

3 NORTH ITALIAN COMMODE
The bombé shape of this mid-18th century walnut commode was as popular in England as in the rest of Europe. The inlay in ivory, mother-of-pearl and pewter on the top is echoed on the front and sides. H 3ft 1in/94cm

4 LOUIS XV COMMODE
A scrolled marquetry cartouche has been combined with parquetry on this mid-18th century French bombé commode, which has ormolu mounts. The marble top is a later replacement. H 33in x W 3ft 9in; H 84cm x W 1.14m

5 DUTCH CHEST OF DRAWERS
Dating from c.1775, this is a typical Dutch commode with convex and concave drawer fronts and paw feet – a style which was popular throughout the 18th century. The piece has been restored, and although correct in style, the ornate handles, escutcheons and locks are of a later date. W 3ft/91cm

6 SWEDISH COMMODE
Since Swedish court architects were sent to Paris for training, their designs were, for a long time, influenced by those of the French. This late 18th-century walnut-veneered commode has three drawers and sharp-cornered veneers, which are typically Swedish features, and asymmetrical rococo handles. H 34in/ 86cm

7 TRANSITIONAL FRENCH COMMODE
Clearly showing the move away from the rococo style to more classical straight lines, this tulipwood and purpleheart piece dates from c.1765. The decorative inlays also derive from classical motifs, while the rail and cabriole legs are still rococo in style. H 3ft 1in x W 4ft 4in; H 94cm x W 1.32m

HIGHBOYS, TALLBOYS AND PRESSES

The highboy or chest-on-stand, a near relative of the chest of drawers, first appeared soon after the Restoration of the English monarchy in 1660, when Charles II returned from Europe with many foreign artisans. Highboys became popular because placing a chest of drawers on a stand meant people were able to reach the bottom drawer more easily. The decoration of highboys was similar to that of contemporary chests, but the tops were not normally veneered.

By the early eighteenth century, the highboy had evolved into the chest-on-chest, or tallboy. During the course of that century, the shapes of tallboys developed from the early rectangular to later serpentine and bow-fronted forms. The first tallboys were made of veneered or burl walnut, but by the 1740s mahogany veneers were being used.

From the mid-eighteenth century, the "press" started to rival the tallboy for storing linen and clothes. A press consisted of a cupboard with sliding shelves placed on a chest of drawers. By early Victorian times, presses had often been fitted, on either side of the central shelf section, with a cupboard for hanging clothes – the armoire as we know it had evolved.

American furniture periods

In the United States, furniture styles lagged some years behind those in Britain. Although Queen Anne ruled from 1702–14, in the United States the Queen Anne style (2) lasted from 1720 to 1755. Similarly, the American Chippendale-style period (4) ran between 1755 and 1780, about five years behind the same style in Britain.

Is it original?

Occasionally, chests-on-chests may be found that are the result of a "marriage," or fitting together, of two chests to create a different piece. Although this was often done for good practical reasons, it can seriously affect the value of a piece.

A quick inspection will soon reveal a marriage. Check that the wood and decorative detail of both parts match exactly and that the backboards of both chests are of the same timber and of similar quality. Pull out a couple of drawers and examine the inside of the drawer front for any extra holes indicating that handles have been changed; also check that the dovetailing on the drawers of both parts matches.

1 CHARLES II OAK CHEST-ON-STAND
Although the arched top section appears to have eight small drawers, it actually has four wide drawers and a brushing slide. The same illusion occurs on the stand, which also contains a secret drawer. The baluster legs, wavy stretchers and bun feet are all Restoration features. H 5ft 6in x W 3ft 8in; H 1.68m x W 1.12m

2 AMERICAN QUEEN ANNE HIGHBOY
Crafted from the local woods of New England, this maple and pine highboy (the American name for a chest-on-stand) has cabriole legs. Typical of this type of piece is the bonnet-top pediment with flame finials, a style that flourished in North America, but never became popular in Europe.

3 GEORGE I BURL WALNUT TALLBOY
Dating from around 1725, this tallboy, or chest-on-chest, has a molded cornice and fluted canted corners which indicate its quality. H 5ft 10in x W 3ft 8in; H 1.78m x W 1.12m

4 AMERICAN CHEST-ON-CHEST
This mahogany Chippendale-period chest-on-chest shows the fluted canted corners often seen on pieces from New England. It has brass handles and a carved and pierced finial in the center of a broken-arch pediment.

5 GEORGE III LINEN PRESS
The lines of this mahogany and parcel-gilt press are architectural, from the broken-arch pediment (now lacking the central ornament) to the fretwork pilasters flanking the doors and ogee feet. H 8ft 3in x W 4ft 6in; H 2.52m x W 1.37m

6 DUTCH WALNUT CLOTHES PRESS
A profile of Mercury, messenger of the gods, graces the center of the cornice of this 1760s' walnut clothes press. Marquetry decoration covers the entire piece from the flowering urns and songbirds on the cupboard doors to the bombé base and carved apron. H 7ft 6in x W 5ft 8in; H 2.29m x W 1.73m

7 EARLY VICTORIAN LINEN CUPBOARD
This satinwood linen cupboard can be dated to the 1840s by the maker's stamp Johnstone Jeanes & Co., 67 New Bond Street, London. The central cupboard is fitted with four slides and is flanked on each side by six cedar-lined drawers. H 4ft 11in x W 7ft 11in; H 1.5m x W 2.41m

◄ **GEORGE I CHEST-ON-CHEST**
Finished with a molded cornice and decorated with feather banding, this burl walnut tallboy has two small and six long drawers in the upper section and the more usual arrangement of three long drawers below. Later examples sometimes have the top drawer of the lower part fitted as a secretaire drawer. H 5ft 2in x W 4ft 1in; H 1.57m x W 1.24m

FURNITURE

Architecturally, a cabinet is a small room in which valuable objects are stored or displayed; in furniture it has a similar definition, describing a piece of furniture with doors, behind which there are shelves or drawers used for storing valuable items.

The cabinet, developed in Spain and France early in the sixteenth century, was described at the time as "a small piece of furniture, more or less portable but always square in shape and containing many neat, small drawers." Such cabinets were known in England from Tudor times, but they were of European manufacture. They were often quite small and would generally have stood on a table, a trestle stand or a chest, although a few may already have had their own stands. Cabinets were not widely made in England until after the Restoration of the monarchy in 1660, when they rapidly became popular.

These later cabinets were usually 5–6ft/ 1.5–1.8m tall and 3–4ft/90cm–1.2m wide. Some of them stood on chests, while others were mounted on stands. The decoration of the stand matched that of the cabinet and was of high quality, reflecting the treasures stored within. Marquetry, parquetry and veneering were used with great skill, as were ivory, enamel plaques, semiprecious stones and painted panels. Trade with the Far East meant that both lacquer cabinets and lacquer panels, which were then made up into cabinets or used as doors, were imported, while the stands were made in Europe and reflected the style of the day.

Is the stand original?

The legs of stands often get damaged, so it is as well to check that there are no differences in color between stand and cabinet and that there is no distressing in areas that are not normally subject to wear and tear. Many stands have been replaced at a later date, but the quality of the veneering will indicate this, since old, handcut veneers were usually at least 1/16in/1.6mm thick, while machine-cut veneers are paper thin.

The veneers were laid over a base of oak or pine and then finished. Variations in thickness are generally due to wear and tear or shrinkage of the carcass timbers.

Oyster veneering

This form of parquetry was very popular among cabinetmakers and other craftsmen in the late 17th century (below). The veneers were cut across the grain of small branches of trees, resulting in a pattern of whorls that resembled the inside of an oyster shell. Favorite woods were walnut, laburnum, olive and kingwood.

Seaweed marquetry

Also known as arabesque marquetry, seaweed marquetry (6) was so called because the swirling patterns in contrasting woods, such as holly and walnut, look like fronds of seaweed.

2 LOUIS XIV WALNUT CABINET
The scarlet tortoiseshell door, itself decorated with a trompe l'oeil doorway in ebony and ivory, conceals a mirrored interior with small drawers, typical on cabinets at this time. The beautiful marquetry, which includes birds and flowers, shows the high standard of decoration found on quality furniture. H 5ft 8in x W 4ft 1in; H 1.73m x W 1.24m

3 DUTCH CABINET
This form was popular in Holland during the 17th century. The doors have central floral marquetry panels surrounded by geometric designs in burl walnut parquetry. The interior is fitted with three drawers and shelves for storage. H 7ft 2in x W 5ft 8in; H 2.18m x W 1.73m

4 GEORGE III MAHOGANY CABINET
The simplicity of this mahogany cabinet, with a fretwork gallery and carving on the door frames and stand in Chinese Chippendale style, is in marked contrast to most late 18th-century cabinets. There is little risk of the cabinet overshadowing the contents, which would have been clearly seen through the glass-paneled doors. H 3ft 8in/1.12m

5 GERMAN CABINET-ON-STAND
The decoration and rectangular shape of this chinoiserie cabinet imitate the lacquer cabinets imported from China during the late 17th and 18th centuries; it was, possibly, made in Berlin. The later stand (c.1830) is an exact copy of the stands for two Louis XIV cabinets imported by the Duke of Northumberland in 1824 and now at the family home, Alnwick Castle. H 5ft x W 3ft 11in; H 1.52m x W 1.19m

6 KINGWOOD CABINET-ON-STAND
A combination of pietra dura (semiprecious stones and marble) and seaweed marquetry has been used to decorate this late 17th-century cabinet. The elaborate giltwood stand is of a later date. H 5ft 9in x W 5ft 4in; H 1.75m x W 1.63m

7 ITALIAN EBONY AND IVORY CABINET
Dating from c.1875, this ebonized neoclassical style cabinet, with inlay and figures in ivory, and two ebony figures supporting the stand, shows how earlier designs and decoration retained their popularity. H 8ft 7in x W 4ft 11in; H 2.62m x W 1.5m

1 SOUTH GERMAN CABINET
Free-standing ebonized barley-sugar twist columns adorn the front of this early 18th-century cabinet, supported by an elaborately carved stand. Among the allegorical marquetry on both the exterior and interior are symbols of Fortitude and Folly. H 5ft x L 3ft 11in; H 1.52m x L 1.19m

◀ **CHARLES II CABINET**
This oyster-veneered laburnum cabinet has a drop-flap intended for writing in place of the more usual blind doors. The flap is leather lined, and the fitted interior has a central cupboard surrounded by drawers and pigeonholes. Stiles on each side of the frieze drawer indicate that the stand originally had six legs. H 5ft x W 3ft 10in; H 1.52m x W 1.17m

Cabinets with blind doors, no matter how highly ornamented, had to be opened and an object removed so that it could be examined or admired. This changed during the early to mid-eighteenth century, when the fashion for collecting and displaying porcelain being imported in vast quantities from China prompted the production of cabinets with glazed panels in their doors.

These cabinets were of various forms: some had their own stands, others were of more architectural form, with pedimented tops, often reaching a height of 7ft/2.1m or more. Yet others had a glazed door on the top half, revealing the contents, and a blind door to the bottom section.

Lower side cabinets appeared in the late 1700s; they were often made in pairs and could be used between windows in place of pier tables. A popular form in Victorian times was the credenza, a low D-shaped cabinet with glazed, quarter-circle cupboards at each end. Another type was the vitrine, which looked back in style to eighteenth-century France.

As with other furniture, cabinet styles varied widely during the 1800s, and examples were made in Gothic, Rococo Revival and Sheraton Revival styles – a trend that carried through into the early 1900s.

Points to note
Side cabinets
Brass grills over pleated-silk door panels did not become a feature until early Victorian times. There should normally be shelves and not drawers behind the doors.

Display cabinets
Occasionally, these have been cut down from larger pieces so that they will fit into today's smaller houses. Make sure there is a stepped joint between the lower and upper sections and that the cabinet is not made in one piece.

From 1770 onward, the base section normally had cupboards and was not as high as the top section.

Earlier decorative panels from older pieces of furniture were sometimes incorporated into cabinets made in the latter half of the 19th century, giving the impression that the piece is older than is actually the case.

To make them more saleable, glass has often been added to cabinets with blind doors, and they are then passed off as original.

◄ GEORGE III CABINET
Made c.1770 for the breakfast parlour at Fawley Court in Buckinghamshire, this display cabinet is spectacularly veneered in broomwood in a chevron pattern. The doors have their original brass grilles, behind which are panes of glass. The shelves are very slightly raked to allow the objects inside to be viewed clearly, while the two cupboards in the base are fitted with shelves and removable trays. H 9ft 8in x W 8ft; H 2.94m x W 2.44m

1 GEORGE IV SIDE CABINET
The decoration of this rosewood and ebonized side cabinet, with its use of anthemia in ormolu, pleated silk doors, roaring leopard monopodia and marble top is typically Regency. It has a royal provenance, for it bears the inventory mark of George IV. H 3ft 1in x W 3ft 7in; H 94cm x W 1.09m

2 BOULLE MEUBLE D'APPUI
Boulle-decorated furniture enjoyed a great revival in the 19th century as is exemplified in this breakfront cabinet (c.1860) whose design harks back to the early 18th century. The pale color of the intricate inlay in the ebonized wood reflects the veining in the marble top. H 3ft 9in x W 6ft 3in; H 1.14m x W 1.91m

3 VICTORIAN GLASS-FRONTED CABINET
Called a credenza after the Italian for sideboard, this type of cabinet either had a blind central cupboard with shelves and could be used as a sideboard or had glazed doors and could be used as a display cabinet.

The detail (3a) from this walnut example, dating from 1860, shows the high quality of the figured veneers, marquetry and gilt mounts. H 3ft 7in/1.09m

4 SHERATON REVIVAL CABINET
The fashion in the early 1900s for furniture with a lighter look led to a revival of Sheraton style. This display cabinet, with serpentine sides and a central panel of hooped beading, is made in orange-toned East Indian satinwood; 18th-century originals were veneered in gold-toned West Indian woods. W 4ft 6in/1.37m

5 CHIPPENDALE REVIVAL CABINET
The extensive, ornate carving and generous curves of this mahogany display cabinet make it a superb example of its type. Despite the size, cabinets such as this would have been found in many ordinary middle class homes at the beginning of the 20th century. W 6ft/1.83m

1

2

3

3a

4

5

WRITING TABLES

The earliest piece of writing furniture was a box with a slanted lid; it stood on a table and its compartmented interior held the necessary materials. By the early 1700s, however, several types of handsome furniture were being developed for an increasingly literate clientele. Among them was the writing table, a large, flat-topped rectangular table with drawers in the front apron, known in France as a *bureau plat*. This was a popular form until the end of the nineteenth century, with only its style and decoration reflecting the changes in taste.

The eighteenth-century love of smaller rooms led to a demand for furniture to fit them, and around 1760 French *ébénistes* produced the immediately fashionable *bonheur du jour* (success of the day). This is, typically, a small table with a cabinet superstructure and a single frieze drawer.

Writing tables became fashionable in England in the mid-1700s, and in the 1780s a new style evolved with a D-shaped superstructure. This was called a Carlton House table after the Prince Regent's London home; but although the prince owned such a desk, no firm evidence exists to confirm that the first one was made for him.

▼ ITALIAN WRITING TABLE

Elaborate marquetry and carving in Renaissance and Mannerist styles decorate this early 19th-century writing table with secret recesses. The coat of arms of the House of Savoy is inlaid on the top and indicates that it may have been a royal commission.

The art of boulle

This type of marquetry (1) uses veneers of brass and tortoiseshell cut together in elaborate patterns. It was named for André-Charles Boulle (1642–1732), although he did not invent it but rather perfected its use.

Thin sheets of the materials were glued together, then the pattern was cut out. A design in brass on a tortoiseshell background is known as *première-partie* boulle, while tortoiseshell patterns set into brass are known as *contre-partie* boulle.

In England, where it is also referred to as Bühl work, it became fashionable in Regency times; many cabinet makers used it, but normally on a rosewood, mahogany or ebony background rather than tortoiseshell. One of the technique's best-known exponents was Louis Le Gaigneur, a Frenchman, who made boulle furniture for George IV.

French makers' marks

The mark JME (2), which is found stamped on pieces of furniture made in Paris from 1743 to 1789, stands for *Jurande des menuisiers ébénistes*, the guild whose role was to guarantee the high quality of the furniture that was made by its members.

The stamp is more often found on pieces produced by *ébénistes*, who specialized in veneered furniture, than on those of *menuisiers*, who specialized in carved furniture.

1 BUREAU PLAT
Boulle decoration of an early 18th-century type, in a combination of both première- *and* contre-partie, *has been used to great effect here on a 19th-century carcass.*

2 LOUIS XV TABLE À ÉCRIRE
This small writing table, with its kingwood and tulipwood parquetry and floral marquetry, is a good example of a type made in the mid-18th century – the golden age of letter writing. It was made by Pierre Roussel and is stamped JME. H 29in x W 26in; H 74cm x W 66cm

3 GEORGE III CARLTON HOUSE DESK
The D-shaped superstructure of this elegant, early satinwood desk consists of small drawers that follow the curve of the table around to the front edge. H 35in x W 3ft; H 89cm x W 91cm

4 GEORGE III BONHEUR DU JOUR
The design of this ormolu-mounted, mahogany bonheur du jour owes much to the German ébéniste David Roentgen, who worked for the French and Russian courts – the architectural form and concealed drawers are typical of his work. This desk may have been made by John Okeley who trained at Roentgen's Neuwied workshop in Germany from 1766–72.

5 GEORGE IV OAK WRITING TABLE
During the 1820s Sir Geoffrey Wyatville remodeled Windsor Castle in the gothic style for King George IV. The design motifs of this substantial table (c.1825) reflect the continuing popularity of the style in England. H 33in x W 5ft 3in; H 84cm x W 1.6m

6 LOUIS XVIII BONHEUR DU JOUR
This charming early 19th-century piece, decorated with porcelain plaques and ormolu mounts, is the epitome of a lady's writing table. The cupboard on the desk top is flanked by small shelves, and a slide pulls out to provide a surface for writing. H 4ft 2in x W 30in; H 1.27m x W 76cm

7 VICTORIAN BONHEUR DU JOUR
Writing tables such as this one, in burl walnut with kingwood crossbanding, were made for a lady's use in either the drawing room or boudoir. The gilt-metal mounts and porcelain plaque show how English designers c.1860 tried to emulate earlier French styles. W 3ft 5in/1.04m

KNEEHOLE AND PEDESTAL DESKS

The desk developed in Italy and France in the early part of the seventeenth century. One French model that evolved was the *bureau mazarin*, a desk with a rectangular top and drawers on either side of a knee-hole supported on legs united by stretchers. The name is a nineteenth-century appellation, since Cardinal Mazarin, Louis XIV's First Minister, died in 1661 before the type first appeared. English examples are found by the 1690s.

The more typical eighteenth-century English kneehole desk originated from the chest of drawers and was probably at first used as a dressing table, standing against a wall. It had a rectangular top with a long drawer, underneath which were two banks of drawers on either side of a central recessed kneehole with a cupboard.

As with other case furniture, shapes and styles changed, and by the mid-eighteenth century large pedestal desks were a feature of libraries and business offices. Since they were meant to be free-standing, these desks were decorated on all four sides. They had a large rectangular top and two pedestals with drawers or cupboards reaching to the floor on both sides and were big enough for a person to sit on either side, hence the term "partners' desks". Smaller versions were made for use in private houses, generally with dummy drawers on one side so that they could stand in the centre of a room. Pedestal desks have remained popular and are still being made.

Points to note
Kneehole desks
Unscrupulous dealers sometimes create kneehole desks out of chests of drawers, so make sure the veneer on the cupboard and sides of the kneehole are of the same colour and grain as the rest of the piece. The construction of the small side drawers should be the same on both the outer and inner edges and there should be an even amount of wear on the carcass from use over the years.

Pedestal desks
These have three parts: a separate top, with a central drawer and two smaller side drawers, and two pedestals, each of which usually contains three drawers. Check that the components match and that one has not been replaced by a part from another desk; changes in veneer colour will indicate this. The desks may also have been cut down to make them more saleable, so look out for signs of saw marks on the carcass and veneers that do not match.

▼ **BUGATTI KNEEHOLE DESK**
Made by the Italian designer Carlo Bugatti (1856–1940) in 1900 for the Conte Crevelli Visconti, this large ebonized and rosewood desk has a detachable superstructure. It features vellum panels painted with the stylized grasses and Moorish detailing that are typical of Bugatti's exotic style.

1 LOUIS XIV BUREAU MAZARIN
This example is made of ebonized wood with parcel-gilt decoration, but these desks were often embellished with elaborate marquetry or boulle. The bureau plat superseded this form in the early 18th century. W 4ft/1.22m

2 ENGLISH KNEEHOLE DESK
Dating from c.1720, this walnut desk, with its original handles and bracket feet, is a good example of its period. The oak back panel and oak-lined drawers with feather banding around the sides are a sign of quality. H 29in x W 4ft 5in; H 74cm x W 1.35m

3 KNEEHOLE DRESSING-TABLE DESK
This fine Georgian mahogany writing desk, with serpentine top, carved decoration and ogee feet, dates from c.1760. It served also as a dressing table, for the long top drawer opens to reveal a baize-lined slide covering a fitted interior. It contains a mirror, glass bottles, lidded boxes, compartments, racks and even secret drawers, thus providing facilities for either writing or the toilette. H 32in x W 3ft 5in; H 81cm x W 1.04m

4 GEORGE II KNEEHOLE DESK
Although it has undergone later modifications, this mahogany desk is still an attractive example, with its cabriole legs and hairy paw feet. The sides contain a combination of real and false drawers, with a cupboard on the left-hand side. There are false drawers at the back. H 32in x W 4ft 1in; H 81cm x W 1.25m

5 MID-19TH CENTURY PEDESTAL DESK
The dummy drawers at the back indicate that this desk was designed to be free-standing. The richly figured walnut veneers and tooled leather top are typical of the period and the name of the maker, Lamb of Manchester, is stamped in the top right-hand drawer. H 29in x W 4ft 5in; H 74cm x W 1.34m

6 ART NOUVEAU DESK
Made by the firm of Shapland & Petter at Barnstaple, Devon, from white-lacquered oak, this desk is decorated with a combination of lead glass and stained glass ovals that reflect the influence of both Charles Rennie Mackintosh and the Vienna Secessionists. H 3ft 2in x W 3ft 3in; H 97cm x W 99cm

WRITING DESKS

Writing desks are sometimes called bureaux, their name in French. In England the word *bureau* is used specifically to describe a desk, or cabinet, with interior drawers or pigeonholes concealed by a drop-flap which slopes at an angle – usually 45 degrees. As a rule, the bureaux made throughout the rest of Europe tend to be larger than their English counterparts, which developed from the early writing boxes sometimes called Bible boxes.

Between 1690 and 1720, the cabinet stood on a stand with six legs; when the drop-flap was lowered, the two legs at the center front would swing out to support it. It was not until the early 1700s that the present form of the desk evolved, with a writing cabinet above a chest of drawers.

At first, desks were made in two sections and often had carrying handles, for, like writing boxes, they were regarded as portable. The upper part stood on the unveneered top of the chest, with a molding hiding the joint. Later desks were made in one piece, but the molding was kept as a form of decoration and did not disappear until *c.*1720. After this date, the top was always flush with the base or slightly set in from it. This basic shape has remained constant, the only changes being in the design of the handles, feet and drawer fronts as tastes have changed.

Cockbeading
Found on English furniture (**2**, **6**) from *c.*1710, this is a protective rounded molding applied to the edges of drawers to prevent the veneer from being damaged.

Points to note
On a genuine writing desk, feet and handles will be in period with the style of the piece. Early examples had bun feet, which in the 18th century were often replaced with the then more fashionable bracket feet. More recently, these have in some instances again been replaced by new bun feet.

Handles, too, are often changed with the intention of "updating" a piece to make it more fashionable or to make it appear older than it is.

Supporting the drop-flap
The drop-flap of a desk is supported in one of three ways: on gate-legs (**1**); on the partly opened top drawer (**3**); or on lopers (**2**, **4**, **5** and **6**).

▼ **LOUIS XV BUREAU DE DAME**
This bureau, made for a lady (c.1750), is smaller than normal. It has a typical fitted interior with drawers, shelves and a well. Some of the ormolu mounts are original, others have been added, probably in the 1800s. W 3ft 8in/1.12m

1 WILLIAM AND MARY OAK DESK
The two legs at the center front of the stand swing out to support the flap of this desk when it is opened. The fitted interior includes shelves, four drawers and a well. The baluster and bobbin legs, united by stretchers, end in feet of a later date. H 34in x W 30in; H 86cm x W 76cm

2 GEORGE I WALNUT DESK
This piece has an elaborate fitted interior, with a central cupboard flanked by two pilasters which are, in fact, secret drawers. The band of newer veneer between the top and lower sections indicates that when it was made this piece may have had a band of molding there. H 3ft 3in x W 3ft 1in; H 1m x W 94cm

3 MID-18TH CENTURY ITALIAN DESK
The bombé, or swelling, curvaceous shape and rococo design of this walnut desk from Lombardy were echoed elsewhere in Europe, notably in Holland. Such shapes are said to have been influenced by the work of the baroque architect Francesco Borromini (1599–1667), the designer of the exuberant baldachin in St. Peter's, Rome. H and W 4ft/1.2m

4 SCANDINAVIAN DESK
The swags and guilloches in the marquetry on this burl walnut and kingwood desk point to a date of c.1775, for they reflect the interest in Classicism that was current in Europe at that time. There are no frieze drawers, but the interior has three wells. H 3ft 5in x W 32in; H 1.04m x W 81cm

5 ROSEWOOD BLOCK-FRONT DESK
At first glance, the block front of this late 18th-century desk, with its concave and convex curves, seems typical of a piece of Dutch-influenced furniture from Pennsylvania. The wood, however, indicates that its origins were oriental. H 3ft 4in/1.02m

6 MAHOGANY DESK
The fall-front of this writing desk of classic shape and proportions (1780) encloses small drawers and pigeonholes. When it was made, it would have relied on the mahogany veneer and crossbanding for decorative effect, but in the 1800s the marquetry panels and boxwood lines on the drawers were added; the handles, too, are later: the originals would have been "swan necks." H 3ft 6in/1.07m

FURNITURE

As books became freely available, the need for more storage space led from the idea of writing cabinets on chests, or bureau-cabinets, to the secretaire-bookcase, with a traditional desk base and a cupboard above in which to keep books. The cupboard was at first enclosed by blind or mirrored doors and later by glazed doors. A molded edge disguised the "join" between the upper and lower sections.

After the mid-1700s, the hinged writing slope was sometimes replaced by a secretaire drawer which pulled out to form a writing surface. Secretaire-bookcases, became the great showpieces of New England cabinetmakers in the late 1700s. Since they were regarded as status symbols, secretaire-bookcases everywhere were often richly carved and ornamented.

Another form of writing desk popular in the late 1600s was the cabinet on a stand with a large vertical fall-front, known as a scriptor. Similar to this was the *secrétaire à abattant,* which found favor in late eighteenth-century France and was copied by cabinetmakers elsewhere in Europe. The large expanse of the fall-front and the cupboard doors below it presented a splendid opportunity for rich embellishment, often incorporating marquetry or, in later pieces, well-figured veneers.

Points to note

If one section of a secretaire-bookcase or cabinet is damaged, the two sections may be split up and the good part "married" to a new partner, decreasing the value. The top of the desk, where the bookcase rests, should always be veneered. The back edge of the top half should always be flush with that of the bottom half. Veneers, handles and any carving should be the same on both sections.

Light for reading

Many early 18th-century secretaire-bookcases were fitted with candle slides (*below*), located at the base of the upper section just below the doors. When more light was needed, the slides could be pulled out and a candlestick placed on them. This was particularly effective when the bookcase doors were mirrored.

Block-fronted furniture

The front of some case furniture (**3**) is made up of three vertical sections; the central one is concave while the two flanking sections are convex, creating a block front. Popular in the early 18th century with New England cabinetmakers, the design originated with André-Charles Boulle and was common in North European countries.

◄ **GEORGE II BUREAU-CABINET**
This sumptuous scarlet lacquer cabinet came from the same collection as the set of chairs that were made in Giles Grendey's workshop and exported to Spain (see pp.176–77).
The chinoiserie decoration of foliage, landscapes, horsemen and figures, on the fall-front and drawers of the desk and inside the cabinet, is heightened with gold and silver. The doors are mirrored on the outside, and the fitted interior has a mirror-glazed cupboard, drawers, racks and pigeonholes.
H 7ft 9in x W 3ft 4in; H 2.36m x W 1.02m

1 SPANISH WALNUT VARGUEÑO
Vertical fall-front desks, known in Spain as vargueños, *were popular in the 16th and 17th centuries. They were often mounted on simple stands, but this iron-bound desk, decorated with bone and parcel-gilt, has a stand with drawers and cupboards. Both sections have carrying handles. H 4ft 11in/1.5m*

2 GEORGE II SECRETAIRE-BOOKCASE
The top left-hand drawer of this rare mahogany secretaire-bookcase with glazed upper doors (c.1735–50) bears the maker's label of Giles Grendey. It forms an interesting contrast to the other piece by Grendey (below). The column to the right of the central cupboard in the fitted interior hides a secret compartment which is released from inside the cupboard. H 6ft/1.83m

3 AMERICAN SECRETARY DESK
A fine example of a Chippendale-style mahogany and pine secretary desk with a bonnet top, made c.1755–85 in Newport, Rhode Island, probably by the famous cabinetmaking Goddard family. The block front and stylized shell motifs in groups of three are characteristic of Rhode Island design.

4 DANISH BUREAU-CABINET
Cabinets such as this early 19th-century one in mahogany, with architectural features and intarsia panels in fruitwood, were known in Denmark as chatol. *The cupboards were drawing-room pieces and were often used to store flatware and glasses, since at the time the Danes took their meals in this room. H 7ft 2in x W 4ft 3in; H 2.18m x W 1.3m*

5 EMPIRE SECRÉTAIRE À ABATTANT
This secrétaire, *with its rich mahogany veneers and striking ormolu mounts, is typical of those made in France in the early 1800s. On earlier 18th-century models, the drawers below the fall-front were generally concealed by cupboard doors. H 4ft 9in x W 3ft 2in; H 1.45m x W 97cm*

6 SECRÉTAIRE À ABATTANT
The finely figured veneers are the sole decoration on this secrétaire. *There is a cushion (convex-fronted) drawer in the frieze, and the fall-front opens to reveal an arrangement of small drawers and compartments, each fitted with an ivory knob mounted above one full-length internal drawer. H 5ft 1in x W 3ft 1in; H 1.55m x W 94cm*

ROLL-TOP DESKS

The roll-top, or cylinder, desk is another form that owes its origins (*c.*1760) to a French cabinetmaker, in this instance Jean-François Oeben. This type of desk has a writing table base with a superstructure of drawers and shelves over which a curved cover rolls back, revealing a writing surface that may be fixed, or slide forward as the top opens or be pulled forward manually.

The rolling tops of these desks are either of tambour form, where slats of wood are glued to either linen or canvas, or are "cylinders" of solid wood. Papers and letters could easily be stored away by simply closing and locking the roll top. The design spread throughout Europe and to North America, and these desks have remained popular into the twentieth century. They became fashionable in England in the late 1700s, and both Sheraton and Hepplewhite produced designs for them.

▼ WOOTON CYLINDER DESK
The apparent cylinder shape of this walnut desk, patented in 1874 by William S. Wooton, is deceptive. The front opens to reveal a fall-front writing flap and cabinet-like doors with slots, pigeonholes and shelves. Satinwood inlay and cast-brass pulls are a feature. These were popular office desks until the 1890s, when even their capacious size proved no match for the increased paperwork generated by typewriters.

A desk for a king

The masterpiece of Jean-François Oeben (1721–63) is the roll-top desk he was ordered to make for Louis XV in 1760. It was completed in 1769 by Oeben's former apprentice Jean-Henri Riesener, who became *ébéniste* to Louis XVI. Known as the *bureau du roi*, it can today be seen at Versailles in the room for which it was made.

Oeben was skilled in the use of marquetry, and the bronze mounts on his furniture were always of a high quality. He was a lover of mechanical features and invented the *secrétaire à capucine*, a small, seemingly flat-topped writing table on which, when a spring mechanism is operated, part of the top rises to reveal a set of drawers.

Point to note

Whether of tambour type or solid wood, the tops of roll-top desks can be difficult to keep in working order, and their condition will affect the value of any piece.

1 DUTCH ROLL-TOP DESK
At first glance this could be mistaken for a French example, with its diamond parquetry and crossbanding, but the wood used is walnut, which is typically Dutch. The locks and fittings are original, c.1785. H 3ft 7in/1.09m

2 RUSSIAN ROLL-TOP DESK
Like much furniture made in Russia during the 1800s, this elegant desk, with its parquetry and brass inlays and mounts, owes its design to foreign influences. There are similarities with the designs of the German David Roentgen, who worked for the Russian Court in the late 18th century. H 4ft 2in x W 4ft; H 1.27m x W 1.2m

3 REGENCY ROLL-TOP DESK
This kingwood and tulipwood desk is a type that was popular with ladies, for it can be used for reading as well as writing. Books were placed on the two shelves, supported by brass columns, and the pull-out slide formed a reading slope. The star-shaped handles, one of which is missing, are a nice period detail. H 4ft 9in x W 30in; H 1.44m x W 76cm

4 AUSTRIAN ROLL-TOP DESK
An attractive mahogany desk dating from the late 18th or early 19th century. Despite the fine ormolu mounts, which appear French, the construction and cedar-lined drawers suggest an Austrian origin. When the cylinder fall is opened, it rolls into the semicircular back of the desk. H 3ft 4in x W 31in; H 1.02m x W 79cm

5 SCANDINAVIAN ROLL-TOP DESK
The Napoleonic Wars in the early 19th century meant that mahogany and other woods could not be imported into Scandinavia. As a result, cabinetmakers turned to native woods such as satin birch, which is here used with a darker wood to emphasize the architectural design of the interior. H 4ft x W 3ft 8in; H 1.22m x W 1.12m

6 ENGLISH CYLINDER-FALL DESK
This large mahogany desk was probably made for a library. There are three frieze drawers with two cupboards below on each side of a central kneehole. The opened top shows the shelves, drawers and pigeonholes for storing papers and other paraphernalia, that were a feature of such desks. W 6ft 6in/1.98m

By the late 1700s, a gentleman's library would have housed several different types of table and desk, which were used for both reading and writing. On those known as architects' tables, the front legs and frieze of the table could be pulled forward so that the top could be raised as an easel.

Another form of writing desk which developed during this period was the davenport, so called, it is thought, after a Captain Davenport who gave an order to the English furniture maker Gillows of Lancaster to produce such a desk. The rectangular design was, at first, of a rather military severity, but as these small desks gained favor in the nineteenth century, they became more elaborate and remained so until the end of the century.

The Napoleonic wars in the early 1800s, and the need for portable furniture for officers and clerks in both the army and navy, led to the introduction of the writing box, or slope, which could be as useful on military expeditions for the gentleman as for his lady on sketching expeditions. Made with brass-bound edges or corners, they had hinged lids, which when opened formed a sloping writing surface, with compartments underneath for quills and ink or paints and brushes.

By the middle of the nineteenth century, designs had become more decorative, and boxes were made of papier-mâché, lacquer or exotic rosewood, coromandel and zebrawood. Some were veneered in burl-cut woods or even covered with leather.

An early furniture maker

The firm of Gillows was founded by Robert Gillow in 1695 in Lancaster. At that time, the city was a port through which American timber was imported, and it became the company's headquarters.

In 1761 a London branch of the firm was opened in what is now Oxford Street. During the 18th and 19th centuries, they produced a large amount of well-made furniture, much of which bears Gillows's stamp. The firm eventually became Waring and Gillow, and their records, which go back to 1731, are today preserved in the Victoria and Albert Museum, London.

Points to note

Some library tables have had their legs altered to make them appear of earlier date. Square tapering legs are found on early examples, but by the 1790s turned tapering legs had become more fashionable. These were then supplanted by the use of end supports early in the 19th century.

▼ **READING OR WRITING TABLE**
The design of this table, dating from c.1790, has been influenced by contemporary French neoclassical furniture. With its lifting top and frieze drawer, it is similar to an architect's table. When the drawer is opened, a baize-covered slide is revealed, under which is a series of boxes marked with the letters of the alphabet. L 3ft 8in/1.12m

1 ROSEWOOD DAVENPORT
The design of the davenport changed in the 1820s. The drawers were made less wide to create a recess for the writer's knees that was flanked either by turned column supports in the classical manner, as seen in this early Victorian example, or, later, by scrolling supports. The top is inlaid with leather, and there is a small drawer for writing materials. W 24in/61cm

2 BURL WALNUT DAVENPORT
While some davenports have lift-up compartments, others have a counter-balanced rising top for stationery and, as in this fine mid-Victorian example, a writing surface that slides sideways. The scrolling supports have pierced fret panels. W 24in/61cm

3 CYLINDER-FALL DAVENPORT
Veneered in burl walnut with marquetry panels, this piece provides an interesting variation on the standard davenport. While the cylinder-fall and stationery box above are quite usual at this date (c.1865), the section below is less so, since the drawers have been replaced by a cupboard with shelves for sheet music.

4 GEORGE IV LIBRARY TABLE
Inlaid with brass and decorated with contre-boulle on the frieze, drawer fronts and stretcher, this Regency rosewood library table dates from around 1820. The claw feet, cast in gilt-brass, are typical of the period. L 3ft 9in/1.14m

5 VICTORIAN LIBRARY TABLE
The design of this leather-topped library table (c.1860) can probably be attributed to the architect and designer Charles Bevan. The top is supported at each end by twin turned columns, carved with spandrels, dots, triangles and chevrons, while the apron has formalized floral motifs. There is contrasting inlaid banding and ebonized details. L 4ft 6in/1.37m

6 BURL WALNUT WRITING SLOPE
Typically mid-Victorian, with its cylindrical lid and inked-in walnut veneer, this writing slope (c.1850) has its original fittings. These include the inkwell, leather-covered tinder boxes with engraved gilt-metal lids (used to light candles for melting sealing wax), agate quill holder and gilt-metal paper knife. W 18in/46cm

BOOKCASES

In the past, books were owned mainly by the rich, so bookcases were often designed as part of the architecture of large rooms, and even those that were free-standing were big. Usually only the upper part in which books were stored had glazed doors, while the cupboards below had blind doors. The breakfront bookcase with a projecting central section was popular.

Among the earliest known cabinets built specifically for books are those made for the famous diarist Samuel Pepys in the 1660s. Until this time, books were few, and they were kept in cupboards and chests, but by about 1730, books were more readily available, and they became an important feature of a gentleman's house as an indication of wealth and taste. Just as cabinets were needed in which to display precious objects so, too, the demand grew for cabinets in which to keep books, which were highly prized not only for their contents but also for their rich bindings.

In the late 1700s, it became fashionable to collect paintings, and so, to create more wall space, bookcases became smaller and lower. The new types, including chiffoniers, low breakfronts and revolving bookcases, allowed books to be kept more readily at hand in rooms other than the library.

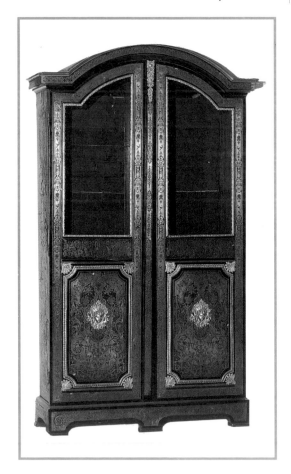

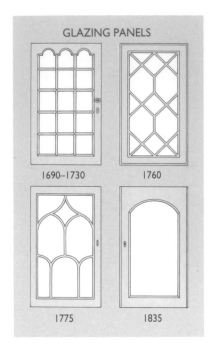

GLAZING PANELS

1690–1730

1760

1775

1835

Glazing styles

The style of glazing can help in dating a piece. The development of clear, lightweight glass in the late 1600s meant that doors could be fitted with glazed panels. Early glazed doors had rectangular panes held in place with substantial moldings.

After 1760, glass was of better quality, thinner and easier to cut. The shape of the panes thus became more varied and elaborate, and heavy moldings were replaced by astragal glazing bars, which looked like curved beading. Small panes were used all through the 1700s, and it was not until the 19th century that doors with one large glass panel were widely made.

Adaptations and alterations

Bookcases may be cut down to suit smaller rooms by removing the pediment or reducing the height or depth of the carcass. Late Georgian and 19th-century breakfront armoires are often altered to look like 18th-century bookcases. Blind doors are made for the lower section, while the upper part is reduced in depth and glazed panels are fitted to the doors. Make sure the veneers on sides and front are the same in grain and color.

◀ **FRENCH RÉGENCE BOOKCASE**
Most of this bookcase, decorated in boulle marquetry, dates from c.1720. The base is later, and the ormolu masks on the lower half of the door may not be original. Similar bookcases with wood veneers are also found. H 8ft 7in/2.62m

1 GEORGE III BOOKCASE
How splendidly a Georgian library could be furnished is demonstrated by this grand mahogany breakfront bookcase with a broken C-scrolled pediment. It is similar in design and workmanship to bookcases supplied by Thomas Chippendale c.1760–65 and can reasonably be attributed to him. H 8ft 11in/2.72m

2 MID-GEORGIAN BOOKCASE
The style of this mahogany bookcase, with its molded cornice and two drawers, shows the development in design from the now-rare bookcases of the late 17th century, such as those belonging to Pepys (now in Magdalene College, Cambridge, England) which had glazed doors on the lower section. By the early 1700s, the base had drawers, or cupboards with blind doors. H 7ft 3in/2.21m

3 REGENCY SATINWOOD BOOKCASE
This bookcase with tapering pilasters and adjustable shelves is a good example of the smaller forms that became popular in the late 18th and early 19th centuries. It may well have stood with its matching counterpart against the pier walls of a room. H 3ft/91cm

4 ARTS AND CRAFTS BOOKCASE
Ernest Gimson (1864–1919), a prominent member of the Arts and Crafts Movement, designed this small walnut bookcase in the style that was popular for Victorian library furniture. His work is notable for its elegant simplicity – here the only ornament is the chamfering on the sides and shelf edges. H 5ft/1.52m

5 REVOLVING BOOKSTAND
Dating from the early 1900s, this bookstand, decorated with stringing and crossbanding in a traditional manner, is an example of the Edwardian Sheraton revival. The three small drawers and cupboards make it a useful piece in an ever-popular style. H 35in/89cm

6 FRENCH REVOLVING BOOKSTAND
Produced in Nancy c.1900, this walnut bookstand was designed by Emile Gallé (1846–1904), better known for his work in glass. The fruitwood marquetry design and flowers and foliage of the pierced panels reflect Gallé's love of nature. The base is of a later date. H 30in/76cm

BEDS

From the Middle Ages on, beds were highly prized possessions, regarded as symbols of the owner's wealth and taste, and much attention was paid to their construction and the richness of the hangings and canopy. The four-poster, or tester, bed favored in Tudor times was usually made of oak; this style remained popular, however, and many later examples in mahogany can be found. The wooden headboards and the posts at the foot of these beds were nearly always richly decorated, since they were clearly visible, while the posts at the head were obscured by the bed curtains and were plainer.

Half-tester beds, that is, beds with a half canopy, first appeared toward the end of the seventeenth century, but did not oust the four-poster until the early 1800s.

During the nineteenth century, many types of bed were made, including some in Elizabethan Revival style and others in fashionable French taste. Bedsteads in iron and brass, which owed their origins to the folding iron beds used on military campaigns, were first made in 1820–30 and proved popular with the general public. The quality varied: the best were of finely wrought iron rods with decorative fittings masking the joints, while the simplest resembled little more than a length of fenceposts.

Points to note
Tester beds
The name "tester," which now refers to a four-poster, derives from the old term for the canopy or ceiling of a large bed.

In addition to making reproduction oak tester beds, the Victorians adapted 17th-century carved oak beds to make them more suitable for their homes. Other, 20th-century, modifications to look for are reductions in height and width to suit smaller modern rooms.

In the 1920s, decorated footposts removed from 18th-century beds were used to make torchères by the addition of a tray top and tripod feet.

The bedroom was used as a living room for greeting friends well into the 18th century, and in large houses much attention and detail was paid to the main bedroom and its bed, which was often a four-poster.

Federal-style country beds
Simple designs are easily faked, so check that corners have become slightly rounded with handling and that feet and slats are appropriately worn. With painted examples, make that paint is original by checking whether an earlier layer of paint is visible in cracked areas.

◀ **FOUR-POSTER BED**
A magnificent example of English chinoiserie furniture, this splendidly carved wooden bed has japanned red, blue and gold decoration and a pagoda-shaped canopy with gilt dragons at each of the four corners.

The fourth Duke of Beaufort commissioned it for a bedroom at his home, Badminton House, from the cabinetmaker John Linnell (1729–96), and it was made in the workshops of Linnell's father, William, between 1752 and 1754. The bed formed part of a set of furniture which included eight armchairs, two pairs of free-standing shelves, and a commode.

1 OAK MARQUETRY TESTER BED
A traditional Carolean oak four-poster bed with a paneled headboard, canopy and decorated columns with cup and cover turning. The arcaded headboard has marquetry panels depicting vases of flowers.
H 7ft 5in x L 6ft 11in x W 5ft 9in;
H 2.26m x L 2.11m x W 1.75m

2 REGENCY FOUR-POSTER BED
The decoration of this bed in fruitwood and parcel gilt uses many motifs popular in the Regency period (1811–30), from the foliate edge and stars on the cornice to the fluted columns with their mounts and carved feather finials. These are a reminder of the feathered plumes found on some of the great beds of earlier times. H 8ft x W 3ft 8in;
H 2.44m x W 1.12m

3 FEDERAL-STYLE BED
This New England country bed with matching ends and a slatted base is of a type known as a "hired man's bed," since it could serve as an extra bed in a living room. It is made from maple, stained to look like mahogany, and though simple, the design shows the same classical influence that inspired earlier, more stylish, Federal designs. It dates from c.1820–50.
H 24in x L 5ft 11in x W 24in;
H 61cm x L 1.8m x W 61cm

4 CAST IRON AND BRASS BEDSTEAD
The looped design of this bedstead, dating from c.1870, is unusual. The cast iron rods of such beds were usually enhanced by gilding or primary colors or, as here, with brass decoration.

5 BRETON-STYLE OAK BEDSTEAD
The spindle-work, tall corner posts and well-carved pediments on this bedstead dating from c.1870 are typical regional characteristics of furniture made in Brittany, northern France. A ship's wheel motif gives an appropriately nautical touch.
W 5ft/1.52cm

6 LOUIS XV-STYLE BEDSTEAD
Made in southern France c.1875, this walnut bedstead, with a well-carved headboard and ornate relief carving on the footboard, is a fine example of Louis XV Revival furniture popular in the late 19th century. The shell motif is often found on high-quality beds of the period. W 4ft 6in/1.37m

FURNITURE

Bedroom furniture, often made *en suite*, generally consisted of a clothes press, stools or chairs, and dressing table in addition to the bed. Although cosmetics had been used for centuries, the earliest form of table made specially for the *toilette* was the side table with an arched frieze and three small drawers that appeared in the mid-1600s.

In the early eighteenth century, dressing tables similar in design to the kneehole desk or pedestal desk were made, but by mid-century these gave way to chests and tables with fitted interiors; mirrors housed in the top drawer could be raised on a ratchet. Although stationary mirrors on the top are found on some late eighteenth-century dressers, it was not until Victorian times that they became standard.

Another important and useful item of bedroom furniture was the linen, or clothes, press. The top cupboard section, with blind doors, held shelves on which folded clothes could be laid, while the lower part had drawers. By the Regency period, larger armoires were being made which consisted of a central clothes press flanked by hanging cupboards. As the 1800s wore on, armoires became more like those of today, with full-length doors and hanging space, but larger versions of the Regency type were made until well into this century.

Commercial manufacturers

In the Victorian era, with its increasing emphasis on machine-made furniture, mass-produced pieces of dubious quality in a confusion of derivative styles flooded the market. There were also, however, several firms who produced well-designed furniture to extremely high standards. Prominent among these was Gillows (2), later Waring and Gillow (*see p.228*), who made pieces in the reformist Gothic Revival style initiated by Pugin. And after 1875, Liberty's promoted the work of the Art Nouveau and Arts and Crafts Movements (*see p.168*).

Art Deco style

Designers in the 1920s rejected the previous century's fashion for reviving the styles of the past. Taking their inspiration from a variety of artistic movements – Cubism, Futurism and Bauhaus among them – they created the style that became known as Art Deco (3). The name, deriving from the French for "decorative arts," was coined after the Exposition des Arts Décoratifs held in Paris in 1925.

Art Deco glorifies the achievement of the 20th century and incorporates Modern Movement themes – rationality, simplicity and functionalism.

◀ **DUTCH ARMOIRE**
The continental European version of the clothes press, the armoire, was extremely popular in 18th-century Holland. This serpentine-fronted example in mahogany has a bombé lower section with claw and ball feet. Delft ornaments were often displayed on top of the cornice, which here has foliate scrolling and a portrait medallion. Many plain armoires were later decorated with marquetry. H 8ft 5in x W 6ft 8in; H 2.57m x W 2.03m

1 GEORGE II CLOTHES PRESS
A fine example in mahogany of an English clothes press. The cornice has a foliate egg and dart border centered by a grotesque mask. Egg and dart molding also decorates the paneled doors that enclose shelves and three drawers. There is a brushing slide in the chest section, which has a gadrooned frieze with a central carved shell and claw feet. H 7ft x W 4ft 5in; H 2.13m x W 1.35m

2 VICTORIAN GOTHIC CLOTHES PRESS
This oak press, part of the furnishings of the Palace of Westminster – the British Houses of Parliament – was made by Gillows c.1850 to a design by A.W. Pugin. The cast iron hinges and handles are typical of Gothic Revival style. H 7ft x W 4ft; H 2.13m x W 1.2m

3 ART DECO ARMOIRE
Part of a suite, this burl maple armoire, with ivory inlay and ormolu lockplates in the form of garlands, is characteristic of 1920s Art Deco style. It bears a label for the firm of Mercier Frères, Paris.

4 GEORGE II DRESSER
A fine yewwood dresser dating from c.1755. There are three small drawers in the deep arcaded frieze, and the square-section cabriole legs end in pad feet. W 31in/79cm

5 SATINWOOD DRESSER
This fine satinwood dresser with rosewood banding has a shield-shaped mirror on easel supports and a superstructure of drawers. The lower part has canted corners and a shaped undertier; the square tapering legs end in spade feet. H 4ft 9in x W 35in; H 1.45m x W 90cm

6 REGENCY DRESSER
This mahogany dresser is in a style popular in the late 18th and early 19th centuries. The twin-flap top opens to reveal an adjustable mirror and fitted compartments. H 31in x W 32in; H 79cm x W 81cm

7 CHIPPENDALE-STYLE LOWBOY
The American origin of this mahogany lowboy (c.1770) is indicated by the carved panel on the lower drawer, the carved knees and feet, and the brass handles and lockplate, which are larger and more decorative than English ones. H 31in x W 34in; H 79cm x W 86cm

Dressers with attached mirrors did not become commonplace until the 1800s; toilette mirrors, which could be placed on a chest or table, were, however, a feature of eighteenth-century bedrooms. Many had a base with drawers for storing cosmetics and other small toiletry articles.

The washstand evolved by the mid-eighteenth century and was usually either of rectangular or tripod form. A basin was placed at the top with a shelf for a soap dish below and, at the bottom, a dished platform on which the water jug stood. Washstands gradually became more elaborate, with hinged lids to conceal the basin, and corner washstands with rising tops that acted as splashboards became popular.

Bedside cabinets, or commodes as they were named in Victorian times, were also introduced in the mid-1700s and replaced the close stool. Normally rectangular, they had tray tops and a cupboard underneath with two doors or a tambour shutter. Below this were simulated drawers which opened to reveal a chamber pot and could be used as a seat. The tops had hand holes so the commodes could be removed during the day.

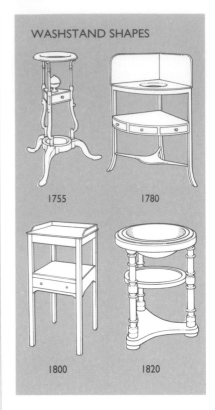

WASHSTAND SHAPES

1755   1780

1800   1820

A German furniture style

The style of furniture and other decorative artefacts made in Germany and Austria c.1820–40 is known as Biedermeier (5). The name comes from a fictional "Papa Biedermeier," a caricature of middle-class comfort.

The furniture had a simpler, more classical elegance than the previous French Empire style; there was less use of metal mounts, and the forms were more architectural. English furniture designs were also favored, as can be seen in some of the sofas of the period, which look similar to those of the English Regency.

Light-colored fruitwoods were used for most of the furniture made in Austria and southern Germany, while dark mahogany was favored in the northern German states.

The style was also adopted to some extent in Scandinavia, Russia and eastern Europe (see p.184).

◀ **QUEEN ANNE TOILETTE MIRROR**
This fine and rare early 18th-century lacquered toilette mirror, with its original arched beveled mirror plate, has a base in the form of a miniature writing desk. Inside are pigeonholes and small drawers, and the front drawer is fitted with three boxes and two brushes. H 5ft 8in/1.73m

1 GEORGE III WASHSTANDS
This pair of washstands is a good example of the type produced in the late 18th century. Each has a twin-flap top enclosing a well for the basin, and a cabinet, drawer and shelf below. Originally, they also had pull-up mirrors. H 35in/89cm

2 LOUIS XV TABLE DE NUIT
Dating from the mid-18th century, this kingwood and tulipwood table has a solid, serpentine three-quarter gallery around the marble top. There is a paper label on the table bearing the letters CP beneath a crown, No 647 and a painted inventory number, 237. This might indicate a royal provenance, since at the time the letters CP were used for pieces made for the château of Compiègne. W 19in/48cm

3 REGENCY BEDSIDE CABINET
This gothic-style mahogany cabinet, one of a pair, has arcaded molding on the door and sides, and stands on reeded bun feet. It has a molded arch interior with a shelf. H 32in/81cm

4 ENGLISH MAHOGANY WASHSTAND
A good example of the tripod type, dating from 1755–60. This design is sometimes known as a wigstand, since a wig could be placed in the bowl to be dressed, and any powder would be caught in the bowl. H 31in/79cm

5 BIEDERMEIER BEDSIDE CABINET
A mahogany bedside cabinet in fluted column form, which dates from 1820–40. It has a scrolling ionic capital and stands on a shaped plinth. The rising top is hinged and originally enclosed a fitted interior. H 34in/86cm

6 MARBLE-TOPPED WASHSTAND
Victorian washstands were usually much larger than earlier models and were often part of a set of furniture. This American one in oak has a shaped marble top and splashboard, with a cabinet below for the chamber pot, and stamped brass handles. It was probably made in Ohio c.1860–90.

7 ANGLO-INDIAN DRESSING BOX
Made of sandalwood with inlaid ivory decoration, this box is typical of the Anglo-Indian furniture made in Vizagapatam in the late 18th century. The two small bottles fit into the segmented interior, which also holds boxes and a mirror. H 16in/41cm

FURNITURE

FURNITURE

Fitted corner shelves were an integral part of paneled rooms and were the inspiration for corner cabinets. These pieces of furniture were popular throughout the eighteenth century and were generally either hanging, or floor-standing cabinets of double height. Early examples were made from oak; later, walnut, mahogany and pine were most common.

Although some cabinets had glass panels in the doors, the majority of doors were blind. These were often decorated with painted flowers or elegant scenes, and some were japanned. Others were inlaid with marquetry and parquetry or, less elaborately, with stringing or bands of different colored wood. When cabinet doors were blind, it was customary to leave them open so that the china could be seen on the shaped shelves within. Later in the eighteenth century, variations were made to include a cabinet below and shelves above.

Whatnots, a development of the early eighteenth-century tiered stand, were first seen in the 1790s. The early ones were quite large and were designed to hold folios of paintings or sheet music. By the Victorian era, whatnots were living-room pieces used to display ornaments. Their decoration featured turned columns, pierced and carved galleries and even mirrors. Many variations were made including those with canterbury or chest bases. The move in the late 1800s toward "purer" revivals of earlier furniture styles, marked the passing of the whatnot's heyday.

Points to note

Glazed corner cabinets and those with bow-fronts are generally more in demand than those with solid fronts or square in shape; they are also rarer and correspondingly more expensive.

The backs of pre-Victorian corner cabinets were made with unfinished wood and then painted; check for signs of the original paint, although many backs have been replaced.

Tall corner cabinets are often broken up to form two smaller hanging cabinets. A genuine piece will have a polished underside and show no signs of recent finishing.

Many hanging and standing corner cabinets were reproduced in the 19th and early 20th centuries, and some even have japanned decoration which copies Adam-style designs.

▼ MID-VICTORIAN CORNER CABINETS

This attractive pair of rare English corner cabinets was probably made in London around 1870. The high-quality mounts and use of ash suggest that it is an English piece, but the marquetry on the doors shows that the inspiration is French Transitional style. The excellent decoration includes the serpentine sides, inlaid with squares, the parquetry top, and the fine marquetry on the doors, which show a vase of flowers above a hat and flute on a harewood background. H 3ft 1 in x W 30in; H 94cm x W 76cm

1 GEORGE III STANDING CABINET
Below the dentil (toothed) cornice, the frieze of this pine corner cabinet (c.1780) is decorated with a central ram's-head urn with pewter paterae and swags. The arched glazed door and flat doors below are flanked by fluted pilasters. H 8ft 2in x W 5ft 1in; H 2.49m x W 1.55m

2 BOW-FRONTED HANGING CABINET
Made of mahogany, this late Georgian corner cabinet has a bow-front – a highly sought feature. Note how the cornice is in sections to produce the correct curved shape. The brass H-shaped hinges are a typical feature on country-made cabinets. The interior, which originally would either have been lined or painted, has three small drawers that may have been used to store tea. H 4ft/1.22m

3 GEORGE III LOW WHATNOT
This low mahogany stand, for holding either manuscripts or books, would have been a useful addition to a library or study. It dates from c.1800. H 20in x W 30in; H 51cm x W 76cm

4 MID-VICTORIAN WHATNOT
Obviously designed to display ornaments, this whatnot (c.1870) has inlaid shelves that are supported by spiral-turned columns. H 6ft/1.83m

5 WALNUT WHATNOT CABINET
Several features identify this whatnot cabinet, which has a series of compartments inside the base, as a Victorian piece dating from c.1870. The veneers are machine-cut, the elaborate columns machine-turned, and the top is surrounded by a gilt-metal gallery. H 3ft 4in/1.02m

6 GEORGE IV CANTERBURY
Stands such as this 1820s mahogany canterbury were designed to hold bound music, while the drawer below was used to store sheet music – today, many people use them as magazine racks. Despite the fact that this example is on castors, the central division has a hand-hole for carrying, as is common when canterburies have three sections. W 19in/48cm

SMALL DRAWING-ROOM FURNITURE

In addition to tables and chairs, many types of small furniture were made for the living room. Torchères, or candlestands, are modeled on the metal standards used for lighting in medieval times. By the late 1600s, they often formed part of a set of furniture, usually including a wall mirror, occasional table and pair of torchères. They were common during the 1700s, and their design followed changing tastes: by the end of the century, influenced by the trend to neoclassicism, the column form had given way to the tripod.

Jardinières, for holding flowers or plants, were usually metal-lined, although some had porcelain cisterns. In the early 1700s, *jardinières* were generally not more than 24in/61cm high, but by the second half of the century they were often taller. In Victorian times, they were popular in both living room and sunroom.

In the late 1600s, sewing accessories were kept in lace boxes; in the early 1700s, women used special baskets to hold their sewing. It was not until the 1760s that work tables (to some extent lace boxes on legs) became fashionable; they remained so in the 1800s. They were made in a variety of styles, and many had a reversible top with an inlaid chessboard on one side. The top section usually had a fitted interior for storing sewing implements and thread. Many had a brightly colored silk bag below in which needlework was kept. Sewing boxes, again with fitted interiors, were also popular, since they were easily portable.

Gueridons

The French term for a candlestand is *gueridon*. It can be applied to the large gilt stands, such as the torchères (1), found in grand châteaux.

Robert Adam

The son of a Scottish architect, Robert Adam (1728–92) became the chief creator of the British neoclassical style (*below*). A designer and architect himself, Adam's distinctive ideas grew during an extended tour of Europe, in the 1750s, studying the major classical sites. His designs were characterized by symmetrical lines, fine proportions, geometric shapes and a wealth of classical motifs. These motifs included garlands of flowers, acanthus leaves, urns and cameos of neoclassical figures. During the 1760s, in partnership with his brother James, he developed the Adam style, which influenced all areas of design for some 20 years.

▼ **GEORGE III JARDINIÈRE**
The painted decoration in green, black and gilt on this lead-lined jardinière *includes scenes in the Etruscan style on front and back. It has ormolu mounts and lion-mask handles. The* jardinière *was part of a set of furniture designed by Robert Adam for Cumberland House in London in the late 1700s. H 20in x W 3ft; H 51cm x W 91cm*

1 GEORGE II TORCHÈRES
The acanthus leaf, flower head and tassel decoration, shell clasps and ball and claw feet on this important pair of white and gilt torchères are typical of the period. A similar design appears in a set of furniture made in the same period for a country house at Stowe in England. H 4ft 1in x Diam. 15in; H 1.24m x Diam. 38cm

2 GEORGE II MAHOGANY TORCHÈRE
The molded circular top of this mahogany torchère is surrounded by a brass-inlaid spindled gallery. The column has a spirally turned knop and ends in a tripod base with downswept cabriole legs. H 32in x Diam. 13in; H 81cm x Diam. 33cm

3 CARVED MAHOGANY JARDINIÈRE
The decoration of this jardinière (c.1770) with paterae and acanthus leaves reflects the influences of the new neoclassical designs. The gadrooned top edge, however, is rather more traditional. H 20in/51cm

4 ROSEWOOD WORK TABLE
Dating from the 1830s, this work table with a drop-leaf top is a good example of a late Regency piece. The single frieze drawer would have held sewing accessories and the silk-lined bag any work in progress. The circular base and carved paw feet are also typical of the period. H 30in/76cm

5 ROSEWOOD SEWING BOX
A fine-quality sewing box (c.1830), complete with all its original fittings. The parquetry decoration on the exterior (5a) is repeated inside the lid and on the thread spools and compartment lids. W 14in/36cm

6 VIENNESE WORK TABLE
The revolving globe top of this early 19th-century mahogany work table is inlaid with engraved satinwood bands and encloses a well-fitted interior. It is supported by an ebonized and gilded winged figure. For many years, this table was thought to be English, but its Austrian origins are now well established. H 3ft 3in x Diam. 18in; H 99cm x Diam. 46cm

SMALL DINING-ROOM FURNITURE

From the 1770s onward, tea caddies were produced in a variety of shapes, sizes and materials, and they were always fitted with a lock, for tea was an expensive commodity. These caddies contained one, or sometimes two, foil-lined canisters (to hold green and bohea – black – China teas) and often a glass bowl in which the teas could be mixed or sugar stored. The tea caddy would be placed on a small tripod table, or stand, close to where the lady of the house sat so that she could make the tea, which was usually drunk after dinner. Toward the end of the eighteenth century, caddy and stand were sometimes combined to form a "caddy on legs" known as a teapoy.

Dumb-waiters, introduced into England in the 1730s and only some 40 years later into the rest of Europe, were used to hold plates, desserts and wines so that parties could continue after the servants had been dismissed. Early examples were somewhat similar to the tripod table except that they had three or four graduated circular trays, which revolved on a central column terminating in a tripod with ball and claw feet and castors. Variations began to emerge in the late 1700s, and in Victorian times rectangular and square shapes were also made.

Wooden wine coolers first appeared in the 1730s and were usually lead-lined so that they could be filled with ice to keep bottles cool. Cellarets, too, were found in the dining room; they were used primarily to store wine bottles, although some later examples also had sections for holding ice.

Another feature of the dining room was the knifebox. These were made by specialist makers and had a fitted interior, with many small partitions lined with baize or velvet, which is often missing today. The most common type had a serpentine front and sloping lid; the vase, or urn, shape was also popular after c.1770 because of its classical associations.

Teapoys

The word teapoy, derived from the Hindu word *tin*, meaning three and the Persian *pae*, meaning foot – hence three-footed – was used originally to describe the small three-legged table on which a tea caddy stood. When the caddy and table became one, the word was retained to describe it.

Caddy is a corruption of the Malay word *kati*, a weight of 1⅓lb/595g. It was first used of the porcelain containers in which tea was imported into England.

Points to note

It is not unusual to find splits in the circular trays of dumb-waiters with a central column. This is because of the weight of the objects that have repeatedly been placed upon them. This does not happen with the more desirable examples that have drop flaps, since they have struts to support the shelves when they are raised.

1 GEORGE III MAHOGANY TEAPOY

The octagonal top of this teapoy covers three lidded boxes. It stands on four spreading reeded legs, decorated with lotus leaves and united by an X-shaped stretcher. H 28in x W 17in; H 72cm x W 43cm

▼ TEA CADDIES

This group gives a good indication of the variety of shapes and styles of decoration of tea caddies. Left to right: *four Regency caddies: the first is ivory with metal mounts; the next is made of harewood and marquetry; the third, with a cameo bust on the front, is ivory edged with tortoiseshell; the fourth is octagonal and veneered in tortoiseshell. The open caddy (c.1845), showing two tea boxes and a mixing bowl, is papier-mâché inlaid with mother-of-pearl.*

2 BUTLER'S TRAY

These trays were used for carrying food and drink to and from the dining room. Here the tray is seen with three of its sides down; all four have hand holes. Many, as here, have an X-frame stand on which the tray can rest.

3 GEORGE III DUMB-WAITER

A typical three-tier mahogany dumb-waiter of the period. The turned column, headed by a vase finial, is supported by three downswept legs with reeded decoration ending in brass feet and castors. The trays, the largest of which is 24in/61cm in diameter, could usually be revolved. H 5ft/1.52m

4 GEORGE III CELLARET

Made from mahogany, this cellaret has a D-shaped section with a spindle gallery to hold plates and a well for cutlery. Wine bottles would have been stored in the cabinet underneath. H 32in x W25in; H 81cm x W 64cm

5 PAIR OF REGENCY KNIFEBOXES

The lids of these mahogany knifeboxes, with marquetry and ebony stringing, rise on a telescopic pole to reveal an interior fitted with a compartment for each item of cutlery, for both forks and spoons as well as knives were kept in them. H 25in/64cm

6 VICTORIAN DECANTER SET

An oak decanter case, or tantalus, with three cut-glass decanters. It is carved with fruiting vines and has silvered metal mounts. The drawer would have been used to hold playing cards and counters. W 12in/30cm

7 MAHOGANY WINE COOLER

Although made in the late 19th century, this hexagonal wine cooler, with ormolu handles and ram's head mounts, is in the neoclassical style. H 29in x W 20in; H 74cm x W 51cm

The two prime functions of screens are to ward off drafts or to protect from heat. In Tudor times, large draft-excluding screens were made of wicker or wood and covered with costly materials, but the establishment of the Dutch and English East India companies in the early seventeenth century encouraged trade with the Far East, and the large folding, or hinged, oriental lacquer screen was introduced into Europe. It became an important item of furniture, prized for its decorative as well as its functional qualities, and its popularity lasted well into the 1800s. Smaller, folding panel screens covered with painted leather, rich fabrics or needlework were also fashionable.

Other types common in the eighteenth century were horse, or cheval, firescreens and pole screens with an adjustable panel. Fires were an important source of light and the only source of heat, so people sat close to them, and these small pole screens, which shielded the face, were useful, especially since wax was one of the ingredients of cosmetics.

Early pole screens were made of iron; an example, "garnished with silver," features in the 1679 inventory of the bedchamber of the English queen, and can be found at Ham House near London. Later, wooden screens were attached to the pole by a ring and screw, which allowed the height to be adjusted to suit the user.

◀ GEORGE III FIRESCREEN
The design of this mahogany and parcel-gilt firescreen (c.1765) has affinities with those published by the cabinetmakers Ince & Mayhew, who plagiarized some of Chippendale's designs. The charming tapestry picture of a shepherdess and animals is surrounded by a Chinese-style blind fret. Both the cresting and apron of the panel have ornate pierced carving, and there is cabochon and acanthus decoration on the cabriole legs which end in ball and claw feet. H 4ft 5in x W 25in; H 1.35m x W 64cm

Lacquering
Oriental lacquer backgrounds (2) are most frequently black, particularly for Japanese pieces, dark or light brown, green, yellow and shades of red. Inspired by lacquering, imitators in the West developed japanning (*see p.194*), which became the rage in the mid-18th century.

Lacquering uses the sap tapped from a type of sumac tree, *Rhus vernicifera*. Clear or opaque varnishes made from the sap are applied to wooden or metal surfaces in a slow process which can take a year or more before the item is completed. The finished lacquer piece may feature inlays of metal or mother-of-pearl.

Cheval screens
The rather odd name given to these screens (5) stems from the fact that they stood on four legs like a horse or, in French, *cheval*. The same term is used to describe a large, free-standing mirror on a four-legged base (*see p.246*).

Reversing the trend
While many screens were imported from the Far East, in the 16th and 17th centuries Spanish gilt embossed screens became an important trade item, bought even by the Chinese and Japanese.

1 GEORGE III PANEL SCREEN
This mahogany firescreen, with fine Chinese-style lattice panels, is possibly part of a set of furniture supplied by Chippendale between 1763 and 1766 to Sir Lawrence Dundas for both his London and Yorkshire houses. The canvas panels decorated with paintings of clematis and peonies are of a later date. H 3ft 9in/1.14m

2 CHINESE EIGHT-PANEL SCREEN
The decoration of this magnificent black and gold lacquer screen, made for export in the late 18th century, depicts figures in landscapes on one side and, on the reverse, birds, bamboo, and flowering and fruiting branches. Each panel: H 7ft 1in x W 22in; H 2.16m x W 56cm

3 WILLIAM IV THREE-PANEL SCREEN
The mahogany frame of this screen holds leather panels into which are set pictures of exotic birds, including collared doves and lapwings, held by gilt slips. The frame's top is decorated with flower heads and leafy finials. Each panel: H 4ft 7in x W 30in; H 1.41m x W 77cm

4 WILLIAM MORRIS SCREEN
This glazed three-fold mahogany screen, with a paneled back and a frieze of carved foliage, was part of the drawing-room furniture made c.1889 by Morris & Co. for the country house at Bullerswood in Kent. The finely embroidered panels of stylized pinks, tulips and poppies, with scrolling, leafy stems, were thought to have been designed by Morris's daughter May. Each panel: H 4ft 8in x W 2ft; H 1.42m x W 61cm

5 GEORGE IV CHEVAL SCREEN
One of a pair of mahogany and parcel-gilt cheval screens, with an embroidered silk panel, attributable to the cabinet-making firm of Morel and Hughes. It is similar to a pair they supplied for Northumberland House which today can be seen at Syon Park, near London.

6 AMERICAN MAHOGANY FIRESCREEN
The wool-embroidered linen panel on this pole screen, made by a New York cabinetmaker, was worked by a lady named Tanneke Pears and is dated 1766. The turned pole and tripod base is much simpler than that of its English counterpart (above) which features elaborate carved decoration. H 5ft x W 22in; H 1.52m x W 56cm

7 PAIR OF ROSEWOOD POLE SCREENS
Pole screens were usually made in pairs, one for each side of the fireplace. This fine pair, dating from 1835, has Berlin woolwork banners in Rococo Revival shield-shaped frames and stands on trefoil bases. They lack the original finials. H 5ft/1.52m

◀ **CHARLES II CARVED MIRROR**
The crisply carved baroque decoration of this limewood mirror frame includes the British royal coat-of-arms flanked by cherubs at the top, putti climbing among trailing foliage and fruit on the sides, and sea creatures and shells at the base. The mirror plate and the back, with its gilt border, are later replacements.
H 5ft 4in x W 4ft; H 1.63m x W 1.22m

In medieval times mirrors were made from highly polished plates of silver, gold, pewter or bronze. It was not until the early sixteenth century that mirror glass was first made at the Murano works near Venice. Glass mirrors were not produced in any quantity in England until after the Restoration in 1660, when mirrors were being made at the Vauxhall glass works.

The process used until the late 1700s involved slicing open cylinders of glass, rolling them flat, and then polishing them. The backs were silvered by spreading mercury over tin foil. The pieces of mirror glass made in this way were small, which is why many early mirrors consist of more than one plate, with the joints usually hidden by a small fillet of wood. In 1773 English manufacturers adopted a French process, already about 100 years old, for casting glass, which meant larger plates could be produced. Although the Americans made their own frames, mirror glass was mainly imported until the end of the 1700s.

Large overmantel and pier mirrors were important decorative items in eighteenth-century rooms, and frames, in a variety of shapes and materials, echoed furniture designs. Toilet mirrors on stands appeared in the early eighteenth century, and cheval mirrors c.1790.

Mirror frames
Early mirror frames were generally made of wood (*see above*), either carved or covered with gesso, and then gilded (**3, 4, 5**). These were largely superseded in the 19th century by frames made of stucco, or plaster, on a wire base, which are often very good, but not as valuable as wooden ones.

Mirror glass
The glass in old mirrors is thinner than modern glass and has a grayish tinge, which gives a darker image. It is seldom perfect and usually has black spots where the backing has worn off, but resilvering reduces a mirror's value.

Reflected light
Attached to the frames of many mirrors are sconces or candle arms (**2, 5, 6, 8**). By setting candles close to mirrors, the light they gave was reflected, greatly adding to the illumination of a room.

1 VENETIAN MIRROR
The glass crest above this early 1700s mirror features an engraved cartouche with a rural scene. The blue and white glass frame incorporates geometrical decoration and oval panels depicting putti (cherubs).
H 5ft x W 4ft 2in; H 1.52m x W 1.27m

2 GEORGE II OVERMANTEL MIRROR
This mahogany mirror (c.1730), has a typical scrolling top with a gilt ho-o bird in the center. The mirror is made up of three plates, and there are brass candle arms at the bottom corners.
H 23in x L 4ft 4in; H 58cm x L 1.32m

3 AMERICAN GILT AND PINE MIRROR
This mirror exhibits the classical elements that were the hallmark of the Federal style (1790–1830). The eagle surmounting the frame represents military prowess and was a popular decoration throughout the 18th century on both sides of the Atlantic.

4 GEORGE III PIER GLASS
Pier glasses, which hung above pier tables on window walls, were an important decorative feature in grand interiors. This fine Irish giltwood mirror was made in Dublin by John and William Booker. H 6ft 6in x W 3ft 10in; H 1.98m x W1.17m

5 ITALIAN GILTWOOD MIRROR
This mirror dates from c.1875, but with its frame of pierced acanthus scrolls, it looks back in style to 17th-century Italian baroque mirrors. It has triple floral candle sconces on each side. H 5ft 10in x W 4ft; H 1.78m x W 1.22m

6 IRISH MIRROR-CHANDELIER
The frame of this mid-18th century mirror is made up of studs of blue and white glass with gilt fillets and stars for decoration. A glass sconce, with two candle arms and one decorated arm, hangs in front of the mirror, its reflection giving it the appearance of a small chandelier. H 31in x W 20in; H 79cm x W 51cm

7 FRENCH RÉGENCE ORMOLU MIRROR
The frame is in the neoclassical style, with a cresting mask and a band of intricate strapwork featuring profiles of Roman emperors and their wives at the sides; roundels in the corners show Prudence, Truth, Wisdom and Justice. Such mirrors, with a rear easel support, could stand on a dresser. H 29in x W 19in; H 74cm x W 48cm

8 REGENCY CHEVAL MIRROR
Cheval mirrors, standing on four legs, were used for dressing, so the candle sconces at the sides were usually adjustable. The ebonized frame that simulates bamboo illustrates the Regency passion for chinoiserie. H 6ft 6in x W 35in; H 1.98m x W 89cm

OAK AND COUNTRY FURNITURE: 1

Made from locally available woods and by provincial craftsmen, country furniture has its own style and charm. Unlike crudely doweled primitive furniture, country pieces were usually well made and represented the local interpretation of a style. Until the 1700s, oak was the principal wood for furniture making in England and much of Europe. Although other woods such as beech, elm and ash were occasionally used, they were not as hard and did not prove as durable as oak. As walnut and mahogany became popular with city furniture makers, oak remained a country wood.

In the early 1600s, Europeans began to move out of the feudal communities of baronial halls into family units. This led to an increased demand for smaller household furniture, which itself triggered many design innovations, including the gate-leg table.

Furniture made in cities and large towns showed the influence of fashions in design and new construction methods. Traditional styles, by contrast, were still produced by country craftsmen – often using jointed construction. During the 1800s, simplified versions of the more popular "town" styles were made, but where a type of country furniture had proved useful, it tended not to change in form or construction.

In Victorian times there was a revival of interest in oak furniture, and many straight reproductions of early pieces were made, while other items were made up incorporating parts from genuinely old furniture.

Points to note

When trying to determine whether a piece of country furniture is a genuine antique or of later manufacture, there are several points to be considered.

Although it may be primitive, carving on country furniture is not crude, and it will generally be of good quality and well balanced in design.

In the carving on reproductions, features will often be depicted that would not have been known at the time it was made.

Avoid pieces that have any later embellishments – these tend to be sharp and incised, in contrast to original decoration, which stands proud of the surface with the edges smoothed through use.

Always watch out for signs of distressing, or wear, which should occur only in areas subject to the normal wear and tear of everyday use, such as foot rails and top rails on chairs, the edges of cabinet doors and drawers, and the feet of almost all furniture.

Although early oak would originally have had its famous golden hue, centuries of use and polishing should have aged it to a warm chestnut or darker. Stripping destroys the color and sheen and greatly detracts from the value of a piece.

1 LARGE OAK CHEST
This chest was constructed in the 19th century, but original 15th-century Gothic carved panels in ecclesiastical form have been incorporated into the front. There is a superb lock plate with decorated borders. L 4ft 7in/1.4m

2 DOUGH BIN
As the name suggests, dough was left to rise in bins such as this oak piece (c.1675). It shows a combination of carved and applied turned decoration on its geometrically designed front panel. The turned baluster legs are united by stretchers. L 3ft 6in/1.07m

3 OAK HALL BENCH
An unusually small 17th-century piece. The paneled back is decorated with stylized foliage and diamond-shaped lozenges. The box seat has a hinged lid and a paneled front and sides. W 35in/89cm

4 OAK WRITING DESK
A typical and fairly rare example of an English desk c.1700–35. The carcass has half-round moldings, in contrast to the later beading on the drawers; there is a blank space above the two short drawers, which conceals the fitted interior well; and the lopers are rectangular. The handles are replacements, but are stylistically correct. H 3ft 10in/1.17m

5 SPANISH OAK CABINET
This type of 17th-century cabinet, with seven separate doors and a plank top, went out of favor in more prosperous households, but continued to be used in poorer homes well into the 19th century. H 4ft 7in x W 6ft 7in; H 1.4m x W 2.01m

6 FRENCH PROVINCIAL BUFFET
Buffets, or bas d'armoires, *such as this late 18th-century walnut piece, performed the same function as the low dresser. The decoration combines elements of both the Louis XV and Louis XVI periods. H 3ft x W 4ft 6in; H 91cm x W 1.37m*

7 NORTH WALES OAK HUTCH
The upper part of this fairly typical late 18th-century hutch has a molded cornice and pierced frieze above the plate rack, which has waved end supports. The two cupboards in the base are separated by one real and two false drawers. H 6ft 5in x W 5ft 4in; H 1.96m x W 1.63m

◄ **OAK SIDE TABLE**
A fine example of the small gate-leg tables that evolved in the early 17th century. The D-shaped flap is here shown open, supported by the gate-leg.

The barley-sugar-twist legs and arcaded apron are attractive decorative features, and two rather crude dovetail joints can be seen on either side of the little frieze drawer. Diam. 3ft 1in/94cm

FURNITURE

By the middle of the seventeenth century in England, different regional traits had developed in country furniture. The best-known type of country chair is probably the Windsor chair, which first appeared in the early eighteenth century. Local wood was used – beech in the area around High Wycombe, Buckinghamshire, where Windsor chairs were chiefly made – elm and ash in other regional centers. The earliest is the comb-back, so-called because the top and back sticks resemble the teeth of a comb; it was replaced in the 1740s by the curved bow-back type.

Windsor chairs were universally popular, and styles that originated in England were soon copied in North America. They could be found in the backyards of the well-to-do as well as in cottages and taverns. Many were painted, usually green, but other colors were also used.

Although the ornamentation is much simpler, the influence of the designs of both Chippendale and Hepplewhite can be seen in the decoration of early country chairs. But country furniture also had an influence on designers: in Victorian times, among William Morris's chair designs was the popular rush-seated Sussex chair, which derived from traditional country chairs of the day.

◄ **YORKSHIRE WINDSOR CHAIR**
The spindle-filled bow back of this mid-19th century yew armchair has decorative pierced strapwork splats. The U-shaped arms rest on baluster-turned supports, and the similar baluster legs are united by H-stretchers. The saddle-shaped seat is traditional on all Windsor chairs.

Reproductions

Many reproductions have been made of the Windsor chair in the 20th century. Signs to look out for on a period chair are that seats should have figured grain both underneath and on top; the sticks should taper and will be of varying thicknesses if they are hand-made; there should be wear on the feet, and the legs will also vary slightly if they are handmade; there should be no signs of machine cutting on the central splat.

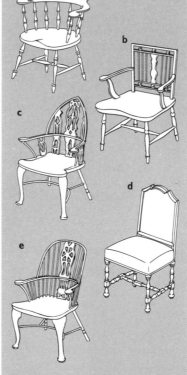

COUNTRY CHAIR SHAPES

a Simple low-back Windsor-style chair, popular since the 1830s. **b** Suffolk chair, late 18th-century, with back made of squared-off pieces. **c** Windsor chair with gothic-arch back and "church-window" pierced splats (1750–90). **d** Upholstered, late 17th-century French country chair with turned legs and stretchers. **e** Windsor chair with cabriole legs, swept-back arms and curved stretcher (1770–1830).

1 YORKSHIRE OAK CHAIR
Although there have been clumsy repairs to the back legs of this chair, it provides a good example of 17th-century regional style. The arched back rails, carved with scrolls and split-bobbin moldings, and the plank seat are typical of chairs made in Yorkshire and Derbyshire at that time.

2 ASH AND ELM DINING CHAIRS
Made in the first half of the 19th century, these typify chairs from the Lancashire/Cheshire region of northern England. The curved top rails, waved ladder backs, rush seats and turned legs ending in pad feet all exhibit a high level of craftsmanship.

3 YEW ROCKING CHAIR
Chairs such as this were more usually made from beech or elm. The rather flat turning indicates a provincial maker and is a clue to the early 19th-century date of the chair. H 4ft/1.22m

4 ORKNEY CHAIR
There are few woods on Scottish islands, so many local chairs were made of driftwood. The high, draft-excluding backs were always made of braided straw, and there was often a drawer under the seat to hold tobacco or whiskey. This example dates from the late 19th century, although this type of chair is still made today.

5 CHARLES II CHILD'S HIGHCHAIR
The back of this oak highchair would originally have had finials; otherwise, it is very similar to the type of chair that the child's parents would have used, albeit with longer legs.

6 AMERICAN CHILD'S HIGHCHAIR
Windsor chairs proved as popular in America as in England, and this pine and maple highchair with a "stick" back is a good example of the "fire house" Windsor type. Made in New England or Pennsylvania c.1820–40, the chair is in good condition and has its original footboard.

7 OAK CRIB
This crib, in a style that remained popular well into the 18th century, can be dated from the carved inscription "W M 1706" on the end; carving was often quite elaborate. The posts at the head and foot of the crib were used to rock it, and the rockers often show signs of wear, indicating that they have seen good use. L 3ft/91cm

PINE FURNITURE

A type of softwood from the coniferous forests of Europe and North America, pine has long been used in furniture making. In areas where it is readily available, such as Austria, Scandinavia, Scotland (where it is known as deal) and parts of North America, pine furniture is common. In England and much of the rest of northern Europe, oak was the main wood, while farther south, cypress, apple and walnut were used. The general lack of native-grown wood in Ireland meant that pine was often imported for making furniture.

Although used mainly for country pieces, pine was cheap and wide planks could be cut from it, so during the seventeenth and eighteenth centuries, city cabinetmakers started using it for carcasses and back panels. These carcasses were then gilded or veneered with more expensive woods such as walnut or mahogany.

Most pine furniture was made by local carpenters and joiners using early construction methods which, although they can look old-fashioned, are not necessarily inferior. Although many pine pieces seem plain, originally they may have been decorated. In England, country furniture was often scumbled, while that made in the rest of Europe was usually painted, either in a solid color or with floral motifs.

In the 1800s, pine was used extensively for both hand- and machine-made pieces in country styles. Then, late in the century, the Arts and Crafts Movement started to experiment with and favor woods such as pine and oak, and although they clung to the idea of simple craftsmanship, some more sophisticated pieces were produced.

Scumbled decoration

English pine furniture was often scumbled, or finished to resemble more expensive woods such as mahogany or walnut. The technique involved brushing or combing a layer of varnish, when half-dry, to produce a grained effect. In the 1960s it became fashionable to "strip" pine of such decorative effects, with the result that few scumbled pieces remain and those that do tend to be quite valuable.

Hand- versus machine-made

In the 19th century, pine furniture was made both by hand and machine (4). Since handmade pieces tend to have a more individual appearance and are often made of wood with better color and grain and fewer knots, they are usually more expensive.

Machine-made pieces are not all of inferior quality, but as the 19th century progressed, the quality of manufacture did decline, as is often evident on inspection of the pieces themselves. Machine-made furniture can usually be identified by the smoothness of the wood, which cannot so easily be achieved manually.

1 IRISH FARMHOUSE HUTCH
This traditional hutch was made in Co. Mayo, Ireland, in the 1870s. It has generous shelving for plates, diagonally constructed door panels, and a scalloped and pierced canopy. Unlike many other hutches, it seems never to have been painted. H 6ft 8in x W 4ft 8in; H 2.03m x W 1.42m

2 AUSTRIAN ARMOIRE
As this armoire was intended for an attic room, it could not be too tall. The problem was solved by placing the drawers next to the cupboard rather than below it. The pin hinges, common on furniture from continental Europe, allow the door to be lifted off. H 5ft x W 3ft 9in; H 1.52m x W 1.14m

3 DANISH KITCHEN TABLE
The square tapered legs, clean elegant lines and traditional doweled joints suggest that this table was made in the late 18th century, but the turned handles indicate that in fact it dates from the 1870s. H 30in x L 3ft; H 76cm x L 91cm

4 MACHINE-MADE CHEST OF DRAWERS
The simple design of this 1890s chest of drawers, part of a set of furniture, is enlivened only by the shaped backboard and original brass handles. Although this is a fine piece, the quality of some machine-made furniture deteriorated during the 19th century. H and W 3ft 6in/1.07m

5 IRISH MIRROR-BACKED SIDEBOARD
Although the flowerhead motifs are typically Irish, the incised decoration and spindle gallery were inspired by characteristic features of the Aesthetic Movement of the late 1800s. H 6ft x W 3ft 10in; H 1.83m x W 1.17m

6 COUNTRY WASHSTAND
Traditional doweled joints and the generous use of thick wood indicate the quality of this washstand, made in Lincolnshire, England, c.1860, and distinguish it from later, inferior pieces of the same design. H 3ft 2in/97cm

7 AUSTRIAN SIDE CHAIR
Despite its rural origin and simple peg joints, the delicately carved back gives this chair an air of elegance. When first made (c.1850), it would probably have had a coat of clear varnish, which has since been stripped. H 3ft/91cm

◄ **PANTRY TABLE**
The splayed legs and crosshatch decoration give this small country piece, dating from the 1860s, a sturdy appearance.

Such craftsmanship typifies the values that members of the Arts and Crafts Movement consciously sought to incorporate into their furniture later in the century. H 23in/58cm

SHAKER FURNITURE

1 PINE SECRETARY DESK
A simple fall-front desk, which was originally built in. It is made of pine and, like many early pieces, stained red (the stain is still visible in places). The cabinets have turned maple handles, and the interior shelves are adjustable.

2 LOW POST BED
This simple bed in painted maple, with large castors of hardwood and iron, has rope strung across the frame to support the mattress. Such beds were usually only 3ft/91cm wide and sometimes had a low footboard as well as a headboard.

3 SEWING DESK
Since neatness was a feature of Shaker life, chests and storage cabinets for everything from clothes to herbs were important. This small desk in pine and maple comes from Hancock, Massachusetts. It was made c.1840–60 to hold sewing and has storage drawers, a small cabinet and a writing slide, doubling its usefulness.

4 SLAT-BACK ARMCHAIR
The delicate appearance of this maple chair (1840–80) disguises its strength. Chairs had to be light because they were hung on pegs on the wall when the floors were cleared for meetings. Each community had its own, slightly different, type of finial; this chair, with a woven-tape seat and arms ending in mushroom posts, comes from either New England or New York.

5 TWO CABINETS
The larger of these cabinets was floor-standing and intended for hanging clothes, while the smaller was made to hang on a hook on the wall.

6 MAPLE DINING TABLE
Shaker tables were of simple trestle form – a design that allows plenty of room for the sitters' legs – and were often as much as 10ft/3.05m long. This example, made in New England or New York in 1820–60, has wrought iron and oak trestles and a maple top. Cherrywood was often used for table tops because it was easy to polish to a beautiful finish.

In the 1760s Ann Lee founded a splinter group of the Quaker movement in Manchester, England. From their habit of shaking and dancing when they worshipped, the members became known as the Shaking Quakers, or Shakers. The sect was not popular in England, and in 1774 a small band sailed to America, settling near Albany in New York State. They flourished, and by 1826 there were 18 communities in New England, Kentucky and Ohio.

Shakers believed in celibacy, racial and sexual equality, and common ownership. Newcomers gave any land or possessions to the community for common use. Each community was divided into "families" of around 100 members, who lived and ate in "dwelling houses," but met for prayer in the Meeting House.

These self-supporting communities made their own furniture along simple, practical lines, devoid of all ornament, and used only light varnishes. Pine was employed for built-in furniture and maple and fruit-woods for free-standing pieces. By the early 1800s the Shakers were selling their furniture to outsiders, who were keen to buy it because it was so well made. Cabinet makers were not allowed to "sign" their work, but their fame spread and the demand for Shaker-made furniture grew; by the 1880s, they were selling by mail-order. Although the number of Shakers has declined, Shaker furniture is still produced today since the esthetics of its design retain their appeal.

The essence of Shaker style was its "sprightly" simplicity, as this reconstructed interior of a Shaker house shows. Furniture with clean, uncluttered lines was often built in, and most "retiring rooms" contained a rocking chair. Here the chair seat is upholstered in handwoven tape, and there are handwoven mats on the floor; beside the chair is a cast-iron candle stand, which could be adjusted to various heights. The simple cast-iron stove is in marked contrast to the ornate examples being produced by outside factories at the time.

Upholstery

The seats (*above*, 4) and backs of Shaker chairs were often upholstered with hand-dyed cotton tape woven in checkerboard or herringbone pattern. This cotton tape proved easier to work with and was longer lasting than either cane or rush.

Wood finishes

The earliest tables and chairs were generally painted or stained dark red, beds were always painted green, and traces of these colors can still be seen on old Shaker furniture. Later, light stains and varnishes were used that allowed the natural beauty of the wood to show through. Veneers and heavy lacquers were not allowed.

PAINTED FURNITURE

Since ancient times, painting has been used as a form of decoration on furniture. Medieval furniture was painted in polychrome colors (and repainted each spring to cover up the grime from open fires). Furniture painting in Scandinavia and central Europe derives from this tradition.

The popularity of painted furniture reached its apogee in Europe in the 1700s. In France, the Martin brothers introduced a technique known as *vernis martin*, whereby the color was mixed with varnish, or a paste was formed from powdered color, varnish and metal fillings and applied to the wood. In England, Hepplewhite, Adam and Sheraton all included painted decoration in their designs. In the late 1800s, the Arts and Crafts Movement produced painted furniture.

The craft of furniture painting in America was much influenced by German and Swiss settlers; the type of decoration they favored is known as Pennsylvania-Dutch, a corruption of the word *Deutsch*.

Points to note

Painted furniture and boxes in good condition, with bright colors, are unusual and valuable, so worn examples are often repainted to make them more attractive to collectors. Newly painted examples can be recognized by the absence of wear in places where they would have been handled, and, since paint becomes brittle with age, by the absence of cracks in the paint or in the varnish covering it.

◀ **REGENCY SECRETAIRE-CABINET**
The door panels and secretaire-drawer of this rosewood cabinet are crossbanded with satinwood and decorated with hand-coloured oval prints showing nymphs and putti. Painted and gilded glass panels in a similar style were sometimes used as decoration on cabinets and chairs. *H 5ft 6in x W 32in; H 1.68m x W 81cm*

1 AMERICAN DOWER CHEST
This large dower chest of joined construction was made by Thomas Dennis of Ipswich, Massachusetts, in 1676. The stylized carved flowers and leaves typical of the decoration on this form of chest are picked out in bright red and blue paint.

2 GEORGE III CYLINDER DESK
The painted decoration on this sophisticated piece of furniture shows a medallion suspended from drapery, within which are putti holding a shield bearing the initials GL – for Grace La Touche, for whom the piece was made. W 3ft/91cm

3 GEORGE III SATINWOOD ARMCHAIR
Made c.1780, this chair was part of a set of 18 made for D. Tupper of Guernsey, in the Channel Islands. The splat is headed by a vase of flowers, and the painted flowers and peacock feathers are a typical conceit of the time. This style of decoration was copied in the Federal period (see p.172) and again in the late 19th and early 20th centuries.

4 AUSTRIAN PAINTED ARMOIRE
The date of this armoire can be clearly seen at the top of the door. The naive, bold and colorful painted finish simulating wood adds to the character of the piece. H 5ft 8in/1.73m

5 AMERICAN BALLOON-BACK CHAIR
These chairs were a 19th-century innovation, so called because the shape of the back resembles a hot-air balloon. The back and seat of this example (c.1820) were painted with flowers in Pennsylvania-Dutch style.

6 NORTH ITALIAN WRITING DESK
This desk dates from the mid-18th century, but its green-painted and silvered decoration of foliage and birds is not original for, in common with much painted furniture, it has been redecorated at some point in its life. H 3ft 7in x W 4ft; H 1.10m x W 1.22m

7 AMERICAN TRINKET BOX
The compartmented interior of this painted pine box, made in New England c.1820–40, indicates that it may have been used for jewelry. Decorative patriotic symbols, such as the eagle, were commonly seen, while the turtle doves entwined in ribbon suggest that the box was a wedding gift. H 6½in x L 15in; H 16cm x L 38cm

OUTDOOR FURNITURE

Marble and carved stone benches were found in renaissance and baroque gardens in Europe, but outdoor furniture as such evolved only in the eighteenth century. Chippendale included designs for chairs to be used in summer houses and arbors in the 1762 edition of the *Director* and, later, Windsor chairs were often painted and used outdoors.

In this period, wooden and iron benches were used as outdoor seats, as seen in the painting by Gainsborough, *Portrait of Mr and Mrs Andrews* (c.1748), with the wife seated on an iron bench. Gothic and Chinese influences are evident in many wooden seats of this time, and in the early 1900s the English architect Edward Lutyens used eighteenth-century examples as the basis for an outdoor seat he designed.

Rustic furniture – a term coined to describe pieces whose frame resembles the branches of a tree – first appeared in the mid-1700s and remained popular well into the 1800s, when it was also produced in terracotta by a number of Staffordshire firms. Such "furniture," made in terrracotta and majolica and often decorated in bright colors, was used mainly in solariums. At the same time, metal furniture for use indoors and out enjoyed great popularity in America and Europe.

Points to note

Both cast- and wrought-iron outdoor furniture is prone to rust, which makes it important to check for sections that may have been replaced, since this will affect the value.

Many 19th-century designs are reproduced today, and some pieces are artificially aged. On original cast-iron furniture, the seams were usually quite well finished, while the nuts were made of brass and were dome-shaped. Modern furniture is generally far more flimsily constructed.

Metal furniture

Ironbridge foundry in Coalbrookdale produced much of the English cast- and wrought-iron furniture that can still be found today. Although little is known about individual designers of this furniture, which includes chairs, benches, tables and plant stands, a wide variety was made with patterns based on leaves and flowers as well as gothic and classical designs. Reeded wrought iron was also used for outdoor furniture from the early 19th century.

1 AMERICAN CAST-IRON BENCH
Fern leaves form the decoration on this bench, which is typical of those made in England as well. By 1850 it was possible in the U.S. to buy such outdoor furniture from catalogs.

2 CAST-IRON URN CHAIR
This American chair in painted cast-iron shows clearly how in the 19th century different designs became interlinked. The back of the chair features a classical-style lyre surrounded by rococo scrolls and garlands of flowers.

3 SOUTH GERMAN RUSTIC BENCH
A stained pine bench, with a carved back showing a bear amid branches and supported by two well-carved naturalistic standing bears. It dates from c.1880 and is a good example of 19th-century rustic furniture. H 33in x W 5ft 4in; H 84cm x W 1.32m

4 IRON-WIRE SIDE CHAIR
By the 1870s, the technique of wire making had improved, and it began to be employed in the design of metal furniture. Its use meant that chairs and benches had a much lighter look than had earlier been the case, as this American example shows.

5 MAJOLICA PEDESTAL SEAT
This ceramic pedestal outdoor seat, made in 1872 by Minton, incorporates motifs inspired by classical design. It is decorated with a band of stylized passion-flowerheads and honeysuckle, which also appeared as a motif on early 19th-century dining chairs (see p.174). The block feet have Greek key pattern decoration. H 16in/46cm

6 STAFFORDSHIRE MAJOLICA PEDESTAL
A pedestal such as this would have been used to support a majolica urn or pot in a sunroom. Made by the firm of William Brownfield of Staffordshire, England, c.1882, the herm, cherub and hoof feet look back to the 18th century in style.

7 MAJOLICA OUTDOOR SEAT
Ancient Egypt was the inspiration for this seat, made by Brownfields of Staffordshire c.1860–70. The seat is supported by a hand-maiden, stylized lotus flowers and snakes. The bright colors are typical of English majolica of the period.

◀ **RUSTIC JARDINIÈRE**
This octagonal Regency jardinière, made of birch and bamboo with applied leaf and flower decoration, is supported by a rustic pedestal in the form of a tree trunk with gnarled roots. W 27in/69cm

FURNITURE

CHAPTER FIVE

CLOCKS AND WATCHES

Much of the appeal of clocks and watches today lies in their juxtaposition of art and mechanics. However, in our age of electronic timepieces and constant transmission of the exact time on the radio, it is increasingly difficult to appreciate fully the dependence on mechanics for timekeeping in daily life, even as late as the mid-twentieth century.

By the end of the 1800s, the well-off generally had a clock in each room in the house and a fob or pocket watch for each member of the family. But before the age of the railroads, whose need to run to a comprehensible timetable necessitated the idea of standard national time in Britain, all timepieces were set to local time (which varies by nearly 30 minutes between Kent and Cornwall), checked against a sundial, or read from the stars at night. Often, in towns, clocks were wound and checked for their owners by the local clockmaker or jeweler against a pocket watch set against a longcase regulator clock in his shop.

While to the Victorians punctuality was a necessity, the attitude to time had been quite the contrary when, in the mid-seventeenth century, household clocks first began to keep respectable time. Until then, most clocks and watches had only one hand, and the dial was calibrated to divisions no smaller than quarter-hours. As legal documents, such as records of evidence given in court, demonstrate, people reckoned time by generalized periods of the day, such as dawn, mid-morning or dusk, rather than o'clock.

One particular section of society, however, had always needed to be time-conscious – the monks and nuns who were such a significant part of medieval life and who were required in their monastic regime to gather for prayer at regular intervals throughout the day and night. Thus it was for, and presumably by, them that clocks were first developed in northern Italy by the late thirteenth century. Not long after this, clock towers also began to rise over the town and guild halls of the cities of Europe. Next, there was a demand from leading citizens for clocks for their homes.

Such origins help explain the root of the words "clock" (from French *cloche*, a bell) and "chapter ring"

for the hour ring of a clock dial, or face (from the monks gathering in chapter each day to recite their monastic rule).

The earliest mechanical clocks had neither hands nor dials; neither did they strike the hour, but rather made a whirring sound to alert the clock keeper to strike the bell. Records survive of drunk or sleepy keepers who failed to perform their duty before an automatic striking system had been devised. By *c*.1450, on the outside of clock towers, clock faces had appeared with a fixed, vertically pointing hand, behind which rotated a ring marked for the hours. At the end of the 1400s, it was realized that a fixed hour ring with a moving hand was easier to read at a glance. Although this became the standard form, the ring could be calibrated to 6, 12 or 24 hours, depending on local usage.

Despite the erratic timekeeping of early clocks and watches, their very existence was a potent reminder of their owners' lives ticking away. As a result, in the late 1500s and early 1600s, many timepieces were fashioned as *memento mori* (a reminder of death): watches in the form of skulls, flowers and even animals. Others were imbued with religious symbolism: cruciform watches or clocks as calvaries.

It was only with the improvements in timekeeping achieved from *c*.1675 that clocks began to be accurate enough to measure time itself. There came a realization that solar time, as registered on sundials, was not constant but varied according to the time of year, and that a regular clock keeps a mean, or average, of the ranging daily rates of solar time. Hence, the term "mean time," which can be established for anywhere in the world. And as minute and second hands have become common and absolute precision has been achieved, humans have become caught in the thrall of time.

▶ MUSICAL BRACKET CLOCK

The maker of this fine bracket clock, Benjamin Barber, worked in Red Lion Street, London, from 1785–94. The clock, in tortoiseshell with ormolu mounts, has a white enameled chapter disk with Turkish numerals. The disks in the ogee top are for a calendar and for selecting the four tunes, which are played every three hours.

Considering that mechanical clocks were first made in northern Italy, remarkably few early Italian clocks have survived. Apart from some early, and usually large, cathedral and monastic clocks, the first clocks to be found in reasonable quantity are the weight-driven chamber clocks made along the River Rhine from Switzerland to the Low Countries. Many of these are later than the gothic style suggests; some of the best came from Switzerland in the mid- to late 1500s.

The earliest clocks to survive in sufficient quantities to interest the collector are the mid-sixteenth century table clocks that originate from the metalworking towns of Nuremberg and Augsburg, long experienced in fashioning springs for locks and crossbows.

Itinerant clock makers had earlier been attracted to the courts of Europe, such as those of the French kings, and there are some exquisite mid-sixteenth century small table clocks in early renaissance architectural style made in Blois and elsewhere. But with the rise in demand for table clocks, it made more sense for clock makers to congregate in towns. Augsburg and Nuremberg were natural centers, and clock making guilds arose, at the latter, for example, in 1543.

Production must have been prodigious, since a huge quantity of German table clocks from the early and mid-1600s still exists. These take several forms, including a series modeled with animals and others with blackamoors or crucifixion scenes. Some of the most complicated are tabernacle clocks, known as masterpiece clocks, since they follow the specifications by which an apprentice attained his mastership, enabling him to practice as a fully fledged clock maker.

The pendulum, devised by a Dutchman, Christiaan Huygens, in 1657–58, quickly spread to England, where London clock makers developed its potential. Next came the balance hairspring, which similarly revolutionized the timekeeping of watches and portable

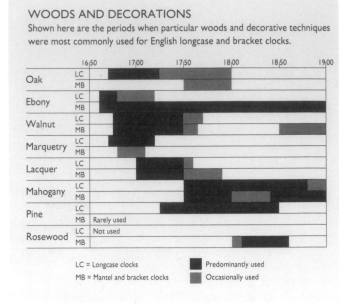

WOODS AND DECORATIONS

Shown here are the periods when particular woods and decorative techniques were most commonly used for English longcase and bracket clocks.

		1650	1700	1750	1800	1850	1900
Oak	LC						
	MB						
Ebony	LC						
	MB						
Walnut	LC						
	MB						
Marquetry	LC						
	MB						
Lacquer	LC						
	MB						
Mahogany	LC						
	MB						
Pine	LC						
	MB	Rarely used					
Rosewood	LC	Not used					
	MB						

LC = Longcase clocks   ■ Predominantly used
MB = Mantel and bracket clocks   ■ Occasionally used

HOROLOGIA FERREA

'Rota æqua ferrea ætherisҙ voluitur,   Recludit æque et hæc et illa tempora

◀ **EARLY CLOCK WORKSHOP**
This engraving appeared c.1570 in a book called Nova Reperta, *written by a Dutchman, van der Straet, who was also known as Stradamus. It shows the interior of a clock workshop with iron clocks, both wall hanging and, it would seem, floor standing, in various stages of construction.*

▶ **CHARLES II LANTERN CLOCK**
The most common type of household clock in the 1600s, lantern clocks were of posted frame construction in brass, with a bell on top, surrounded by fretwork; all were wall hanging. This small clock by Thomas Ford of Buckingham has the rare feature of key winding; lantern clocks were more normally wound by pulling on the "spare" loop of cord or chain, which raised the weight. These clocks are often much altered by conversion from verge to anchor escapement by means of a long pendulum. Timepiece clocks were made to strike by conversion of the alarm train; and some were made into mantel clocks in the 1800s by the substitution of a spring-driven movement, which necessitated piercing the dial with winding holes. Many fakes have also been made. H 12½in/32cm

SHAPES OF CLOCKS

Clocks came in a variety of shapes depending on their intended location and particular function.

1 A dial clock of the type found in every rail station in the age of steam from the mid-19th century onward.

2 A grand bronze wall clock which may have decorated an 18th-century French interior. This style remained popular in the 19th century.

3 An 18th-century tavern clock, also known as an Act of Parliament clock.

4 A classic English longcase or "grandfather" clock of imposing 18th-century design.

5 A complicated and elegant French skeleton clock, dating from the Empire period of the early 19th century.

6 A Cromwellian lantern clock, the first English household clock, which began to be made from c.1620.

7 A classic French carriage clock of the type that was made from c.1850.

| 1 Station dial clock | 2 Bronze wall clock | 3 Tavern clock | 4 Longcase clock | 5 Skeleton clock | 6 Lantern clock | 7 Carriage clock |

clocks. By 1680 the best clocks and watches were being made in London. This was the period of the great names in English clock making: Fromanteel, East, Tompion, Knibb, Quare and Graham.

The English hegemony in horology grew throughout the 1700s, and until 1900 the best clocks and watches were considered to be London-made. Dutch longcase and bracket clocks largely incorporated English movements, housed in locally made cases, and there was a large trade in complete clocks exported elsewhere in Europe. Lacquered, or japanned, clocks, often with musical movements, were a specialty for Italy, Spain and Portugal; similar clocks, with glass domes, and finials, were sold to the Turkish world. In the 1730s, the Chinese emperor's palace was said to have more than 4,000 clocks, many of them English, which were disregarded for their ability to tell the time, fascinating the Chinese by their automata and musical performances.

By 1700 the basic problems in making tolerably accurate household clocks and watches had been solved. However, there followed a quest for precision timekeeping, spurred by the need to develop a marine chronometer as maritime trade advanced and permanent colonies were established by European powers.

English work on precision timekeeping dates from the early 1700s, but this was paralleled in France from mid-century. While English success was greater in the long run, there was a flowering of precision clock making in France in the late 1700s, culminating in the work of the greatest watchmaker ever, Abraham-Louis Breguet.

In the 1800s, the French made quantities of carriage clocks and mantel clocks with standardized movements, while the English stuck rigidly to producing the best handmade clocks and watches. But from the mid-1800s, clock making in both countries was increasingly threatened by cheap mass-produced clocks from America and Germany and watches from Switzerland.

Following the invention of the pendulum in the mid-1600s, clock cases were often made of wood (*see table on p.262*) rather than of metal as they had, almost invariably, been before. With this changeover, the craft of making clock cases passed out of the clock maker's hands, with very different results in France and England. In England, the clock maker was in control and sold the finished article; in France the cabinet maker ordered movements of standardized types to fit into his cases.

As a result, French clock cases were always in step with developments in furniture and metalwork, while English cases, prior to *c.*1760, were usually 25–30 years behind. It was only in the late 1700s, influenced by great cabinet makers and designers such as Chippendale, Hepplewhite, Adam and Sheraton, that clock-case design and decoration caught up with that of furniture.

The form of dials in the two countries was also affected. English clock makers kept to a basically rectangular shape, while French dials were, from *c.*1715, confined to a circle in various standard sizes. Enameling techniques were more advanced in France, and one-piece enamel dials were produced *c.*1715–20 for watches and *c.*1725–35 for clocks. Previously, individual enamel hour plaques in a cast ormolu frame had been used – a style that was revived in the mid-1800s.

Enameled dials were uncommon in England; watches had them only after the 1740s, and clocks after the 1750s. Clock dials normally had an applied chapter

THE FACE

A classic early 18th-century longcase clock face illustrates many of the common elements of all clock faces.

1 Spandrels of cast and chased brass.
2 Chapter ring with numerals in black.
3 Second ring at the top.
4 Two apertures for the winding keys for time and strike.
5 Ornate hour hand and long minute hand.
6 Maker's signature
7 Date aperture.

ring and spandrels fixed to the dial plate, and even after the 1760s a more frequent alternative than enamel was a flat brass dial, engraved and silvered. "White" dials, painted and lightly fired with polychrome designs in the spandrels and the arch, were first advertised in Birmingham in 1772. By the 1780s, they had become common, and they remained a popular form of dial for English provincial longcase clocks until the 1840s.

Although dials were most frequently positioned on the front of clocks, dials on table clocks *c.*1550–1650 were usually on top. These horizontal dials conformed to the shape of the case and had touchpieces by the hour numerals, to enable the time to be "felt" by the fingertips at night (*see p.284*), and sturdy single hands. Single-handed dials were, with few exceptions, standard before the invention of the pendulum and, by *c.*1675, the balance hairspring for watches; minute hands came into general use as a consequence of the improvements in timekeeping that resulted. Almost at a stroke, this was refined from an inaccuracy of about 30 minutes a day to an accuracy of within 3 minutes a week. Second hands, rarely found on bracket or mantel clocks, were adopted on longcase clocks in the 1670s, along with the anchor escapement and second-beating long pendulum. But second hands were not common on pocket watches before the early 1800s.

Calendar hands for the day of the week, date and so on, which had been common on German tabernacle clocks, again became fashionable in the late 1700s and have remained so. Indeed, there was a late flowering in English precision watches at the end of the 1800s, when many complicated pieces were produced with moon phase and calendar indicators and, often, minute or quarter-repeating mechanisms (*see p.286*).

A repeat is one of the "trains" a clock or watch movement can incorporate. A train is a series of gear wheels and pinions running from the source of power

HOW CLOCKS ARE DRIVEN

The earliest clocks were weight-driven and were regulated by some form of verge, or crown-wheel, escapement, so called because the teeth were cut to give the appearance of a crown. It was used in all early clocks and in most English bracket clocks and watches until 1800. The rod is attached to a short pendulum and moves in a wide arc with the swing of the pendulum.

In the anchor escapement, developed *c.*1670, the pallets

ANCHOR ESCAPEMENT

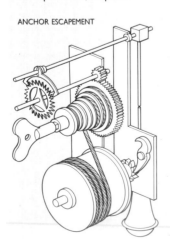

VERGE ESCAPEMENT

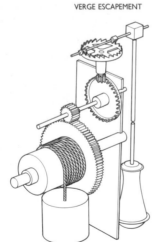

resemble a ship's anchor. First used for longcase, tavern and lantern clocks with a second-beating long pendulum, from *c.*1800 it was used in bracket clocks with a half-second beating, shorter, pendulum.

English spring-driven bracket clocks were usually fitted with a fusee, attached by cord or fine chain to the spring barrel to equalize the tension of the spring as the clock ran down.

SPANDRELS

The ornate corner pieces on a clock dial evolved to disguise the screws attaching the dial to the front plate. Spandrels were made by brass finishers who cast the pieces in quantity, finished them by hand and fire-gilded them. Patterns were standardized, and all clocks by particular makers at particular periods bore the same spandrels, so they form a useful aid to dating (see p.272).

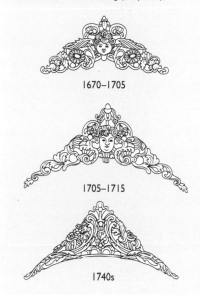

1670–1705

1705–1715

1740s

▶ **AN ENGRAVED BACKPLATE**
From clock No. 619, by George Graham, London, c.1725. The engraving on the backplates of bracket clocks is one of the chief glories of English clock making. Initially, plates were left plain except for the maker's signature, but by c.1680 engraved motifs of scrolling foliage and tulips had spread over the entire plate. In the 1690s, the tulips were replaced by grotesque ornament and birds; but from 1710, as this example shows, these declined in proportion to the scrolling foliage that became common from the late 1720s. At first baroque, by c.1750 the engraving was in a lighter rococo idiom. It declined c.1800 into a repeated motif on the edge of the plate and by 1840 had ceased, except for the signature.

to the function performed. Normally there is one train for each function: for instance, striking the hours or telling the time. The trains are held rigidly in a frame, the earliest of which was the posted frame, used mainly for clocks that ran for 30 hours or less, such as lantern clocks.

By the mid-1500s, small table clocks were being made with the movement held between a pair of plates cut to the same shape as the case and the dial on top. This construction was adopted in a vertical format for the movements of bracket and longcase clocks in the mid-1600s, and since then most clock movements have been of plated type. The same is true of watches, save that in the 1760s, in France, J.A. Lepine invented a system of individual cocks (thin metal braces) for each wheel in the train, allowing much slimmer watches to be made.

Before electric power, most clocks were run by weights or by coiled springs. Since a weight accelerates on falling and a spring weakens as it unwinds, a device known as an escapement is needed to allow only some of the driving power to escape at intervals. With each swing of balance or pendulum, the hands move on slightly as the escapement is unlocked briefly and then locked again.

A fusee is sometimes incorporated in a spring-driven movement to compensate for the spring weakening on unwinding. The fusee is a concave-sided cone cut with a spiral groove; the spring pulls against the narrow end of the fusee when fully wound, working its way toward the wider end as it unwinds. The Germans used the fusee in the "going" trains driving the hands of table clocks; the French had dispensed with it altogether by 1700. The English used it until the early 1900s, and it is a hallmark of the quality of English clock making.

CLOCK HANDS

Early hands were specially made for each clock; in 1690–1740, ornate hands were still carved, but after 1760, hands were often stamped out. Later, the two hands differed more in size than design.

   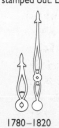 

| 1690–95 | 1690–1740 | 1740–60 | 1780–1820 | 1810–70 |

MANUFACTURERS' TRADEMARKS

The trademarks of 19th-century makers can be found stamped on the backplates of many German and some French clocks, including carriage clocks, or on a trade label pasted inside the case. Some German examples are shown here.

Gustave Becker

Hausuhrenfabrik Winterhalder

Junghans

D.R.G.M.
D.R.G.M.
Deutsches Reichs Gebrauchs Musterschutz
(post-1918 patent mark)

Hamburg American Clock Company

The introduction of the pendulum to England in 1659 led directly to the evolution of longcase and bracket clocks. The cases of the clocks were wooden, the wheels of the movement were framed in vertical plates, and clocks normally ran for eight days. Bracket clocks derive their name from the wall bracket with which some of them were provided; in fact, most stood on pieces of furniture and were known initially simply as spring clocks.

In contrast to longcase clocks, ebony, and then ebonized, cases for bracket clocks continued to be made in equal numbers to walnut, mahogany and other finishes. While some lacquer or japanned bracket clocks were made in the 1700s, few marquetry examples were produced. As with longcase clocks, the change from walnut to mahogany took place *c*.1750, and from the 1760s, fashions in case materials closely followed those of furniture.

In England, bracket clocks were made mainly in London; although there were a few centers of manufacture outside the capital, most of those signed for a country maker were only retailed in the provinces.

◄ GEORGE II BRACKET CLOCK

This ebony timepiece, dating from the late 1740s, stands on its original wall bracket. The "skin" of the bracket slides forward to reveal a well for storing the winding key. By the mid-18th century, clocks had become more numerous and were therefore more often kept permanently in one place, rather than being moved to where they were needed. This is confirmed by the lack of a carrying handle on the break-arch "triple-pad" top of the case.

Although signed for George Graham, the clock's movement is more in the style of one of his most gifted pupils, Thomas Mudge. It was probably made by Mudge shortly before Graham's death in 1751, at which point he succeeded to part of Graham's business. H 21in/53cm

Case styles

At first, like longcases, bracket clocks were severely architectural, but by 1675 they had become a simple plinth-shaped box surmounted by a dome of evolving shape. This was at first cushion-molded (known as a caddy, or basket, top); a small concave curved section was added from *c*.1715–25, giving an ogee outline (the inverted bell top). These curves were reversed by 1760, resulting in the bell top. Break-arch cases were current from the 1760s; lancet shapes and "chamfer tops," with a roof-like slope to all four sides, were popular from Regency times.

Point to note

Most 18th-century bracket clocks originally had verge escapements, many of which were converted in the 1800s to anchor escapements with heavier, slower, pendulums. Twentieth-century taste has dictated that these should be reconverted to verge escapements, but original verge escapements are always more desirable.

1 RENAISSANCE TABERNACLE CLOCK

This German tabernacle clock of c.1560 was made some 100 years before the invention of the pendulum. The pendulum hanging in front of the dial at the front of the gilt-metal case was added in an attempt to match the far better timekeeping achieved by bracket and longcase clocks with pendulums.

2 ARCHITECTURAL-STYLE CLOCK

An early clock, made by Samuel Betts c.1665, within six or seven years of the pendulum's invention. Both the architectural form, with entablature and pediment, and the dial, with a narrow chapter ring set against a dial plate engraved in the spandrels with vegetables, conform to the earliest type of bracket clock. H 19in/48cm

3 WALNUT BRACKET TIMEPIECE

A classic late Charles II clock made by Joseph Knibb in the 1680s, by which date the case was plinth-shaped, with a cushion-molded top. The chapter ring is wider, and there are winged cherub heads in the spandrels. H 11½in/29cm

4 EBONY AND SILVER CLOCK

By tradition made for Queen Anne c.1705, this exquisite small bracket clock by Thomas Tompion and Edward Banger is profusely mounted with silver ornament. It survives with its oak traveling case; at this date, clocks were moved around and often traveled with their owners. The clock is numbered 460 (see p.268). H 9in/23cm

5 MAHOGANY BREAK-ARCH CLOCK

A bracket clock, with a "triple-pad" arched top (c.1780), signed "Vulliamy." The face has three enamel discs, for the main chapter ring and the subsidiaries in the arch, which are for setting to strike/silent and for regulating the pendulum. Enamel clock dials were first used in England in the 1760s.

6 SCARLET BOULLE BRACKET CLOCK

The case of this French Régence period clock c.1730, with ormolu mounts and the dial set with enamel cartouches, is decorated with boulle marquetry (see p.218). By 1725–35, French dials were wholly enamel. H 21in/53cm

7 FRENCH ELEPHANT CLOCK

Mantel clocks incorporating animals within rococo ormolu mounts were highly popular under Louis XV. This mid-18th century clock incorporates a Chinese porcelain elephant; more commonly the animal is of bronze.

8 AUSTRO-SWISS MUSICAL CLOCK

The architectural case of this clock (c.1810) owes much to French, Louis XVI neoclassical style. A chain fusee movement drives a pin-barrel that plays 6 tunes on 11 bells. H 23in/58cm

1

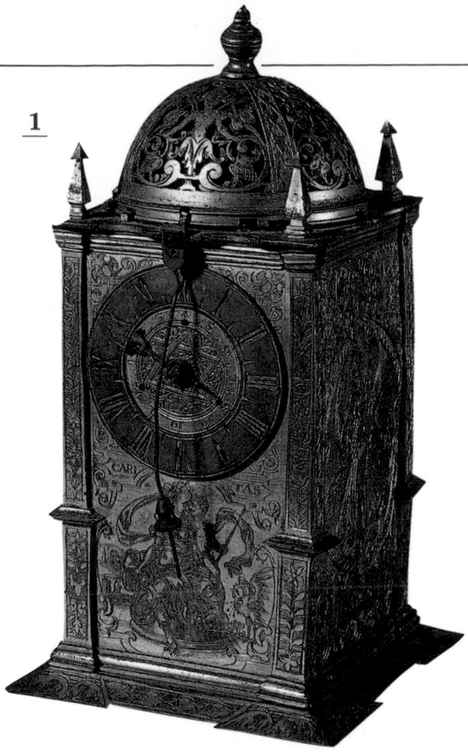

2

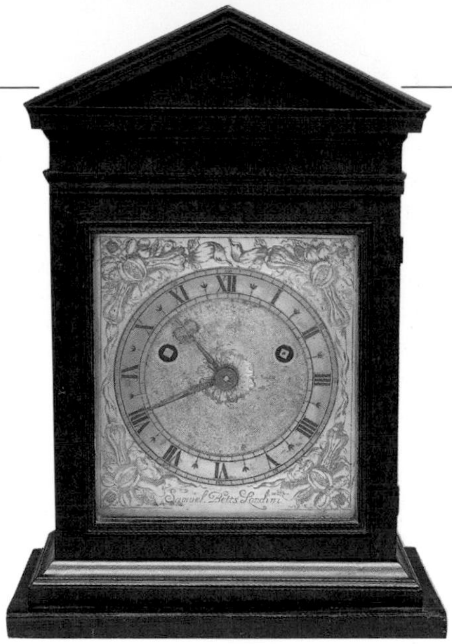

3

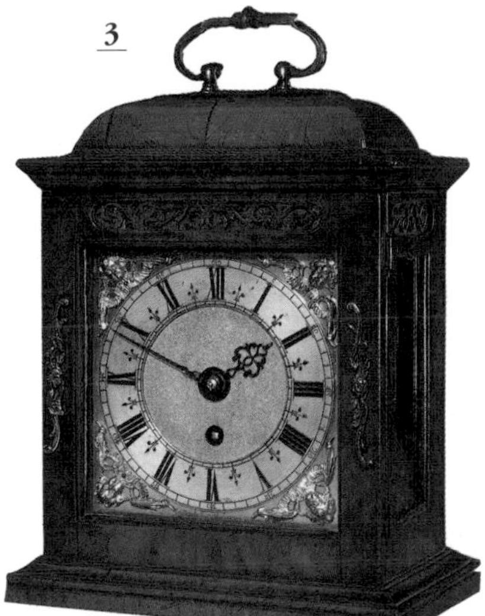

4

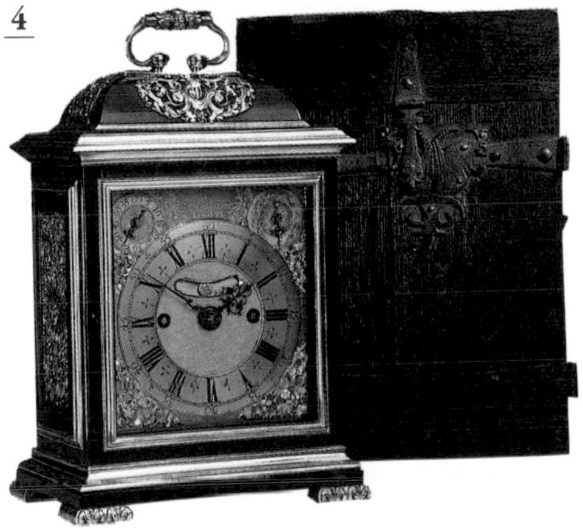

5

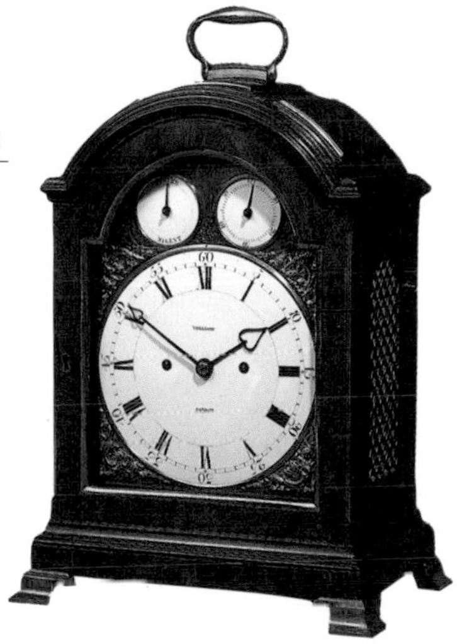

6

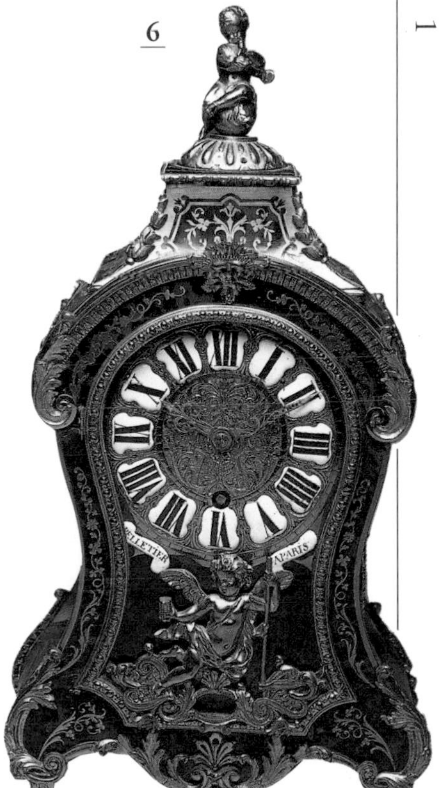

7

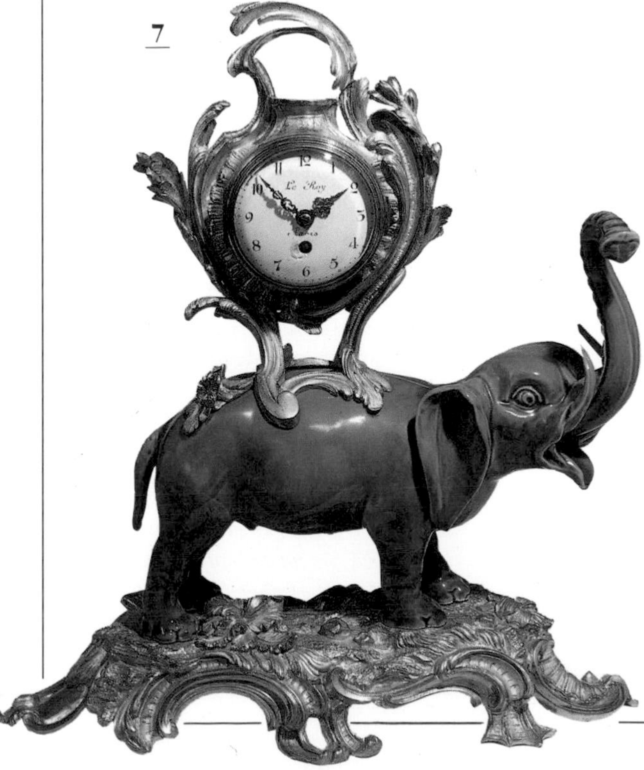

8

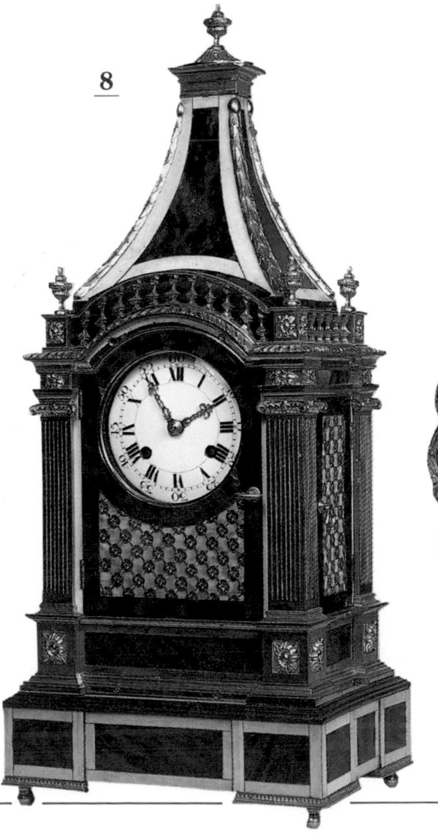

Mantel clocks are related to bracket clocks, but are generally smaller and shallower and have no carrying handles. They were first developed in France in the 1750s and in England during the following decade. Before these dates, mantels were not made with shelves capable of taking a clock. By the 1830s, the habit of flanking a mantel clock with paired ornaments led to the *garniture de cheminée*, a set consisting of a clock and matching sidepieces which enjoyed a vogue in the nineteenth century.

It is in mantel clocks that the most varied shapes and forms of decoration are found. Early French examples developed from *Régence* bracket clocks – newly fashioned in the rococo style and without a wall bracket so that they could be placed on a mantel. A large number of highly ornate rococo clocks were made, in combinations of ormolu, bronze, marble, porcelain and *vernis martin* – a type of japanning. Following the severe neoclassical style of the Louis XVI, Revolutionary and Empire periods, the nineteenth century saw an even larger production of mantel clocks in a variety of eclectic revivalist styles.

In comparison with French mantel clocks, English clocks were often rather sober affairs. They were, however, superb quality, usually non-striking, timepieces for the library, study or boudoir.

Thomas Tompion

Probably the most famous English clock maker of all time, Thomas Tompion (1639–1713) was admitted to the Clockmakers' Company in 1671. He produced barometers and watches, many bracket and longcase clocks (*see p.266: 4; p.270: 5*), and some lantern clocks, and was the first to number his pieces. Collaboration with the physicist Richard Hooke and the inventor Edward Barlow led to several important innovations, including the balance spring and the cylinder escapement. Tompion's timepieces were renowned for their reliability, even in his own day.

▼ LOUIS XV CLOCK

Signed by André de Ribaucourt, who worked in Paris 1770–89, this clock typifies the lighthearted spirit of the rococo. An ormolu bower, festooned with flowers, is peopled by a hurdy-gurdy player, a bagpiper and a dancing girl. The porcelain figures, modeled by J.J. Kändler, are from the Meissen factory (see p.62), the soft-paste flowers from Sèvres.

The side pieces, also with Meissen figures, do not necessarily belong with this clock, but from such juxtapositions grew the idea of making sets with urns or candelabra matching a central clock. H clock 20in/51cm

1 LOUIS XVI URN CLOCK

Urn clocks such as this (c.1790), cast in ormolu in a sturdy neoclassical style, were popular into the 1800s. The minutes and hours are shown on two rotating bands, with the time read against the serpent's tongue. The driving movement is in the plinth base.

2 LYRE MANTEL CLOCK

In its own way a novelty clock, this ormolu and white marble piece (c.1800) has a skeletonized movement and enamel dial which swing on the "gridiron" hanging from the top of the lyre and act as its pendulum. H 24in/61cm

3 EMPIRE TABLE REGULATOR

The severely architectural case of this precision clock (c.1810) is of maple with ebony moldings and bronze mounts. The caryatids show the influence on French decorative arts of Napoleon's 1798 Egyptian campaign. The escapement is visible in the center of the seconds dial, which is intercepted by a dial for hours and minutes. The glazed bob of the gridiron pendulum contains a thermometer. H 21in/53cm

4 FRENCH ORMOLU MANTEL CLOCKS

Two clocks with precision escapements, showing the difference between first and second Empire styles. Left to right: strictly architectural portico clock (c.1815); freer-style clock (c.1865) with ornate porcelain panels and dial (4a) with visible jeweled escapement. H 21in, 20in; H 53cm, 51cm

5 FRENCH PORCELAIN PANELED CLOCK

Mantel clock of portico form (c.1850) with mounts in 18th-century Sèvres style. Such panels were widely used on carriage clocks. H 22in/56cm

6 MAHOGANY MANTEL REGULATOR

The dial of this fine American clock (c.1860) is of painted tin, but it has a deadbeat escapement and a mercury-compensated pendulum that adjusts automatically for changes in length due to temperature change, so it keeps constant time. H 19in/48cm

7 ENGLISH OAK MANTEL CLOCK

Designed by the architect C.F.A. Voysey for his own use, in 1895, this style of clock was later made in aluminum by W.H. Timpey, while Liberty sold similar pewter-cased examples. The letters on the dial spell Tempus fugit (Time flies). H 20in/51cm

Soon after the pendulum was developed in Holland in the late 1650s, longcase clocks appeared. These attractive floor-standing clocks, designed with long trunks to protect the weights and pendulum, were first made in Britain – where they were known as grandfather clocks. Longcase clocks were made in America, where they were called tallcase clocks, and also, although in smaller numbers, in continental Europe.

The first longcase clocks had verge escapements and used short pendulums. It was only with the development of the more accurate anchor escapement (c.1671) that they began to be made with the longer pendulum that beats the seconds.

Early cases, made before the mid-1670s, had a Classical, architectural character, often with Corinthian columns and pedimented tops. From the early 1670s, these elements were confined to columns, either straight or barley-sugar twist, at the front of the hood supporting an entablature. Around 1700, the molding between the trunk and hood changed in profile from convex to concave, and all columns were straight.

Marquetry cases

When marquetry decoration was first applied to English clock cases (c.1675), it was confined to shaped panels of flowers (3). By 1690, however, it had spread across the entire front of the case and often incorporated borders of swirling seaweed marquetry (see p.214). The area of the case taken up with seaweed marquetry increased until, by 1700, it had entirely displaced the floral style (4). Japanned decoration (6, 8) had supplanted all marquetry by 1710–15.

Points to note

Some plain walnut clock cases were "marquetried-up" in the late 19th century. On many of these pieces, unless very crude indeed, the marquetry is of an age and quality that make it indistinguishable to all but an expert and may not affect the clock's value.

Check that the marquetry on the hood, trunk and plinth all match, since many plinths rotted from standing on damp stone floors and were replaced. Original marquetry should have an uneven feel, due to the shrinkage of the wood beneath the veneer. A very smooth, even surface may indicate recent repairs or restoration.

1 CHARLES II LONGCASE CLOCK
Classical columns and a pedimented hood are typical of the architectural emphasis of early English pendulum clocks. This example from the early 1660s, by a member of the Fromanteel family, may have started as a wall clock, but was soon converted into a longcase clock by the addition of the trunk and plinth. H 6ft 1in/1.85m

◀ **DUTCH LONGCASE CLOCK**
Signed "Fromanteel & Clark," this walnut clock (c.1710) is evidence of the close links between clockmaking in England and Holland. Johannes Fromanteel, an English clockmaker of Flemish extraction, first brought the pendulum to England. His brother Abraham went into partnership with Christopher Clarke, who by 1704 was running the Dutch side of the business.

This clock has a typically Dutch profusion of calendar indications (day, date and phase of the moon), although the case style is English. Later Dutch longcase clocks developed a local style of case and dial, but continued to use English movements. H 8ft 6in/2.59m

2 WALNUT LONGCASE CLOCK
Made by John Knibb, the younger of the famous clockmaking brothers, this clock (c.1685) has a shallow domed top with ball finials, a square dial signed by the maker and twist columns to support a pierced wood sound-fret. John Knibb was a provincial maker, but his clocks are of the highest quality. H 6ft 6in/1.98m

3 FLORAL MARQUETRY CLOCK
Made c.1700, this provincial musical clock has a case of unusually high quality. Marquetry extends from just above the ball feet, across the plinth, in panels up the trunk door and on to the hood, where two cherubs recline. The dial (3a), flanked by twist columns and decorated with intricate spandrels, measures 12in/30cm. Pierced blued-steel hands contrast with the silvered chapter ring, and the matted ground contains a seconds ring, calendar aperture and ringed winding hole. H 7ft 5in/2.26m

4 SEAWEED MARQUETRY CLOCK
The 12in/30cm dial, concave molding between the hood and the trunk, and extensive use of seaweed marquetry all indicate that this clock was made soon after 1700. H 7ft 2in/2.18m

5 QUEEN ANNE LONGCASE CLOCK
Thomas Tompion started to number his clocks c.1685; this burl walnut example, number 542, is one of his later pieces (c.1710–12). The flat-topped hood with brass-capped columns is typical of the masculine, yet graceful, lines of his clocks. H 6ft 8in/2.03m

6 IVORY-JAPANNED LONGCASE CLOCK
Japanned in ivory – the rarest and most desirable color – this clock was made c.1710 by Daniel Quare, one of London's greatest makers. The hood lacks its finials. H 8ft 1in/2.46m

7 GEORGE I WALNUT LONGCASE CLOCK
The date of this clock is indicated by both the arched dial (post c.1720) and the flat-topped trunk door (pre c.1730). It was made of burl walnut by William Webster, a pupil of Thomas Tompion, and has an ogee molded top with ball-and-spire finials. H 8ft 4in/2.54m

8 CHINOISERIE LONGCASE CLOCK
An arched top to the trunk door is characteristic of mid-18th century japanned cases. This piece lacks its giltwood finials. H 7ft 11in/2.41m

The makers of clock cabinets were a specialist group who generally followed the trends in furniture making, but often, as much as 25 years later. Few japanned cases were made before 1700, although the style had become fashionable in the 1670s. Similarly, mahogany cases were rare before 1750, despite the fact that this wood had been in common use for two decades. Even when marquetry was in vogue, between 1680 and 1710, plain burl walnut cases remained as popular as ever.

The tops of early longcase clocks could be pushed up to give access to the winding holes. By 1710, however, clocks had become too tall for this to be practical, and a door was made in the hood. This height increase meant that dials, which include the chapter ring and spandrels, also grew. Early spandrels were winged cherub heads which became more elaborate and, by c.1690, also included scrolls. The wings were omitted c.1700, and by 1745 spandrels were rococo.

DATING DIALS

c.1660–65
8in/20cm dial,
small numerals

c.1665–90
10in/25cm dial,
date aperture added

c.1685–95
11in/28cm dial,
seconds ring added

c.1695–1720
12in/30cm dial,
larger minute ring

c.1720
12in/30cm dial,
first arched dials

c.1730
12in/30cm dial,
arched moon dials

An easy way to date an English longcase clock is to look at the size of the dial, then to check the presence of other features.

1 MAHOGANY LONGCASE CLOCK

The columns on the hood, and those with giltwood capitals on the trunk, are typical of George III Lancashire longcase clocks. Other common features are the angles of the plinth and the frieze of verre églomisé (glass with gilded decoration) below the swan's-neck pediment. The maker was the famed Joseph Finney, who worked in Liverpool, 1770–96. H 7ft 8in/2.34m

◀ MID-GEORGIAN CLOCK

This walnut longcase clock by Jonathan Melling of Chester reuses French ormolu mounts originally intended for a grand precision regulator clock. This is an instance, rare in clockmaking, of an English cabinetmaker either purloining mounts from a new piece, possibly damaged in transit, or refashioning an entire piece of furniture, exported as a result of the French Revolution. This clock case follows the London style of c.1730, with an arched trunk door and arched dial. The mounts were probably added in Regency times. H 7ft 5in/2.26m

2 DUTCH MUSICAL LONGCASE CLOCK

A bombé plinth and carved paw feet give a distinctive appearance to this late 19th-century Dutch musical clock. A revivalist piece, its form and marquetry inlay closely follow the typical mid-18th century style. The hood lacks its giltwood figure finials. H 8ft 4in/2.54m

3 SWEDISH PAINTED LONGCASE CLOCK

Pine cases are a feature of many north European countries. The moldings on this mid-18th century example have been picked out in gold leaf. The square dial with an arched hood is another European feature. H 8ft/2.44m

4 SCOTTISH MAHOGANY LONGCASE

Painted-dial longcase clocks made in Scotland invariably have mahogany cases, often with crossbanding. This clock (c.1800) shows an historical scene in the arch (4a) and figure spandrels of the Four Seasons. H 6ft 8in/2.03m

5 FRENCH LONGCASE CLOCK

Originally a plain early 19th-century provincial clock, this case was later redecorated with fine kingwood and purplewood parquetry. The dial came from an earlier clock by Lepine, active in the late 1700s. H 6ft 8in/2.03m

6 BIEDERMEIER VIENNESE REGULATOR

Viennese floor regulators are less common than wall regulators (see p.276). This early Biedermeier regulator (1815–30) has the usual restrained rectilinear case with a pedimented top and a silvered dial (6a). Atypically, it has a three-train grande sonnerie movement (see p.274): the central weight drives the hands while the outer two strike the hour and quarter. H 6ft 2in/1.88m

7 VIENNESE LONGCASE REGULATOR

The heavy architectural style of this mahogany regulator case is typical of the late Biedermeier period (c.1840). The stepped top, with gilt leaf and flower cresting, is bordered by ebony and mother-of-pearl and surmounted by a giltwood eagle. H 9ft 3in/2.82m

8 PAINTED TALLCASE CLOCK

A tall swan's-neck pediment and urn finials grace the top of this large American clock (c.1910). The entire case is painted with flowers, trophies and strapwork. The dial with Arabic numerals is common to this type of longcase clock. H 8ft 4in/2.54m

1

2

3

4

4a

5

6

6a

7

8

TRAVELING CLOCKS

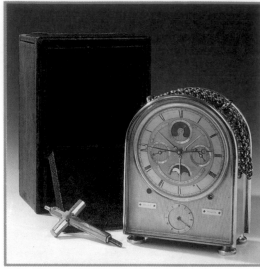

It was the development of spring-driven mechanisms in the early sixteenth century that enabled clock makers to make portable clocks. Hardly accurate before the invention of the balance hairspring in the 1670s, traveling clocks in the 1700s were usually in the form of large watches, 3–5in/8–13cm in diameter, known as coach watches.

The search for precision timekeeping in the eighteenth century, driven by the need to develop a timepiece accurate enough to determine a ship's east–west position, or longitude, led to the emergence of the marine chronometer. Despite the inventiveness of French makers, it was the English who developed the first chronometers to maintain accuracy in the difficult conditions at sea; from the 1830s, they became virtual sole producers.

Carriage clocks were developed from rectangular portable clocks, but had the balance and escapement at the top of the movement, rather than on the backplate. They were usually made of brass, with glazed sides and top and a carrying handle. The first carriage clock, created by Abraham-Louis Breguet in 1796, was supplied to Napoleon for his Egyptian Campaign of 1798. By insisting that all his generals should have a carriage clock, Napoleon was one of the first to recognize their value. The demand for carriage clocks finally took off in the second half of the nineteenth century, when the coming of the railroads revolutionized travel.

By the 1850s, carriage clocks were being made in standard sizes, and they reached a peak of popularity in 1880–1900; this was never regained after the disruption caused by World War I (1914–18).

◄ **SILVER CARRIAGE CLOCK**
Although made in the style of Abraham-Louis Breguet (see p.284), the originator of the carriage clock, this extremely complex silver timepiece, hallmarked 1823, is by James Ferguson Cole, the earliest maker of carriage clocks in Britain. It is thought Cole may have spent time working for Breguet in Paris before setting up in London in 1820. The clock features a minute-repeat mechanism (see p.286), perpetual calendar and alarm. H 6in/15cm

Points to note

Carriage clocks were made to standard sizes; for each size, both case and movement were made in different degrees of elaboration.

The simplest type of clock was non-striking. Others had various striking sequences: hour and half-hour; quarter-hour; and *petite sonnerie* (quarter-striking with a strike/silent lever). Clocks with a *grande sonnerie* mechanism (**5, 6**) had a three-position lever that could be set to strike the hour and quarter at each quarter, to silence the hour at the quarter, or to silence the strike completely.

Cases were sometimes embellished with engraving or set with porcelain or enameled panels instead of plain side glasses.

In general, English carriage clocks are superior to French ones; however, many clocks that carry an English retailer's name on the dial arc, in fact, French. Genuine English clocks can be distinguished by their use of the fusee and chain (*see p.264*).

1 FRENCH MARINE CHRONOMETER
This rare example, signed by Louis Berthoud, clockmaker to the French Navy, dates from the early 19th century and features a detent escapement. This mechanism, developed in the 18th century, was widely used in chronometers because of its precision. Diam. dial 3½in/9cm

2 ENGLISH CARRIAGE CLOCK
Engraved dials were typical features of English carriage clocks. The dial on this clock, by James McCabe (c.1860), is engraved with scrolling foliage and flowerheads. The hands are tipped by small fleur-de-lys, a characteristic English decoration. H 8½in/21cm

3 FRENCH CARRIAGE CLOCK
This comparatively late carriage clock (1887), shown with a mirror image, is housed in an "Anglaise" style case, presumably intended for the English market. Multicolored champlevé enamel is, unusually, combined with Italian micromosaic panels on the sides and rear door. H 7in/18cm

4 DECORATIVE CARRIAGE CLOCK
The Limoges-style enamel face and sides of this carriage clock, dating from c.1870–1900, are ornately decorated with Cupid and Psyche and with cherubs. This was one of a variety of decorative styles favored by French makers. H 6½in/17cm

5 GROUP OF CARRIAGE CLOCKS
These clocks date from c.1860–1925. Left to right: French calendar clock with Corinthian-style case; miniature silver-gilt clock by Cartier with guilloché side and top panels; French clock with alarm; gilt-brass miniature carriage clock with painted blue porcelain front and side panels; gilt-brass grande sonnerie clock with dials for day, date and alarm made in France. H 1½in–7in/4cm–18cm

6 GIANT CARRIAGE CLOCK
A French grande sonnerie timepiece made for the English market, bearing the retailer's name D.G. Rait & Sons. This large carriage clock (c.1880) has a gorge, or grooved, case and is exquisitely engraved with scrolling acanthus and vines against a matted ground. H 8½in/21cm

7 NOVELTY CARRIAGE CLOCK
Occasionally, carriage clocks were made in unusual guises – as a sedan chair, for example – or were equipped with automata. This clock, dating from c.1890, has a singing bird mechanism. H 10½in/26cm

8 FRENCH OVAL CARRIAGE CLOCK
A half-size clock, made by A. Dumas, with an enamel dial and engraved oval case. This example from c.1860 survives with its original leather traveling case. H 4in/10cm

9 FRENCH COMBINATION CLOCK
This unusual combined clock and aneroid barometer (c.1880) is complete with its traveling case. The top features a magnetic compass inset above the barometer and a central thermometer. H 7in/18cm

The first household clocks were weight-driven wall clocks with bulky openwork iron frames in the gothic style. But from the mid-1600s, wall clocks could be either weight driven (usually going 30 hours) or spring driven (running 8 days).

The first specifically English clock, the single-handed brass lantern clock, topped by a bell that gives it a characteristically domed appearance, was developed *c*.1620. It was made until *c*.1720 in London and into the 1800s elsewhere in Britain. English spring-driven clocks included the drop dial and the common Victorian wall dial, with the movement box hidden behind a glazed round painted dial; both developed from the tavern clock.

In the mid-1700s, a cottage industry in the Black Forest of Germany made clocks with wooden movements and carcasses that led to the cuckoo clock. By contrast, Viennese clock makers in the early 1800s produced precision wall regulators with fine glazed cases and enamel dials. The rough equivalent in America was the banjo clock.

From *c*.1715, French clock makers made increasing numbers of cartel clocks, often in fancifully shaped cases by leading cabinet makers, or *bronziers*. There was a great revival of cartel clocks in the 1800s.

◀ ACT OF PARLIAMENT CLOCK

An alternative term for the tavern clock, which originated in the 1720s. The name derives from an Act of 1797 taxing all clocks in Britain, which supposedly led private owners to put away their own clocks and rely on those in inns and taverns. The tax threatened to put clock makers out of business, however, so the Act was repealed the following year, but the name stuck.

This is an early example (1725), with a typically prominent signature, William Scafe, at the base of the dial. The green japanned case and break-arch dial flanked by columns reflect contemporary longcase clock design. This type of clock was produced well into the 19th century. H 5ft 6in/1.68m

Vienna wall regulators

These were weight-driven precision clocks against which other timepieces could be regulated; they were also used for timing astronomical observations. Those made in Vienna were of two types: the lantern clock with a large top and bottom, and the rooftop clock (6) with elegant lines and a simple architectural top. Carcasses were in three sections, veneered inside and out, usually with mahogany, and glazed on front and sides. The hands were always of blued steel. The carcasses of German regulators made later in the 19th century were less restrained.

1 FRANCO-SWISS CARTEL CLOCK

This clock, dating from c.1770, has a Swiss movement, but is housed in a contemporary French-made case, since the French were better at fashioning ormolu. The style of the case is early neoclassical, although still with a hint of the Rococo evident, especially in the angled female heads. H 24in/61cm

2 TEARDROP-SHAPED WALL CLOCK

The shape and flame mahogany veneer on the long door indicate a date of c.1790. The dial is protected by glass held by a turned wood bezel; on later clocks, the bezel was frequently brass. H 4ft 2in/1.27m

3 AMERICAN BANJO CLOCK

Banjo clocks, first made in the Federal period, were revived to celebrate the centenary of the Declaration of Independence. This example, c.1815, has decorative panels of transfer-printed glass. H 3ft 4in/1.01m

4 FRENCH ORMOLU CARTEL CLOCK

Despite the dial with enamel hour-numerals in a cast frame, the "upside-down" appearance of this elaborate clock case (c.1875) indicates a 19th-century revivalist style; 18th-century examples have a more pronounced downward taper. H 30in/76cm

5 VICTORIAN DROP-DIAL CLOCK

Clocks of this shape, with a short pendulum "box" extending below the dial, are known as "drop dial." The beat of the pendulum bob can be seen through the window. The papier-mâché case of this example (c.1860) incorporates mother-of-pearl inlay in the colorful decoration. H 24in/61cm

6 BIEDERMEIER WALL REGULATOR

A rare early Vienna regulator (1830) in a walnut case with architectural detail. Such clocks usually have a single driving weight; they seldom strike and run for periods up to a month. H 34in/86cm

7 GERMAN WALL REGULATOR

This year-going clock in a glazed mahogany case, dating from the early 1900s, indicates four time zones: local time, Vienna, St. Petersburg and Paris. H 5ft 4in/1.63m

WALL CLOCK SHAPES

The earliest wall clocks had long pendulums like those in grandfather clocks and were weight driven. The first spring-driven wall clocks with short pendulums date from c.1750.

Act of Parliament
c.1725–70

Teardrop
c.1770–90

Trunk dial
c.1760–1830

Drop dial
c.1800–80

Wall dial
c.1810–1930

NOVELTY CLOCKS

From the 1600s, novelty clocks have been made to delight and amuse, either by their form, by their automaton action, or by the oblique way they indicate the time.

In the 1600s, the Germans had a fondness for clocks in the form of animals, calvaries, or the Madonna and Child – many with some sort of automaton, such as eyes flicking to and fro in time to the escapement, or limbs moving on the hour in time to the strike. Animal clocks were taken up by the French in the 1700s in exquisitely modeled bronze and ormolu, often with porcelain flowers; nineteenth-century revival examples are less fine. Slave and "Inca" clocks were popular in 1800–30, and toward 1900 there was a fashion for "industrial" clocks resembling pieces of machinery.

Mystery clocks have no obvious linkage between the dial and the movement driving the hands, or seem to have a free-swinging pendulum. Most glass-dial mystery clocks are of anonymous French make with cases of only fair quality. Without doubt, the pinnacle of this art was attained by Cartier in the Art Deco period with clocks fashioned with precious and semiprecious stones.

Black Forest clocks

Early clocks were wall hung, with a wooden movement and case and decoratively painted arched wooden dial; the hands were usually brass. They were produced in Germany during the winter months by workers keen to augment their incomes and sold by local peddlers. The industry flourished, and by the 1800s several different types of novelty clock had been introduced. These included cuckoo and trumpeter clocks (6) and musical pieces that played several tunes. Picture clocks, such as the leopard with moving eyes (4) or figures striking a gong on the hour, were also common.

Rolling ball clocks

The most famous of these is the clock developed by William Congreve in 1808, whereby a ball rolls down a zigzag channel in a tilted tray, which reverses when the ball reaches the end of the groove. The action does not drive the clock, but acts as the escapement for the spring-driven movement. Modern reproductions are most often seen.

1 ITALIAN CRUCIFIX CLOCK
The mechanism of this striking clock, made in northern Italy c.1650, is in the base of the crucifix, while the chapter band is on the rotating ball at the top. This type of clock was usually made in Germany. H 19in/48cm

2 FRENCH EMPIRE SLAVE CLOCK
The fashion in the early 1800s for slave clocks in part reflected the increased trade with the West Indies and America. This example, c.1830, shows a man carrying a cotton bale. H 10in/25cm

3 ARCHITECTURAL SKELETON CLOCK
Clocks with the frame holding the movement reduced to a bare "skeleton" originated in France in the late 1700s, but most were produced in Victorian England. This London-made example dates from 1860. H 7½in/19cm

4 BLACK FOREST PICTURE CLOCK
The frame and picture on this high-quality clock (c.1860) swing away from the dial like a door. The leopard's eyes move in time with the pendulum. H 12in/30cm

5 GOLD STRUT CLOCK
This exceedingly slim traveling clock is held upright by a folding strut on the back. It was given as a present in 1883 by the then Prince of Wales to a card-playing friend. H 6in/15cm

6 BLACK FOREST TRUMPETER CLOCK
In a variant of the cuckoo clock, four metal trumpets sound the hour as a trumpeter appears below the dial. This one (c.1890) has typical carved bone hands and numerals. H 28½in/72cm

7 GERMAN FLICK CLOCK
This example of the "flick" or "ticket" clock, an early form of digital clock patented in 1904, was made a year later. H 5in/13cm

8 FRENCH MYSTERY CLOCK
Cast in spelter (a cheaper substitute for brass or bronze), the face of this clock (c.1900) and the pendulum swing mysteriously from side to side, driven by a tiny pendulum concealed behind the dial. H 12in/30cm

9 JEWELED MYSTERY CLOCK
Made recently by Imhof Swiss in homage to Cartier's 1930s mystery clocks, this rock crystal, gold, jade and citrine clock has diamond-set hands and hour markers. H 6in/15cm

◀ **AUTOMATON CLOCK**
A fine French Directoire *red marble and ormolu waterfall clock, dating from c.1805. It features Cupid "sharpening" his arrow against a rotating grindstone, while revolving glass rods simulate water spouting into a basin below. The automaton mechanism is released every hour. H 23in/58cm*

In the early 1800s, the Japy family, who worked in France near the Swiss border and were, therefore, influenced by Swiss techniques, began to use machinery for the production of clock parts. They progressed to making complete movements, in standard sizes, which were supplied to the makers of decorative cases.

It was, however, the Americans who pioneered the mass production of complete clocks, following the lead of Eli Terry (1772–1852). In 1807, Terry received an order for 4,000 clocks to be made within three years. He built a factory to produce the necessary components, using water-powered machine tools; eight years later, he built another factory, where he developed the "pillar-and-scroll" shelf clock.

Made with a swan's-neck pediment and slender columns flanking the dial, this was the finest of shelf clocks, although the OG type, a rectangular case with ogee molding, was more common. Such weight-driven clocks, the first to be mass produced, were followed in the 1850s by smaller spring-driven models, such as "gingerbread" and "steeple pattern" clocks.

The first American clocks were shipped to England in 1842. This started an influx of thousands of cheap clocks and led to the decline of the English clock industry. It also forced south German clock making, until then a cottage industry, into mass production. Between the 1870s and 1930s, a host of German companies began making spring-driven clocks. As both German and American companies were competing for the same markets, their products can be difficult to tell apart.

German and American clocks

American clocks usually had the manufacturer's name on the dial and may also have had a printed trade or instruction label pasted inside the case (*below*). The cases tended to be veneered in local woods and were often stained to resemble mahogany (4), and there was often a print behind the glass door below the dial. Movements were generally rectangular and had skeletonized plates.

While American movements were usually unsigned, German clocks tended to have trade marks stamped on square backplates. Cases were solidly made, and stained not veneered. Dials were not normally signed, but can have directional arrows by the winding holes.

1 "DROP-DIAL" WALL CLOCK
"Thomas [of] Lincoln" was the retailer, not the maker, of this 1860s clock. It has a high-quality fusee spring-driven movement which strikes a bell. On many clocks made after c.1870, it was more usual for the movement to strike gongs rather than bells. The case is of flame mahogany, with brass stringing between mother-of-pearl roundels. W 16in/41cm

2 ORMOLU MANTEL CLOCK
The movement of this clock was made by the French firm of Japy Frères – the Japy brothers. Pioneers of mass-produced clocks, their movements were put into various grades of case. This clock, with its original glass dome, is made of cast ormolu, but many similar cases were made of spelter, a cheap substitute. H 20in/51cm

3 ENGLISH MAHOGANY DIAL CLOCK
Although most of these classic Victorian clocks have fusee pendulum movements, this one (c.1875) has a platform balance escapement. The glass over the dial is held in place by a brass bezel. Diam. 15in/38cm

4 AMERICAN VENEERED SHELF CLOCK
Made by the Ansonia Clock Company c.1885, this clock has a painted tin dial. The print below is probably a later replacement since it does not fill the whole space. The case is veneered in local spruce wood colored to simulate mahogany. H 12in/30cm

5 IMITATION MARBLE CLOCK
The plinth and central section of this clock have been lacquered to imitate black marble, undercutting genuine marble clocks. Such clocks were a specialty of late 19th-century French makers, although this one (c.1890) was made by the Hamburg American Clock Company of Württemberg, Germany, for export to England. H 12in/30cm

6 "GINGERBREAD" SHELF CLOCK
Wood was steamed and then clamped into a mold to produce the raised pattern on this American clock, made by the New Haven Clock Company c.1900. The name derives from this process, similar to the way gingerbread was traditionally made. H 14in/36cm

7 FRENCH LYRE-SHAPED CLOCK
Clocks of this type, with velour-covered backboards, cast ormolu decoration and enamel dials, were made at the end of the 19th century. They were used both as wall-hanging clocks and, with the addition of an easel back-strut, as boudoir or bedside clocks. H 16in/41cm

8 FRENCH LIGHTHOUSE CLOCK
In the second half of the 19th century, some French clock makers, inspired by the Industrial Revolution, began to produce clocks that mimicked pieces of industrial and marine machinery. This clock was made c.1900 with a simple mass-produced movement. The lantern rotates to display first the clock face, then a barometer. H 17in/43cm

9 AMERICAN "STEEPLE PATTERN" CLOCK
On the pendulum hanging below this non-striking alarm clock is a small disk marked "R=A." This stands for retard/advance, and by turning a nut below the disk the clock was made to go slower or faster. H 17in/43cm

◀ **ALARM CLOCK**
Made c.1890 by the Seth Thomas Clock Company, Connecticut, set up in 1813, this clock is rare since it runs for eight days and the alarm resets itself automatically. The case retains its label with instructions for setting the alarm. The label also proclaims the company as the "maker of superior timepieces of all types, sizes and prices, from a fine ladies' watch to a 40-ft tower clock, the largest in the world." H 9in/23cm

CLOCKS AND WATCHES

POCKET WATCHES: 1

The development of the mainspring *c*.1500 led to the invention of the first watches. In effect miniaturized portable clocks, they were usually worn around the neck on a chain or cord, or from a belt, rather than being carried in a pocket.

Before the 1670s, when the introduction of the balance hairspring revolutionized timekeeping, watches were erratic performers. Being expensive, they were often highly decorative. Cases were sometimes fashioned from faceted and hollowed-out hardstones such as rock crystal. Gold, silver or gilt-metal cases were profusely engraved, and from *c*.1630 the technique of polychrome enameling was developed to great perfection, first in Blois, France, and later in Geneva. Form watches, watches made in the shape of another object, were popular in the early 1600s; they often took the guise of skulls.

The invention of the balance spring allowed more accurate timekeeping, and watches began to feature minute hands. From the 1680s, the numerals (which by then included the minute divisions) took up a larger space on the dial. By *c*.1710 the French were using enamel hour plaques, and from *c*.1725 were making complete enamel dials; by the middle of the century, English watchmakers had followed suit.

Types of watch case
Pair-case
The use of the more accurate balance spring demanded a case that closed tightly to keep out dust. In response, the pair-case (**3**) was developed: an inner case housed the watch movement and an outer case protected against wear and tear. As a result, decoration moved from the inner to the outer case.

The English pair-cased watch with verge escapement became the envy of Europe in the 1700s and early 1800s, and some continental makers faked London signatures on their watches; these are known as "Dutch forgeries," since most came from Holland.

Hunting-case
To protect watch faces from breakage, hinged solid metal covers were sometimes fitted over the dial. These were known as hunting-cased watches (**5**) because they were first developed for use in the hunting field.

Half-hunting case
A refinement of the hunting-case in which the cover had a small round hole in the center revealing a miniature chapter ring and allowing the time to be read without exposing the entire dial.

Polychrome enamel
The technique of painting on a white enamel ground (**6**) was perfected by Jean Toutin of Blois *c*.1630. His family specialized in exquisite landscape, floral and religious scenes and trained a school of enamelers whose influence spanned Europe. They passed on their expertise to the famous Huaud family of Geneva, who worked *c*.1670–1724. Geneva remained famous for enamel work until the late 1800s.

◀ **RARE OCTAGONAL WATCH**
This early 17th-century pocket watch (c.1615) has a gilt-metal case, with hinged covers to the front and back; the octagonal shape was common at the time. The movement is signed by Edmund Bull of Fleet Street, London.

Before the invention of the balance hairspring in the 1670s, watches were inaccurate and, like this example, usually featured only a single hand. By contrast, watch cases were often lavishly decorated. Here the silver dial is engraved with a scene of the Ascension of Christ extending under the narrow, applied gilt-metal chapter ring. L 2½in/6cm

1 EARLY VERGE WATCH
*Made by Michael Graz, this watch from c.1630 is cased in faceted rock crystal. The dial (**1a**) with indicators for day of the week, date, month and phase of the moon, is typical of early German watches. L 2½in/6cm*

2 EARLY ENGLISH WATCH
This early verge watch (c.1660) has a single hand for telling the time and a small blued-steel pointer for reading the date (just visible on the number 12 of the calendar ring). The silver case and center of the dial are exquisitely engraved with tulips. Both were protected by a silver outer case, decorated with pinheads and covered in leather. Diam. 1½in/4.5cm

3 PAIR-CASED VERGE WATCH
*From the protective case (**2**) developed the pair-case, of which this silver watch by Peter Garon, hallmarked 1690, is an example. The outer case of the watch contains a watch paper left by a repairer. Diam. 2½in/6cm*

4 SILVER PAIR-CASED WATCH
Many plain silver pair-cased watches made in the early 19th century have decorative enamel dials. A frigate embellishes the face of this watch (hallmarked 1793), and the letters that replace the numbers on the dial spell "Thomas Baldwin," the name of the original owner. Diam. 2½in/6cm

5 HUNTING-CASED VERGE WATCH
These hunting-cased watches were most fashionable in the 1860s, but this is an early example, hallmarked 1820. The intricate mechanism and fine engraving on the backplate are concealed within the case. Diam. 2½in/6cm

6 DECORATIVE POCKET WATCHES
*In the 18th and 19th centuries, watch cases were decorated in a variety of styles. A scene in polychrome enamel surrounded by split pearls (**a**) was an expensive form of decoration; the use of translucent animal horn with painted designs or scenes (**b**) was cheaper. Diam. (both) 2in/5cm*

7 TWO POCKET WATCHES
*Illustrating the popularity of metal dials in the early 1800s, watch (**a**), dating from c.1832, is cast in colored golds. The enamel dial of (**b**) is more typically mid-18th century. Diam. 2in, 3in; Diam. 5cm, 7cm*

◄ **ENAMEL AND DIAMOND WATCH**
This souscription *pendant watch, by A.-L. Breguet, was bought in 1800 by Hortense de Beauharnais, daughter of the Empress Josephine, and wife of Napoleon's brother, Louis. Such a fine provenance greatly enhances the appeal of a watch, even one by France's greatest watchmaker.*

This piece uses the montre à tact *system developed by Breguet, which allowed the time to be "felt" by pushing around an arrow on the back of the watch as far as it would go. From the diamond to which it was then pointing, the time could be deduced. The time could also be read conventionally from a dial protected by the enameled front cover, which is adorned with a diamond-set crowned letter "H." Diam. 2in/5cm*

Father of the modern watch

Abraham-Louis Breguet (1747–1823) was born in Switzerland but lived in Paris. After the French Revolution, he became principal clock and watchmaker to the Empire. In addition to designing the first carriage clocks (*see p.274*), he invented the *tourbillon* mechanism, which reduced the errors caused by a watch being carried about. The quality of Breguet's engineering, coupled with a functional yet elegant style, gave him a worldwide reputation and clientele.

Breguet specialized in *souscription* watches (*above*, **2**) which were paid for, in advance, by the customer. Their design was of high quality, but to reduce costs they were technically very simple. Made with just one hand, the dial was calibrated so that the time could be read to within 2½ minutes, accurate enough for everyday use.

1 PAIR-CASED VERGE WATCH
This silver pair-cased watch (1770) is a fine example of the quality and legibility of ordinary 18th-century watches. It has a white enamel dial with Roman numerals for the hours, Arabic numerals for the minutes, and classic beetle and poker pattern hands. The case includes a later clock-repairer's paper. Diam. 1¾in/4cm

2 BREGUET MONTRE SOUSCRIPTION
Signed "Breguet et fils" above the VI, this fine souscription *watch (1806), is shown with its gold case open and its winding key. Diam. 1¾in/4cm*

3 HALF-HUNTING VERGE WATCH
Dating from 1820, the silver case of this verge watch is an early example of a half-hunting case. The dial has a smaller chapter ring in the center, which remains visible when the case is closed, and the hour hand has two marks on it so that it can always be recognized. Diam. 2in/5cm

4 AMERICAN GOLD HUNTING WATCH
Despite having mass-produced movements, American gold watches were often set in fine, heavy cases with elaborate engraved decoration. This example (c.1890) was made for the English market. Many American watch cases are made of rolled gold – heavy gold plating on a base-metal case. Diam. 2¼in/6cm

5 SOPHISTICATED SWISS WATCH
Toward the end of the 19th century, Swiss watchmakers improved the technical quality of their timepieces enormously and began to produce highly complex watches. This example, made by Patek Philippe c.1892, incorporates a minute-repeating mechanism (see p.286), chronograph and perpetual calendar. Diam. 2¼in/6cm

6 AMERICAN GOLD POCKET WATCH
This open-face watch in a 9-carat gold case was made c.1900 by the Elgin Watch Company. It is a highly reliable, though average quality, mass-produced watch. The luminous numerals and hands are set on a black dial for good legibility at night. Diam. 2¼in/6cm

7 LADY'S FOB WATCH
An iris set with diamonds adorns the enameled Swiss case of this fob watch (c.1910). It combines the quality of American mass production (the movement is by the Waltham Watch Company) with the Swiss tradition of fine decorative cases. Diam. 1in/2.5cm

8 GOLD ROLEX DRESS WATCH
Made for evening wear, this stylish man's Rolex (c.1925) has Art Deco numerals on a curved square dial with contrasting shading. W 2in/5cm

9 CARTIER PURSE WATCH
The dial of this watch (c.1925), with a black champlevé enameled gold case, is revealed from behind shutters by pressing push-pieces at each end. Cartier was renowned for producing stylish Art Deco timepieces. L 2in/5cm

By the close of the seventeenth century, all the basic problems that had stood in the way of a sufficiently accurate watch had been solved. There remained, however, the need to perfect a timepiece that would enable ships to fix their longitude. The search for the marine chronometer (*see p.274*), with its counterpart the pocket chronometer, kept research going on timepieces.

The lever escapement, a spin-off from this quest for precision, was invented in the 1760s by Thomas Mudge. Unfortunately, Mudge did not fully appreciate its potential, and it was only in the 1830s that the lever escapement came into general use. But within 20 years, it had supplanted all other watch escapements, and it continued to be used in wrist watches until the advent of quartz movements in the 1970s.

Although in the 1800s and 1900s most pocket watches were circular, their decoration was diverse. Metal cases might be plain, engraved or embossed. Enamel work was also popular, but because it was expensive, a cheap substitute, under-painted animal horn, was sometimes used, often depicting rustic scenes.

Early outer cases were covered with leather held in place by pins; later, in the 1700s, a green shagreen covering became common. Many eighteenth-century gold cases were set with gemstones, while those made around 1800 frequently had enamel backs within a border of half-pearls. Porcelain cases were also occasionally made.

The Art Deco period saw the final glory of the pocket watch, with many exquisite pieces being made for evening wear.

WRIST AND FASHION WATCHES

The origin of the wrist watch lies in the 1860s, when ladies' bracelets began to be set with a concealed watch. Men found such an arrangement effeminate, and few men's wrist watches were made before 1910. It was only during World War I that their practicality was proven. Their popularity was ensured by the spread of motoring, and in the 1920s a model called the driver's watch appeared; this fitted the shape of the wrist and could be read with both hands on the steering wheel.

The wrist watch brought about world dominance for Swiss watchmakers, despite the fact that in the 1800s the term "Geneva" applied to a watch had been derogatory. Five of the seven best watchmaking houses are Swiss (Patek Philippe, Jaeger Le Coultre, Vacheron & Constantin, Rolex and Audemars Piguet); the other two (Cartier and Breguet) are French, but both use fine Swiss movements. Secondary Swiss makers include Omega, Longines and IWC (International Watch Company).

The passion for collecting wrist watches, which dates from the early 1980s, was a reaction to the ubiquity and cheapness of quartz watches. The vogue for stylish and mechanically complicated watches, from both before and after World War II, has led some makers to put such models back into production, but in limited numbers. While the ever-popular Rolex Oyster has never been out of production, Jaeger Le Coultre's Reverso has been revived, as have some perpetual calendar watches.

Points to note

The most reliable indicators of the desirability of a wrist watch are not the metal of the case but the maker, the style, and the degree of mechanical complication. Many ordinary gold wrist watches are of little interest to collectors and so are worth no more than the value of the bullion. Features that are popular include chronographs (**5**, **7a**), world-time indicators (*below left*), moon indicators (**7d**), perpetual calendars (**6**), and watches with minute-repeating mechanisms (**4**). Caution should be exercised when considering minute-repeating wrist watches, since some have been recently converted, albeit skillfully, from pocket watches.

Minute-repeating mechanism

This mechanism, more common in clocks, allows the wearer to "hear" the time through striking the last hour, quarter and minute (**4**). If the time were 3:19, for example, the watch would strike: three single notes (ding, ding, ding) to show the hour; followed by one double note (ding-dong) for the quarter hour; and four more single notes for the extra minutes.

1 LEATHER-ENCASED WRIST WATCH
Many ingenious ways of converting old pocket and fob watches were found when, after World War I, wrist watches became acceptable, even fashionable. Made in the 1860s, this Swiss gold cylinder fob, or "granny," watch would have been used by a woman. In the early 1900s, the watch, except for the face, was enclosed in a leather-strapped pouch. This made it so large that it was then probably worn by a man.

◀ WORLD-TIME WRIST WATCH
This rare 18-carat gold watch, made by Patek Philippe in the late 1940s, has a world-time indicator on the case bezel inscribed with 41 cities. Since the bezel revolves in step with the hands, once set, the local time for any of these locations can be read against the 24-hour ring of the dial proper. This ring is colored silver and black, to distinguish between day and night hours. Patek Philippe produced watches of this type from the 1930s, but only in small quantities, which makes them highly collectible.

2 SILVER ROLEX OYSTER
Probably the best known of all wrist watches, the Rolex Oyster was first marketed in 1926. It featured a revolutionary self-sealing winding stem which rendered the watch waterproof, hence the name oyster (see also 6). This early example, made in 1928, has a white enamel dial with luminous Arabic numerals and sits in a cushion-form case. The movement is signed "Rolex Prima."

3 DIAMOND COCKTAIL WATCH
This exquisite 1930s diamond-set platinum cocktail watch on a 9-carat white gold bracelet is true to the origins of the wrist watch as a piece of female jewelry. Many watches of this type were made with woven black silk straps.

4 MINUTE-REPEATING WRIST WATCH
If a slide on the side of the case is pushed, this 1930s 18-carat white-gold watch will strike the time to the last full minute. Such a complex mechanism is extremely unusual in wrist watches, especially one with such a flat rectangular case.

5 WRIST CHRONOGRAPH
Made by the Swiss company Vacheron & Constantin (c.1938), this rare gold watch is also a chronograph, or stopwatch. The stop/second hand is started, stopped and reset using the single button next to the winder.

6 GOLD ROLEX OYSTER PERPETUAL
Diamonds encircle the champagne-colored dial of this modern Rolex Oyster perpetual watch (see also 2), which shows the day and date and has a self-winding mechanism. The numerals are marked by more diamonds, all enclosed within an 18-carat gold case with a self-sealing winding stem.

7 GROUP OF FINE WRIST WATCHES
*The revival of interest in high-grade mechanical watches has led both to a collector's market for old examples and to top manufacturers putting similar watches back into production. This group of fine pieces illustrates both types: (**a**) a gold chronograph and (**b**) a gold watch are both by Patek Philippe and date from the 1940s; (**c**) is a modern automatic calendar watch by Vacheron & Constantin and (**d**) a moonphase watch of a similar date.*

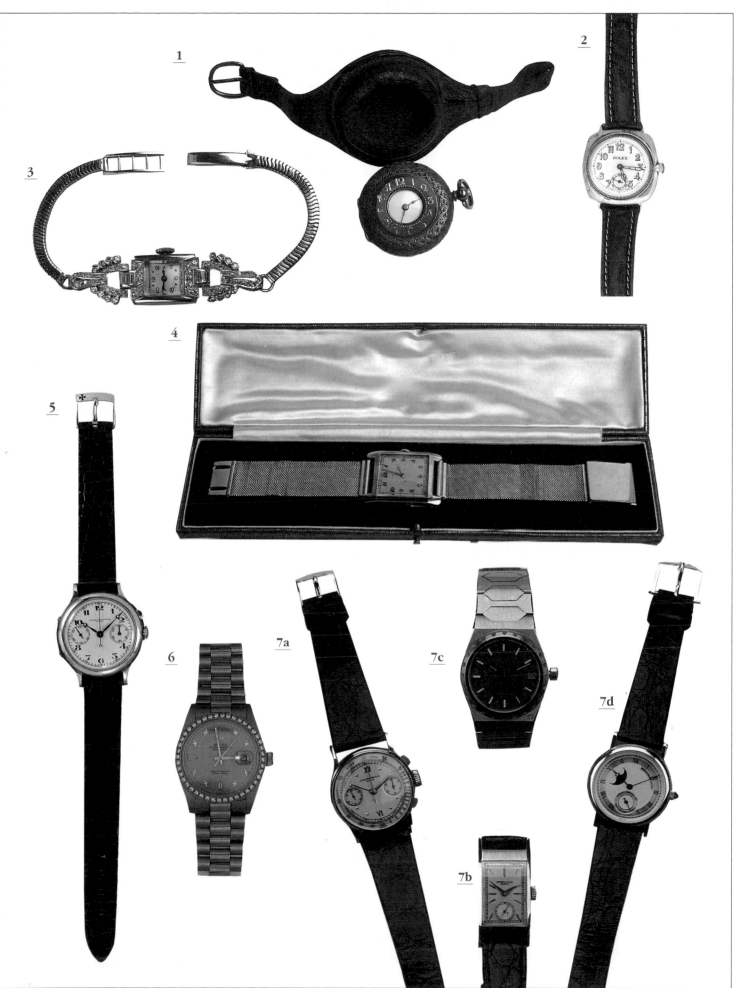

CHAPTER SIX

ORIENTAL WARES

The applied arts in China and Japan present Westerners with a challenging difference of cultural emphasis and a striking sense of continuity. The bronze vessels from the Shang Dynasty (1766–1122 B.C.), for instance, along with calligraphy, were traditionally regarded as the twin pinnacles of Chinese art, and their influence was evident over succeeding centuries.

Indeed, the Chinese written language has been a great unifying factor in oriental art. Enthusiasm for it remained constant, and those who managed to learn its thousands of characters enjoyed high social status. Highest of all were the Mandarins, who governed China on behalf of the Emperor. They were not aristocrats but civil servants, selected through grueling examinations that tested their knowledge of the texts of the Zhou Dynasty (1111–255 B.C.).

The priorities of this scholar élite are mirrored in the arts. Brushpots, waterpots, seal-paste boxes and other fine works were made for use on the writing table, and the prevalence of archaistic styles of decoration reflected a fascination with the past. Chinese antiquarianism began as early as the tenth century A.D., when Shang bronze vessels were collected by scholars, who were initially interested only in the calligraphy and the documentary value of their cast inscriptions. But they were soon to become fascinated with the shapes and decoration of the bronzes, and during the Song Dynasty (A.D. 960–1279), the first objects in bronze and other materials were made in imitation of the archaic.

The élitist literati looked down on public arts such as sculpture, which was associated with the exotic and distrusted religion of Buddhism. This, with its art, existed in a context of official disapproval and even persecution, except when foreigners, such as the Manchu Qing Dynasty (1644–1912), were in power. Buddhism had far greater official sanction in Japan, and monasteries were inviolate even at times of terrible feudal turbulence.

Outside the field of religion, fine carvings tended to be small and were generally intended to be used by an individual or shown off to friends. Snuff bottles, scholars' brushpots and Japanese netsuke were made to be used and handled, so tactile quality was esthetically as

important as appearance. Japan was deeply influenced by China, but there were persistent differences of emphasis. Japanese history differs from the mainland Chinese model, in which a highly centralized and planned system was occasionally attacked or taken over by invading barbarians. Japan was isolated, without the unifying force of outside threat, with the corollary that several artistic styles existed, including the Chinese-influenced Court manner and the aristocratic taste for fine swords and gold-decorated lacquer. Zen Buddhism and the Tea Ceremony also had a profound effect on the Japanese esthetic, with the concept of *shibui* – the refined and subtle – counterbalancing a brash display of wealth and power.

During the peaceful Edo period (1615–1867), the Tokugawa shoguns consolidated their rule by forcing aristocratic families into permanent residence in the capital, present-day Tokyo. A city culture of rich merchants arose to attend to the wants of these hostage courts. In this worldly milieu of new wealth, the makers of decorative sword-fittings, netsuke and *inro* flourished for some 200 years, until the ending of Japan's isolation from the West created the new conditions of the Meiji period (1868–1912).

The applied arts were greatly influenced by contact with the West. European houses are full of Far Eastern wares brought in by the Portuguese, the Dutch and the British in the 1500s to 1800s. Most of these objects combine western shape and function with oriental decoration, but in the late 1800s there was a move toward pure display. This was especially true in Japan, where fine craftsmen, abandoned by consumers at home in the vogue for western goods, created an opulent new world of sculptural groups, censers and vases, alien to Japanese traditions but decorated with Japanese subjects in cloisonné, lacquer and ivory.

▶ **SONG DYNASTY GILT-BRONZE STATUE**
A serene statue, dating from A.D. 960–1279, of a luohan, *or Buddhist holy man, with one hand raised, the other lying palm-upward. Such bronzes are among the finest examples of Chinese metalwork. H 32in/81cm*

CHINESE JADE, HARDSTONE AND OTHER CARVINGS

Since Neolithic times, jade has been of central importance in China, rather in the way that gold has been in the West. But Western eyes tend to associate value with glitter, and it takes some time to appreciate the subtler attraction of soft polish, pale shades and translucent depth.

Because of the hardness of nephrite jade, it was not possible to carve it in the normal sense until the introduction of the diamond-tipped drill. So before the twentieth century, jade was worked with abrasive sand used in combination with ropes and bamboo gouges, and every object took many months of laborious grinding and polishing to form.

Jade was seldom made for export until the late 1800s, so most pieces reflect Chinese taste and are usually functional as well as decorative, although a tendency toward pure display became pronounced in Court taste in the 1700s. Such items as brushpots, brush washers and brush rests reflect the high status of learning in Chinese society, while archaistic shapes and styles of decoration reflect a Confucian culture's intense respect for the past.

From the 1700s, there was increasing interest in carvings in other hardstones, such as jadeite and turquoise, and in coral. Indeed, jadeite largely supplanted nephrite jade, for with its often brilliant apple and emerald green, it is ideal for jewelry as well as traditional vases and censers.

Nephrite jade
A metamorphic rock whose crystalline structure has been altered by pressure or heat to form a silicate that is tougher than steel. The nephrite jade used by the Chinese comes from near the city of Yarkand in East Turkestan.

Jadeite
Also a metamorphic rock, but chemically distinct from jade, being a silicate of sodium and aluminum. Most jadeite used in China is Burmese.

"New jade"
Various other materials are similar to jade, but are softer and less valuable. The foremost is bowenite, a soapy-looking and usually pale green stone, which is carved into the incense burners, figures of maidens dancing and so on that are sold as "new jade" in curio shops in Asia and elsewhere.

▼ **WHITE JADE MARRIAGE BOWL**
This almost faultless bowl, carved with chrysanthemums, bamboo and asters, dates from the reign of Emperor Qianlong (1735–96), regarded as the time when the finest craftsmen had access to the finest stone. Chinese armies had recently reconquered Turkestan, allowing merchants to mine there after centuries of trade in poorer stone found in riverbeds. Diam. 12½in/32cm

1 ARCHAIC JADE OWL PLAQUE
The horned bird, carved with admirable economy from a flat slice of jade, dates from the Shang Dynasty (1766–1122 B.C.), the dawn of Chinese history. The whorl design on the wings is comparable to that on bronzes of the period. W 4½in/12cm

2 SPINACH JADE TABLE SCREEN
Rich dark green stone was favored in the 1700s for luxurious objects such as this table screen. It is carved with a scene of an Immortal and his attendant gathering herbs near a mountain pavilion. Diam. 7½in/19cm

3 CALCIFIED JADE FITTING
A Ming Dynasty (1368–1644) piece that may be a sword fitting. The archaic dragons were carved in a manner imitating the style of the Han Dynasty (2nd century B.C.–2nd century A.D.), and the opaque calcified stone also indicates an early date, but this is probably a chemically induced effect. It is impossible to know now whether deception or respectful imitation was the intention. W 2¼in/6cm

4 JADEITE NECKLACE
Good 20th-century jadeite jewelry in European styles is now highly regarded in China. Flecked apple greens are popular, but rich, even, emerald green is most sought after. L 20½in/51cm

5 TURQUOISE VASE AND COVER
A 19th-century piece, carved with elaborate decoration of songbirds and peonies from a single block of bright, even-toned turquoise. H 5½in/14cm

6 GROUPS OF FEMALE IMMORTALS
These late 19th- or early 20th-century groups show female Immortals, or minor deities. The figures have been ingeniously fitted into branching heads of coral to create graceful compositions. H l to r top 7½in–9in/ 18–23cm; W below 13½in/34cm

7 LAPIS LAZULI MOUNTAIN
Carved c.1800 for a scholar's desk, this piece provided a rest for a writing brush, which fitted into the spur on the left. It exemplifies the romantic ideal of retreat from the world to a lonely communion with nature. The gilt inscription is a poem imitating the style of Emperor Qianlong. W 10½in/26cm

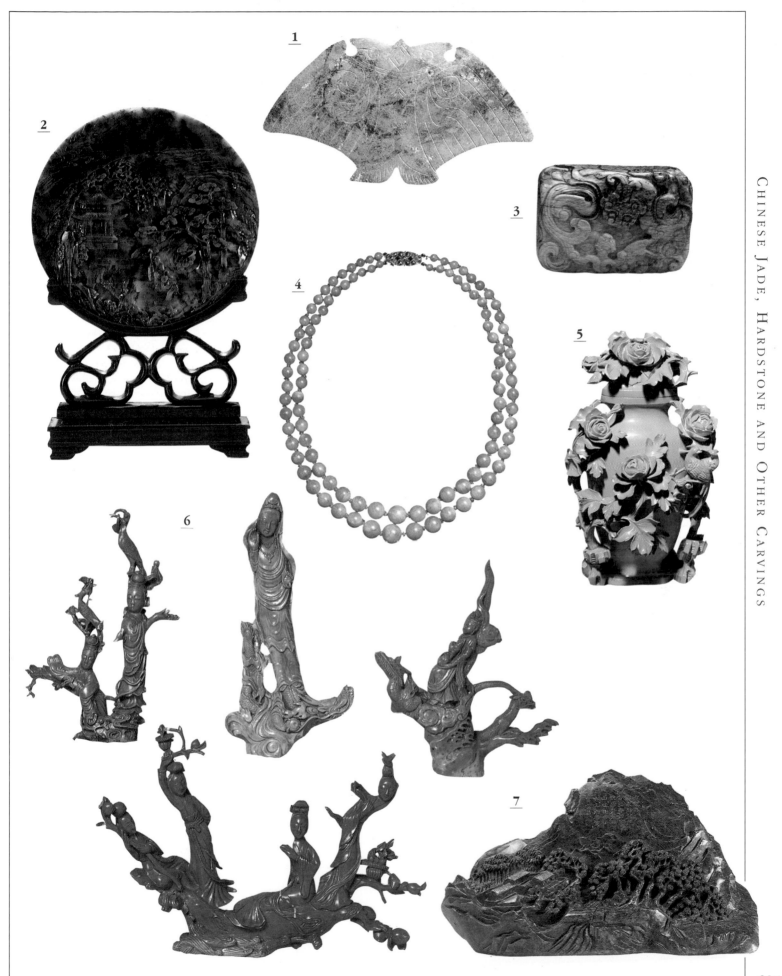

CHINESE IVORY AND BONE CARVINGS

Ivory was a favored material in China from the time of the Shang Dynasty (1766–1122 B.C.), when herds of elephant roamed the south. Its close texture, allowing the carving of crisp, fine detail, and the creamy tone of its surface, which polishes to a soft sheen, can be compared with fine white jade, and older pieces take on an almost glassy patina.

One important use for ivory after the 1600s was for objects for the scholar's table, such as brushpots, boxes for seal paste and wrist-rests. It was also used for the *hu* tablet, a long, undecorated slice from the entire length of the tusk, which in the Emperor's presence was carried by court officials as an emblem of literacy and power.

The shape of tusks was suited to making figures, and a large industry arose in the late Ming period (the 1600s) in the city of Zhangzhou, Fujian. Some of the figures are similar to those in *blanc-de-Chine* porcelain, which was made nearby. Buddhist, Daoist and even Christian images were produced, many of which can still be found in churches in the Philippines and Mexico, for which they were originally ordered.

Canton export ivory carvings

From the early 18th century until c.1880, Canton was a major producer of ivory artefacts such as ladies' fans, workboxes, snuffboxes and card cases. It was also a center for purely decorative objects, pierced concentric balls, for instance, and for openwork models of junks and pagodas to feed the taste for chinoiserie in Europe.

Snuff and opium

New types of ivory artefacts, made for the Chinese themselves in the late 18th and early 19th centuries, included snuff bottles and saucers and also opium pipes and boxes, which are much admired for their rich brown patina.

1 IVORY SEAL BOX AND COVER
A box from late in the Ming Dynasty (1368–1644), decorated in low relief with a scholar riding in a rocky landscape. The box probably held the red paste used for sealing documents, although similar containers appeared on the ladies' dressers for lip salves and glosses. Diam. 2½in/7cm

◀ IVORY WORKBOX
A lady's workbox, containing its original ivory implements for sewing, weaving and tatting. It dates from c.1840, though similar items were produced for export from the 1780s and continued to be made for another 40 years. This type of densely packed, high-relief carving, with crowds of figures in the gardens of a palace, derives from lacquer and jade carvings. It is also found on snuffboxes and on flat, pocket-sized card cases which are, perhaps, the most common form of export ivory. W 12in/30cm

2 IVORY FIGURE OF A BODHISATTVA
The bejeweled, bare torso and floral tiara are the marks of a Bodhisattva, a semi-divine Buddhist helper of humanity. The figure was carved from a single tusk, with the clothing picked out in gilt lacquer which has worn to reveal cinnabar red beneath. H 7in/18cm

3 RHINOCEROS-HORN LIBATION CUP
This material was used for fine carving in the 1600s and 1700s especially. Large horns were carved in the 19th century as display pieces for export, but this piece, with dragons on both inside and outside, was made for a scholar. Such cups were used for alcohol: rhinoceros horn was thought to have health-giving properties and to make any poisoned drink poured into it foam. H with stand 9in/23cm

4 IVORY FIGURE OF AN IMMORTAL
The maiden He Xiangu, one of the Eight Daoist Immortals, holds her attribute, a lotus flower, to her shoulder. This is a late 19th-century carving from Canton. H 19in/48cm

5 IVORY WRIST-REST
To steady the hand when writing, a scholar would rest his wrist on a section of tusk or bamboo. The top of this early 19th-century example is carved in low relief with a fisherman putting on his shoe; the underside is more deeply carved with fishing boats on a mountain river. L 9in/23cm

6 IVORY "FAN OF A THOUSAND FACES"
This fan, made for export in Canton c.1850, has a clear affinity with the export porcelain of the period in coloration and subject matter. The type derives its name from the ivory faces that have been stuck onto the painted paper ground. The reverse (6a) shows the deeply worked guards and finely carved pierced brisé work on the sticks. H 11in/28cm

7 THREE IVORY BRUSHPOTS
Most literate Chinese had a brushpot for storing writing brushes. Ivory and bamboo lent themselves to this form, but brushpots are also found in ceramic and jade. The middle pot of these three late 19th-century examples is in a slightly coarse export style; the outer two were probably made for the home market. H 4–6in/10–15cm

The Japanese term for carvings made solely for display is *okimono*. Such carvings were produced in the second half of the nineteenth century for export to the West. Their combination of fine materials and craftsmanship with exotic subject matter was much in the Victorian taste, and they found a ready market in Europe and America. Much of the impetus for this new style of carving came from the shrinking market for netsuke in the Meiji period (1868–1912), resulting from the fashion in Japan for European dress.

There are two main types of *okimono*. First are those made in ivory from several separately carved sections, put together on a circular stand to make up complex groups of beasts, peasants, basket sellers and so on. The best of these Ogawa School carvings are signed within a rectangular red lacquer panel set into the underside.

A second group, of lower quality, is made from walrus ivory. These are carved from the whole tusk with the unsightly textured center hollowed out into a variety of tall groups: a peasant with a boy or a monkey on his shoulders, for example.

Tokyo School ivory carving

The finest of all *okimono* carvings came from artists trained at the Tokyo School of Art, which was set up in 1887 to combat the slide of quality in commercial carving.

Tokyo School carvings (4) are larger than the run of earlier ivory sculpture and tend to be carved from one piece. These highly realistic sculptures share the peasant and samurai subject matter of the sectional carvings, but tend to be far less busy in design. Signatures are incised directly into the base, on the edges of which the rough, brown, outer tusk surface is often left intact.

Shibayama

Western taste for novelty and color led to the late 19th-century vogue for Shibayama-style (2) inlay work on *okimono* carvings. Pieces of mother-of-pearl, hardstone or stained ivory would be inset into figures, cabinets or vases to glittering effect.

1 IVORY CARVING OF JUROJIN

One of the popular Seven Gods of Good Fortune, Jurojin is the patron of long life and learning and is always depicted with a staff and scroll. His robes are covered with lightly stained incised decoration to bring out the whiteness of his venerable beard. The figure is signed Kyoko within a red tablet on the base. H 15in/38cm

2 INLAID IVORY TUSK VASE

This massive late 19th-century item, from the luxury end of the trade, almost qualifies as a small piece of furniture. Tusk vases, descended from the Chinese brushpot, are a popular Shibayama form, and this piece is inlaid with a caparisoned elephant bearing a large vase of flowers on its back. A rectangular shell tablet on the base is signed Masamitsu. H 2ft 11in/89cm

◄ **WOODEN FIGURE OF JIZO**
The compassionate Bodhisattva Jizo, one of the most popular Japanese Buddhist deities, is depicted as a monk bearing his attributes of a jewel and a staff. The large wooden figure, standing on a lotus flower, with his elegantly draped robe painted in color and gilt, dates from c.1700. H overall 3ft 2in/97cm

3 INLAID IVORY FIGURES

A group of small okimono figures dating from the late 1800s, all inlaid in Shibayama style and signed on the base. Left: A man standing by a well and holding a pump. H 6½in/16cm Top center: An old man in an inlaid robe holding a basket of mice away from an eager cat. H 6½in/16cm Bottom: Daikoku, god of commerce and agriculture, with his coin box and treasure bag, going through his accounts with an abacus. W 5in/13cm Right: A man with a pipe, in a robe inlaid with flowers, selling fish and terrapins from the tubs beside him. H 4in/10cm

4 TOKYO SCHOOL MOTHER AND CHILD

This fine, realistically carved group dates from c.1890. The beautiful calm peasant mother's head and torso was carved from a single large piece of ivory; her limbs and the cheerful baby were separately made and secured with pegs. H 17½in/45cm

5 BUDDHIST PRIEST

A fine example of the Japanese carver's puckish delight in depicting his gods in comic situations. Buddha's disciple, Rakan, rides on the priest's back and uses his scepter to try to catch a crab that is biting the priest's toe. The base is modeled as a stream among rocks, with water bubbles inlaid in shell. H 14½in/37cm

6 IVORY KINGFISHERS

This group dating from c.1900 is signed by the artist Kofu. The birds perch upon a lotus pod made from coarse-grained stag antler, which emphasizes the smooth creamy texture of the ivory and the fine engraved detail of these perky birds with inlaid eyes. L 11in/28cm

7 THREE GODS OF GOOD FORTUNE

An ivory group on a wooden base (c.1900) showing Hotei, the god of happiness, and his children, Daikoku, the god of commerce, and Ebisu, the god of food and fishing, about to eat a meal. Japanese craftsmen often depicted gods either drunk or being made fun of in some way. W 9in/23cm

The dried sap of the native East Asian tree *Rhus vernicifera*, bled from the tree in summer and fall, is the basis of lacquer. It is a natural plastic that becomes extremely tough when hard; for this reason, Japanese aristocrats used lacquer for lightweight armor and, since it will resist even boiling water, for vessels for food and drink.

Lacquer has always been expensive because of the time and skill needed to make objects from it. Drying times can run into weeks for a single coat, and many coats are required to build up enough thickness for use. Each layer must be carefully polished before the next is applied.

Most lacquer is somewhat adulterated, to speed the making process and to give it color. It is normally mixed and thickened either with charcoal, to create a lustrous black, or with mercuric cinnabar to create red. Yellow ocher is also used on carved red lacquer to create bright contrasting layers. Lacquer is always applied to a core of some other material: leather, metal or wood. Even fabrics and paper are used as a core for light lacquer objects such as small dishes and cups.

Chinese lacquer

From the time of the Yuan and Ming dynasties in China (1260–1644), official preference was for carved lacquer in red or black (2), although incised, inlaid and painted styles were also found and were influential in Japan.

Boxes, dishes, bowls and trays were common objects in the Ming period (1368–1644), along with large numbers of tables and chairs and massive cupboards. Under the Qing emperors (1644–1912), the list of lacquer objects was extended to include vases and other vessels in archaistic styles, Buddhist temple fittings and screens.

Japanese lacquer

The characteristic Japanese taste in lacquer was for decoration in gold, usually on a black ground (*see p.298 for terms*) and often with Shibayama mother-of-pearl inlay. Apart from chairs and cupboards (which were not used), objects of much the same type were made as in China.

▼ JAPANESE CEREMONIAL PALANQUIN
This massive piece dates from the Meiji period (1868–1912). Lacquer palanquins and furniture, decorated in gold maki-e *on black and bearing heraldic* mon, *were made for aristocratic weddings from the mid-17th century. Maki-e was reserved by statute for the upper classes, though the law turned a blind eye to rich merchants wearing gold-decorated* inro. *L pole 13ft 8in/4.17m; carrying case 3ft 5in/1.04m*

1 CHINESE BLACK LACQUER DISH
A rare Song Dynasty (960–1279) dish with a petal-shaped rim from a temple collection in Japan. A ghostly image remains in the center of a flower spray, which was probably originally gilt. Fine early uncarved Chinese lacquers had a strong influence on Japanese styles. Diam. 12½in/32cm

2 CHINESE HEXAGONAL EWER
The shape of this rare piece, bearing the incised mark of Emperor Jiajing (1521–66), is derived from Islamic metalwork. The style of carving is known as yuntiao, *"cloud pattern," in China and* guri, *"curved like a wheel," in Japan. H 9in/23cm*

3 CHINESE BROWN LACQUER TABLE
An elegant table (c.1600) designed to stand beside a chair and hold a teacup. The lacquer artist has selected each tiny sliver of mother-of-pearl inlay for its natural green or red iridescence. H 22in/56cm

4 CINNABAR LACQUER HU VASE
This finely carved vase copies an eastern Zhou bronze design from c.400 BC. Dating from the time of Emperor Qianlong (1735–96), it probably came from the palace and reflects the new direction given to craftsmen by his scholarly interest in the past. The gilt metal liner is pierced for arranging flowers. H 28in/71cm

5 SAGE-JUBAKO, OR PICNIC SET
An elegant Japanese picnic set dating from c.1700. Within a neat carrying frame, it contains two sake bottles, a box, a tray and a four-tiered jubako, *or nest of boxes. Food remained warm for some time in these, thanks to their close fit. H 10in/25cm*

6 JAPANESE ARMOR
Laced armor gave good protection against arrows and sword cuts and was light to wear. The iron helmet, mask, gauntlets and leggings here (c.1860) were black-lacquered against corrosion, while the laced leather plates were lacquered for strength.

7 SUZURIBAKO, OR WRITING BOX
The high status of literacy in Japan is reflected in the quality of decoration on this 19th-century suzuribako. *Inside the lid, a samurai horse wanders in a forest, while the box, containing an inkstone and water dropper, bears the heraldic* mon *of the Tokugawa shoguns. L 9in/23cm*

8 LACQUERED WOOD SADDLE FRAME
Light, waterproof lacquer was the normal protective coating for saddles such as this handsome 19th-century example, decorated in takimaki-e *and with heraldic cranes. The seat would have been covered in leather. L 14½in/37cm*

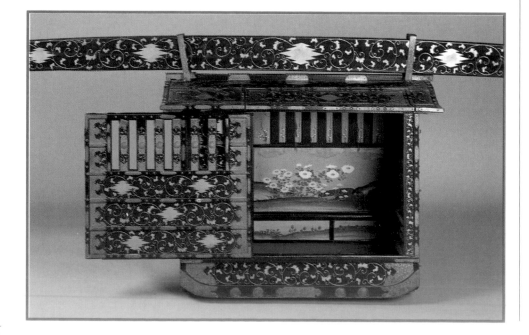

1

2

3

4

5

6

7

8

The Western trade in Oriental art began in the mid-1500s, with Portuguese merchants trading in Chinese porcelain and Japanese lacquer. Objects from the Momoyama period (1568–1600), with the dark ground largely covered with bright gold coloring and inlay of mother-of-pearl, such as the coffer (*below*), lecterns, folding shrines and fall-front writing cabinets found immediate favor in Europe.

In the 1600s, Japanese styles became more spacious and were dominated by landscape and garden subjects in gold *maki-e* on black. This type of lacquer was imitated in China both for export and at Court, and in European japanned work. From the mid-1700s to the 1880s, Canton was the most important center for export wares, including furniture and the massive 12-fold "Coromandel" screens. In this process, a thin skin of black or brown lacquer was carved through to the layer beneath, and the resulting areas were filled in with bright colors. Palace scenes, birds and flowers were popular subjects.

Boxes were made with a wide variety of fittings, including metal tea caddies and ivory sewing implements or puzzles. Boxes for the card game loo (an early form of whist) had inner boxes containing hundreds of carved mother-of-pearl counters.

Japanese export lacquer became less common during the eighteenth century, possibly undercut by Chinese imitations. But after 1854, when Japan was opened up to the West, it reappeared with some superlatively crafted objects, which are highly fashionable with collectors today.

Types of Japanese lacquer

Maki-e is the generic term for a design sprinkled in metal dust, usually gold or silver, on a coat of wet lacquer. The most important types of *maki-e* are:

Nashiji: Flakes of gold are strewn sparingly at various angles on wet lacquer, which is allowed to dry and relacquered, creating a sparkling effect (**5, 6**; *p.296*: **5, 7, 8**).

Hiramaki-e: "Flat" *maki-e*; gold powder is thickly sprinkled on a design painted in wet lacquer, hardly raising it above the level of the background (**5, 6**; *p.296*: feature, **5, 7, 8**; *p.300*: **4**).

Takamaki-e: The design is raised in low relief by mixing lacquer with a thickener, such as charcoal, and applying alternate coats of gold powder and lacquer. When dry, it can be carved into three-dimensional pictures (**5, 6**; *p.296*: **5, 8**).

Togidashi maki-e: "Polished-out" *maki-e*; designs are covered with clear lacquer, then polished flush with the background (*p.300*: feature, **2**).

These methods would often be used together, and in conjunction with Shibayama inlay of mother-of-pearl, metal or other materials.

1 CHINESE CHEST ON STAND
This chest, made for the European market c.1700, is decorated with birds and flowers in red and gold lacquer on a black ground, in imitation of the popular Japanese export style. It has carrying handles on the sides and rests on an English-made stand. H 3ft 2in x W 4ft 5in; H 97cm x W 1.35m

2 CHINESE LACQUER WORK TABLE
A good example of the high-quality export lacquer made in Canton c.1830–50. The original carved ivory sewing fittings and damask work bag are still in place. As with export ivory at the time (see p.292), crowded palace-garden scenes are a favorite subject for lacquer; this scene with dragon boats racing is particularly charming. W 2ft 5in/74cm

3 JAPANESE TELESCOPE
This late 18th-century half-inch refracting telescope has a lacquered pasteboard body colored and tooled to imitate European leather. It bears the VOC monogram of the Vereenigde Oostindische Compagnie – the Dutch East India Company – the only Europeans allowed any contact with Japan by the isolationist Tokugawa shogunate (1600–1868). L extended 3ft 3in/99cm

4 CHINESE EXPORT LACQUER BOX
A 19th-century brown and gilt lacquer box containing four pewter tea caddies. Finely painted scenes depict the harvesting, grading, drying and tasting of tea, the most important commodity of the China trade with the West. W 15½in/39cm

5 JAPANESE VASE AND COVER
Various maki-e finishes decorate the body and cover of this late 19th-century vase. Mythological scenes on the front and back panels are inlaid in Shibayama style, while silver and cloisonné enamel are used for the dragon handles and the finial in the form of the god of Long Life. H 10½in/26cm

6 JAPANESE LACQUER TABLE SCREEN
Another example of excellent export lacquer work, this late 19th-century screen is adorned with figures from Japanese and Chinese mythology. Ivory and shell inlay is used, together with hiramaki-e, takamaki-e and nashiji. Each leaf: H 18in x W 9½in; H 46cm x W 24cm

7 JAPANESE DISPLAY CABINET
A high-quality export cabinet dating from the Meiji period (1868–1912). The fine gilt lacquer work and Shibayama inlay utilize skills developed making small objects for the Japanese home market. H 6ft 6in/1.97m

◄ **JAPANESE COFFER**
A small piece, dating from the 16th-century Momoyama period, this coffer is wholly European in shape. The vibrant decoration with its gold and brown lacquer and chunky mother-of-pearl inlay is, however, typically exotic Japanese. H 6½in x L 9in; H 16cm x L 23cm

NETSUKE, INRO AND OJIME

Since traditional Japanese kimonos have no pockets, an intricate system was devised by which personal belongings could be suspended from the *obi*, or sash. Various *sagemono*, or "hanging things," were carried in this way, although the most usual were *inro*, a purse and keys. *Inro* were originally small tiered boxes which held the seal and seal-paste used by every literate person. They were also used for storing medicines, with each compartment holding a different herb. By the Edo period (1615–1867), however, *inro* had become miniaturized, so they could be carried on the person.

A silk cord passed through holes on both sides of the individual boxes that made up an *inro* and held them together. A small bead, or *ojime*, drew the strings together, and above the *obi*, a netsuke neatly secured the knot that held everything in place. At its best, the whole ensemble combined function with a discreet, yet stylish, display.

Even without considering the decoration of *inro*, their craftsmanship is impressive. They were composed of as many as seven miniature boxes, each made separately and fitted together in perfect line. Usually made of lacquered wood, *inro* were easy to decorate – indeed, all styles of Japanese lacquer can be found on them in miniature.

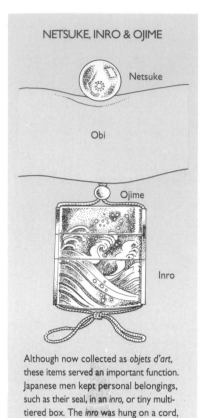

NETSUKE, INRO & OJIME

Netsuke

Obi

Ojime

Inro

Although now collected as *objets d'art*, these items served an important function. Japanese men kept personal belongings, such as their seal, in an *inro*, or tiny multi-tiered box. The *inro* was hung on a cord, which passed through an *ojime*, or bead, that slid down to keep the *inro* closed. The cord then passed beneath the sash tied around the kimono and was secured above it, using a netsuke, or toggle.

◀ **TWO FINE INRO**
Resplendent in red lacquer, with added gold and togidashi-e, the small 19th-century single-case inro *(right) features a young boy (not shown) trying to restrain a large running ox. Attached is a small black* ojime *and a red and black netsuke.*
W inro *4in/10cm*

The straight-sided four-case inro *(left), decorated with bright gold* takamaki-e *lacquer, was made in the late 19th century. An exquisitely detailed scene of a flower seller and his customer is embellished with Shibayama of mother-of-pearl, ivory and colored horn. The silver* ojime *is cast in relief with flowers and rocks, while the ivory netsuke, signed Hidemasa, is in the form of a mask.*
L inro *3½in/9cm*

1 LARGE FOUR-CASE INRO
A dragon, with eyes of sparkling rock crystal, rises from the sea in clouds of vapor on this late 18th-century inro. *It also bears the maker's signature, Koma Kyoryu saku. The 19th-century walrus ivory netsuke was carved and inlaid in blue-black copper alloy with a Chinese Immortal conjuring a dragon from a bowl.* L inro *5in/13cm*

2 TWO LACQUERED INRO
Dating from c.1850, the inro *on the left is decorated in* takamaki-e *(see p.296) on a dull gold ground with a spring scene of a cuckoo calling over rice fields. The other (c.1820) shows a lion on a rock. Both have a* manju *(flat) netsuke which represents a rice cake.* L inro *3½in, 4in; L 9cm, 10cm*

3 STAINED BOXWOOD INRO
Inro *in materials other than lacquer often diverge from the standard shape, as in this naturalistic cicada dating from the 19th century. The netsuke, a mouse on top of a half-eaten gourd, is carved from a tooth.* H 4in/10cm

4 FOUR-CASE INRO AND SHEATH INRO
In the 19th century, inro *decoration evolved toward increasingly lush and striking effects. The left-hand* inro, *signed Kinsai, is adorned with a black crow design on a gold ground. The unusual sheath* inro *of gold* hiramaki-e *opens to reveal an inner three-case* inro. *H 2½in, 3½in; H 6cm, 9cm*

5 MID-19TH CENTURY THREE-CASE INRO
A fine inro *by Kajitawa, decorated in gold, silver, bronze and black* togidashi-e *with a scene of Kiso Gorge, after a print by Hiroshige.* L 3in/8cm

6 THREE 19TH-CENTURY INRO
Decorated with temples and pavilions behind swirling waves, the central four-case inro *is the oldest (1840) and is marked "Asakusa," the place it was made. The other two three-case* inro *are both later; the one on the left shows armor on a dull gold ground; the other depicts the warrior Masatsura writing a poem with an arrow before departing for battle.* H 3–4in/8–10cm

7 SILVER AND GILT TOBACCO PIPE
Tobacco was an exotic innovation in the Edo period, and pipes followed the shape of European clay examples, but in more precious materials. The pipe was thrust through the obi, often with a metal ashtray netsuke. L 10in/25cm

The inspiration for netsuke (pronounced nets-ki) came from Chinese toggles, made of stones and shells, which were probably introduced into Japan in the 1500s. The Chinese selected their toggles for magical qualities, whereas the Japanese considered the subject, material and esthetic quality.

By the late 1600s, netsuke carving had become a recognized branch of the arts, although it was only in 1781, when *Soken kisho*, the first book with a section on netsuke, was published, that the names of individual artisans were mentioned. By this time, workshops were well established, each with a master teaching a number of pupils.

Netsuke were made from a plethora of materials and in many shapes. The most common form was the *manju*, a slightly domed disk named after traditional rice cakes of the same shape. They were decorated with engraving, deep carving and even piercing, and some were inlaid with hardstone.

The most popular netsuke were the *katabori*, three-dimensional carvings. Those made in the 1700s featured figures from Chinese mythology or Westerners and tended to be tall and thin. By c.1800, they had become smaller and more compact.

The subject matter of netsuke varied hugely: some gave a delightful view of daily life; others showed mythological or realistic beasts or Japanese gods, who were often treated with affectionate ridicule. Yet other types of netsuke included miniature theatrical masks, and seal netsuke, which combined two functions in one object.

◀ **IVORY NETSUKE OF A BAKU**
A baku is a benevolent mythical beast which prevents nightmares by swallowing them. This netsuke was carved in the late 18th century by Getchu and exemplifies the spirit of the netsuke, with its combination of impish wit, sculptural form and painstaking quality of finish. This particular piece made a world record price for a netsuke when it sold in London in 1987 for £110,000. H 3½in/9cm

Materials used for netsuke

Early pieces were made predominantly of wood and ivory, but after c.1800 the range of materials seemed almost infinite. Not only elephant ivory was used, but also the tusks of the walrus and wild boar, the horns of the narwhal, stag and rhinoceros, and the teeth of the sperm whale and tiger. Each had its own distinctive grain and color, often recognizable only by an expert. Netsuke were also made of lacquer, bamboo, jade, porcelain, various metals and coral.

Signatures on netsuke

The practice of signing their work developed slowly among the makers of netsuke, the *netsuke-shi*, and only about half of all netsuke are signed. Since both styles and signatures were often copied by other makers, the presence of a signature is no guarantee of either quality or value.

1 IVORY NETSUKE OF A EUROPEAN
Carved in the mid-18th century, this unsigned netsuke of a grotesque bearded European, singing and beating a drum, reveals the fascination of the isolated Japanese with the exotic Far West. At the time, the only Europeans allowed any contact with Japan were the Dutch, and they were confined to a single trading post on the artificial island of Deshima in Nagasaki harbor. H 4½in/11cm

2 IVORY NETSUKE OF A WESTERNER
Although this rather engaging carving of a Westerner clutching a bow shows considerable signs of wear, this does not greatly affect its value, since collectors tend to appreciate the evidence of a long history. Made in the second half of the 18th century, the piece is unsigned. H 3in/8cm

3 IVORY NETSUKE OF A SEATED GOAT
In Japan, the goat is one of the 12 animals of the zodiac, each of which represents a particular year, so this netsuke may have been a New Year gift. It was made by the Kyoto artist Mitsuhara, who was active c.1800. The quality of this piece is evident in the shape, which makes the most of the precious tusk, and the detailed carving of the fur, worn smooth in places.

4 FINE IVORY NETSUKE OF DARUMA
Daruma, the 6th-century Indian monk who founded Zen Buddhism, is shown miraculously crossing the ocean from China to Japan on a stem of millet. With his lugubrious expression, he was a popular comic subject. This piece from the early 1800s is by Minkoku. H 2in/5cm

5 BOXWOOD NETSUKE
Signed Shoko, a maker from Hida, this mid-19th century netsuke features the fabulous characters Ashinaga and Tenaga (seated), who had exceedingly long arms. H 2½in/6cm

6 RIBALD IVORY NETSUKE
This finely executed piece, by the 19th-century Kyoto artist Masakazu, depicts a man who appears to have nipped himself painfully between the legs as he dries himself after a bath. This is a good example of a balancing netsuke, which, although the shape is top-heavy, stands erect on a flat surface. H 3in/8cm

7 TWO NETSUKE MADE FOR EXPORT
Comparatively rough carvings were made for export in the last two decades of the 19th century. Artificial staining was used to make them seem older than they were. Both show aspects of the jovial god Hotei, who is often confused with Buddha, but is the god of happiness and children. The netsuke on the left shows two boys holding fans, one of Hotei's attributes, and playing with his bag of wind. The other depicts the fat, bald god holding two children. H 1in, 2in; H 2.5cm, 5cm

8 WOODEN NETSUKE OF AN ONI
This oni, or demon, leaning on a mokugyo, or Buddhist gong, and holding a coral and ivory beater is expressively carved. He is meditating before being converted to the faith. This fine late 19th-century work by the artist Toshiyuki shows the fashion in later netsuke for striking mixed media effects. H 2in/5cm

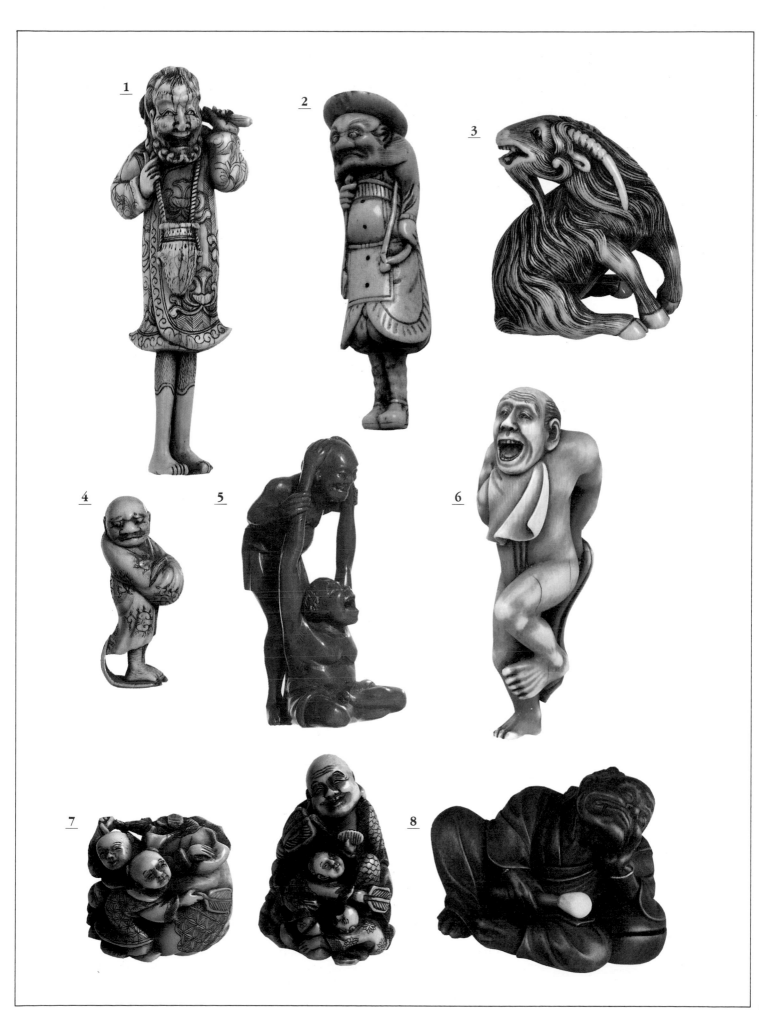

JAPANESE AND CHINESE METALWORK

◄ **CHINESE BRONZE TIGER'S HEAD**
This Sino-European style head comes from a set of 12 figures of the animals of the Chinese zodiac. They were made for a fountain at the European Palace in the Yuanming Yuan, the "Old Summer Palace" outside Beijing. The fountain was designed c.1750 by the Jesuit priest Michel Benoist. A different figure spouted water at each hour, and at midday all spouted together. H 12in/30cm

Bronze casting began in China *c.*2000 B.C. or earlier. Indeed, the classic bronze vessels of the Shang, Zhou and Han periods (1766 B.C.–A.D. 220) are claimed by some to be the finest achievement of Chinese art, for the quality of their casting and the barbaric vigor of their shape and decoration. They were a formative influence on later Chinese taste and were imitated in bronze, jade, lacquer, cloisonné, bamboo and porcelain.

From the fifth century A.D., Buddhism was a great patron of bronze founding, with fine gilt images in a willowy, Indian-influenced style during the Tang period. In the Ming and Qing periods (1368–1912), high-quality figure work was produced, either in a rounded native Chinese style or a hybrid Sino-Tibetan manner. Later bronzes, with inlaid or fire-gilt finishes, included vessels and some figures that are gold-splashed, inlaid with silver wire or molded and parcel-gilt.

The metalwork of Japan was dominated by the arts of war. The country was ruled for centuries by a warrior upper class who regarded the sword as the highest art form, so blades and fittings attracted the finest craftsmanship. Early blades, and blades by famous makers, were treasured by the aristocracy and samurai, but with the rise of the merchant classes in the 1700s greater interest was focused on decorative mountings in soft metal and lacquer.

Japanese metalwork terms
Machibori: Makers of decorative swordfittings, who also made netsuke.
Shakudo: An alloy of copper and a small amount of gold that can be patinated a lustrous black (**7**, **9**).
Shibuichi: An alloy of copper and silver in the ratio of 3:1 which can be patinated from silver to gray and brown.
Tsuba: Sword guards, made by the *machibori*. In the 1500s and 1600s, *tsuba* were usually of iron, often with piercing; copper, decorated with molded *shakudo*, *shibuichi* and gilt, become popular in the 1700s.

1 CHINESE BRONZE FOOD VESSEL
A finely cast archaic Shang Dynasty (1766–1122 B.C.) bronze gui, decorated with stylized dragons below a bovine head in high relief. Such vessels come from the tombs of princes and have a much-prized patina from long years of burial. Diam. 9in/23cm

2 CHINESE BEATEN GOLD CUP
The lotus shape of this rare cup from the Tang Dynasty (A.D. 618–907) displays western Asian influence. An undated inscription identifies it as a gift by a high civil servant, probably to a Buddhist temple. Diam. 4in/10cm

3 CHINESE GILT-BRONZE FIGURES
These finely cast late Ming figures (1368–1644) were made to stand on the altar of a Buddhist temple. The tall warrior, whose tiara identifies him as a Buddhist guardian, was originally one of a pair flanking a Buddha or Bodhisattva, such as the Guanyin seated on a lotus throne. H 24½in, 20½in; H 62cm, 52cm

4 CHINESE BRONZE ALTAR GARNITURE
A group made for a Buddhist altar; the base of the censer bears the six-character mark of Emperor Qianlong (1735–96). Joss sticks were burned in the censer, the prickets held candles, and the pear-shaped vases held flowers. H candlestick 15½in/40cm

5 JAPANESE TWO-HANDED SWORD
The fine blade, designed for cutting, not thrusting, is an old-style tachi from c.1550. It was mounted in the Edo period in ostentatious ceremonial style, to be worn hung loosely from the sash, cutting edge down. L blade 30in/76cm

6 PAIR OF JAPANESE MENUKI
Menuki were small ornamental metal pieces positioned on each side of a sword hilt, theoretically to improve the grip. This 19th-century pair in shakudo and gilt depict an oni, or demon, and the mythical catcher of demons, Shoki, always depicted as a Chinese scholar.

7 JAPANESE TSUBA, FUCHI AND KASHIRA
The 19th-century copper tsuba (sword guard) was signed by Rifudo Shozui. Fuchi and kashira are fittings for the sword hilt, the fuchi separating the grip from the tsuba and the kashira forming the pommel. They are usually designed to match, as in this late 18th-century pair decorated with shishi or Dogs of Fo. L tsuba 3in/8cm

8 JAPANESE KOMAI-STYLE KODANSU
A fine example of export inlaid metalwork from the 1800s. The box opens to reveal three drawers. It is decorated with landscape panels showing scenes from Lake Biwa against a typical Komai geometric inlay ground. L 6in/15cm

9 JAPANESE OKIMONO-STYLE NETSUKE
This 19th-century group shows two South Sea Island divers in shakudo, with shells and an octopus in copper, struggling to free a piece of coral from the silver seabed. W 2½in/6cm

ORIENTAL WARES

The first securely datable cloisonné enamels in China bear the incised mark of the Ming Emperor Xuande (1425–35). They were confident, high-quality Imperial work, with a rich palette of colors, and some objects are of considerable size.

The large-cell (*cloison*) designs of the Xuande period were followed by a denser style in later Ming, with more *cloisons* filling the area. This may have reflected technical problems of attachment as well as stylistic preference. Many cloisonné pieces are in ritual form, implying a ceremonial function in temples and palaces.

Interesting experiments with color appeared from the late 1400s, most notably "Ming pink," in which red and white glass pastes were fused within a cell without mixing, giving a speckled effect.

A huge variety of new forms and styles appeared with the setting up of the Qing Imperial workshop in the Forbidden City, Beijing, in the late 1600s. These included Tibetan Buddhist shapes, animals and birds, a wide range of archaistic vase and censer forms, and copies of Xuande cloisonné. Western shapes, and sometimes subjects, were also made; these were, however, curiosities for the court, and cloisonné was not made for export until the mid-1800s.

306

Cloisonné enamel

A French term, cloisonné means "enclosed in a cell" and refers to the enclosures made from bent copper wire that are soldered or glued to a metal vessel in order to separate different colored areas of enamel. The enamel is a glass paste colored with various metallic oxides – cobalt for blue, for instance. The process of filling the *cloisons* (cells) and firing at low temperature is repeated several times, since enamels shrink, but eventually the surface can be polished smooth and the wires gilded with mercury.

Champlevé enamel

The process resembles cloisonné, but is, in fact, a form of inlay, since the cells are created by cutting away areas of the cast bronze body and then filling them with enamel.

Beijing and Canton enamel

In this technique, the design is painted in colored glass, generally on a copper body. It derives from Limoges in France and was introduced to the court of Emperor Kangxi (1661–1722) by Jesuit missionaries. By the 1720s, the technique was used in Canton for export work.

1 EARLY MING CLOISONNÉ DISH
The overall design of lotus flowers borne on tightly scrolling stems on this dish, dating from the mid- to late 15th century, closely parallels the blue and white porcelain of the time. Diam. 10in/25cm

2 ARCHAISTIC HU-FORM VASE
This vase dates to the Qianlong period (1735–96), when interest in the archaic was at its height. Geometric distortions disguise the classic Qing decorative motif of two rampant dragons flanking a "flaming pearl." H 13in/33cm

◄ IMPERIAL CLOISONNÉ MANDALA
This miniature building is a three-dimensional Buddhist mystic diagram, or mandala, bearing a Qianlong Imperial mark dating it to c.1772. Such mandalas were made for use at Jehol, where the Emperor had summer palaces built in Tibetan style. H 22in/56cm

3 SLENDER CLOISONNÉ VASE
The unusually restricted cobalt and turquoise palette on this Qianlong period vase sets off the fine gilt-bronze elephant's-head handles. Gilt-bronze is used also for the archaistic dragons at the shoulder and at the foot. H 19in/48cm

4 LATE MING ALTAR GARNITURE
A cloisonné garniture from c.1600. The forms of the central fangding censer and the trumpet-shaped fangzun are derived from archaic Shang bronzes (1766–1122 B.C.). All of the pieces are decorated with a fanciful version of the Shang taotie monster mask. Censer W x H 15in x 19in; W x H 38cm x 48cm

5 QIANLONG RUYI SCEPTERS
Ruyi scepters were considered lucky and were given as wedding and birthday gifts. The gnarled gilt-bronze branches of these 18th-century scepters end in delicately shaded cloisonné fruit. Peaches are emblematic of long life, and a many-seeded pomegranate expresses a polite hope for numerous male progeny. L 12in/30cm

6 IMPERIAL BEIJING ENAMEL CENSER
This rare piece bears the Yuzhi "by Imperial command" mark (6a) of the Emperor Kangxi (1661–1722). It is an early example of the enamel style introduced by Jesuit missionaries, as well as of the famille-rose palette associated with porcelain of subsequent periods. Diam. 4½in/12cm

7 CANTON ENAMEL VESSELS
Qianlong period pieces made in Canton for export, with the probable exception of the blue and copper-gilt vase in the Chinese taste. Left to right: tea kettle on a stand with burner, imitating a George II silver form; box combining archaistic dragons on the lid with a bucolic scene copied from the Dutch artist David Teniers; ewer in Islamic metalwork shape, which has lost its original S-curved spout. It bears an Armenian inscription and the date 1776 on the side and was evidently made for the Middle East. H tea kettle 12in/30cm

Before *c.*1840, when Japanese cloisonné was "reinvented" under the stylistic influence of Ming cloisonné from China, only a small amount was produced in Japan. The catalyst was the artist Kaji Tsunekichi from Nagoya, which became the center of a thriving export industry by the end of the 1800s.

Early cloisonné was characterized by muddy colors and poor surfaces with extensive pitting. From the mid-1850s, Japanese shapes and styles of decoration, such as textile-based diaper patterns, were added to the Ming-style repertoire. Larger pieces became practicable, especially on a porcelain base, which was fashionable for some 15 years from the mid-1860s. The surface finish was improved, but colors remained dull.

In the late 1870s, Gottfried von Wagner was brought in by the Meiji government to introduce new technology to improve the color and brightness of porcelain. By 1880 a semi-transparent black enamel had been produced – the first of several transparent colors that were to transform the palette of the cloisonné artist. Wagner also perfected a technique that dispensed with visible *cloisons* in wide areas of uniform color, which had previously been necessary to anchor the enamel to the base. The new manner emulated painting on porcelain and led to the sheer, uncluttered style of the late 1800s and early 1900s.

Namikawa Sosuke

The last great advance in Japanese cloisonné was made by Namikawa Sosuke in Tokyo. He first received recognition in 1881 when he developed a new painterly technique known as *shosen-shippo* – erased cloisonné, in which the wires were dissolved away with acid after firing. He pursued the ideal of painterly space for another 10 years before arriving at the softer, more naturalistic, wire-less cloisonné style, or *musen-shippo* (5, 8), which was used to make replicas of brush paintings.

Plique-à-jour

In the craft of *plique-à-jour* (3), known as *shotai-shippo* in Japan, the metal body is removed after the first firing, leaving the enamel and wires. The demanding technique was introduced from France in the early 1900s.

1 JAPANESE MOONFLASK
An early (1860s) cloisonné moonflask, so-called because of its shape. The piece shows a careful observance of earlier Chinese shapes and styles of decoration. The legendary carp in the roundel, which became a dragon when it leapt the Longmen Falls, is symbolic of a student passing the imperial examinations. H 13in/33cm

◀ **SILVER KORO AND COVER**
This late 19th-century silver and cloisonné koro, or incense burner, and cover is formed as a sacred pearl, around which two dragons are coiled to form the feet and the handle on the lid. When a pastille of incense was burned, the lid was removed.

Silver is used both for the wire and for the body metal on the finest cloisonné of this period. The cloud and wisteria decoration is raised in cloisons on the minutely hammered surface. H 4in/10cm

2 TWO CHAMPLEVÉ FIGURES
Champlevé is a variation of cloisonné (see p.306). Although made in Japan, c.1880, these bronze and enamel figures are of Chinese deities. The dark patination is original. H 9in, 10in; H 23cm, 25cm

3 PLIQUE-À-JOUR VASE
A fine, early 20th-century baluster vase with silver mounts, decorated with a profusion of wildflowers. The rich translucent colors – crimson, green, blue and purple – produced by this process resemble those of stained glass. Diam. rim 2½in/7cm

4 LATE 19TH-CENTURY JAR AND COVER
A piece from Nagoya, decorated with gold wire butterflies fluttering around hydrangea flowers. The delicately shaded translucent enamels on a midnight blue ground are contained within formal brocade-patterned borders. H 4½in/11cm

5 NAMIKAWA SOSUKE VASE
The Tokyo artist Sosuke was the leading exponent of musen-shippo, or wire-less cloisonné, used in this fine vase, where the decoration aspires to the manner of a painting. The laboriously polished, perfect, glossy finish is characteristic of fine late 19th-century cloisonné. The vase is signed by the artist within a silver wire seal. H 12in/30cm

6 CLOISONNÉ TEA JAR AND COVER
An interesting feature here is the accompanying drawn design from which the panel on the lid of this jar (1870s) was made. The areas of wire-less green enamel and a bird among flowers are offset by dense diaper work elsewhere. H 2½in/7cm

7 FINE LATE 19TH-CENTURY VASE
Silver wire in varying thicknesses and enamels in subtle colors are used for the bird and flower decoration on the four gray and pale blue panels. The black surrounds present a contrast of complex patterned cloisonné grounds. H 12in/30cm

8 CLOISONNÉ TRIPOD KORO
This fine unsigned late 19th-century musen-shippo piece has a silver cover decorated with plovers in flight. There is a traditional poetic comparison between these small white birds and the spray of breaking waves. H 3½in/9cm

BEIJING GLASS

The earliest surviving examples of Chinese glass are some small beads with eye-like decoration, dating from the fifth century B.C. Other glass artefacts do exist, such as fish-shaped pendants made during the Tang Dynasty (A.D. 618–907), but in essence glass-making in China was spasmodic before the Qing Dynasty (1644–1912).

The production of Beijing glass began in earnest when a factory was established in the Forbidden City in 1696 by Emperor Kangxi. Like the Qing Imperial enamel workshop (see p.306), it was set up under Jesuit supervision, although the shapes and methods of manufacture differed greatly from those in Europe.

Beijing glass vessels were usually thick-walled, reflecting a preference for molding over blowing techniques. Clear glass was rare; most was strongly colored with mineral oxides. Some glass was made to resemble hardstones such as turquoise, aventurine and realgar, a spectacular and poisonous arsenic sulfide ore suffused with vivid red and yellow.

Overlay work was a specialty of Beijing glassmakers. The base was covered with one or more layers of contrasting glass and then carved through to reveal the design. Some of the cleverest work of this type is found in miniature on snuff bottles.

Enamel decoration

Some Beijing glass was decorated using enamels applied to an opaque white ground (see p.114: feature). The high point of this technique was reached during the reign of Qianlong (1735–96), when many fine wares were produced for the palace. These pieces all bore the *Guyuexuan* "Old Moon Pavilion" mark. The style of decoration was generally similar to that used on enameled porcelain.

Interior-painted snuff bottles

Toward the end of the 19th century, a school of snuff-bottle painters began to produce clear glass bottles expertly painted on the inside, a technique still practiced today. The themes they favored included figures and landscapes (see p.114: 7).

---

1 BLUE AND WHITE BOWL
Dating from the 19th century, this overlay bowl has rounded sides, which rise to a curved everted rim. It features a popular traditional Daoist subject, the "eight horses of Muwang." They are shown in blue relief on a white ground. The interior is also white. Diam. 7½in/19cm

---

◀ **OVERLAY SNUFF BOTTLE**
Snuff taking, the inhalation of powdered tobacco, was introduced into China by Westerners and became highly fashionable during the 18th and 19th centuries – a fact supported by the quality of the snuff bottles produced. A long ivory spoon was attached to the inside of the bottle stopper for ladling out the snuff.

Made in the late 19th century, this bottle is decorated with an exquisite multicolored overlay depicting dragons and sea creatures. This effect was created by overlaying several different colors side by side, and then carving them away to the opaque white glass beneath. H 4in/10cm

2 GREEN AND WHITE GLASS JAR
Vignettes of birds and flowers adorn this fine 19th-century jar and cover. It was carved through a spinach-green overlay to a bubbled opaque white body beneath. Diam. 8in/20cm

3 18TH-CENTURY BOTTLE VASE
This striking bottle vase was carved through a red overlay to the bright yellow ground. The design incorporates two symbols of long life, a peach tree bearing fruit and lingzhi fungus. The Chinese word for peach is shou (pronounced "show"), which sounds the same as the word for long life. The lingzhi fungus, shown on the tree trunk and ground, is frequently used in Chinese art to signify a wish for longevity. H 6in/15cm

4 DOUBLE-OVERLAY SNUFF BOTTLE
Layers of both white and green glass have been carved to produce this unusual design of silkworms feeding on mulberry leaves. Miniature bottles, such as this 19th-century example, show some of the finest Beijing glass work. They also always have stoppers made in a contrasting material.

5 PEAR-SHAPED GLASS VASE
Lotus scrolls and bands of petals carved from a layer of red glass create a subtle pattern on the dark pink ground of this 19th-century vase. H 9in/23cm

6 PAIR OF GLASS SEALS
Although more normally made of ivory or hardstone, these rare 18th-century glass seals are of a size and shape associated with official and imperial use. The decoration, showing three kui dragons in brown overlay on a white ground, is intentionally reminiscent of carvings from nephrite jade, which has an oxidized russet skin over flawless white stone. 2½in/6cm square

7 19TH-CENTURY PURPLE BOWL
Two fan-shaped panels, featuring birds, plum trees and chrysanthemums, adorn this rich purple bowl, which has rounded sides and an everted rim. Diam. 6½in/16cm

8 TRANSPARENT RED GLASS BOWL
A bird and a butterfly, carved in low relief, dart among chrysanthemum sprays on this ruby glass bowl. It was made in the late 19th century. Diam. 6in/15cm

GLOSSARY

The glossary should be used in conjunction with the index. Where relevant, some references to the text and illustrations are given. SMALL CAPITALS *refer to other glossary entries.*

A

Acanthus Leaf pattern widely used in Classical antiquity and revived *c.*1765 as an ornamental motif in carving and decoration. *See pp.136 (1), 149 (8), 152 (1, 5, 6), 172 (4), 180, 246 (5)*

Acid polishing A process that restores a polished surface to glass after cutting by immersing it briefly in a hydrofluoric solution, which removes a thin outer layer of glass.

Adam, Robert (1728–92) Scottish architect and designer who, with his brother James, largely revived Classical ornamentation and design in a style that bears their name. *See chart pp.160–61; 2, 132 (2), 174, 240*

Aesthetic Movement Short-lived decorative arts movement, much influenced by Oriental styles, which flourished in Britain and America *c.*1870–80. *See p.202 (5)*

Affenkapelle A set of porcelain figures in the form of monkey musicians introduced by Meissen in the mid-18th C. They were also made by many other European factories during the 19th C, and sets of a similar type were made in other materials. *Cf. p.128 (7)*

Agate ware Staffordshire pottery made to resemble the colour and marbling of natural agate. It was popular in the 18th C and was produced by potteries such as WEDGWOOD and Whieldon. *Cf. pp.50, 51*

◄ THE BADMINTON CABINET
Made in 1728–32 in the workshops of the Grand Duke of Tuscany for Badminton House, the country home of the Third Duke of Beaufort, this cabinet is, perhaps, the greatest masterpiece of Florentine Baroque workmanship. It is also the most expensive piece of furniture ever sold at auction: it fetched £7,722,000. The cabinet is made of ebony, decorated with inlaid hardstone panels, semiprecious stones and an ebony and hardstone clock. It is topped with gilded bronze ornaments and a ducal crest. H 12ft 8in x W 7ft 8in; H 3.86m x W 2.33m

Air bubble A decorative effect in glassware. Molten glass is pierced with a metal point, then sealed, leaving a bubble of air trapped inside. This can either be pulled into a tear shape or left as a spherical bubble. *See p.96*

Air twist Spiral pattern in the stem of a glass made by manipulating a bubble of air. This technique was developed *c.*1740–70. *See p.96*

Albarello Waisted, pottery drug jar. *See p.40*

Ale glass Glass for strong ale, resembling a wine glass, with a decorated stem and elongated bowl, first made in the 18th C. The bowl is often decorated with designs of hops or heads of barley.

Amberina An art glass, produced by partial reheating, ranging in colour from dark red to amber. It was made by the New England Glass Company after 1883. *See p.110*

Amboyna Red-brown East Indian wood used for decorative VENEERS and INLAY work in the 18th C and 19th C. *See p.204 (5)*

American Colonial style Term describing building and furniture styles from the early 17th C to the beginning of the Federal style. *See chart pp.10–11*

American Federal style Term describing building and furniture styles from 1780 to 1820 – the early years of independence. *See chart pp.10–11; 172 (1, 5), 232 (3)*

Amphora Two-handled jar from Classical times used for transporting wine or oil. It was revived in the 18th C as a decorative motif in the repertoire of NEO-CLASSICAL design. *See pp.18, 92 (6)*

Anglo-Indian furniture Furniture produced in India to European designs from the mid-18th C until the end of the 19th C. These items were made mainly for colonial administrators and aristocratic Indian families. *See pp.196, 236 (7)*

Angoulême sprig An ornament used to decorate 18th-C porcelain consisting of a cornflower, two leaves and two sprays of forget-me-not. It was first developed at the porcelain factory of

Louis, Duke of Angoulême, in Paris and is also known as a Chantilly sprig. The design was copied by English makers at DERBY, WORCESTER and Lowestoft.

Annealing The process of heating silver at various stages during manufacture to strengthen it after hammering has rendered the metal brittle. *See p.118*

Anthemion Stylized flower motif based on honeysuckle and derived from a Classical Greek ornament. Used in the 18th C and 19th C on silverware and furniture. *See pp.132, 134 (5), 174 (1), 196 (3)*

Apostle spoons A set of 13 silver or pewter spoons, each with a FINIAL at the end of the handle representing Christ or one of his 12 disciples. Popular in Europe from the 15th C to the 17th C and revived in 19th-C Britain to decorate mass-produced coffee spoons. *See p.124*

Applied decoration An ornamental finish prepared in advance and applied to an object in a completed state, as with WEDGWOOD's jasperware. *See pp.15, 58 (4, 6)*

Apprentice piece Scaled-down item of furniture made to display an apprentice's craftsmanship before he commenced work on full-sized pieces.

Apron (1) Shaped wooden edging hanging below a table top or drawer line on a piece of furniture. **(2)** A cast, chased or pierced metal framework between the supports of an epergne or centrepiece. *See p.190 (2), 194 (4)*

Arabesque Design of leaves, branches and scrolls intertwined, common on Islamic and Hispano-Moresque pottery. Popular ornament on silverware from the Renaissance; especially *c.*1760–90.

Arcading Decorative feature, found on furniture and carved panels of the late 16th C and 17th C, taking the form of a series of rounded arches. *See p.232 (1)*

Architectural style Term used to describe furniture and clock cases with features such as arches, PEDIMENTS and columns. *See pp.218 (4), 224 (4), 266 (2), 270, 272 (7)*

Arita ware Porcelain from the Arita potteries in Japan, established in the early 17th C. Both KAKIEMON and IMARI wares come from Arita kilns. *See p.32*

Armada chest Strongbox dating from the 17th C and 18th C, with heavy iron banding, false keyholes, looped hasps for padlocks and an elaborate lock in the lid. Such chests were first made in Germany and have no connection with the Spanish Armada of 1588.

Armoire A large, tall cupboard or press used for storing clothes. Formerly armor was stored in such cupboards, hence the name. *See p.234*

Armorial Term used to describe a full coat-of-arms or designs incorporating heraldic symbols. Armorials are often found on both Chinese export and European porcelain and on silverware. *See pp.28, 54 (1), 132*

Art Deco A style of art and decoration, reflecting the modern esthetic of the machine age, which developed in the 20th C between the two world wars. This style was first popularized at the 1925 *Exposition des Arts Décoratifs* in Paris, from which the term Art Deco is derived. *See pp.112 (5), 234 (3), 284 (8)*

Art Nouveau Style of art and decoration characterized by natural forms and sinuous, flowing lines. It was fashionable from the 1880s until the outbreak of war in 1914. *See pp.180 (7), 200*

Arts and Crafts Movement Started in Britain in the late 19th C by a group of artists and craftsmen committed to hand-crafted, rather than machine-produced, articles. William Morris (1834–96) was an early influence. *See pp.184, 194*

Assay The testing of metals by fire, touch or cupellation to determine their purity according to set legal standards. *See pp.120–23*

Astragal Half-round reeded MOLDING attached to the edges of door frames or cabinets to conceal the joint; also used for glazing bars on glass-fronted cupboard doors. *See p.230*

Aventurine An art glass resembling the gold-speckled, reddish-brown quartz aventurine. The glass owes its appearance to copper oxide added during the molten stage. *See p.310*

B

Baccarat French glassworks founded in 1764 and situated east of Paris. Famous for high-quality lead glass and for MILLEFIORI paperweights. *See p.114*

Backboard The unpolished back of a piece of wall furniture or a framed mirror, not designed to be seen.

Backplate The plate at the back of a clock MOVEMENT, one of two holding the mechanism in place. *See p.265*

Back stool A three- or four-legged stool with a back, which evolved into an early form of the single, or side, chair. Back stools were introduced in the 16th C when all chairs had arms and were so called because they had no arms. *See p.170*

Balance wheel The wheel in a timepiece that controls the action of the ESCAPEMENT mechanism, regulating the MOVEMENT.

Ball and claw Carved foot shaped like a ball gripped by a claw. Introduced *c.*1720 and mostly seen on furniture with CABRIOLE legs. *See pp.172 (1, 3), 188*

Balloon-back chair Chair with an open "O"-shaped back and nipped-in waist. Popular as sets of dining chairs from the 1820s and throughout the Victorian period. *See pp.174 (3), 256 (5)*

Baluster Turned column with a curving shape, used on table legs, chair backs, glass stems and metalware. *See pp.96, 188, 248 (2)*

Banding Narrow decorative strips of VENEER or INLAY, usually forming a border. Straight banding is cut with the grain. Crossbanding is cut directly across the grain. Herringbone, or feather, banding is cut diagonally across the grain; often two feather bands are run together in opposite directions to create chevrons. *See p.165*

Banjo clock Wall clock in the shape of an up-turned banjo, first produced during the Federal period (1780–1820) in Boston by the U.S. clock maker Willard. Reproductions were common in the 19th C. *See p.276 (3)*

Barley-sugar twist Type of TURNING in which the wood is shaped in a spiral; used on furniture as legs or for decoration. *See pp.188, 208 (6), 270*

Barber's bowl Ceramic or metal shaving dish with a semicircular section removed from the rim to fit the client's chin; used by barbers from the 17th C onward. *See pp.33 (2), 134*

Baroque Heavily ornate style of architecture from 17th-C Italy which influenced all the decorative arts in 1660–1730. *See charts pp.10–11, 160–61*

Basalt Black, fine-grained stoneware developed by several Staffordshire potters and improved by Josiah WEDGWOOD in the mid-1760s. This relatively cheap material was used to manufacture vases, copies of classical bronzes and CAMEOS. *See p.58 (1, 5)*

Bateman family Firm of silversmiths producing household silverware in the 18th C and 19th C. Hester Bateman (1708–94), trained by her husband John, is the best known. Her sons Peter and Jonathan, Jonathan's wife Ann, and their son William carried on the business into the 19th C. Silverware made by the family includes tableware, tea sets and wine accessories. *See pp.144 (5), 146 (6)*

Bat printing 18th-C process that applied a delicate pattern on top of a ceramic glaze. A design was printed on a flexible pad or sheet called a bat, then an oil-based outline was transferred to the piece and dusted with color.

Beaker Drinking cup without handles or stem, made from wood, pottery, glass or silver; popular until the 18th C, when it was largely replaced by the glass. *See pp.94 (1, 5), 142 (5)*

Beech An inexpensive hardwood often used to make country furniture, especially chairs. *See pp.164, 250*

Belleek Factory in County Fermanagh, Northern Ireland, established in 1857 and specializing in woven parian porcelain with motifs drawn from the local flora and fauna. It also produced delicate, pearlized tableware. *See p.76 (9)*

Bends The curved runners on a rocking chair.

Bentwood Term used to describe lightweight or laminated wood which has been bent into curved shapes by steaming or soaking in hot water. *See pp.174 (6); Cf. pp.180 (6), 280 (6)*

Bergère French term for a tub-shaped armchair, made from *c*.1725. In the 19th C, this term was applied to an upholstered, deep-seated chair, with a loose seat cushion and padded arms joined to a sweeping back rail. *See pp.167, 178 (5), 184 (2)*

Bevel The slanted edge of a mirror or pane of thick glass cut to form a decorative border.

Bezel A metal rim or setting used to hold a clock or watch glass, or to line the shutting edge of a container. *See pp.276 (2), 286*

Bible box Oak box with a hinged lid used in the 17th C for holding the family Bible or writing implements. *See p.222*

Biedermeier Decorative style originating in Germany in the early 19th C. *See chart pp.10–11; 184 (3), 236*

Biscuit pottery Term describing all ceramics that have been fired once but not glazed. When biscuit pottery was used to make dolls' heads and bodies in the mid-19th C, it was known as bisque. *See p.66 (1)*

Blanc-de-Chine French term for unpainted, highly translucent porcelain made in Fujian province, China, which is characterized by a thick glaze. It was much copied by European factories in the 18th C. *See pp.22, 292*

Bloom Dull, flat surface on old glassware, which results from faults in the glass or from wear.

Blue and white Decorative color scheme for pottery and porcelain using COBALT BLUE as an underglaze pigment. *See pp.24, 38, 44, 46*

Bobbin turning A decorative feature of 17th-C and 18th-C chair and table legs and stretchers, consisting of a series of wooden spheres turned on a lathe. *See pp.176 (1), 188, 194 (1)*

Bocage ROCOCO motif of flowers or foliage surrounding or supporting a central figure; popular in ceramics from the 1750s to the 1770s. *See pp.64 (4), 268*

Body The mixture of raw materials from which pottery or porcelain is made. Often called "paste" when referring to porcelain. *See p.14*

Bombé French term for the swollen or bulging shape often used for chests of drawers, particularly in continental Europe. *See pp.210 (3, 4), 212 (6), 272 (2)*

Bonbonnière Container for candy, usually made of silver or porcelain and crafted into novelty shapes. *See p.60 (2)*

Bone ash Calcium phosphate derived from burnt animal bones; used as a fusing and stabilizing agent in soft-paste porcelain. *See p.76*

Bone china A mixture of BONE ASH and kaolin which makes a hard, stable porcelain. Introduced by SPODE in 1794. *See chart pp.16–17; 19, 76*

Bonheur-du-jour A ladies' writing table, with shelves and pigeonholes, introduced in France in the 1760s. *See p.218*

Böttger, Johann (1682–1719) Inventor of hard-paste porcelain in Europe; previously it had only been known in China. He was made a director of the newly formed Meissen factory in 1710. *See pp.54, 62 (1)*

Boulle (buhl) Style of marquetry using tortoiseshell and brass inlay, perfected by Louis XIV's cabinetmaker, André-Charles Boulle (1642–1732) in the early 18th C. *See p.218*

Boulton, Matthew (1728–1809) Birmingham entrepreneur and metalware manufacturer who made furniture mounts, sword hilts, buckles and minted copper pennies. In the 1760s, he became Britain's leading producer of SHEFFIELD PLATE.

Bow The largest 18th-C porcelain factory in Britain, also known as New Canton. Founded in 1744 by Thomas Frye, it took advantage of the new soft-paste porcelain, invented in 1748, to produce imitation oriental porcelain and BLUE AND WHITE wares. Both figures and tableware were made. *See p.70*

Bow front A curving, convex front on a chest of drawers, bureau or sideboard. *See pp.204 (2), 210*

Boxwood Yellow close-grained hardwood used for marquetry in the 16th C and 17th C, and for STRINGING in the late 18th C and early 19th C. *See pp.192 (5), 198 (6)*

Bracket clock Term for a spring-driven, portable clock designed to stand on a table or mantelpiece or on a wall bracket. *See pp.266–69*

Breakfast table Small, four-legged table with two hinged flaps which could easily be moved. *See p.188*

Breakfront Protruding center section on a piece of furniture such as a bookcase or sideboard; popular in the 18th C and 19th C, especially in America. *See pp.158, 230 (1)*

Bright-cut engraving Method of ENGRAVING silver developed in the late 18th C, using a double-edged tool to remove slivers of metal and burnish the cut at the same time. *See p.146*

Britannia standard Compulsory standard for British silverware between 1697 and 1720. The proportion of silver to base metal was 95.8%, higher than that in sterling silver at 92.5%, to prevent coinage from being melted down to make household silver. *See pp.120, 148*

Brocard, Philippe-Joseph (1867–90) French glassmaker who began his career by reproducing 13th-C Syrian mosque lamps to fulfill a demand for Moorish and Levantine furnishings. Later, his original work included bowls with complex raised designs, finished with ENAMEL paints. *See p.110 (1)*

Brushing slide Pull-out shelf inserted between the topmost drawer and the top of 18th-C chests of drawers; used for brushing clothes. *See p.208*

Bureau plat French term for a flat-topped writing desk with drawers beneath. *See p.218*

Burl walnut VENEER cut from a cross-section of the gnarled grain at the base of the tree or from a gall. *See pp.164, 172, 180 (2), 228 (2), 270 (5)*

Burmese glass Colored art glass developed in the late 19th C and created by reheating heat-sensitive glass. Uranium and gold oxides in the molten glass gave a color range from yellow to pink. *See pp.106 (6), 110*

Bustelli, Franz Anton (1723–63) Chief modeler at the NYMPHENBURG porcelain factory in Germany in 1754–63; he is best known for his *Commedia dell'arte* figures. *See p.64*

C

Cabinet Cupboard with drawers and shelves for storing or displaying precious items; often highly decorated with inlay and ornamental features. *See pp.214–17*

Cabriole Furniture leg with a double curve: outward at the knee and inward above the foot; reputedly based on the hind leg of a goat. *See pp.172, 188*

Cagework A chased and pierced sleeve of decorative silver overlying a plain or gilt inner body; used on cups, BEAKERS and tankards of the late 17th C. *See p.118*

Calcite glass Creamy white art glass used for lampshades, made by adding BONE ASH to molten glass; it was developed in the U.S. during the early years of the 20th C by Frederick Calder.

Cameo A low-relief carving or portrait on shell or stone with two or more layers of different colors.

Cameo glass Layered glass, carved or etched with acid to expose the base layer underneath in much the same manner as a CAMEO. The top layer is frequently opaque white. Uncut cameo glass is known as cased glass. *See pp.91, 110, 114*

Cancellation mark One or two strokes incised or painted over a maker's mark on ceramics to show they are below standard or from a discontinued line.

Candle slide Retractable wooden support for a candle found on 18th-C tables and writing desks. *See p.224*

Caneware Stoneware vessels molded to resemble bamboo created by Josiah WEDGWOOD in the 1770s. *See p.58 (7)*

Canted corner Slanting, CHAMFERED or BEVELED edge. *See p.212 (3)*

Canteen Case or chest of flatware.

Canton porcelain Term for 18th-C and early 19th-C porcelain enameled in Canton, China, for export to Western markets; also known as Chinese export porcelain. *See chart pp.16–17; 28*

Carcass Main structure of a piece of furniture excluding drawers, doors, etc. *See pp.164, 166*

Carnival glass A popular form of American glassware made *c.*1908–24, often given as prizes at fairs. *See p.108*

Carolean English decorative style from the reign of Charles I (1625–49). *See chart pp.10–11*

Cartouche Decoratively shaped tablet, often enclosed by scrollwork and used to frame crests or coats-of-arms. *See pp.128 (4), 140 (3, 8), 152 (3), 246 (1)*

Carver Dining chair with arms, which is also often called an elbow chair. *See pp.172 (3), 174*

Case furniture A piece of furniture designed to contain something, for example, a chest of drawers.

Caster Shaker for sugar, pepper and other spices; casters became common in the late 17th C, with the increased availability in Europe of sugar and spices. *See p.128*

Caudle cup Two-handled cup, sometimes with a saucer and lid, for serving caudle, a spiced gruel, to invalids or nursing mothers. Made in silver and pottery. *See p.46*

Caughley Shropshire pottery factory famous for its soft-paste porcelain, known as Salopian ware, from 1772 to 1812. Caughley porcelain closely resembled the designs and shapes of nearby WORCESTER, and most of it was BLUE AND WHITE Oriental-style tableware, sometimes embellished with gilding.

Celadon Originally a type of Chinese stoneware with a gray-green glaze, derived from iron oxide, developed during the Song Dynasty (960–1279). Now the name is applied to any glaze with similar coloring. *See p.20 (8)*

Chaise longue Elongated, upholstered chair with a complete or partial back. *Cf.* DAYBED

Chamberstick Bedroom candle-holder with a saucer-style base and carrying handle. *See p.136*

Chamfer The angle on the edge of a piece of wood, achieved by planing or cutting. *See pp.172 (2), 194 (5), 230 (4)*

Chantilly French porcelain factory founded by the Duc de Condé in 1725. It is best known for its tin-glazed

KAKIEMON-style pieces, modeled on the large collection of Japanese Kakiemon porcelain owned by the duke. After 1755, when an edict was passed forbidding competition with the royal factory at Vincennes, the factory concentrated on BLUE AND WHITE tableware, snuffboxes and other small items. *See pp.60 (4), 66 (8)*

Chapter ring Circle on the dial of a clock or watch on which the hours are marked. *See p.264*

Charger Large oval or circular plate for serving meat. *See pp.28 (3), 32, 42 (5), 46, 54 (3)*

Chasing Technique for decorating metalware, particularly silver, using a hammer and blunt punch to depress or raise the surface, leaving a design in relief. *See pp.119, 142*

Chelsea One of the earliest porcelain factories in Britain. It was founded in 1745 and flourished until 1769 when it was sold to DERBY. It was devoted to producing tableware, tea sets and vases for the luxury market. *See p.68*

Cheval mirror or screen Tall, free-standing item on a four-legged base. *See pp.244, 246 (8)*

Chiffonier In France and North America, the term refers to a tall chest of drawers popular in the mid- to late 18th C. In Britain, a chiffonier is a form of cabinet with cupboards and a sideboard top, often used as a buffet in the dining room. *See p.230*

China clay A white clay, also known as kaolin, which is free from impurities and is one of the essential constituents of porcelain.

Chinoiserie European imitations of Chinese decoration and design – in particular, fretwork, oriental motifs and carving. Not to be confused with Chinese articles exported to Europe. *See pp.142, 194 (8), 270 (8)*

Chip carving Design made in a wooden panel by chipping out a pattern; found on pieces dating from the medieval period. *See p.206 (2)*

Chippendale, Thomas (1718–79) English cabinetmaker and designer. Most of the 160 designs in his book, *The Gentleman and Cabinet-Maker's*

Director, first published in 1754, are in Chinese, gothic or French ROCOCO style. LACQUERING, painting or gilding was used to finish many of the pieces. Very influential in the mid-GEORGIAN period in England and America and much imitated in later times. *See chart pp.160–61; 158, 172 (2), 230 (1)*

Chronometer Portable timepiece of great accuracy; developed in the 18th C for determining longitude at sea. Chronometers are often mounted in protective wooden boxes. *See p.274 (1)*

Claret pitcher Glass wine pitcher with hinged silver or silver-gilt lid and decorative mounts; made in the 19th C. *See p.102 (4, 5)*

Claw and ball *See* BALL AND CLAW

Clichy French glassworks, established in 1837 at Billancourt, Paris, and later at Clichy-la-Garenne; specialized in MILLEFIORI paperweights, inkstands and vases. *See p.114 (1, 2)*

Clobbering Overpainting an existing design on ceramics with colored ENAMELS or gilding. Chinese BLUE AND WHITE was often treated in this way, particularly by the Dutch.

Cloisonné Decorative technique in which a pattern made up of wires, or thin strips of metal, soldered to a metal base, is filled with vitreous ENAMELS. *See pp.306–9*

Coalport Shropshire-based porcelain factory established in 1795; famous for its smooth, translucent BONE CHINA developed after 1810. In 1821 a maroon ground was introduced which became a Coalport characteristic. During the 1830s the factory produced popular flower-encrusted, ROCOCO vase and other pieces using two famous Sèvres ground colors – *bleu céleste* and "rose Pompadour." The factory was acquired by the WEDGWOOD group and ceased production in 1926. *See p.76 (1, 8)*

Coaster Circular stand with a raised silver rim or gallery, used for port or wine bottles on the table. First introduced in the 1760s. *See p.144 (3)*

Cobalt blue Pigment derived from cobalt oxide which could be fired at high temperature without changing color; much used on early ceramics. *See pp.24, 70. Cf.* BLUE AND WHITE

Cockbeading A beaded MOLDING that projects from the surface of a piece of furniture; usually seen around drawer fronts. *See p.222*

Cold painting Technique of painting on ceramics using oil- or lacquer-based paints, which do not fuse to the surface on firing, instead of ENAMELS, which do.

Collar Decorative ring of glass used to disguise the point where two pieces of glass have been fused together, such as a foot and a stem, or a stem and a bowl.

Commode French term for a chest of drawers or CABINET, often highly decorated with VENEERS and metal mounts (*see p.210*). In Victorian times, the term was used for a bedside cabinet containing a chamber pot. *See p.226*

Concertina mechanism The means by which the hinged back legs on a table fold out, accordion-style, to support a flap top. Commonly found on 18th-C card tables. *See p.196*

Copenhagen Danish porcelain factory which began by producing soft-paste porcelain 1759–65, before switching to hard-paste porcelain in 1771. It became the Royal Copenhagen Porcelain Manufactory in 1779 and continues in business to this day. *See pp.72, 80 (6)*

Coquillage Decoration incorporating a shell motif, much used on ROCOCO-style furniture and silver. *See pp.130 (3, 4), 208 (3)*

Corner chair Early GEORGIAN chair with two side legs, one front and one back leg, which fitted neatly into a corner. These chairs were also known as writing chairs. *See p.178 (2)*

Cornice Top molding or decorative projection on tall CABINET furniture. The term can also describe the supports for bed hangings. *See pp.212 (3, 6), 238 (1, 2)*

Country furniture Articles of furniture made by provincial craftsmen using local woods and construction techniques. Country furniture is usually designed to be functional and long lasting, rather than decorative. *See pp.248–53*

Crackle Network of fine lines or cracks on a glazed ceramic surface, caused

by differing expansion rates between the body and the applied glaze. Found on Chinese and Japanese ceramics and copied by 19th-C art potters. *See pp.20 (6), 28 (8), 30 (6)*

Creamware Cheap, cream-colored EARTHENWARE, made from Devon clay and ground burnt flints, with a transparent glaze. It was refined in the 1760s by Josiah WEDGWOOD, when it was known as "Queen's ware" and soon became the standard household pottery used in Britain. *See p.52.*

Creil French EARTHENWARE factory established in 1795 to compete with British suppliers of CREAMWARE. Merged twice with a nearby creamware factory, Montereau, before closing in 1895.

Cresting Carved decoration along the top rail of a chair or mirror frame. *See pp.180 (6), 246 (1, 2)*

Cup and cover Bulbous, turned-wood decoration found on legs of furniture and on bedposts in Elizabethan and 19th-C Revival styles. *See pp.188, 232 (1)*

Cut-card work Type of silver decoration from the 17th C and early 18th C, in which a pattern cut from a sheet of metal was soldered flush to the article. Also applied to furniture where FRETWORK is glued to solid wood to create the illusion of carving. *See p.152*

Cylinder fall Slatted or rigid curved lid that slides down from within the top of a desk to cover the desk top. *See p.226*

D

Daum Glassworks in Nancy, France, run by the Daum brothers, Auguste and Antonin, best known for producing ART NOUVEAU and ART DECO vases and lamps. *See p.112*

Davenport Small writing desk consisting of a sloping top, often with drawers which opened from the side. Davenports first appeared in the late 18th C and remained popular during the 19th C. *See p.228*

Daybed Upholstered or cushioned couch with a slanting backrest used for resting during the day. *See p.180 (4)*

Deck, Theodore (1823–91) French ceramics artist best known for his brightly colored earthenware with designs inspired by Eastern art. In 1887 Deck became administrator at the Sèvres factory. *See p.84 (2)*

De Lamerie, Paul (1688–1751) Outstanding HUGUENOT silversmith, working in London, who produced household silverware in the QUEEN ANNE and Huguenot style, before creating the flamboyant ROCOCO-style pieces for which he is chiefly known. In 1716 he was appointed goldsmith to King George I. *See p.152*

Delft Center in Holland for tin-glazed EARTHENWARE from the mid-16th C to the mid-18th C, where Dutch potters adapted the designs on Chinese BLUE AND WHITE porcelain. This largely domestic pottery was very successful until the emergence of CREAMWARE and porcelain which became freely available at the end of the 18th C. *See p.44*

Delftware Tin-glazed pottery made in England during the 17th C and 18th C, inspired by the Dutch wares. *See p.46*

Della Robbia, Luca (1399–1482) Florentine sculptor who produced MAIOLICA plaques. *See p.40*

De Morgan, William Frend (1839–1917) Leading ARTS AND CRAFTS pottery designer, who worked for Morris & Co. in the 1860s making stained glass and luster-glazed tiles in Hispano-Moresque style, before establishing his own studio in 1872, first in Merton and then in Fulham, London, 1888–1907. Here, De Morgan, much influenced by Italian MAIOLICA, specialized in vessels and tiles. *See pp.42 (7), 82*

Derby English city famed for its porcelain manufacture. The first factory began producing Meissen imitations in soft-paste porcelain in 1750. In the 1770s the Japanese IMARI style became strongly identified with Derby. In the early 19th C, BONE CHINA replaced soft-paste porcelain, and the company produced less expensive products until 1848, when it closed. The Crown Derby Porcelain Company was set up in 1876 to produce decorated and gilded bone china once again. *See p.68*

Deutsche Blumen "German flowers" – lifelike floral decoration on ceramics based on botanical illustration. This type of decoration dates from the 1720s and is found on Meissen, WORCESTER, BOW and CHELSEA wares.

Ding ware (dingyao) Dishes, bottles, ewers and vases dating from the Song Dynasty (960–1279); examples of the earliest known Chinese porcelain. *See p.20*

Directoire Simple and austere style fashionable during the Directoire government in France (1793–99). *See chart pp.10–11*

Dogs of Fo Porcelain figures of a Chinese Buddhist lion representing legendary temple guardians; usually found in pairs. *See p.304 (7)*

Doulton Ceramics factory in Lambeth, London, founded by John Doulton (1793–1873). Initially, it produced household stoneware, but later involvement with the Lambeth School of Art led to the development of the Doulton Studio art pottery in the 1860s. The factory also created Lambeth FAIENCE and silicon and marquetry wares; in 1882, it launched high-quality figures and tile panels in porcelain. *See p.82*

Dovetail Close-fitting joints with interlocking tenons used in the making of high-quality furniture. *See p.166*

Dram glass *See* FIRING GLASS

Dresden 19th-C German ceramics manufactured by various factories in the Dresden area of southeastern Germany. Until the 1970s the term referred to the Meissen factory itself. *See p.80 (7)*

Drop-in seat Padded seat that can be easily removed from the chair frame. *See pp.166, 172, 174, 182*

Drop-leaf table The surface area of such tables can be increased by raising an extra leaf, supported on hinged legs or arms or brackets. *See pp.186, 188*

Drum table Circular table with a deep border containing drawers. *See p.200 (4)*

Dwight, John (c.1637–1703) London potter who made the first attributable British stoneware in the late 17th C; he also developed salt-glazed stoneware and red stoneware. The ELERS brothers worked with him. *See pp.54, 56 (1)*

E

Earthenware Porous pottery, fired at c.900–1,500°F/500–800°C, which is waterproof only when glazed. The color of the clays and the metal oxide content produce a varied range of colors. *See chart pp.16–17; 15, 42–47*

East India companies At the beginning of the 1600s, both the Dutch and the English set up trading companies to deal in Far Eastern spices, silk, furniture, fabrics and porcelain. They ousted the Portuguese, who had been the first to establish maritime trade with China during the 1500s. *See pp.32, 298 (3)*

Eastlake, Charles Locke (1836–1906) British architect and furniture designer whose book, *Hints on Household Taste* (1868), revived interest in the "Early English" style in the late 19th C. *See p.190*

Ebéniste French term for a cabinetmaker specializing in veneering; the word is derived from 17th-C French furniture, which often had an ebony VENEER. *See p.218. Cf.* MENUISIER

Ebonized wood Wood, often of poor quality, that is stained and polished to resemble ebony. *See pp.176 (4), 266*

Edo period Period in Japanese history (1615–1867) when the decorative arts flourished and Edo, present-day Tokyo, became the capital. *See chart pp.10–11*

Egg and dart Carved or moulded ornamentation found on furniture, in particular CABINETS, consisting of a series of ovals with intervening arrowheads. *See p.194 (5)*

Electroplating Electrochemical process developed in the 1840s, by which a base metal (either Britannia metal or nickel) was coated with a thin layer of pure silver. *See pp.128 (8), 146*

Elers, David and John (fl.1686–1700) Two Dutch brothers who worked with the potter John DWIGHT, before setting up their own pottery in Staffordshire producing red stoneware with relief patterns in white. *See p.54 (6)*

Ellicot, John (1706–72) Master clock maker to King George III, who invented a form of compensated pendulum and improved the cylinder ESCAPEMENT.

Embossing *See* CHASING

Empire style Decorative style, rooted in classical taste, popular in France c.1800–15 and in the U.S. c.1820–40. See chart pp.10–11; 78, 268 (3)

Enamel Form of decoration that can be fused to metal, glass or ceramics. It is made from a mixture of powdered glass and pigmented metallic oxides, suspended in an oily medium. During firing, the oily medium burns off and the other constituents fuse.

Engraving Form of decoration in which lines or dots are incised into a hard surface, such as metal or glass, either with a diamond-tipped tool or rotating abrasive wheel or by the application of acid. See pp.104, 140

Entablature Architectural term adopted by cabinetmakers for the components surmounting a column: the architrave, frieze and CORNICE.

Escapement Regulating mechanism of a clock that allows stored power in a falling weight or wound spring to be released at regular intervals. See pp.264, 266

Escutcheon Decorative metal plate surrounding a keyhole on furniture, or a carved shield on a PEDIMENT. See p.167

F

Façon de Venise Glassware made in the 16th C and 17th C chiefly in Britain, Germany and the Netherlands which copies the style of Venetian glass. See p.92

Faience French term for tin-glazed EARTHENWARE. See pp.19, 42. See also MAIOLICA, DELFTWARE

Famille rose "Pink family"; opaque ENAMELS used on Chinese porcelain in 1723–35, the most conspicuous color being rose-pink (derived from gold). See pp.26–29

Famille verte "Green family"; transparent ENAMELS, especially brilliant green, used to decorate Chinese Kangxi-period(1661–1722) porcelain. See pp.26–29

Feldspar porcelain BONE CHINA which contains pure feldspar rather than china stone and so is much tougher. First produced by COALPORT, but soon taken up by SPODE.

Finial Carved, turned or metal ornament mounted on top of a piece of furniture, such as a secrétaire, bookcase or clock case. See also KNOP

Firing glass Squat 18th-C wine glass with a thick stem and heavy foot, also known as a dram glass. See p.96

Flambé Lustrous, deep red glaze with splashes of blue, violet and other colors. Originally used by the Chinese in the 17th C and 18th C, it became popular with ART NOUVEAU potters in the late 1800s. See pp.14, 22 (6), 82 (9)

Flatbacks Molded pottery figures with undecorated and unglazed backs made by the STAFFORDSHIRE POTTERIES for mantelpieces. Cf. p.50 (5)

Flatware In silverware, all flat pieces such as spoons, forks, slices and knives; in porcelain, generally plates, saucers, salvers and dishes. See pp.124–127

Flaxman, John (1755–1826) Sculptor and artist who designed friezes and portrait medallions for WEDGWOOD from 1775. Flaxman also produced models for silverware by Paul Storr. See p.58

Fluting Vertical cut or groove on a cylindrical object such as a column, wine glass stem or on silver.

Flux Material such as BONE ASH, lime, potash, soda or borax, which promotes fusion of the particles and enables a ceramic or glass body to be fired at a lower temperature. See p.18

Frankenthal German porcelain factory, operating 1755–99, which produced tableware in the style of Meissen and Sèvres, Commedia dell'arte and other figures. See p.64

French polish LACQUERED finish on furniture introduced in the late 18th C.

Fretwork Technique of cutting thin pieces of wood or metal into shapes or patterns with a fine-bladed saw. See p.200 (2)

Fusee Cone-shaped spool in a clock around which the gut or chain is wound in order to equalize the tension of the spring as it unwinds. See pp.264, 265, 274, 280 (1, 3)

G

Gadrooning Carved or molded border consisting of a series of raised convex curves; used on silver, ceramics and furniture. See pp.119, 130 (6), 132, 140, 144 (3), 174

Gallé, Emile (1846–1904) French designer of glass, ceramics and furniture influential in the ART NOUVEAU movement. Gallé founded a glass factory at Nancy in 1867 and developed techniques such as etching, wheel-engraving, ENAMEL painting on opaque glass and carving CAMEO GLASS. See pp.84 (1), 110 (3, 4), 230 (6)

Garniture Set of three, five or seven pieces, often vases, used to decorate a mantelpiece. See pp.44 (6), 152 (6), 268, 304 (4)

Gate-leg Pivoting table leg which supports a hinged leaf or flap. See p.186

Georgian Largely classical British style (1720–1800). See chart pp.10–11

Gesso A type of plaster made from powdered chalk and size which, when many layers are applied to wood or other materials, gives a hard, smooth base for painting or gilding and can be carved. See p.194

Gimson, Ernest (1864–1919) Architect and designer prominent in the ARTS AND CRAFTS movement. See p.230 (4)

Glasgow School Designers and architects connected with the Glasgow School of Arts in the late 19th C, who developed a style of ART NOUVEAU. See p.190. See also MACKINTOSH

Gothic Revival Decorative style of the 18th C and 19th C, reworking the original gothic style which flourished in medieval times (11th C–15th C). This style is typified by pointed arches with slender lines and pierced tracery; examples include, in the 18th C, some CHIPPENDALE furniture and the 19th-C designs of A.W.N. Pugin. See pp.172 (3), 178

Graham, George (1673–1751) Clock and watch maker who did much to increase the accuracy of the tallcase clock with his deadbeat ESCAPEMENT (1715) and mercury pendulum (1726). Graham also invented the cylinder escapement. See pp.265, 266

Grotesque Fantastic human or animal form, sometimes combined with scrollwork, used as a decorative motif. See pp.174 (7), 214 (1), 234 (1)

Guilloche Decoration with a pattern of intertwined ribbons, worked in single or double bands, resulting in a series of small circles. *See p.274 (5)*

H

Harlequin set Group of objects in a common style, but with individual decoration. Also refers to unrelated items that have been made into a set.

Hepplewhite, George (d.1786) English cabinetmaker and furniture designer, an exponent of the NEOCLASSICAL style. After an apprenticeship with Robert Gillow of Lancaster, Hepplewhite opened a shop in London. He is chiefly known for his *Cabinet-Maker and Upholsterer's Guide* published in 1788, which contains nearly 300 designs for furniture and furnishings, which are characterized by their simplicity, elegance and utility. *See p.172 (4); Cf. pp.228, 234*

Höchst German ceramics factory active in 1746–96, which specialized first in ENAMEL-painted FAIENCE and later in ROCOCO-style statuettes and tableware. *See p.64 (4)*

Hood The top section of a tallcase clock which houses the MOVEMENT and the dial.

Huguenots French Protestants who fled to Britain after Louis XIV of France revoked the Edict of Nantes in 1685, denying them freedom of worship. Huguenots were frequently skilled craftsmen who created exquisite woven fabrics and silks, furniture decorated with VENEERS and LACQUER, as well as cast and engraved silverware. *See pp.140, 170*

Humpen Cylindrical German drinking glasses, sometimes lidded, first made in the 16th C. They are frequently decorated with trailed and pincered bands and painted with colourful ENAMELS. *Reichsadlerhumpen* display the double-headed eagle of the Holy Roman Empire; *Kurfürstenhumpen* show the emperor himself; and *Apostelhumpen* depict religious scenes. *See p.94 (2)*

Hutch Large table with cupboards or drawers beneath and a tier of narrow open shelves above to display fine tableware. *See p.202*

I

Ice glass, also known as frosted glass, cracked glass or *verre craquelé*. *See p.106*

Imari ware Japanese porcelain, made at Arita from the 17th C onward, with paneled decoration drawn from local textile designs in underglaze blue, iron-red ENAMEL and gilding, with some use of black, green and yellow enamels. Imari patterns inspired many European manufacturers in the 18th C and 19th C, among them DERBY and SPODE. *See p. 32 (6, 8). Cf. p.28 (1)*

Impressed mark Pottery mark, where a row of letters or marks are stamped into the soft, unfired clay. Used on early pieces from BOW. *See p.70*

Incised mark The earliest method of marking pottery in which the mark is scratched into the soft clay before firing; the edges often feel rough.

Inlay Decorative technique dating from the 15th C, whereby contrasting woods, metal, ivory or mother-of-pearl are set into recesses cut into the surface of a piece. *See pp.165, 176 (6), 190, 192 (5), 196 (1), 202 (5), 276 (4), 298, 306*

Intaglio A design etched or ENGRAVED into the surface of a piece; used in the decoration of glass. *See pp.104, 202 (5)*

Intarsia Inlaid still life or architectural scene found on furniture from the 16th C and 17th C. *See p.224 (4)*

Irish glass Ornate LEAD CRYSTAL glass produced from the end of the 18th C in the Irish cities of Belfast, Cork, Dublin and WATERFORD. Some shapes, such as canoe-shaped bowls, are specific to Irish glass. *See p.104*

Istoriato Historical, biblical or mythological scene painted on Italian tin-glazed EARTHENWARE from the early 16th C. *See pp.12, 42*

J

Japanning Technique originating in the early 18th C whereby European craftsmen imitated oriental lacquerwork with paint and varnish. *See pp.176 (6), 194, 270 (6, 8). See also* LACQUER *and* VERNIS MARTIN

Japonaiserie European designs and forms influenced by Japanese style. *See pp.50 (7), 84 (4, 6), 128 (8), 190, 194*

Jeweling Decoration on ceramics resembling gemstones, made by fusing drops of colored ENAMEL to gold or silver foil. *See pp.78, 80 (2)*

K

Kakiemon ware 17th-C Japanese porcelain vividly colored in turquoise, dark blue, red and black and decorated with plants and birds. Widely imitated in European porcelain in the 18th C. *See pp.32, 60 (4)*

Kändler, Johann Joachim (1706–75) Chief modeler at the Meissen factory in 1733–75, who raised the making of porcelain figures to an art form. *See pp.62, 268*

Kent, William (1684–1748) Influential architect and designer in the classical style, responsible for buildings such as Holkham Hall, Norfolk, in England. Kent believed in coordinating the inside and outside of a building and often designed interiors himself.

Knop Ornamental knob or bulge, found, for example, on the stem of a glass or a teapot lid.

Knurling Irregular grooved edging on silver and gold. *See also* GADROONING

Kraak Chinese porcelain, decorated in underglaze blue, exported to Holland in the late 16th C and early 17th C. The name is a corruption of "carrack," the ship used to transport it. *See p.24 (3)*

L

Lacquer Several layers of a hard glossy resin, from the tree *Rhus vernicifera*, built up and then carved or inlaid with various materials. A technique used mainly in the Orient. *See pp.224, 244, 296–99. See also* JAPANNING

Latticinio Threads of white or colored glass embedded in clear glass in a twisted or network pattern. *See pp.92 (3), 102 (1)*

Lead crystal Clear, brilliant glass made with lead oxide, suitable for cutting and engraving; thought to have been invented by George Ravenscroft (1618–81). *See pp.90, 96;* IRISH GLASS

Lenticle Glass window in the door of a tallcase (longcase) clock through which the pendulum can be seen. *See p.271 (2, 3, 4)*

Limoges City in France famous for its ENAMEL work and TRANSFER-PRINTED ceramics.

Loading Pitch or resin filler which adds density to a hollow metal object such as a knife handle or candlestick. *See pp.126, 136*

Longton Hall STAFFORDSHIRE POTTERY which produced tableware with overlapping leaf designs in soft-paste porcelain in 1750–60. Also noted for its figures, recognized by their poorly defined features. *See p.70 (4)*

Lopers Pull-out wooden rails supporting a fold-out desk or leaf on a small table. *See pp.192, 222*

Louis XIV style Opulent BAROQUE style dating from 1643–1715; typified by fine VENEERS, marquetry and the increasing use of exotic materials such as tortoiseshell and LACQUER. *See pp.214 (2), 220 (1)*

Louis-Philippe style French decorative style from the reign of King Louis-Philippe (1830–48), featuring heavy ornamentation and flamboyant curves. *See chart pp.10–11*

Lusterware Pottery or porcelain to which a metallic glaze containing silver, copper, gold or platinum is applied to produce a glistening sheen. *See p.40 (6)*

M

Mackintosh, Charles Rennie (1869–1928) Scottish architect and designer in the ART NOUVEAU style. He is best known for the new GLASGOW SCHOOL of Art built in 1897 and for his gently curving, elongated furniture. *See chart pp.160–61; 190, 200*

Maiolica Richly painted, tin-glazed EARTHENWARE made in Italy from the 15th C. The name is said to derive from ceramics introduced to Italy via the Spanish island of Majorca. The cities of Faenza and Florence were the most prominent producers of MAIOLICA. *See chart pp.16–17; 40–43*

Majolica Vividly decorated EARTHENWARE, molded or pressed to produce a sharp relief. Based on 16th-C Italian MAIOLICA, it was developed by Herbert Minton in 1851, and early pieces included vases, dishes and TAZZAS. Household majolica, made from 1861,

ranges from umbrella stands to wall plaques. *See pp.42, 258 (5, 6, 7)*

Marbled glass Glass containing two or more colors, combined, when molten, to resemble marble. *See p.94 (7)*

Matting Textured decoration found on some silverware made between the 16th C and the 18th C. *See pp.104 (5), 140 (7), 156, 274 (6)*

Meiping Chinese vase with wide shoulders and a narrow neck, made to take a single stem of cherry blossom. *See pp.22 (6), 26 (1)*

Menuisier French joiner making only small items from carved or plain woods. *See pp.178, 218. Cf. ÉBÉNISTE*

Milk glass Opaque white glass made with tin oxide. First used in Venice during the 15th C, it remained popular throughout the 19th C. *See p.106 (5)*

Millefiori Glassmaking technique in which sections from canes of colored glass arc embedded in molten clear glass. *See p.114*

Minton Ceramics factory established in 1793 by Thomas Minton, well known during the 19th C for MAJOLICA, parian ware and CLOISONNÉ work. Minton has continued to produce high-quality porcelain in the 20th C. *See pp.42, 50 (7), 82 (1, 5), 198*

Molding Raised strip of plaster or wood, applied to a piece as decoration or to conceal a joint. *See p.224*

Movement Mechanism of a clock or watch that causes it to work.

N

Nabeshima Japanese kilns near Arita established in the 17th C. Only small amounts of this porcelain were exported to the West. *See p.32 (7)*

Nailsea Glasshouse Glassworks near Bristol, England, making household wares, novelty objects decorated with colorful twists and flasks in pale green glass 1788–1873. The name was later given to any glass object in the same style. *See p.106 (1)*

Nankin ware Traditional name for early Chinese export BLUE AND WHITE porcelain; taken from Nanking, through which the ceramics were shipped.

Neoclassicism Revival style inspired by the art and architecture of ancient Greece and Rome. Popular in the mid- to late 18th C, after the excavations at Pompeii and Herculaneum and interest in the work of Renaissance architect Andrea Palladio. *See chart pp.10–11; 172. See also EMPIRE STYLE*

Northwood, John (1836–1902) English glass maker specializing in CAMEO GLASS and best known for copying the 1st-C Roman urn known as the "Portland vase," so winning a prize of £1,000.

Nymphenburg German porcelain factory near Munich in Bavaria, which made hard-paste porcelain from 1747. Nymphenburg specialized in ROCOCO figures, classical busts and tableware. *See p.64 (2)*

O

Ogee Double curve, convex at the top and becoming concave at the bottom, often found on MOLDINGS and on the feet of GEORGIAN furniture. *See pp.208, 212 (5), 266, 270 (7)*

Okimono Japanese figurative statue carved in ivory, wood or bone, for household decoration. *See p.294*

Opalescent glass Popular form of iridescent art glass, pioneered by the STEUBEN Glassworks in the U.S. during the 19th C. It resembled the color of natural opal, although later examples were colored green, pink and turquoise, and often painted or gilded.

Ormolu Originally the powdered gold used to gild furniture mounts made from bronze and other metals. The name now refers to the actual mounts. *See pp.224 (5), 246 (7), 266 (7), 268 (1), 280 (2)*

Overglaze color Decoration painted or printed on ceramics after glazing, rather than before. *See p.26*

Oyster veneer Type of VENEER using vertical sections cut from the branches of walnut or laburnum trees, whose pattern resembles an oyster. First used by the Dutch in the 17th C. *See pp.214, 200 (1), 206 (5)*

P

Parcel gilding Part-gilding of a piece of furniture or silver; ungilded areas on furniture are protected with varnish or shellac. *See pp.118, 138 (1), 204*

Parquetry Form of marquetry based on a repeated, geometric pattern, executed in woods of contrasting grains or colors. *See pp.210 (4), 226 (1, 2), 238, 272 (5)*

Patera Circular or oval ornament decorated in low relief and widely used on NEOCLASSICAL furniture. *See pp.172 (4), 178 (5), 182 (4), 204 (3), 238 (1)*

Patina Build-up of polish and dirt over many years, giving furniture a glowing, aged appearance. With continuous polishing, silver also develops a patina. *See pp.118, 164*

Pediment Surmounts the CORNICE in CABINET furniture. It has taken different forms, such as swan-neck and broken arch, according to prevailing fashions. *See pp.158, 212 (2, 5), 224 (3), 270 (1), 272 (1, 6, 8)*

Pellatt, Apsley (1791–1863) Innovative English glass maker who introduced the French technique of embedding ceramic plaques in glass, improved methods of producing pressed glass and revived Venetian ICE GLASS.

Petite sonnerie Clock striking double rings on every quarter hour, and a single ring on the hour. *See p.274*

Pie crust Scalloped decorative rim found on silverware and furniture, fashionable in the mid-18th C and 19th C. *See p.198*

Pilaster Partial column on the face of a piece of furniture, often rectangular in section. *See pp.212 (5), 238 (1)*

Plinth A solid base section used instead of legs on cabinet furniture.

Puritan or Commonwealth style Plain, utilitarian style favored during the Commonwealth period (1649–60), when England was without a king. Luxury and excessive ornament were rejected, and tableware, furniture and dress were kept simple. *See p.170 (1)*

Q

Quare, Daniel (1647–1724) English clock and barometer maker, much favored by King George I. He was the first to patent a REPEATER mechanism for watches. *See p.270 (6)*

Queen Anne Style of design that emerged during the reign of Queen Anne (1702–14). *See chart pp.10–11; 162, 172, 182 (1), 194 (2), 206 (6)*

R

Rabbet Groove, channel or recess cut along the edge of a piece of wood to receive the end or edge of another piece of wood, as in drawers. *See p.208*

Raku Japanese EARTHENWARE pottery with a thick lead glaze; used to make cups and bowls for the tea ceremony. *Raku* dates from the 16th C. *See p.30*

Rattail Decorative elongation of a spoon handle onto the bowl to give added strength. Developed during the late 17th C. *See pp.124, 126 (2)*

Reeding Decoration similar to FLUTING, but instead of carved grooves, convex parallel ribs are carved in the wood. *See pp.184 (2), 188, 242 (1)*

Régence French decorative style dating from the regency of Philippe d'Orléans, 1715–23. It predates the ROCOCO style of Louis XV and replaced the heavy ornamentation of Louis XIV pieces with flowing curves and asymmetric decorations of foliage and figures. *See chart pp.10–11; 128 (2)*

Regency British decorative style named after the Prince Regent, who ruled in place of his incapacitated father, George III, from 1811–20. In practice, Regency refers to a series of styles found *c*.1800–30. *See chart pp.10–11; 126 (7), 130 (7), 140 (6, 7), 172 (6), 174 (1), 196 (4)*

Repeater Clock or watch mechanism that repeats the previous hour, quarter hour and minutes when a cord or button is touched, so enabling the time to be told without the need to see the face. Repeating clocks were first made in the 1680s. *See p.286*

Repoussé Term used in silverware, to describe a raised design created with a hammer and punch, which is then "pushed back" in places. *See pp.118, 142*

Rococo Highly decorative and elaborate architectural style which originated in France in the early 18th C. It emphasized ornamentation and curving lines. Motifs especially associated with rococo are rocks, shells and floral designs; Indian and Chinese patterns were also used. *See p.128 (3, 4)*

Roemer Much copied German drinking glass developed in the late 15th C. It has a globular bowl, mounted on a thick stem decorated with prunts. A development of the *Roemer* was the English rummer, a large-bowled, short-stemmed ale or cider glass, introduced in the 18th C. *See pp.90, 96, 98 (3, 6), 108 (1)*

Roentgen, David (1743–1807) Son of Abraham Roentgen (1711–93), founder of the family furniture-making firm at Neuwied, Germany, in 1750. Roentgen developed the ROCOCO style of his father, using rich carving and exotic INLAYS; later, he switched to more rigid classical forms, embellished with bronze appliqué. *See pp.218 (4), 226 (2)*

Roundel Small ornamental disk or medallion. *See pp.30, 174 (7), 246 (7), 280 (1), 308 (1)*

Rozenburg Ceramics factory founded in 1883 by William Wolff Freiherr von Gudenburg near The Hague, Holland. Rozenburg is best known for its eggshell porcelain pieces in ART NOUVEAU shapes, with painted designs derived from Javanese batik work. *See p.84*

Ruby glass Glass with a rich red color created by the addition of copper or gold oxide. Cranberry glass is slightly paler in color. *See pp.104 (7), 156 (6)*

S

St. Cloud Early producer of French FAIENCE and soft-paste porcelain in 1664–1766. St. Cloud is noted for its white porcelain decorated with applied prunus patterning. KAKIEMON and IMARI-style pieces were also produced. *See p.60*

St. Louis Glassworks founded in 1767. Until 1839, St. Louis produced LEAD CRYSTAL wares, then diversified into high-quality tablewares, ornamental pieces in colored glass and paperweights. The glassworks still produces today. *See p.114 (1, 2)*

Seddon, George (1727–1801) Cabinetmaker who founded one of the most successful furniture-making companies in Britain, employing a workforce of hundreds to make high-quality pieces. A rival to Waring and Gillow. *See chart pp.160–61; 194 (6)*

Serpentine front Sinuous double-curved front found on chest furniture, especially in the 18th C, and also on chair seats. *See pp.184 (5), 194 (8), 204 (3, 4), 210 (6)*

Settle Wooden bench with a high back and arms and sometimes a chest for storage under the seat; popular in the 16th C to19th C. *See p.248 (3)*

Sgraffito Pottery technique whereby the surface of unfired slip is scratched or scored with a design to reveal the body color. *See pp.38 (2), 48*

Sheffield plate Process developed by Thomas Boulsover, a Sheffield cutler, in 1740. A thin layer of silver is fused onto copper, and it is then worked as a single metal. *See pp.118–19, 128 (8), 136 (8), 148*

Shelf clock Cheaply manufactured clocks developed in America to sit on a narrow shelf or ledge. Most have a plain rectangular frame and glass front. *See p.280 (4, 6)*

Sheraton, Thomas (1751–1806) English cabinetmaker who developed the NEOCLASSICAL style in furniture. This style of refined elegance and balance is taken from his books *The Cabinet Dictionary* (1803) and *The Cabinet-Maker and Upholsterer's Drawing Book* (1791–94) *See chart pp.160–61; 172 (5), 192*

Slip Potter's clay reduced to a creamy consistency, used to coat pottery or as an adhesive for external decoration. It is also used to cast hollow figures. *See pp.19, 48 (6, 7), 54 (3), 56 (5), 58, 82 (7)*

Slipware Any pottery decorated with SLIP; this can take the form of dipping the article in slip or trailing thickened slip across the surface of a body. *See chart pp.16–17; 26 (1), 50*

Spelter Zinc alloy used as an alternative metal to bronze. *See pp.278 (8), 280(2)*

Splat Central upright of a wooden chair back rising from the seat to the top rail.

Spode Ceramics factory founded by Josiah Spode in 1770, initially producing household EARTHENWARE, including CREAMWARE and TRANSFER-PRINTED Staffordshire blue, which Spode pioneered. After 1797 Spode produced BONE CHINA tableware and, from 1800,

translucent FELDSPAR PORCELAIN and worked with ENAMEL decoration in the REGENCY style. In 1846 the Spode factory, known as Copeland since 1833, perfected parian ware. Copeland, using the Spode trademark, continues to produce high-quality tableware to this day. *See chart pp.16–17; 15, 52, 76 (4, 5)*

Sprigging Ceramic decoration, shaped separately, then attached or "sprigged" to the main body with SLIP. *See p.15*

Spur marks Marks on the base of ceramic plates, dishes etc. made by pegs used to separate pieces in the kiln; can help identification. *See p.38 (7)*

Staffordshire potteries British ceramics factories concentrated around the towns of Stoke-on-Trent, Burslem, Hanley, Tunstall, Longton and Fenton,which exploited the local clays and the abundant supplies of coal. Most of the innovative techniques in British ceramics have come from the Staffordshire potteries. *See p.50*

Steuben American glassworks making art glass, founded in 1903 by the Englishman Frederick Carder. In 1918 it was taken over by the Corning Glassworks and from the 1930s commissioned designs from artists such as Jean Cocteau, Salvador Dali and Eric Gill. *See p.112 (6)*

Stourbridge glass Center of glass-making in Worcestershire established by French HUGUENOT glass workers in the 17th C. In the 19th C, it was noted for its high-quality table glass.

Strapwork Design of interlacing bands or straps on silver. *See p.128*

Stretcher Horizontal strut or rail between the legs of tables or chairs.

Stringing INLAY on furniture consisting of fine lines of metal or contrasting wood. *See pp.192 (3), 198 (6)*

T
Tazza Shallow basin with a wide bowl and single spreading foot or support. *See pp.78 (5), 92 (3), 106, 154*

Temmoku glaze Black or dark brown glaze found on Chinese stoneware from the 10th C–13th C; copied by the Japanese. *See pp.14, 30 (4)*

Thonet brothers Austrian furniture makers established in 1842, which by 1871 had become the largest such company in the world. Thonet specialized in mass-produced BENTWOOD furniture and found export markets all over Europe and the United States. In 1923, the company became Thonet-Mundus and turned to making tubular steel chairs. *See p.174 (6)*

Tiffany & Co. American jewelers established in New York in 1837 by Charles Tiffany. Known throughout the world for its jewely, including Tiffany watches and silverware. *See pp.122, 148*

Tiffany, Louis Comfort (1848–1933) Son of Charles Tiffany and founder of an interior design company in 1879, later known as the Tiffany Studios. His output, mainly in the ART NOUVEAU style, included Favrile art glass, stained glass, mosaics, bowls and lamps. After 1902, he specialized in furniture, fabrics, wallpaper, and jewelry. Tiffany Studios closed in 1932. *See p.112*

Train Mechanism in a clock or watch linking the power source to the hands. *See pp.264–65*

Transfer printing Method of applying decoration to mass-produced ceramics. Paper, printed with a design in metallic oxides, is wrapped around the porcelain and burned away during the firing process, leaving the pattern in the glaze. It was invented in Britain in the mid-18th C and is still the most common method of decorating ceramics throughout Europe and America. *See pp.15, 19, 70. See also SPODE*

Transitional style Chinese porcelain, mainly BLUE AND WHITE, produced between c.1620 and 1680: the last two decades of the Ming Dynasty and the beginning of the Qing Dynasty. On Transitional pieces, imperial decorations are replaced by landscapes and everyday scenes. Little was exported to the West. *See p.32 (2)*

Turning Using a lathe to shape wood, metal or other material. Also known as turnery. *See pp.170 (4, 5), 176 (1), 188, 194*

Twist Decoration on the stems of drinking glasses; rods of colored glass are inserted into the stem when it is molten and then twisted. *See p.96*

V

Vauxhall London porcelain works operating between 1751–64, using a soapstone soft-paste porcelain mix to create tea sets, chamber pots, flower-pots and snuffboxes. Decoration, TRANSFER PRINTED and hand painted, resembled Chinese BLUE AND WHITE.

Veneer Thin sheet of attractively grained wood – such as satinwood, rosewood or walnut – applied to a surface for decorative effect. First practiced in ancient times, veneering was fashionable in Europe in the 17th C. *See pp.165, 214*

Vernis martin Form of LACQUER patented by Guillaume Martin and his brother in the 18th C, used for interior decoration and small objects such as clock cases or boxes. *See pp.256, 268*

Voysey, Charles Francis Annesley (1857–1941) British architect, designer and author, known for his contribution to ART NOUVEAU. Influenced by William Morris, Voysey designed wallpapers and fabrics, as well as simple well-built houses. *See p.268*

W

Waterford Glassmaking factory in Ireland founded in 1729 and producing first flint glass then, from 1783, LEAD CRYSTAL. Pieces include tableware, bowls, glasses and decanters. The factory closed in 1851, but a new factory has been reproducing Waterford styles since 1951. *See p.90*

Webb, Philip (1831–1915) Architect and designer noted for his solid oak furniture with stained or painted surfaces. Webb also designed glassware, jewelry, metalwork and embroidery. His belief in hand-crafting pieces brought him into contact with William Morris, and many of his designs were used by Morris's company. *See pp.190, 194*

Wedgwood British pottery founded by Josiah Wedgwood (1730–95) in 1759 in Staffordshire, England. Its reputation stems from the numerous innovations in ceramics, designed to rival imported Chinese porcelain, which included CREAMWARE, BASALT, pearlware and the blue jasperware synonymous with its name. *See chart pp.16–71; 52, 58*

Wellington chest Narrow chest of drawers, dating from the early 19th C, with six to twelve shallow drawers and with a lockable flap to secure them. *See p.208 (5)*

Wemyss ware Pronounced "weemz." Ceramics produced at the Fife pottery, Scotland, in 1880–1930. A wide variety of tableware, household pieces and figures were made and handpainted with brightly colored floral, fruit and bird underglaze motifs. *See p.82 (8)*

Wiener Werkstätte The "Vienna Workshops"; a cooperative of Austrian craftsmen founded in 1901 by designers Josef Hoffman and Koloman Moser. The workshops specialized in ART NOUVEAU furniture, metalwork, textiles, glass and ceramics. *See pp.98 (7), 112 (7), 174 (5), 202 (6)*

Willow pattern Chinese design, featuring a garden scene, which inspired English tableware, TRANSFER PRINTED in underglaze blue. Thomas MINTON made the first engraving for willow pattern for the CAUGHLEY pottery c.1780. The design has since been much copied. *Cf. p.24 (5, 6)*

Wing chair Upholstered chair with a high back and projecting wing pieces at each side to protect the sitter from drafts; introduced in the late 17th C. *See p.182 (1)*

Wood, Ralph (1715–72) Staffordshire potter to whom many figures, Toby jugs and FLATWARE are attributed. *See p.50*

Worcester British ceramics factory founded in 1751 and still active. Early output concentrated on soft-paste porcelain decorated in underglaze blue and modeled on silverware shapes. The factory also produced coffee and tea sets using a porcelain-soapstone mix. After 1763 there was a move toward the luxury market with imitations of Meissen, Sèvres and Japanese designs. BONE CHINA was introduced in 1800 and decorated by a neighboring factory, Chamberlains; the two companies merged in 1840. During the 19th C, Worcester produced richly gilded and enameled tablewares, figures, parian ware and renaissance-style vases. Worcester is still known for its high-quality painted decoration. *See pp.68, 76 (3)*

Wright, Frank Lloyd (1867–1959) American architect and design theorist whose organic approach to buildings, and their interiors and furnishings made him a principal influence in the American ARTS AND CRAFTS MOVEMENT. *See p. 86 (7)*

Y

Yixing Potteries in China producing red stoneware pieces. Many of these were exported to Europe in the 17th C and influenced indigenous companies such as Meissen, where BÖTTGER made red stoneware. *See p.54 (7)*

INDEX

This index should be used in conjunction with the glossary. Normal type indicates an entry in the text, **bold** indicates a major entry, and *italic* an illustration or caption entry.

Pennsylvania-Dutch style 256, *256*

pen trays *24*

Persian earthenware *42*

pew group 56, *56*

pier glasses *246*

pietra dura 200, *200*

Pietsch, Karl *104*

pilasters *222, 238*

Pilgrim bottles *152*

Pillement, Jean *150*

pincushions *156*

pine furniture **252**

pitchers: ceramic *44, 46, 48, 50, 50, 54, 54, 56, 68, 82*; beer *56*; claret 102, *102*; glass **100–103**, *108*; silver 144, *144*

Pitts, Thomas *132, 138*

Pitts, William *138, 154*

plaques *40, 42, 52, 58, 64, 82*

Platel, Pierre *136, 140, 152*

plates: ceramics *44, 46, 64, 66, 68, 72*; glass *92*; Japanese *32, 36*; silver *140*

plique à jour 308, *308*

pocket watches *see* WATCHES

pole screens 244, *244*

porcelain 14, **20–29, 32–37, 60–81**; 18th-C **60–75**; 19th-C **76–81**; eggshell *28, 34, 34*; enameled 14–15, **26–29**; glazes *14*; history 18–19; restoration of 74. *See also* *individual countries*

Portugal: furniture 170, *182, 194*; maritime trade *24*; silver *154*; silver hallmarks *123*

Posen, Lazarus *138*

posset pots 46, *46*

pottery **40–59**; art **82–87**; Chinese *20*; Delftware *46*; early history 12, 18–19; European **48, 82–85**; Islamic **38**; Japanese *30*; lead-glazed **48–51**; stoneware **54–57**; tin-glazed **40–45**; Wedgwood **58**

Preissler, Ignaz 60, *60*

presses *212, 234*

Prutscher, Otto *98*

Pugin, A.W.N. 154, 178, *178, 190, 190*, 234, *234*

punch bowls *28, 46. See also* MONTEITHS

puzzle goblet *94*

puzzle jug *56*

Q

Qianlong period 22, 26, 28, *304*; cloisonné *306*; enamel *306*; glass *310*; jade *290*

Qing wares 22, *22, 24, 306*

Quare, Daniel *263, 270*

Queen Anne style *162*, 172, *172*, 182, *182, 194*, 196,

206, 236; American 172, *212, 212*; clocks *266, 270*; silver *148, 150*

R

Ramsden, Omar *144*

rattles 156, *156*

Ravenscroft, George 90, 96

Read, John *148*

Régence style: clocks *266, 268*; furniture *210, 230, 246*; silver *128*, 152

Regency style: furniture *172, 174, 174, 176, 178, 180, 184, 192, 192, 196, 196, 204, 216, 218, 228, 230, 240, 242, 244, 246, 256, 258*; glass *104*; silver *126, 130, 132, 134*

regulators *268, 272, 276, 276*

Reinicke, Peter 62, *62*

Reissner, Stellmacher and Kessel *84*

religious silver **154**

Renaissance style: clocks *266*; furniture 162

repoussé silver *118, 142, 148*

Restauration style *182*

Restoration *see* CHARLES II

Revere, Paul, Jr. *122, 146*

Rhodes, David *52*

Ricardo, Halsey *82*

Riesener, Jean-Henri 226

Ringler, J.J. *64*

Rococo Revival style: ceramics 78, 80, *80*; furniture *174*, 180, *180, 196*, 216, *244*; silver 116, *124, 146, 148, 150*

rococo style 10–11, 160–61; ceramics *64, 66, 68, 68, 74, 74, 76*; clocks *266, 268, 268, 276*; furniture *163*, 172, *174*, 208, *210, 222*; silver 116, *128*, 130, *130, 132, 132, 136, 138, 140, 140, 146, 148*, 152

Roentgen, Abraham *158*;

Roentgen, David *158, 218, 226*

Rolex watches *284*

roll-top desks *see* DESKS

Rookwood Pottery 86, *86*

Roussel, Pierre *218*

Royal Worcester *see* WORCESTER PORCELAIN

Rozenburg pottery *84*

Rundell, Bridge & Rundell 128, *144*

Ruskin pottery *14, 82*

Russia, desks *226*

rustic furniture 258, *258*

Ryokuzando *36*

Ryozan 36

S

Sadler, John *46*

St. Cloud porcelain 60, *60*

St. Louis 114, *114*

Saint-Porchaire wares 48, *48*

salt cellars *48*, **128**

salt-glazed stoneware **54–57**, *82*

Saltram House *2*, 4, *19*

salvers *140*

samovars 146

Satsuma ware **36**

sauce tureens **130**

Sawyer, Richard *138*

Scafe, William *276*

Scandinavia: clocks *272*; furniture *210, 222, 226*; silver *142. See also* DENMARK, SWEDEN

Schwarzlot 60, *94*

Scofield, John *136*

sconces *136, 246, 246*

Scotland: clocks *272*; furniture *208, 250*; silver *120, 146*

scratch blue decoration 56, *56*

screens *244, 290, 298*; cheval *244*

screws *167*

scumbled decoration 252

seals, glass *310*

secretaire-bookcases **224**

secretaire-cabinets 256

secretaires *212*, 224, *224*

Seddon, George *194*

semainier 208

Seth Thomas Clock Company *280*

Seto porcelain *30*

settees/settles/sociables **180**

Sèvres: clocks *268*; figures *66*; porcelain *15*, **66**, 76, 78, *78, 80*

sgraffito 15, 38, 48, *48*

Shaker furniture **254**

Shapland & Petter *220*

Sharp, Robert *136*

Sheffield plate 118–19, 136, *136, 148, 148. See also* SILVER PLATING

Sheraton style *163*, 172, *176, 192, 200*, 216, *216, 230*, 256

Sheraton, Thomas 172, *192*

Shigaraki porcelain *30*

Shino porcelain *30*

Shute, Walter *142*

Sibley, Richard *132*

sideboards **202–5**, *252*

sifters **128**

Silesia glass *104*

silver **116–57**; bright-cut engraving 146, *146, 156*; Britannia standard 116, 120, *121*, 146, *152*; casting *118, 119, 128*; chasing 118, *118, 128, 134*, 142, *142, 148*, 152, *154*; chinoiserie 142, *142, 150*; decoration 118, *119, 134, 142*, 152, *156*;

embossing *119*, 142, *142, 156*; gadrooning *116, 119, 130, 132, 134, 140, 144*; hallmarks **120–23**, 130, 136, 144; manufacturing 118–19; parcel gilding 118, *118, 128, 138*; plating 118–19, *128*, 136, *136*, 146, 148, *148*; repairs and alterations 119; sterling 120. *See also* CHOCOLATE POTS, COFFEE POTS, DISPLAY SILVER, DRINKING VESSELS, FLATWARE, RELIGIOUS SILVER, SMALL SILVER, TABLEWARE, TEA SETS

silver-gilt *1*, 4, 118, *124, 126, 128, 134, 136, 140, 142, 144, 152, 154, 156*; clocks *266, 274*; watches *282*

silver plate 118–19, *128*, 136, *136*, 146, 148, *148*

silversmiths 140

Sitzendorf porcelain *80*

Sleath, Gabriel *150*

slip: casting 15, 19, 56, *56*; decoration 48, *48*; trailing 26, *26, 82, 82*; wares 50, *50*

small silver *144, 150*, **156**

Smith, Daniel *136*

Smith, George *124, 174, 178, 180*

snuffboxes and bottles 60, *114*, 288, 310, *310*

snuffers *136*

Sobei Kinkozan 36, *36*

sofas **180**

Solon, Marc Louis 76, *76*

Spain: ceramics 40, *40, 72*; furniture *186, 206*, 224, 244, *248*; silver hallmarks *123*

spandrels *see* CLOCKS

spelter *278, 280*

Spode: Josiah 50; porcelain *76*; transfer printing *15*

spoons *124, 126*, 150, *150*

Sprimont, Nicholas *128, 130*

Staffordshire: porcelain 70, *70, 76*; pottery 14, 19, 50, *50, 52, 56, 56, 258, 258*

Stephens, Benoni *148*

Steuben glass 112, *112*

Stiegel, Henry *98*

Stolzel, Samuel *72*

stoneware **54–59**; Chinese 20, *20*

stools **168**, 170, *170*

Storr, Paul 116, **128**, *130, 132, 134, 138, 140, 144, 156*

Strasbourg pottery 42, *42*

Stroud, William *136*

sucket forks *124*

sugar bowls/boxes *150*; casters **128**; tongs *150*

Sweden: clocks *272*; furniture *210*; silver *142*

Swift, John *148*

ACKNOWLEDGMENTS

Marshall Editions would like to thank the following for their assistance in the compilation of this book:

Copy editors: Lindsay McTeague, Isabella Raeburn, Maggi McCormick (American)
DTP editor: Mary Pickles
Editorial research: Simon Beecroft, Helen Burridge, Jon Richards
Index: Jill Ford
Picture manager: Zilda Tandy
Picture research: Jo Egerton
Production: Janice Storr, Sarah Hinks
Production editor: Tim Probart

Illustrators: Coral Mula: 88, 116, 260, 288
  Richard Phipps: 12, 158 and symbols

Silver consultant: Stephen Clarke

Information for feature caption on p.60: Gordon Lang

Picture credits

Underlined **bold** numerals refer to page numbers. **Bold** numerals refer to illustrated item numbers on text pages. Where known, sale dates and lot numbers are given for all material from Christie's and Sotheby's, the lot number following the sale date and separated by a colon.
Abbreviations: CC/ME = Clive Corless/Marshall Editions; CMG = The Corning Museum of Glass.

1 Christie's Images 26.2.92:8-10; **2** The National Trust Photographic Library; **6** Sotheby's; **7** Christie's; **8** Christie's Images 21.6.85:98.

POTTERY AND PORCELAIN

13 Christie's Images 29.6.87:126; **14** *top* Paul Atterbury, *bottom* Mahaux Photography/The Image Bank; **15** *top (both)* Spode, *bottom* Ira Block/The Image Bank; **18** Christie's Images 9.12.88:77; **19** The National Trust Photographic Library; **20** Christie's Images 8.12.86:232; **21** Christie's Images 1 8.6.87:231, 2 21.4.86:261, 3 1.10.91:715, 4 10.6.91:26, 5 8.6.87:171, 6 14.12.83:311, 7 16.4.85:28; Sotheby's 8 10.12.91:158; **22** Christie's Images 8.10.90:466; **23** Christie's Images 1 26.9.89:586, 2,3,7 8.10.90:629,591,605, 4 8.6.87:60, 5,6 11.6.90:296, 8,9,10 1.10.91:807,1059,803; **24** Christie's Images 1.10.91:735; **25** Christie's Images 1,4 1.10.91:745,853, 3 23.4.90:189, CC/ME 2,5,6,7,8; **26** Christie's Images 19.3.91:606; **27** Christie's Images 1,2,4,5,7 8.6.87:130,272,85,70,291, 3 14.12.83:389, 6 15.12.83:492, 8 1.10.91:1054; **28** Sotheby's 21.5.91:131-5; **29** Sotheby's 1,2,3 27.11.90:96, 4,5 9-12.5.89:107, Christie's Images 6,7 2.1.87:215,554, CC/ME 8; **30** Christie's Images 7.3.88:100; **31** Christie's Images 1,2 7.3.88:145,128, 3 6.3.89:305, 4,5,6 16.6.88:122,109; **32** Christie's Images 13.11.89:223; **33** Christie's Images 1 19.11.90:702, 2,8 16.6.88:5,24, 3 13.11.89:200, 6 9.6.86: 111, 7 5.6.90:12, Sotheby's 4,5 7.6.90:64,72; **34** Sotheby's Billingshurst 28.11.90:1568; **35** Christie's Images 1 7.3.88:93, 2 11.11.91:390, 3,6 18.11.86: 25, CC/ME 4,5,7,8; **36** Christie's Images 9.11.88:527; **37** Christie's Images 1 17.6.91:236, 2,5 19.11.90:898,890, 3 9.6.86:126, 4 20.3.91:257, 6,7 23.6.87: 97,96, 8 6.3.89:451; **38** Christie's Images 24.4.90:386; **39** Christie's Images 1 28.4.92:188, 2,3 24.4.90:482,484, 4 10.10.89:481, 5 8.10.91:193, 6,7 9.10.90: 166,164, 8 28.4.92:239, 9 24.4.90:406; **40** Christie's Images 4.7.88: 211; **41** Christie's Images 1 1.7.85:275, 2 21.6.89:61, 3 13.3.89:274, 4 12.3.90:307-8, 5 30.3.87:252, Sotheby's 6 5.12.91:85-7; **42** Sotheby's 6.10.92: 146; **43** Christie's Images 1 12.3.90:327, 2 6.10.85:30, 3,4 2.10.89:36,11, 7 13.4.88:53, Sotheby's 5 29.10.91.80, CC/ME 6; **44** Sotheby's 16.7.91:86-90; **45** Sotheby's 1 1.10.91, Mallett 2, Christie's Images 3 3.7.89:256, 4 29.5.90: 200, 5 3.10.88:6, 6 25.2.91:21, 7 3.7.89:273; **46** Sotheby's 1.10.91:11-13,22, 42; **47** Sotheby's 1 1.7.86:69, 3 1.10.91:6,7, 4 16.7.91:147, Christie's Images 2 29.5.90:17, CC/ME 5,7; **48** Christie's Images 25.2.91:14; **49** Sotheby's 1 7.10.92:189, Christie's Images 2,4 4.7.88:183,245, 5 13.3.89:207, Paul Atterbury 6,7, CC/ME 3; **50** Sotheby's 16.7.91:160; **51** Christie's Images 1 29.5.90:70, 4 25.11.91:40, Sotheby's 2 6.6.89:327, CC/ME 3,5,6,7; **52** Christie's Images 29.5.90:105; **53** Christie's Images 1 1.10.90:15, 5 14.10.85: 53, 6 12.2.90:28, Sotheby's 2 16.7.91:167, 3 21.10.86:176, 4 16.7.91:162-4, 7 7.3.81:106; **54** Sotheby's 1.7.86:70; **55** Sotheby's 1 2.3.93:254, 2 6.10.92: 161-3, 3 23.6.92:115-7, 4 15.6.93:131, 7 14.6.88:123, Jonathan Horne 6, CC/ME 5; **56** Christie's Images 2.6.86:25; **57** Jonathan Horne 1,4, Sotheby's 2,3 15.9.92:187,197, 5 16.7.91:154, Christie's Images 6 10.10.88:112, 7 1.10.90:9; **58** Christie's Images 12.2.90:47; **59** Sotheby's 1,5 19.11.91:166-71, 2 9.2.93:166, 4 5.10.93:182, 6 13.11.92:326, CC/ME 3,7,8; **60** The Burghley House Collection; **61** Christie's Images 1 29.6.87:277, 3 4.7.88:177, 4 3.7.89:37, 5 15.10.90:12, 6 2.10.89:192, 7 22.6.92:9, Sotheby's 2 6.10.92: 149; **62** Christie's Images 1.7.85:221; **63** Sotheby's 1 19.2.91:89-92, 3,7 6.3.90:182, CC/ME 2,4,5,8, Christie's Images 6 25.11.91:341; **64** Christie's Images 3.7.89:98; **65** Christie's Images 1 29.6.87:208, 3 1.7.85:115, 4 13.3.89:85, 6 25.11.91:300, 7 4.7.88:145, CC/ME 2,5; **66** Christie's Images 3.7.89:53; **67** Sotheby's 1 14.5.91, 2 15.12.91:296, Christie's Images 3 1.7.85: 42, 4 3.6.86:221, 5 3.10.80:88, 6,7 2.10.89:232,217, 8 4.7.88:3, 9 3.7.89:84; **68** Christie's Images 20.5.91:267; **69** Christie's Images 1 6.6.88:254, 2,5 22.5.89:180,193, 3,4 20.5.91:203,204, 7 29.5.90:509, 8,9 10.10.88:204,203, CC/ME 6; **70** Christie's Images 29.5.90:446; **71** Christie's Images 1 25.11.91: 105, 2,3,4,6 22.5.89:7,8,9,243, 5 18.5.92:64, 7 1.10.90:304, 8 9.10.89:311; **72** Sotheby's 9.11.93:410; **73** Christie's Images 1 2.7.90:32, 3 2.10.89:99, 4 4.7.88:17, 6 13.3.89:44, 2,5 9.11.93:416-8,419; **74** Christie's Images 2.7.90:36; **75** Christie's Images 1,2 2.10.89:109,85, 3 25.2.91:91, 4 20.5.91:102, 6 3.7.89:122, Sotheby's 5 5.12.91:271; **76** Sotheby's;

77 Christie's Images 1,4 18.5.92:143,112, 3 20.5.91:252, CC/ME 2,5,6,8,9, Sotheby's 7 15.11.88:217; **78** Sotheby's 25.11.92:166; **79** Christie's Images 1,2 25.11.91:304,285, 3 14.10.85:305, 4 4.7.88:16, 5 12.3.90:19, Sotheby's 6 14.5.91:23, Esto; **80** Christie's Images 20.2.92:291; **81** Sotheby's 1 2.3.93, 2 26.3.91:312, 3 4.10.90:74, 6,7 28.10.91:81,145, Christie's NY 4, Christie's Images 5 14.10.85:294; **82** Sotheby's 18.11.91:4,29,46,58,68; **83** Sotheby's 1 19.12.89:103, 4,9 14.4.92:426-544, CC/ME 2,3,5,7,8, Christie's Images 6 26.9.86:78; **84** Sotheby's 3.5.91:204-5; **85** Sotheby's 1,5 19.10.90:180, 184-5, 2,3,4,6 3.5.91:218,215,217,219-20, 7 25.10.91:176; **86** Christie's NY; **87** Christie's NY 1,2,3,4,7, Esto 5,6.

GLASS

89 Bridgeman Art Library/Museo Archaelogico di villa Giulia; **90** *top* The Image Bank, *bottom* Christie's Images 11.4.86:28; **91** *left* CC/ME, *center* CMG, *right above* Christie's Images, *right below* Sotheby's; **92** CMG 51.3.118; **93** CMG 1 83.3.51, Christie's Images 2 13.2.90:183, 3 16.10.90:239, 4 4.6.91:140, 5 20.11.85:221, Sotheby's 6; **94** Christie's Images 16.10.90:257; **95** Sotheby's 1 16.7.84:7, 5 16.6.84:94, 6 25.3.91:277-80, Christie's Images 2 25.11.86:200, 3 4.6.91:150, 7 13.2.90:232; **96** CMG 79.2.89:97; **97** CMG 1 63.2.8, Sotheby's 2, 3 19.11.91:1-2, Christie's Images 4 7.6.88:212, 5,6 16.10.90:148,162, 7 13.2.90:129, 8 26.11.91:132; **98** Sotheby's 19.11.91:79; **99** Christie's Images 1 13.2.90:133, 3 22.11.88:11, 4 23.5.89:265, 7 13.4.88:225, CMG 2 87.4.55, 5 55.4.57, Sotheby's 6 19.11.91:59-62; **100** Sotheby's 19.11.91:21; **101** Christie's Images 1 9.7.91:58, 2 2.6.87:255, 3 16.10.90:258, CC/ME 4,5,7, Sotheby's 6 19.11.91:42; **102** Sotheby's 28.10.91:11; **103** Sotheby's 1,2 14.4.92:133,176-7, 3 19.11.91:66-7, 5 CMG 4 88.2.3, 6 8.4.4.241, CC/ME 7; **104** Sotheby's 19.11.91:72-5; **105** Christie's Images 1 4.6.91:149, 3 26.11.91:204, Sotheby's 2 19.11.91, 4 15.2.91:205, CC/ME 5,6,7; **106** Sotheby's 28.11.91:48; **107** CC/ME 1,3,4,5,7, CMG 2 87.4.15, 6 79.4.72A-E; **108** Christie's Images 5.3.85:40; **109** CMG 1 73.2.2, 2 55.4.187, 3 60.4.123, 4 68.4.406, CC/ME 5-8; **110** CMG 79.4.322, 73.4.145, 72.4.162, 79.2.78, 76.4.63, 72.4.163, 79.4.342; **111** Sotheby's 1 23.6.92:487, Christie's Images 2,3 28.9.88:335,329, 4 15.4.87:149, 5 4.6.91:217-221, CC/ME 6; **112** CMG 80.4.192; **113** Christie's Images 1 15.2.89:113, 4 19.8.89:279, 5 18.12.85:135, 7 17.4.84:183, Sotheby's 2,8 19.10.76:76,77-79, CC/ME 3, CMG 6 75.4.113; **114** Robert Kleiner; **115** Sotheby's 1 2.3.93, Christie's Images 2,4 23.5.89:360,284, 6 16.10.90:292, CMG 3 86.2.24,.25,.32,.31,.30, CC/ME 5, Robert Kleiner 7.

SILVER

117 Christie's Images 4.3.92:156; **118** Christie's Images 14.12.88:59; **119** Christie's Images *left* 4.3.92:189, *center & right* 25.10.89:74; **120** CC/ME; **121** *top* CC/ME, *bottom* Christie's Images 25.10.89:238; **122** Christie's NY *top & bottom* 19.10.90:103,100; **124** Courtesy, Winterthur Museum 63.52; **125** Sotheby's 1,2 1.11.90:261-2,277-9, CC/ME 3,4,6,7,8, Christie's Images 5 23.10.91:98; **126** Christie's Images 23.5.90:58; **127** CC/ME 1,4,6 Christie's Images 2,3 22.5.91:83,243, 5 23.5.90:62, 7 7.3.90:60; **128** Christie's Images 22.5.91:274; **129** Christie's Images 1 9.3.88:195, 3 23.5.90:186, 4 22.5.91: 46-7, 6 4.3.92:146, 7 3.3.93:118, Sotheby's 2 20.6.92, 5 28.2.91:83, 8 3.5.91: 354,355; **130** Sotheby's; **131** Christie's Images 1 24.10.90:213, 3 23.5.90: 184, 4 22.5.91:41, 5,6 12.7.89:157,192, Sotheby's 2,7 28.2.91:206,80; **132** Sotheby's 11.11.82:24; **133** Christie's Images 1 25.10.89:167, 3 23.10.91:50, 4,5 22.5.91:11,27-8, Sotheby's 2,6; **134** Sotheby's 20.5.92:135(NY); **135** Christie's Images 1 24.10.90:212, 2 23.10.91:142, 5,6,7 11.7.90:127,128,63, Sotheby's 4 20.6.92:126(NY), 8 10.7.90:272; **136** Christie's Images 7.3.90:186; **137** Sotheby's 1 19.11.87:41, 5, Courtesy, Winterthur Museum 2 61.801.1, 2A Christie's Images 3,4 22.5.91:67-70,273, 6 24.10.90:177, 7,10 12.7.89:118,145, 9 10.7.90:179, CC/ME 8; **138** Christie's Images 14.12.88:146; **139** Sotheby's 1,2, Christie's Images 3 23.5.90:110, 4 14.12.88:62, 5,8 22.5.91:17,6, 6 11.7.90:112, 7 8.5.88:136; **140** Christie's Images 22.5.91:144; **141** Christie's Images 1 23.5.90:210, 2 11.7.90:188-90, 3 2.7.89:199, 4,5,6 22.5.91:50,38,22-23, 7 18.5.88:121, Sotheby's 8 26.7.73:204; **142** Sotheby's 20.5.92:143(NY); **143** Sotheby's 1,2 28.2.91:231, Christie's Images 3 27.11.91:120, 4 25.10.89:238, 6 14.7.93:83, 7 19.10.90:100, 8 24.10.90:118, CC/ME 5; **144** Christie's Images 14.12.88:101; **145** Christie's Images 1,4,6 22.5.91:86,29,4, 8 7.3.90:68, Sotheby's 3 11.11.93:325-6, CC/ME 2,5,7; **146** Sotheby's; **147** Christie's Images 1,2 22.5.91:109,85, 3 24.10.90:198, 4 1.93:121(NY), 5 2.6.90:84, 6 18.5.88:141, CC/ME 7,8; **148** Christie's NY 1.93:193; **149** Christie's Images 1 22.5.91:125, 2 20.7.89:197, 3 10.7.91:8, 5 23.5.90:169, Sotheby's 4,8 19.10.90:255, CC/ME 6,7; **150** Christie's Images 1.10.79:152; **151** Christie's Images 1 23.5.90:216, 3,4

22.5.91:109,87-9, Sotheby's 2 27.2.92:367, CC/ME 5-9; 152 Christie's Images 23.5.90:229; 153 Christie's Images 1,7 7.3.90:185,78, 2,3 22.5.91:140,117, 4 24.10.90:117, 5 25.10.89:116, 6 4.3.92:141; 154 Sotheby's 4.7.89:202; 155 Sotheby's 1 20.10.89:517, 3 18.11.91:177, 4,5,6 28.2.91:305,263-4, 7 23.5.91:109-11, 8 1.11.90:301, Christie's Images 2 10.7.91:109; 156 CC/ME; 157 Christie's Images 1 11.7.90:131-2, 5 7.3.90:1, CC/ME 2,3,6,7,8,9,10, Sotheby's 4 25.10.91:324.

FURNITURE

159 Christie's Images 5.12.91:120; 162 The National Trust Photographic Library; 163 Christie's Images 23.3.84:65; 165 top Christie's Images 16.11.89:124, bottom Sotheby's 22.2.91:167; 167 Sotheby's 25.5.90:119; 168 Christie's Images 19.6.88:71; 169 Christie's Images 1 21.11.85:8, 3 12.12.91:59, 4 27.1.88:100, 6 13.10.88:167, Phillips 2 27.11.90:54, CC/ME 5; 170 Christie's Images 24.10.91:15; 171 Geffrye Museum 1, Angelo Hornak 2, Christie's Images 3 28.11.88:336, 6 7.4.88:32, Esto 4,5; 172 Christie's Images 28.6.84:58; 173 CC/ME 1, Christie's Images 2 16.11.89:40, 4 5.7.90: 140, 6 4.7.91:71, Sotheby's 3 12.7.91:280, Esto 5; 174 Christie's Images 14.11.91:169; 175 CC/ME 1,2,4,7, Chun Y. Lai/Esto 3,6, Christie's Images 5 26.9.86:269; 177 Christie's Images 1 3.5.90:66, 2 18.11.82:181, 4 11.4.91:95, 6 22.5.86:40, CC/ME 3,5,7,8; 178 Christie's Images 16.1.89:55; 179 Christie's Images 1 11.4.91:88, 3 3.11.88:44, 4,5 13.6.91:41,43, 6 4.7.91:65, Courtesy, Winterthur Museum 2 58.2216; 180 Christie's Images 9.7.92:78A; 181 Chun Y. Lai/Esto 1,6, Christie's Images 2,4 14.11.91:96,212, 3 4.12.86: 92, 5 9.3.89:5, 7 17.4.84:536-7; 182 Christie's Images 3.5.90:48; 183 Sotheby's 1 6.7.90:49, 5 5.12.91, 7 13.12.91, Christie's Images 2 22.6.89:98, 3,4 23.2.89:102,61, CC/ME 6; 184 Angelo Hornak/Victoria & Albert Museum; 185 Christie's Images 1 6.7.89:123, 2 8.10.88, CC/ME 4,5,6, Sotheby's 3 13.12.91:331; 187 Christie's Images 1 9.6.88:160, 2 7.4.88:87, CC/ME 3,4; 188 CC/ME; 189 CC/ME 1, Bridgeman Art Library 2, Christie's Images 3 7.4.83:96, 4 13.10.88:86; 191 CC/ME 1,2,4,5, Paul Atterbury 3; 192 Christie's Images 5.2.87:65; 193 Christie's Images 1,2 4.7.91:86,147, 4 16.6.84, CC/ME 3,6,7, Bridgeman Art Library 5; 194 Bridgeman Art Library/ Fine Art Society; 195 CC/ME 1,4, Christie's Images 2 21.11.85:170, 3 25.10.90:112, 5,7 14.4.88:146,85, 6 4.7.91:59, 8 14.11.91:170; 196 Christie's Images 28.6.84:83; 197 Christie's Images 1 29.5.86:169, 2 27.3.86:124, 3 7.7.88:80, 4,5 4.7.91:99,97, CC/ME 6,7; 198 Bridgeman Art Library; 199 CC/ME 1,3,4, Sotheby's 2 5.7.91:85, Christie's Images 5 5.12.91:10, 6 7.7.88:97; 200 Bridgeman Art Library; 201 Christie's Images 1 29.5.86:168, 2,4 19.4.90:112,118, 3 10.12.87:105, 5 14.4.88:74, 6 11.4.91:81, 7 9.6.88: 140; 202 Christie's Images 10.12.87:147; 203 Christie's Images 1 5.11.87: 124, 2 25.10.90:145, 3 24.10.91:96, 5 18.7.90:29, 6 15.7.87:329, CC/ME 4; 204 Christie's Images 5.7.90:101; 205 CC/ME 1, Christie's Images 2 5.12.91:124, 3 1.5.86:87, 5 3.7.86:120, 6 16.11.89:113, Esto 4; 206 Chun Y. Lai/Esto; 207 Christie's Images 1 3.11.88:129, 5 14.11.91:95, 6 19.11.87:64, CC/ME 2,3,4; 208 Christie's Images 18.6.87:134; 209 CC/ME 1,4,5,6, Christie's Images 2 14.11.91:39, Courtesy, Winterthur Museum 3 59.2645; 210 Christie's Images 3.7.86:129; 211 Christie's Images 1 29.5.86:159, 2 5.12.91:130, 3 9.6.88:142, 4 27.3.86:48, 7 18.6.87:181, CC/ME 5,6; 212 Christie's Images 1.5.86:163; 213 Christie's Images 1 11.4.91:148, 3 5.2.87:179, 5 14.11.91:211, 6 15.3.90:184, 7 7.2.91:146, Chun Y. Lai/Esto 2,4; 214 Christie's Images 14.11.91:213; 215 Christie's Images 1 10.12.87:148, 2 18.6.87:210, 3,5 9.6.88:176,181, 4 14.11.91:58, 6 2.7.87:459, 7 12.11.87:175; 216 Christie's Images 5.7.90:132; 217 Christie's Images 1 19.11.87:76, 2 12.11.87:97, CC/ME 3,4,5; 218 Christie's Images 27.3.86:174; 219 Christie's Images 1,2 3.7.86:140,95, 3,5 7.7.88:69,107, 4 5.7.90:146, 6 4.12.86:138, CC/ME 7; 220 Christie's Images 17.4.84:527-8; 221 Christie's Images 1 18.6.87:205, 3 5.12.91:98, 4 5.7.91:102, 6 15.2.89:62, CC/ME 2,5; 222 Christie's Images 12.11.87:90; 223 Christie's Images 1 7.4.88:81, 2 7.7.81:101,114, 3 9.6.88:98, 4 7.7.88:114, CC/ME 5, 6; 224 Christie's Images 7.7.88:129; 225 Christie's Images 1 9.6.88:162, 4 12.11.87:133, 5 10.12.87: 137, CC/ME 2,6, Chun Y. Lai/Esto 3; 226 Chun Y. Lai/Esto; 227 CC/ME 1,6, Christie's Images 2 10.12.87:133, 3 16.11.89:120, 4 23.6.88:132, 5 9.6.88: 153; 228 CC/ME; 229 CC/ME 1, 2,3, Sotheby's 4 22.2.91:309, 5 23.10.87: 363, Norman Brand/ME 6; 230 Christie's Images 23.6.88:73; 231 Christie's Images 1 7.7.88:132, 2 5.7.90:117, 3 19.11.87:48, 4 15.2.89:68, 6 16.12.87: 129, CC/ME 5; 232 Bridgeman Art Library/Victoria & Albert Museum; 233 Christie's Images 1 25.10.90:146, 2 30.1.86:106, Esto 3, Seventh Heaven 4,5,6; 234 Christie's Images 9.6.88:108; 235 Christie's Images 1 27.6.85:38, 2 11.4.91:154, 3 7.12.88:118, 4 3.11.88:176, 5 12.7.90:211, 6 21.6.90:164,

Chun Y. Lai/Esto 7; 236 Christie's Images 28.6.84:17; 237 Christie's Images 1 21.6.90:161, 2 9.6.88:115, 3 11.4.91:58, 5 21.6.90:140, 7 15.11.90:9, CC/ME 4, Chun Y. Lai/Esto 6; 238 Sotheby's 2.11.90:248; 239 Sotheby's 1 17.5.91:173, 3 12.7.91:352, 6 1.8.88, CC/ME 2,4,5; 240 Christie's Images 27.6.85:182; 241 Sotheby's 1 28.6.84:89, 3 5/12.7.91:119, Christie's Images 2 15.11.90:83, 6 12.12.85:129, CC/ME 4,5; 242 far left to centre Christie's Images 12.7.90:147, right Sotheby's 5.7.91:6; far right CC/ME; 243 Christie's Images 1 12.7.90:70, 3,5 11.10.90:125,73, 4 7.2.91:50, 7 24.10.91:136, Sotheby's 2 20.9.91:52, CC/ME 6; 244 Sotheby's 5/12.7.91:86; 245 Christie's Images 1 21.6.90:27, 2 26.6.86:165, 3 13.10.88:180, Sotheby's 4 29.11.84:2, 5 22.11.90:142, Courtesy, Winterthur Museum 6 65.2903, CC/ME 7; 246 Christie's Images 27.6.85:47; 247 Christie's Images 1 12.12.85:123, 4 27.6.85:130, 5 23.11.89:158, 6 11.4.91:21, 7 22.6.89:93, 8 7.2.91:57, Sotheby's 2 15/22.2.91:237, Chun Y. Lai/Esto 3; 248 Christie's Images 27.6.85:60; 249 CC/ME 1,2,4, Christie's Images 3 28.11.88:334, 5 4.5.89:70, 6 15.3.90:162, 7 24.10.91:76; 250 Christie's Images 21.5.87:259; 251 Christie's Images 1 7.4.88:36, 2,5 25.10.90:55,39, CC/ME 3,4,7, Esto 6; 252-3 CC/ME; 254 Ezra Stoller/Esto; 255 Chun Y. Lai/Esto; 256 Christie's Images 28.6.84:110; 257 Courtesy, Winterthur Museum 1 88.276, Christie's Images 2 30.10.88:161, 6 6.6.91:200, S 3 15/22.2.91:277, Chun Y. Lai/Esto 7, Angelo Hornak/American Museum in Britain 5, CC/ME 4; 258 Christie's Images 6.11.86:128; 259 Chun Y. Lai/Esto 1,2,4, Christie's Images 3 23.3.89.109, 5 22.1.86:62, Sotheby's 6 19.11.91:325, 7 19.12.89:111.

CLOCKS AND WATCHES

261 Christie's Images 3.7.91:289; 263 Christie's Images 12.12.88:122; 265 Christie's Images 5.12.91:28A; 266 Christie's Images 5.12.91:301; 267 Sotheby's 1,6, Christie's Images 2 5.7.89:31, 3 3.9.92:76, 4 5.12.91:40, 5 4.12.89:143, 7 23.11.89:54, 8 12.12.88:144; 268 Sotheby's 2.5.691:22; 269 Christie's Images 1 22.6.89:94, 3 30.9.92:55, 4 24.11.92:84-6, Sotheby's 2 30.8.91:240, 5 4.10.90, 7 CC/ME 6; 270 Christie's Images 3.7.91:251; 271 Christie's Images 1,2 5.12.91:37,31, 3,7 4.7.90:79,77, 4 30.9.92:120, 5 24.11.92:129, 6 9.4.87:60, 8 25.6.87:106; 272 Christie's Images 27.6.85:17; 273 Christie's Images 1 4.7.90:76, 5 2.10.91:32, 6 24.11.92:121, Sotheby's 2 30.5.91:302, 7 4.10.90:99, 8 28.6.93:248, CC/ME 3,4; 274 Christie's Images 3.7.91:177; 275 Sotheby's 1 20.7.89, 2 30.5.91:282, Christie's Images 3,4,7 4.7.90:37,29-33,39, 5 24.11.92:65-9, 6 2.10.91:13, CC/ME 8,9; 276 Christie's Images 7.5.92:40; 277 Sotheby's 1,4 30.5.91:232,255, 3, First Strike 2, CC/ME 5, Christie's Images 6 7.5.92:14, 7 7.5.92:39; 278 Sotheby's; 279 Christie's Images 1 4.7.90:61, 2 7.5.92:128-130, 3 3.9.92:53-4, 9 3.7.91:162, CC/ME 4,7,8, Sotheby's 5 30.5.91:201, 6 18.12.90; 280-1 CC/ME; 282 Sotheby's; 283 Christie's Images 1 4.7.90:20, CC/ME 2-5, Sotheby's 6-9; 284 Sotheby's 13.11.90; 285 CC/ME 1,3,4,6,7,8, Sotheby's 2,9 5.10.89:79, Christie's Images 5 14.11.90; 286 Sotheby's; 287 CC/ME 1,3,4, Sotheby's 2,6 5.10.89:79, 7 25.4.91:270-3, Christie's Images 5 14.11.90.

ORIENTAL WARES

289 Christie's Images 2.10.91:1668; 290 Christie's Images 31.3.92:1190; 291 Christie's Images 1 8.6.87:92, 2,3 25.9.89:353,277, 4,6 9.12.86:568,536, 5 11.12.89:320, 7 16.4.85:315; 292 CC/ME; 293 Christie's Images 1 11.6.90:228, 2 14.12.83:381, 5 20.6.84:391, CC/ME 3,4,6,7; 294 Christie's Images 20.3.91:196; 295 Christie's Images 1 6.3.89:235, 2 18.11.85:528, 3 17.6.91:53, 4 5.6.90:332, 5 18.3.92:321, CC/ME 6,7; 296 Christie's Images 19.11.90:972; 297 Christie's Images 1,2,3 14.12.83:12,54,78, 4 9.12.85:216, 5 18.3.92:281, 6 21.3.90:382, 7 7.3.88:212, 8 13.11.89:665; 298 Christie's Images 19.11.90:1006; 299 Christie's Images 1 5.7.90:80, 3 13.11.89:486, 4 11.6.90:225, 5 11.11.91:215, 6 9/10.6.86:177, 7 9.11.88:562, CC/ME 2; 300 Sotheby's; 301 Christie's Images 1,7 21.3.90:264,265, 3 19.11.90:422, 4,6 17.6.91:367,349, CC/ME 2 Sotheby's 5; 302 Sotheby's; 303 Christie's Images 1 20.3.91:43, 3 9.6.86:319, 4,5 19.11.90:534,502, CC/ME 2,7, Sotheby's 6 20.6.88:6, 8 12-3.6.86:238; 304 Christie's Images 2.10.91:1680; 305 Christie's Images 1 8.12.86:54, 2 10.12.91:23, 3 14-17.6.85:391-2, 4 8.6.87:139, 5 9.3.87:273, 6 17.6.91:156, 7 18/19.11.85:754-7, 8 14.6.89:168, 9 6.6.88:385; 306 Christie's Images 10.12.90:289; 307 Sotheby's 1 21.10.82:14, Christie's Images 2 9.12.85:234, 3 10.6.91:136, 4 8.6.87:136, 5 16.6.86:3, 6 19.3.91:321A&B, 7 21.3.88:23; 308 Christie's Images 17.6.91:86; 309 CC/ME 1,2, Christie's Images 3,8 19.11.90:916, 5 18.3.92:183, 7 6.3.89:200, Sotheby's 4 13.3.87, 6 20/21.6.88:713; 310 Robert Kleiner; 311 Christie's Images 1,7,5 11.6.90:299,301, 2,8 11.12.89:279, 3,6 19.3.91:339, Robert Kleiner 4; 312 Christie's Images 5.7.90:151.